Northwestern University
STUDIES IN *Phenomenology &*
Existential Philosophy

History and Truth

Paul Ricoeur

Translated, with an Introduction, by

History and Truth

CHARLES A. KELBLEY

NORTHWESTERN UNIVERSITY PRESS

Evanston   1 9 6 5

Introduction

IN HIS GIFFORD LECTURES, Gabriel Marcel stated that we live in a world which seems founded on the refusal to reflect. On several occasions, he insisted that the fate of philosophy and civilization are intimately related,[1] implying that the philosopher does not have the privilege of abstaining from participation in the crises of his epoch. Surely there is no need to underscore the role of existentialism and of phenomenology in the "persistent, unyielding struggle against the spirit of abstraction."[2] The present volume will, I believe, lend support to Marcel's conviction. Paul Ricoeur, Professor of Philosophy at the Sorbonne in the University of Paris, is neither unfamiliar with existential philosophy nor with the thought of Marcel in particular. Among his first publications is a book devoted to Karl Jaspers' philosophy,[3] and a second book to that of Jaspers and of Marcel.[4] Furthermore, Ricoeur is very much a part of the phenomenological movement. In addition to his translation of and commentary on Husserl's *Ideen*,[5] Ricoeur has made an original contribution to the literature of phenomenology in his monumental *Philosophy of the Will*[6] which to the present time includes *The Voluntary and the Involuntary* and *Finitude and Guilt*.[7]

1. *Les Hommes contre l'humain* (Paris: La Colombe, 1951).
2. *Ibid.*
3. M. Dufrenne and P. Ricoeur, *Karl Jaspers et la philosophie de l'existence* (Paris: Seuil, 1947).
4. P. Ricoeur, *Gabriel Marcel et Karl Jaspers* (Paris: Temps Présent, 1948).
5. E. Husserl, *Idées directrices pour une phénoménologie*, trans. P. Ricoeur (Paris: Gallimard, 1950).
6. *Philosophie de la volonté*. I. *Le Volontaire et l'involontaire* (Paris: Aubier, 1950). II. *Finitude et culpabilité:* 1. *L'Homme faillible;* 2. *La Symbolique du mal* (Paris: Aubier, 1960).
7. Volume I, *The Voluntary and the Involuntary*, is being translated for this series by Erazim V. Kohak and will be published by Northwestern University Press. Volume II, *Finitude and Guilt:* Book I: *Fallible Man* has been translated by Charles Kelbley (Chicago: Gateway, 1965).

History and Truth brings together a number of Ricoeur's less technical essays on subjects both theoretical and practical. While not pretending to offer a systematic presentation of his philosophy, the essays of this volume do, as I shall try to show, presuppose and draw upon his major philosophical work. Moreover, they exemplify the hope of Marcel—that the philosopher insert himself in the trajectories of civilization if he is to claim concern with the nature of truth.

Certain of these essays were originally published in *Esprit,* the prevailing left-wing Christian journal founded in 1932 by the French personalist, Emmanuel Mounier, to whom one of the essays in this collection is dedicated. Ricoeur, a friend and collaborator of Mounier until the latter's death in 1950, is a frequent contributor to *Esprit.* The Esprit movement, as conceived by Mounier, represents both a renewal of the Renaissance spirit and a break with university philosophy, the latter of which seemed to Mounier to be removed from the times. Yet Mounier's personalism evolved gradually into a philosophy, a "philosophy of existence," evoking themes which encouraged an interpenetration of reflection and action. Ricoeur's association with the Esprit movement, however, by no means indicates that he broke with traditional philosophy in the name of more pressing problems of contemporary civilization. While Ricoeur acknowledges a kinship with such noted philosophers as Husserl, Jaspers, and Marcel, this ought only be viewed, I believe, as partial backdrop to a philosophy which spans more than a single school of thought.

Congruent with Ricoeur's essay in memory of Emmanuel Mounier is his essay "Work and the Word" which perhaps best illustrates the meaning of the phrase which he applies to this entire collection: "In praise of the word which reflects efficaciously and acts thoughtfully." Man is both work and word, both a being who works and speaks, and if there should appear to be a dramatic opposition between these two sides, *praxis* and *theoria,* they are but one of the exemplifications of man's bivalent nature of which these essays speak. Clearly, it would seem that to Ricoeur, the fundamental philosophical experience is man as a broken unity (reminiscent of *le monde brisé* theme in the writings of Gabriel Marcel) for which he seeks a reconciliation.[8] Throughout this

---

8. In his *Gabriel Marcel et Karl Jaspers, op. cit.,* Ricoeur states that he received the decisive philosophical shock from the thought of Marcel. See also volume II of Herbert Spiegelberg's *The Phenomenological Movement* (The Hague: Martinus Nijhoff, 1960) for an account of Ricoeur's development and work up to the time of the publication of *Finitude and Guilt.*

volume, one witnesses a host of descriptions of the divisive character of man's existential status: torn as he is between Logos and Eros, between objectivity and subjectivity, between the abstract and the concrete, between the roles of the *socius* and the neighbor, between universality and singularity, and not least between two "ethics of distress," that of love and that of coercion. The last reflects a split which is the ever-bitter fruit of political existence driven to madness. Each of the essays might therefore be characterized as obsessed with a desire for reconciliation, either in the more methodological order (characteristic of Part I), or in the ethico-cultural order (as in Part II). Yet, unlike many philosophers who write of history, Ricoeur is wary of bringing these several dialectics of human existence to a premature synthesis; he wishes to undertake the history of philosophy without engaging in the philosophy of history.

There are indeed many indices throughout this volume which incline one to situate Ricoeur in an existentialist framework. His repeated return to Spinoza's famous dictum, "The more we understand individual objects, the more we understand God," marks his sensitivity to the singularity of individual existence. At the same time, it answers to his urgent sense of universality and meaning, the uniqueness and oneness of human reality. To the question "Does history have meaning?" he seems to give a deliberately ambiguous answer: yes, insofar as we are able to approach universality and system; no, insofar as this universality does violence to the life of individuals whose singularity always remains invincible. Attention, however, ought to be drawn to the ambiguity of the words *meaning* and *history* (or historicity). There is meaning in the sense of logical progression and contextual relationships; but is it not equally clear that there is meaning in singularity devoid of contextual causality and logical sequence? And, in consequence, shall we see history not only in its structural aspect, but also equally well in its event-aspect, the latter irreducible to a "logic of philosophy"?

Perhaps the first essay, "Objectivity and Subjectivity in History," adequately points up the presupposition underlying the persistent problematic "Can history be objective?" Is not the philosopher who would deny that history can be objective actually requiring an objectivity which could not on principle be attained, that is, an objectivity which involves *no* subjectivity? The "events" of men and the "advent" of consciousness inevitably cause us to brood over how we shall predicate meaning. We pause. Perhaps, too, the split between objectivity and subjectivity, between universality and singularity, is, in the last analysis, reflective of the nature of the historian's task. The historian is led to discover that the *object* of history is always the human *subject*. Was it not the glory of Kierkegaard to signalize this idea? We *must* pause.

The issue most central to this volume concerns the antinomy that Ricoeur establishes between history and truth, or between historicity and meaning. Insofar as the notion of truth signifies the progress of a unique and self-same meaning, to that extent it abolishes the disconnected series of individual upheavals and engulfs the events of men within a system. Likewise, there is a patent hiatus between the task of establishing a single truth and the history of divergent philosophies. In a first approximation, Ricoeur characterizes truth as a regulative idea, as the task of unifying (or indeed imposing unity upon) the diversity of our field of knowledge and of resolving differences of opinion. Truth would put an end to the "vertigo of variation" that history and the history of philosophy exude. But this notion of truth does away with history; it destroys historicity. A second model of truth, which reflects another way of gaining an understanding of history, bears upon the singularities that emerge in the flux of time. Yet, when we engage in this "singularity" conception of history, wherein the system is annihilated, we end up in a kind of historical schizophrenia. In voiding the idea of history as a coherent series or as a logical development, we also void the idea of a unique truth and instead promote a multiplicity of truths.

These opposing ways of viewing history, therefore, lead to antinomous conceptions of truth, leaving us divided between the imperialism of unity and the vertigo of variation. Both models of truth would destroy history. The system destroys history because history becomes engulfed in an immanent logic; singularity, too, is the end of history since all history is repudiated in it. Thus, Ricoeur argues, history is history only to the extent that it has reached neither the system nor absolute singularity; it remains history to the extent that the meaning of it remains confused and entangled. Previous to its fusion into system or singularity, history is essentially equivocal and in virtue of this, historical investigation cannot but be inexact; history cannot be objective; it can never completely *objectify* man, either in the sense of regarding him as a "moment" in universal history, or in the sense of unfettering him from all relational ties and establishing him as a completely "singular essence."

Thus, "to do the history of philosophy without the philosophy of history" implies, according to Ricoeur, that the lesson of the history of philosophy is that unity is not to be found in history; we are thus instructed in the "ambiguous status of mankind." Complementing this refusal to "say the last word" is the ineffable moment of human existence which operates as a limit to human pretensions. The unity of truth is a "timeless task only because it is at first an eschatological hope." In short, Ricoeur introduces an eschatological stage which would seem to frustrate all hope for unity *in* history. "What eschatological language calls 'hope' is recaptured reflectively in the very delay of all syntheses, in the postponement of the solution to all dialectics." Man is characterized as constantly struggling for his unity and his perenniality.

Yet, we should pause here to determine what it is to search for truth if the very notion of it is at odds with the concepts of history and historicity. The search for truth is problematic because of the duality in human nature between "finitude" and "infinitude," the narrowness of the human condition, and the infinite desire man has for totality. "Let being be thought in me"; "let me be bound by being." Such expressions refer to an abstract, timeless, and impersonal truth which, if attainable, could be reached only by means of a concrete, temporal, and personal striving. There is, Ricoeur contends, only one way of emerging from the narrowness of the human condition, and this is *communication*. This leads Ricoeur to an intersubjective definition of truth according to which each person continually moves toward self-clarification by unfolding his perception of the world in communication with others. It is this conception of truth as intersubjective which enables different philosophies to elude the two models of truth which were listed above, the system and singularity. How else can Plato escape the capsule formulae of typology as well as the immobility of a singular essence? How else can the philosophers of the past continue to engender new meanings if they are not "open" to dialogue with the present? Can anything human be given a meaning once and for all, nailed down to a system or to a singular essence? Can anything human be objectified? Again, we seem to be thrown back upon the "ambiguous status of mankind."

Truth would be attainable, Ricoeur contends, if communication were total. But this remains impossible; there can be no totality of communication and the "task" of truth is therefore a constant one. The duty of thought, which has truth as its goal, is endowed with purpose by what Ricoeur calls a kind of "ontological hope." The expression "I hope I am within the bounds of truth" suggests the eschatological influence which both keeps history open and provides the source for the courage to do the history of philosophy without the philosophy of history.

"The Image of God and the Epic of Man" adds the crowning

touch to the apology of man in search of unity. In the elucidation of three fundamental quests—having, power, and value (*avoir, pouvoir, valoir*)—we find that these very human quests may actually constitute the surest road to man's alienation. Here we encounter an idea, to which Freud, Marx, and Sartre have so forcefully given expression, that consciousness is ever tempted toward "false consciousness" and is ever in need of being "exorcised" and reminded of its duty to "self-creation." Perhaps the "ambiguous status of man" then serves to point up the truth that the real defense of freedom lies in the imagination. This would in turn seem to justify and confer meaning upon "the risk of being man."

*   *   *

The more systematic thought of Ricoeur is found in the volumes of his monumental *Philosophy of the Will*. More clearly than the others, the first volume, *The Voluntary and the Involuntary*, exemplifies the phenomenological method as inaugurated by Husserl, although it is made equally clear that Ricoeur's commitment to phenomenology is a limited one. This first volume is but the first stage in what promises to be one of the more over-arching philosophical enterprises of modern times, ranging over the eidetic, symbolic, empirical, and poetic dimensions of human existence.

The Voluntary and the Involuntary inaugurates the philosophy of the will by establishing at the outset a double abstraction, what Ricoeur calls a "reduction," from fault and transcendence. By this is meant the empirical state of man's finitude and guilt and his relation to the transcendent. The purpose of the abstraction is, of course, to allow for an eidetic description of man's most fundamental possibilities without taking account of his empirical condition of "brokenness" or his poetic dimension as longing for a beyond.

Dedicated to Gabriel Marcel, *The Voluntary and the Involuntary* actually combines divergent streams of thought in brilliant fashion. Both Husserl's phenomenological method of pure description and Marcel's existentialism find place within the analyses, signaling a constant interplay between Marcel's notion of the mystery of the body as incarnate subject and what Husserl called the "eidetic reduction." The reason for this combined methodology stems from Ricoeur's belief that the Husserlian method of pure description is limited if it is not complemented by empirical and scientific data which serve as "diagnostic" to the intentional structures of man's practical and affective life. Briefly, the author acknowledges that "meditation on the work of Gabriel Marcel is at the root of the analyses" of his book. Yet Ricoeur wished to put the thought of Marcel "to the test of the precise problems posed by classical psychology." Hence his method involved situating himself between two exigencies: "that of a thought nurtured by the mystery of the body, and that of a thought which takes account of the distinctions inherited from the Husserlian method of description." In light of these remarks, one can better understand why Ricoeur, at the beginning of his *Philosophy of the Will*, states that "everything sets us apart from the celebrated and obscure transcendental reduction." For it is this reduction that "checkmates a true understanding of one's own body." The bond between the will and the body requires a kind of attention other than the intellectual consideration of structures. What is required is that "I actively participate in my *incarnation as mystery*"; that "I pass from objectivity to existence." In saying that Ricoeur's goal is to describe the relations between the voluntary and the involuntary, one sees that the methodology throughout raids diverse segments of experience to buttress the coherence and interdependence of the voluntary and involuntary parts of human nature. Phenomenological and existential, pure and impure description collide gracefully to envision a restoration of the unity of man's being which stands against the apparent apotheosis of "negation" in our time.

Professor Herbert Spiegelberg speaks of Ricoeur's "existentialism" as one of affirmation.[9] It is here that Ricoeur may be distinguished from his contemporaries and situated within the philosophies of existentialism and phenomenology. One sees how the direction of Ricoeur's philosophy contrasts with that of Sartre in the essay entitled "Negativity and Primary Affirmation." This essay is an open polemic on Sartre's philosophy of negation. If Sartre's philosophy is characterized by the predominance of negation, Ricoeur's is one in search of the "primary affirmation"; it is the *affirmation originaire* of which Jean Nabert writes in his profound *Eléments pour une Ethique*. While respecting Sartre's celebrated exposition of nihilating acts, Ricoeur nevertheless questions the validity of hypostatizing these nihilating acts into a nothingness which would constitute the "ontological characteristic" of the human reality. He then turns to an analysis of the origins of negation and proceeds to outline a brilliant "reflection on reflection" which aims at recapturing the primary affirmation upon which alone negation can be founded. He suggests that "the soul of

9. *The Phenomenological Movement*, II, p. 568.

refusal, of recrimination, of contestation, of interrogation, and doubt, is fundamentally affirmation."

The phenomenology of *finitude* points up Ricoeur's differences from Merleau-Ponty. In "Negativity and Primary Affirmation," Ricoeur, making reference to Merleau-Ponty, states that the experience of finitude presents itself as a contrasted experience of both limitation and "transgression." This experience must be described as it is in its duality and not broken in two. One cannot, "in a first stage, work out a description of being-in-the-world (e.g., in perception or in affectivity) and then, in a second stage, initiate the transcendence of this being-in-the-world (e.g., through the word or the will)." On the contrary, "in the same movement, the act of existing becomes embodied and transcends its embodiment." Point of view and perspective are known as point of view and perspective by virtue of our constant ability to transcend them. The "word" ceaselessly evinces this transcendence, so that the dialectic of signifying and perceiving would seem absolutely primal, and the project of a "phenomenology of perception," in which there is a neglect of this moment of "saying" and a destruction of the reciprocity between saying and seeing, is in the end an "untenable venture."

In the spirit of Merleau-Ponty, the description of the body-subject (*le corps propre*) is therefore wholly geared toward the establishment of a philosophy of finitude without an absolute, one in which consciousness is perpetually riveted to a point of view. This is, summarily, a philosophy wherein "all consciousness is perceptual, even the consciousness of ourselves." Yet can we not ask "how the moment of reflection on the unreflected, how the wish for universality and truth, and lastly, how the philosophical act itself are possible if man is so completely identified with his insertion in his field of perception, action, and living"? [10] Otherwise it is to suppose that the other operations of consciousness, science, and all that pertains to speaking, for instance, involve the same fundamental structures as perceptual experience. Man is not to be wholly defined by his status of "being-in-the-world." His insertion is not so total that he loses the aloofness of signifying which is the principle of expression. Such are the tenets that Ricoeur proclaims in face of Merleau-Ponty's *Phenomenology of Perception*.

Recognizing that Husserl's phenomenology became progressively existential so far as the problem of perception took precedence over all the others, Ricoeur tends to ally himself more closely

10. Cf. the author's "Phénoménologie existentielle" in *Encyclopédie française*, XIX (1957).

with the first works of Husserl, from *Logical Investigations* to *Cartesian Meditations,* wherein consciousness is not defined by perception, by its inherence in the world, but rather by its absence. Consciousness signifies emptily, which may or may not (in the case of absurd propositions) be fulfilled by intuition. In short, Ricoeur tends to emphasize that period of Husserl's thought wherein consciousness is at once speech *and* perception. As is well known, many feel that Merleau-Ponty has emphasized only Husserl's later period, neglecting the fact that Husserl's great work, *Logical Investigations,* "does not begin with the presence of things but with the power of signifying them." As Ricoeur puts it, "Husserl began his work not with a phenomenology of perception but with a phenomenology of significations." [11]

One finds a much more extensive development of the dialectic between signifying and perceiving, between saying and seeing, in *Fallible Man.* Beginning with the Cartesian theme of finite-infinite man, Ricoeur dissociates himself from tendencies among contemporary existentialists to make finitude the global characteristic of human reality. His working hypothesis leads him to stress the infinitude of man as well as his finitude. This is to respect man's global disposition of "non-coincidence and disproportion" and to respect that he is intermediate, not between "being and nothingness," but within himself. For Ricoeur, to start from the whole of man means to start from his non-coincidence with himself, his disproportion, and the mediations he effects in existing. Yet "philosophy does not start anything independently"; rather, it is supported by the non-philosophical and derives its existence from the substance of what has already been understood prior to thought, in a "precomprehension" of man by himself.

Thus the key concept of fallibility is located in a pre-philosophical comprehension of man which Ricoeur finds adumbrated in the Platonic myth of the soul-as-a-mélange, in the Pascalian pathos of "misery," and in the Kierkegaardian "self" of *The Sickness unto Death.* This precomprehension is the "matrix of a philosophy which makes disproportion and intermediacy the ontic characteristic of man." First there is a phenomenological description of man in himself, the "pathétique" of misery. Secondly, on the basis of this nebula of meaning, Ricoeur describes a progressive recovery of this pathétique by a reflective [*réflexive*] method starting not from the self, but rather from the object before the self. This movement is intended to exemplify a transcendental stage of Kantian inspiration. In virtue of reflection on the object,

11. Cf. the article "Negativity and Primary Affirmation."

Ricoeur finds the elements of a finitude consisting of perspectival point of view *and* the infinitude of intellectual determination. That is, both finite perspective and the ability to transgress perspective, to go beyond point of view and to signify the object in a non-perspectival manner. In succeeding analyses, he carries the portrayal of "disproportion" and non-coincidence into transcendental, practical, and affective dimensions, treating respectively the disproportions of knowing, acting, and feeling.

The train of thought in *Fallible Man* is gradually to expand reflection until it ultimately coincides with the richness of the pre-philosophical comprehension of man as "miserable," as prone to "become" the flawed creature. The author conceives of reflection as an effort to recapture a sentiment of an experience previously given. Yet, reflection shows itself incapable of matching the meaning contained in man's precomprehension of himself. It is this residue of meaning that led Ricoeur, in a second book of *Finitude and Guilt,* to attempt a much different approach to the phenomena of fault and evil. *La Symbolique du mal* bears upon the symbolic manifestations of evil. It is in this book that the transition from fallibility to fault is effected. Ricoeur initiates a hermeneutics of symbols and myths, practicing a method which is no longer one of pure reflection (which abstracts from image, myth, and symbol), but is rather a deliberate confrontation with the symbols by which man avows his actual fallen condition. Between the capacity for evil and the actual assertion of it, there is a leap which must be caught in the act. Hence, his method involves bearing on the *avowal* of man about himself and on the symbols of evil in which this avowal is given expression.

The two approaches to Finitude and Guilt—the abstract description of fallibility, and the phenomenological "repetition" of the avowal of fault in myths and symbols—leave a hiatus between pure reflection on fallibility and the actual avowal of fault. Ricoeur asks how we can continue so as to enrich reflection with the positive wealth of meaning contained in the symbolism of evil, while still respecting the immediacy of the symbol. His answer is one which would be creative of meaning, a philosophical hermeneutics claiming not to unearth a philosophy hidden under the garb of symbols, but rather to establish a philosophy on the basis of symbols and achieve meaning via creative interpretation. Moreover, he promises to carry out this project in a subsequent volume which would constitute an "empirics" of human volition, starting from the evocative power of the symbol. In this direction, Professor Ricoeur's latest work, an outgrowth of his Yale Terry Lectures and in some sense a preparation for the continuation of his *Philosophy of the Will,* deals with "The Interpretation of Symbols" and affords a confrontation of phenomenology with psychoanalysis, specifically that of Freud.

*   *   *

At the outset of this introduction, it was suggested that the essays of this volume presuppose and draw upon Ricoeur's major philosophical work. To be sure, this may be seen more clearly in the last two essays. Yet, the organic bond that connects the entire collection with the author's *Philosophy of the Will* is, I suggest, what was cited as Ricoeur's fundamental philosophical experience, man as a broken unity. In the more systematic volumes of Ricoeur's work, the brokenness of man is given rigorous philosophical status. In particular, his phenomenology of finitude clarifies the underlying structures of man's bivalent nature by elucidating the notions of disproportion and non-coincidence. But presupposing his philosophical treatment of man's nature, Ricoeur here sets out to assay the significance of the historian's craft with its exigency for objectivity and what its value may be when seen through the prism of the history of philosophy. Based upon the prior analyses of man and his non-coincidence with himself, he examines the validity of a philosophy of history which would lay claim to being definitive. His definition of man as intermediate within himself and his subsequent characterization of human existence as a multiple act of effecting mediations allow us to see why Ricoeur, in this volume, does not wish to bring the several dialectics of human existence to a premature synthesis.

From critical, theological, political, and philosophical perspectives, Ricoeur elucidates the ambiguous status of mankind which no logic of philosophy or of history can coordinate short of imposing a violent synthesis of the truth. While the ultimate meaning of man's historical experience is condemned to remain ambiguous, while history and truth remain torn between the vertigo of variation and the imperialism of unity, these essays nevertheless tend to punctuate an "existentialism" of affirmation founded on the feeling of hope and the primary affirmation which is constitutive of reflection.

Charles Andrew Kelbley

Contents

History and Truth

Preface to the First Edition (1955)

EACH OF THE ESSAYS in this collection is the result of some particular circumstance. They do not flow from any preconceived plan governing the themes or the order of their presentation. Rather, all of them were provoked by some event: a group discussion, a conference or a congress, an anniversary celebrated with sadness or joy. And yet there is a certain uniformity within these disparate texts,[1] thanks to a continuity in rhythm and subject matter, and especially thanks to a certain involuntary harmony which I shall attempt to clarify by doing a critique, so to speak, of myself.

These texts have been grouped around two poles: a methodological pole and an ethical pole (in the broadest sense of the word ethical). The first part contains articles devoted to the significance of historical work, some dealing with the historian's craft proper, with its exigency for objectivity, and others with the philosophico-theological problem of a total or ultimate significance of history. The studies of the second part pertain to what I would call a critique of civilization. In this part there is an attempt to reachieve a reflective awareness of certain civilizing drives which are characteristic of our era. All of these essays are oriented toward a political

1. Three types of texts have been excluded. First, articles which are too technical in their philosophical bearing, one of which is nevertheless directly related to the central theme of this collection: "Husserl et le sens de l'histoire" (*Revue de métaphysique et de morale*, 1950). Secondly, philosophical chronicles pertaining to book reviews or to the criticism of contemporary works. Lastly, essays touching upon my *Philosophie de la volonté*, particularly those bearing upon the preparation of the second volume: *Finitude et culpabilité*.

[3]

pedagogy, the meaning of which is clarified in the pages devoted to Emmanuel Mounier.

While it was thus convenient to divide these diverse essays into two groups, what is most important in my opinion is what I called at the outset the continuity in rhythm. In effect, there is a single rhythm which unites the two preoccupations mentioned above. The emphasis on one or another of these two preoccupations is merely reversed in the two parts of this book. I categorically refuse to dissociate the elucidation of directive concepts, according to which we are trying to *think* our insertion in history, from the concern for actively intervening in the crisis of our civilization and thereby *giving testimony* to the force and efficacity of thought. Nothing is more foreign to the "style" of these essays than the so-called opposition between committed thought and uncommitted thought. Considered individually or as a whole, these essays attempt to show the futility of this quarrel. Both of these words (committed, uncommitted) should be done away with. An opposition that is less stylish but more radical was introduced by Marx between thought, which merely weighs and contemplates, and praxis, which transforms the world. In my opinion, there is even more reason to reject this opposition. Several of these essays attempt to show that the appearance of contemplative modes of thought, such as those of Parmenides, Plato, or Neo-Platonists (to take an extreme example), have transformed the world. For, along with the denial of sensible appearances, they have given us Euclidian mathematics, mathematical physics, and, through the instrumentality of measurement and calculation, the world of machines and technical civilization.

The rhythmic unity to which I am here alluding is more clearly stated in the essay entitled "Work and the Word." I look within the very act of speaking for this alternation between contact and distance that should be found in all responsible behavior of an "intellectual" confronted with some problem. Thus the more methodological reflection of the first essays is inseparable from the ethico-political grasp of human relationships toward which the studies of the second part tend. Inversely, the philosophical way of being present to my time seems to be linked to a capacity for reachieving the remote intentions and the radical cultural presuppositions which underlie what I earlier called the civilizing drives of our era. Thus reflection on the "event" takes us back to the search for significations and notional sequences with which the first essays are concerned. This amounts to saying that one need not be ashamed of being an "intellectual," as is Valéry's Socrates in

Eupalinos, doomed to the regret of having made nothing with his hands. I believe in the efficacy of reflection because I believe that man's greatness lies in the dialectic of work and the spoken word. Saying and doing, signifying and making are intermingled to such an extent that it is impossible to set up a lasting and deep opposition between "theoria" and "praxis." The word is my kingdom and I am not ashamed of it. To be more precise, I am ashamed of it to the extent that my speaking shares in the guilt of an unjust society which exploits work. I am not ashamed of it primordially, that is, with respect to its destination. As a university professor, I believe in the efficacy of instructive speech; in teaching the history of philosophy, I believe in the enlightening power, even for a system of politics, of speaking devoted to elaborating our philosophical memory. As a member of the team of *Esprit,* I believe in the efficacy of speech which thoughtfully elucidates the generating themes of an advancing civilization. As a listener to the Christian message, I believe that words may change the "heart," that is, the refulgent core of our preferences and the positions which we embrace. In a sense, all of these essays are in praise of the word which reflects efficaciously and acts thoughtfully.

The title given to these essays may appear overly ambitious if one expects to find a systematic treatment of these two cardinal notions: History and Truth. Nevertheless, I have retained them because for me they signify less a program to be exhausted by thought than an intention and a direction of research. These two words—history and truth—accompany all of the essays of this book; their meanings gradually become manifest and are continually enriched with new significance.

First, history and truth lead us to pose this question: does the history of the past, with which the historian's craft is concerned, lend itself to a true knowledge which is in accordance with the intentions and rules of the objective type of thought that is achieved in the sciences? I have placed the essay which most bears the stamp of this critical question at the beginning of this work. The reason for this was to base all of the other essays upon this foundation of rigor and modesty which pertains to the historical discipline. The measure of "objectivity" exemplified by the historian goes with us as a critical warning in the dangerous enterprise of giving global interpretations to history.

Accordingly, relative to this limited truth of the historian's history is situated the task of composing a philosophical history of philosophy. At the end of the first essay, I show how this procedure continues that of the historian proper. The history of philosophy is shown to be a recovery of the historian's history, guided by a philosophical awareness. This is why it belongs to philosophy and not to history. The problematic peculiar to the search for truth in the history of philosophy occupies the entire second essay—the central one in my opinion. In this second essay, truth is characterized principally by the passion for unity in contrast to the factual segmentation of philosophy into multiple philosophies. But this passion would be useless if it did not succeed in eliciting a series of provisory determinations of the concept of truth as well as of history itself. The method of providing successive approximations, which is practiced here, permits us to decipher concurrently the notions of history and truth, to unfold in depth the various levels of significance based upon this sort of proscenium that is constituted by historical objectivity. (This method of giving various meanings is likewise practiced in "Truth and Falsehood" and in "True and False Anguish.")

The truth of the history of philosophy therefore appears here as a principle of the possibility of historical research in philosophy. It is a principle which is constantly being lost and recovered as the meaning of this history is transformed.

The second essay ends on a difficult theme which foretokens "Christianity and the Meaning of History." This theme, each time that I give myself entirely to the truth of the other, is enunciated approximately in these words: "I hope that he is within the bounds of truth." Within the bounds of truth: this relation of belonging, of inclusion which assimilates every historical form to a contour surrounded by light, is accessible only to a regulative feeling capable of purifying historical skepticism, a feeling which is reason but not knowledge—the feeling that all philosophies are ultimately within the same truth of being. This feeling I call "hope" and I deal with it in a subsequent essay under the heading of Christian preaching. It is the feeling that I also call "primary affirmation" in the essay "True and False Anguish" (here borrowing M. Nabert's excellent expression). But if Christian preaching refers hope to an ἔσχατον [eschaton] which judges and completes history without belonging to it, this hope with eschatological intention has its impact in philosophical reflection in the form of an actual rational feeling. I receive the "pledge of hope" when I momentarily perceive the harmony of the diverse philosophical systems which are nevertheless irreducible to one single, coherent discourse. It is in this sense that I use Spinoza's famous theorem: "The more we understand individual objects, the more we understand God." I am aware of the fact that eschatology is incurably mythical in comparison with the philosophical consciousness of the truth, and that in return, all reference to the actual rationality of the whole of history is, in the eyes of he who preaches the Last Day, a relapse into a guilty, natural theology. I am aware that it is difficult if not impossible to overcome this mutual exclusion. Yet I feel that it is possible to convert this mortal contradiction into a living tension, that is to say, to live this contradiction—to live Christian hope philosophically as the directive principle of reflection—for the conviction of the ultimate unity of truth is the very Spirit of Reason. Perhaps in this way I can acquire the courage to do the history of philosophy without the philosophy of history, to respect unreservedly the truth of the other without becoming schizophrenic. Later we shall see the ethical and political equivalents of these formulae. Perhaps this is the meaning of the "truth in charity" of which St. Paul speaks. Perhaps it is also the meaning of the history of philosophy.

I hesitated to include the essay on "Christianity and the Meaning of History" because it goes much further than the others (with the possible exception of the essay entitled "The *Socius* and the Neighbor") toward a profession of Christian faith and thereby breaks a certain modesty which to me seems essential to philosophical dialogue. (I allude to this modesty at the end of "True and False Anguish" in referring to the silence of the religious man confronted with the suffering of the innocent.) Personal integrity, however, here required that I deal directly with the issues. It is a fact that the meaning I see in my craft as a historian of philosophy is defined by the dual affinity it has with the *critical* discipline of the historian proper, which I am not, and the profession of an *eschatological* meaning which pertains to a theology of history, which I do not feel qualified to elaborate and which, perhaps, cannot be elaborated owing to a lack of criteria. I am not hiding behind any of the difficulties created by this last affinity. Yet the methodological rigor of the history of philosophy does not seem weakened by linking the rationality of the historian's craft to the mystery of eschatology. For the subjective motivation of a craft is one thing, and the methodical structure which secures its autonomy another. The twofold affinity, by which I here define the median or intercalary situation of the history of philosophy, merely concerns the spiritual economy of man tormented by problems. This dependence within the order of spiritual motivation does not prevent the history of philosophy from achieving its own independence in elaborating its own problematic and its own methods. From this second point of view, another system of references may appear, as is shown in the short note on "The History of Philosophy and the Sociology of Knowledge" which anticipates more rigorous future works. There I defend the idea that the history of philosophy is formed in the interval between a sociology of knowledge (which is a scientific and not a philosophical discipline) and a philosophy of history (which is a philosophical and not an historical discipline). This second system of references and intercalation, unlike the one mentioned previously, no longer concerns itself with the subjective motivation of the author of the history of philosophy, but with the architectonic and discipline of its object. This should be enough to show that a discipline may be dependent on the spiritual economy of man who exercises it, and autonomous as to its problems and its methods.

The meanings of the concepts of history and truth thus merge together. Their duality, however, does not end here. History is the expired history that the historian recaptures as *truth*, that is, as objectivity; but it is also the history in process that we are experiencing and making. How shall we *make it into truth*? The second series of essays brings about this change in perspective.

I have decided to start the second part with the essay that I presented some time ago along with those contributed by my collaborators on *Esprit* in memory of our friend Emmanuel Mounier. Set in this new context, this essay constitutes an open admission of my debt to him. He had a way of linking philosophical reflection, which was to all appearances the farthest removed from current events, to vital problems of our times; he refused to dissociate a criteriology of truth from a political pedagogy; he would not separate the "awakening of the person" from the "communal revolution"; he refused to take part in the anti-technicist movement under the pretext of "interiority"; he distrusted "purism" and catastrophism; he possessed a kind of "tragic optimism." All that I regard as my debt to Emmanuel Mounier.

The problem of the truth of history, not in the sense of a true knowledge of past history but in the sense of a true fulfillment of my task as a workman of history, finds its crucial point in the question concerning the fundamental unity of the historical movement of a civilization.

This question makes its appearance throughout the whole sequence of essays starting with "Truth and Falsehood." Sometimes it is considered from the point of view of what might be called a history of culture: and so we see perception, action, and knowledge branch out into attitudes which successively implicate one another, attempt to absorb one another, and exclude and rival one another. The movement of civilization then appears as a phenomenon of indefinite pluralization, constantly counterbalanced by the emergence of unifying powers—for example, medieval theology or modern politics. Sometimes the question spurts up in the form of the project of the "civilization of work." Is it possible to regroup all human potentialities around the pole of man as worker? Here the dialectic of saying and doing makes its appearance. The same question turns up in another form when we find ourselves called upon to choose between two interpretations of human relationships. According to the first, another is my neighbor over and above all social mediation, and authentic intersubjectivity is an encounter without any criterion immanent in history. According to the second, another man is a social function, the precious fruit of all the sorrowful mediations in the economic, political, and cultural orders. Here we find a new dialectic unfolding, a dialectic of "direct" and "indirect" relationships, person-to-person encounters and social bonds consolidated into institutions, a dialectic of the intimate and the social. Lastly, the same question springs from the debate between the prophetic exigency—as has been said, not without a danger of abuse—and the political exigency. We are witnessing the debate between two historical "efficacities," a violent efficacity and a disarmed efficacity, without our sensing the right to exclude one in the name of the other.

Basically, this many-sided question is the same one which confronted us earlier in respect to the history of philosophy. At that time I was asking whether my memory of mankind, or at least that portion of history for which the historian of philosophy is responsible, had a systematic unity throughout the succession of "forms" wherein philosophy rises and declines. Now I am asking whether this project of mankind, which we call our civilization, has a systematic unity throughout the multitude of cultural attitudes which it develops and the multitude of interhuman bonds which it intersects. In a word, this question concerns the truth *of* history and *in* history, and is approached as the dialectics of the One and the Many.

But in moving from the epistemological register to the ethical register, the problem of truth and history becomes enriched with multiple harmonics. First, the question of unity, in becoming a practical question—in the concise sense of the word practical which is opposed to theoretical—cuts into the question of authority in all its forms. I do not think I have ever given in to the anarchic disparagement of authority. The problem of authority should be approached positively whenever it is encountered. In the phenomenon of authority we find an authentic function of ordering and unification which counterbalances the aimless proliferation of human talents. Authority, however, leads to temptation; it is the trap of the passions for power. The history of authority is a history where splendor and guilt are inextricably intertwined. The fault which clings to the exercise of authority is sometimes called untruth, sometimes violence. But it is all the same thing, according to whether one considers it in its relation to the rights which are encroached upon, or in its relation to the men crushed by the demons of power.

In "Truth and Falsehood," the problem of untruth is approached in terms of the quest for unity which may serve to define Reason. And if it is true that the demons prefer to haunt the courts of the gods, then it is within the heart of Reason, in the core of its wish for unity, that the highest untruth is born: that of presumed and pretended unity. We shall consider two fundamental historical forms of it: the "clerical synthesis of truth" and the "political synthesis of truth." However, these untruthful unifications of the kingdom of truth, which are also violent unities in relation to the life of men and their right to error, are undoubtedly only the most conspicuous modalities of a historical guilt with a thousand faces. To be sure, many of the analyses of the first part are given new perspective if we view them in light of the close proximity of truth and untruth, of truth and violence. Hence the unity that I reject in the history of philosophy, eclectic or dialectic unity, shares in the same universe of guilt as clerical and political violence.

This is why an essay which to all appearances is so contingent in its origin (Gary Davis, alas!) as "Non-violent Man and his Presence to History" is, I believe, in direct contact with the most central theme of this entire collection. In this article I tried to understand the obscure, indirect, and disconnected way in which the non-violent man acts in history when he bears witness, by his acts, to the far-off goals of this history and identifies the means at his disposal with the ends for which he hopes. Now this presence of the non-violent man to history demonstrates, in my opinion, that history is quite rich and that there are many ways of being effective in it. But above all, the way in which the Jehovah's Witness, for example, lets himself be cut to pieces rather than bear arms suddenly throws light on the meaning of my own work: is not the respect for the disparity among the historical "forms" of philosophy a kind of non-violence? Does not this non-violence, which is intimately related to every other form of non-violence, eventually become associated, like all forms of non-violence, with the inevitable violence which animates the most clairvoyant history: that of states and churches, of capitalistic powers, of the sword and the robe? And does not their union make up this comprehensive movement of history that no knowledge totalizes?

At the outset I spoke of the "involuntary" harmony of these essays. Why this unusual adjective? For me, this term designates a structure of thought that is less apparent than the rhythm which relates the epistemological concern and the ethico-cultural concern throughout these texts. While gathering these texts together, I noticed that from the mere literary point of view they present a resemblance in composition which was certainly not deliberate. All of them try, with varying degrees of success, to attain a certain point of unresolved tension. On the one hand, they are obsessed with the desire for reconciliation, either in the methodological order or in the ethico-cultural order. On the other hand, they convey an emphatic distrust of premature solutions. This unplanned structure constitutes a sort of dialectic with a postponed synthesis. It is seen most clearly in the oppositions of two words: work-speech, *socius*-neighbor, progressionist violence-non-violent resistance, history of philosophy-history of philosophies. But this same dialectic actuates the analyses by means of successive approximations or by graded levels. Within the context of the historian's craft, we have the following levels: the objectivity of recorded history, the historian's subjectivity, and the subjectivity of actual history; in the history of philosophy, there are the levels of eclecticism, pluralism, and the unity of the light of truth; in philosophy and in the theology of history, we have the levels of progress, ambiguity, and hope; lastly, there are various levels of anguish—vital anguish, psychic anguish, historical anguish, ethical anguish, metaphysical anguish, etc.

This common feature might be nothing more than an expository method if it did not express directly, on the rhetorical level, a feature of reflection itself—if it did not ultimately betray, both on the level of literary expression and on the level of reflective sequence, what I earlier called the philosophical impact of hope. Thus, a few remarks on the formal composition of these essays takes us directly to their essential characteristic.

I do not wish to dwell here on the methodological difficulties raised by the insertion of an eschatological stage into philosophical reflection. By starting this time from the texts of the second part, perhaps we shall be better equipped to bring out the theoreticopractical function of this theme and to clarify the meaning of what I called a rational feeling that is regulative and purificative both of skepticism and fanaticism: skepticism which refuses to look for meaning, and fanaticism which declares it prematurely.

I maintain that the philosophical impact of hope has an important bearing on reflection—and this is exemplified in the style of these essays. By this I mean that what eschatological language calls hope is recaptured reflectively in the very *delay* of all syntheses, in the *postponement* of the solution to all dialectics. For philosophy, the Last Day cannot be the dream of some happy ending which lies on the imaginary horizon of our battles. It is in this sense that "The Kingdom of God is at hand." It is this nearness which keeps history open.

In the philosophical dimension in which I share, this idea of openness presents two sides: a negative and a positive side. From one point of view, the concept of "Last Day" works as a *limiting concept* in the Kantian sense, that is, as an active limitation of phenomenal history by a total meaning which is "thought" but not "known." [2] The presence of this limitation shatters the pretension of philosophies of history to express the coherent meaning of all that has passed and all that is to come. I am always short of the Last Judgment. By setting up the limit of the Last Day, I thereby step down from my seat as final judge. The last word therefore is not uttered anywhere; I do not yet know how to Say it and Make it consistent with everything else: how, for example, perceptual truth, scientific truth, ethical truth, etc., coincide. I do not know how Plato, Aristotle, Descartes, Kant, and Hegel share in the same truth. Thereupon it is easy to revert from this function of a limiting concept to what I called the main feature of reflection: the limiting concept of an end of history protects the "discontinuity" of unique visions of the world. It supports the "circles" among diverse cultural attitudes and manifold civilizing drives (Speaking leads to Doing, and Doing to Speaking; perceptual truth leads to scientific truth, which leads to ethical truth, which in turn leads back to perceptual truth, etc.). There are "circles" but no "hierarchy," no infrastructure or superstructure in the global movement of history; yet from a certain point of view, everything may be looked upon as an infrastructure. To summarize this negative function of the eschatological idea, let us say that it is the category of the "not yet."

But the philosophical impact of hope for the Last Day is not

2. I insisted upon the central significance of the idea of limitation in Kant in "Husserl et Kant," *Kantstudien*, Vol. 46, no. 1.

limited to this dethronement of our rational supremacy. In the very midst of this sort of agnosticism in the philosophy of history, it is the source of affirmation which emanates from this collection.

The next to last essay, entitled "True and False Anguish," tries to make this power of affirmation emerge by means of a reflection on the negative emotion *par excellence,* anguish. To actually reflect on anguish is, in my opinion, to use it as a detector of the primary affirmation which has always already conquered anguish. The degrees of anguish which reflection covers, from the vital anguish of contingency and death to the metaphysical anguish of radical nonsense, are also the degrees of a kind of vehemence to exist which surges up at every offense. If to reflect is therefore to go beyond the very thing that one understands, then the philosophical benefit of a meditation on the truth of anguish is to direct us back to the center of the problem of the truth of history.

In this essay, historical anguish is first put back into the context of a broader spiritual economy. Thus, on the one hand, it figures between the contingency of life and the fragility of the psychic, and, on the other hand, between the existential anguish of choice and guilt and the still more radical anguish of Foundation. The stimulus peculiar to it is the frightening possibility that there may be pure loss in history, at least in comparison with every philosophy of history, that there may be a negative which apparently does not mediatize anything and remains unamenable to inclusion within the immanence of some Logos.

At the same time, the act by which I put trust in a hidden meaning, which no logic of historical existence can exhaust, appears, in its turn, related to the act by which I *wish to live* despite the fact that the imminence of death confronts me; to the act by which this will to live becomes *justified* in an ethical and political task; to the act by which bound freedom becomes *repentant* and *regenerates* itself; to the act by which I invoke, along with the tragic chorus and the Hebraic psalm, the goodness of the totality of being. This serial and hierarchized act is the primary affirmation. Reflection on anguish is no longer merely a critique of authenticity; in the midst of total threat, it recaptures the power to affirm which constitutes reflection, and leads it to *establish* a limit to its own powers. This recuperative reflection is certainly the philosophical impact of hope, no longer merely in the category of the "not yet" but in that of the "from now on."

And yet no "enthusiasm" could gloss over the *philosophical* precariousness of the eschatological moment; does philosophy wish to "demythologize" it, as it certainly seems required to do? If that is the case, it loses the twofold virtue of limitation and primary affirmation and falls back into deceitful and violent rationalizations. Here philosophy seems to be well guarded against itself by nonphilosophy.[3] This presents us with a perplexing situation as to the possibility of identifying philosophy with the search for a "point of departure." It seems that in order to be independent in the elaboration of its problems, methods, and statements, philosophy must be dependent with respect to its sources and its profound motivation. This fact cannot fail to be disquieting.

Within the confines of philosophical rigor, from which we shall never ask too much, and in the vicinity of the non-philosophical sources of philosophy, thought must undoubtedly be content with the "timid" hope which is mentioned in the last lines. This hope seems to extend the *docta ignorantia* taught for the first time by the pre-Socratic Xenophanes who was at the turning-point between the Ionians and the Eleatics:

> There never was nor will there ever be any man who has certain knowledge about the gods and about all the things that I tell of. And even if he does happen to get most things right, still he himself is not aware of this. Yet all may have shadows of the truth.[4]

3. "Aux frontières de la philosophie," *Esprit* (November, 1952). "Sur le tragique," *Esprit* (March, 1953).
4. Diels, *Die Fragmente der Vorsokratiker* (Xenophanes, B 34), I, p. 64.

Preface to the Second Edition (1964)

THE ELEVEN ARTICLES which made up the first edition (1955) have been republished without alteration. I have decided that it is neither possible nor correct to judge what has become obsolete or belied by events, nor what may still, after ten years, retain interest or be of lasting value. I have simply added six articles which by their content and nature complement the previous edition without disrupting the theme or tone of the book.

The original division of texts into two groups has been preserved; the two titles which have been given to them—*Truth in the Knowledge of History* and *Truth in Historical Action*—designate the two relations, epistemological and practical, which are sustained by Truth and History.

The first part—*Truth in the Knowledge of History*—is more clearly articulated in two sections dealing respectively with critical and theological perspectives. One text—"The *Socius* and the Neighbor"—which was originally in the second part of the book has been moved to the first part because of its affinity with the theological theme. Two new texts have been placed at the end of each of the two sections.

As in the first edition, the second part—*Truth in Historical Action*—is again introduced by the essay on Emmanuel Mounier. The second section is devoted to the general relationship between Speaking and Praxis. The third section, which for the most part is new (it is augmented by three articles), gravitates around the enigmas of political power for philosophical reflection and for action in the world of culture. In the fourth section I attempted to outline the general idea of the implicit philosophy which inspires these essays. This philosophy is developed in a more rigorous and systematic manner in the series of volumes which constitute my *Philosophie de la volonté*.[5] A new text reinforces this section and ends the book. I have entitled this last section *The Power of Affirmation* in remembrance of Jean Nabert with whom I have, during the past ten years, realized more and more affinities.

5. *Philosophie de la volonté:* I. *Le Volontaire et l'involontaire* (Paris: Aubier, 1950); II. *Finitude et culpabilité:* 1. *L'Homme faillible,* 2. *La Symbolique du mal* (Paris: Aubier, 1960).—Trans.

PART I
Truth in the Knowledge of History

1 / Critical Perspectives

Objectivity and Subjectivity in History

THE PROBLEM BEFORE US concerns a methodology which enables us to undertake a fundamental re-examination of the strictly pedagogical questions relating to the coordination of educational disciplines. Behind this problem, however, we may catch sight of and philosophically reconsider the most important "interests" brought into play by historical knowledge. I borrow the word "interest" from Kant: when he was resolving the antinomies of reason—one of which is the antinomy of necessary and free causality—Kant paused to weigh the interests thrown into the balance by one or the other position. Naturally we are dealing here with intellectual interests or, in Kant's words, with "the interest of reason in this conflict with itself."

We must proceed in the same way with the obvious alternative which presents itself. The two words objectivity and subjectivity represent disparate interests, *expectations* which differ in quality and in direction.

We expect history to have a certain objectivity—the objectivity which is proper to it; this, rather than subjectivity, must be our point of departure. Now what do we look for under this heading? Objectivity should be taken here in its strict epistemological sense: the objective is what thought has worked out, put into order, understood, and what it can thus make understood. This is true of the physical and biological sciences as well as of history. Hence, we expect history to make the past of human societies attain the dignity of objectivity, though this does not mean the objectivity of physics or biology, for there are as many levels of objectivity as there are methodical procedures. Accordingly, we expect history to add a new province to the diversified empire of objectivity.

[21]

The above expectation implies another one: we expect the *historian* to have a certain quality of *subjectivity*, not just any subjectivity but one which is precisely suited to the objectivity proper to history. It is a question, therefore, of an *implied* subjectivity, one that is implied by the expected objectivity. Thus we have a feeling that there is good and bad subjectivity and we expect the very exercise of the historian's craft to decide between them.

Furthermore, under the heading of subjectivity we are looking for something of more consequence than the good subjectivity of the historian. We expect history to be a history of men, one which helps the reader who is instructed by the historian's history to achieve a high level of subjectivity—not just a personal subjectivity but that which is proper to mankind. However, this interest or expectation of a passage from myself to man—by means of history—is no longer exactly epistemological but properly philosophical. For what we expect from the reading and contemplation of the historian's works is a *subjectivity of reflection*. This interest now concerns not the historian who writes history, but the reader—notably the philosophical reader—in whom every book or work finds its completion at its own risks.

Such is the path we shall follow: from the objectivity of history to the subjectivity of the historian; from both of those to philosophical subjectivity (to use a neutral term which does not prejudice the subsequent analysis).

[1] THE HISTORIAN'S CRAFT AND OBJECTIVITY IN HISTORY

WE EXPECT HISTORY to have a certain objectivity which is proper to it. The way in which history is born and reborn confirms this; it always flows from the way in which traditional societies *rectify* the official and pragmatic arrangement of their past. This rectification is of the same nature as the rectification represented by physical science in relation to the first arrangement of appearances in perception and in the cosmologies dependent on perception.[1]

But who is to tell us what this specific objectivity is? The philosopher, in this respect, cannot enlighten the historian; for it is always the very exercise of a scientific profession which instructs

1. It was recently shown that Thucydides—unlike Herodotus—was impelled by the same passion for strict causality as Anaxagoras, Leucippus, and Democritus, by the same quest for the principle of motion as pre-Socratic physics. He looks for this principle of motion in human societies, just as the physicist looks for it in the things of nature.

the philosopher. Thus we must first listen to the historian as he reflects on his craft, for he is the measure of the objectivity proper to history, just as his craft is the measure of the good and bad subjectivity implied by this objectivity.

"The Historian's Craft": we all know that this is the subtitle which Marc Bloch gave to his *Apologie pour l'histoire*. Unfortunately, this book was never completed; yet it still contains all that we need to lay the foundations for our reflection. The titles of the chapters concerning method (Historical Observation, Historical Criticism, Historical Analysis) do not leave us in any doubt; they mark the stages of an objectivity in development.

We must be grateful to Marc Bloch for having used the term "observation" to designate the historian's approach to the past. By making use of an expression of Simiand, who called history a "knowledge through traces," Bloch shows that the historian's apparent bondage of never being in the presence of his past object but only its trace by no means disqualifies history as science. Grasping the past in and through its documentary traces is an *observation* in the strong sense of the word—for to observe never means the mere recording of a brute fact. To reconstruct an event, or rather a series of events, or a situation, or an institution, on the basis of documents is to elaborate an objective behavior of a particular type which cannot be doubted. For this reconstruction presupposes that the document is interrogated and forced to speak; that the historian goes to meet its meaning by establishing a working hypothesis. Not only does the historian's inquiry raise the trace to the dignity of a meaningful document, but it also raises the past itself to the dignity of an historical fact. The document was not a document before the historian came to ask it a question. Thus, on the basis of his observation, the historian establishes a document, so to speak, behind him, and in this way establishes historical facts. From this point of view, the historical fact is not fundamentally different from other scientific facts. In a similar comparison, G. Canguilhem maintains that "the scientific fact is what science makes in making itself." Objectivity is just that: a work of methodical activity. We may understand, then, why this activity bears the excellent name of "criticism."

We should also be grateful to Marc Bloch for initially using the word "analysis," instead of "synthesis," to designate the historian's activity of trying to *explain*. He is ever so right in maintaining that the historian's task is not to restore things "such as they happened." For history's ambition is not to bring the past back to life but to recompose and reconstruct, that is to say, to compose and construct a retrospective sequence. The objectivity of history consists precisely in repudiating the attempt to relive and coincide with the past; it consists in the ambition to elaborate factual sequences on the level of an historical understanding. Marc Bloch emphasizes the tremendous amount of abstraction that such a work presupposes. There is no *explanation* without the constitution of several "series" of phenomena: economic, political, cultural, etc. In fact, if one could not identify or recognize the *same* function in *other* events there would be nothing to understand; there is history only because certain "phenomena" continue. "In so far as their development comes about from the older to the more recent, human phenomena are governed primarily by chains of similar phenomena. Thus, to classify them according to kind is to unveil the principal effective lines of force." [2] Historical synthesis exists only because history is first of all an analysis and not an emotional coinciding. Like every other scientist, the historian tries to find the relations between the phenomena that he has distinguished. Consequently, we shall insist on the necessity of understanding wholes and the organic bonds which transcend all analytical causality. It may be seen, then, that we shall oppose understanding and explanation. Yet this distinction cannot be looked upon as the key to historical methodology. As Marc Bloch says, "The work of recomposition can only come after analysis. Or to be more percise, recomposition is only the continuation of analysis, its ultimate justification. In primitive analysis, where it is a question of contemplation rather than of observation, we cannot discern interrelationships inasmuch as nothing is distinct." [3]

Understanding is therefore not the opposite of explanation; on the contrary, it is its complement and counterpart. It bears the mark of the analysis or the analyses which made it possible. And it retains this mark to the end; the consciousness of an era, which the historian tries to reconstruct within his most far-reaching syntheses, is nourished by all the interactions and varied relations he has won through analysis. The full historical fact, the "integral past," is properly an Idea in the Kantian sense, that is to say, the *never attained limit* of an ever more extensive and complex effort to integrate. The notion of the "integral past" is the *regulative idea* of that effort. This notion is not given immediately, since nothing is more mediate than a totality; it is the product of a "master conception" which expresses the historian's supreme effort to put history in order. It is, to speak another (but scientific) language,

2. *Apologie pour l'histoire*, p. 74.
3. *Ibid.*, p. 78.

the fruit of "theory," in the sense in which we speak of "physical theory."

No "master conception," moreover, can encompass the whole of history. An epoch is still a product of analysis. History will never propose to our understanding anything more than "total parts" (in the words of Leibnitz), that is, "analytic syntheses" (which is a bold expression from Kant's "Transcendental Deduction").

And so history is thoroughly faithful to its etymology: it is a "research," ἱστορία [historia]. It is not an anxious interrogation on our discouraging historicity, on our way of living and sliding along in time, but rather a reply to this "historical" condition—a reply through the *choice of history,* through the choice of a certain *knowledge,* of a will to understand rationally, to build what Fustel de Coulanges called the "science of human societies" and what Marc Bloch calls a "rational enterprise of analysis."

This desire for objectivity is not limited to a critique of documents, as a narrow positivism would have it. On the contrary, it even encourages great syntheses. Its near rationalism is of the same nature as that of modern physics, and in this respect there is no reason for history to have an inferiority complex.

[2] THE OBJECTIVITY OF HISTORY AND THE HISTORIAN'S SUBJECTIVITY

LET US NOW DISCUSS the relationship of contemporary criticism to the historian's craft, a relationship which bears upon his desire and endeavor for objectivity. For a half century, contemporary criticism has emphatically insisted on the role of the historian's subjectivity in the elaboration of history.

It would seem that we cannot consider this subjectivity in itself without at first knowing in what it is engaged, namely, a rational enterprise of analysis. Prudence requires, then, that we proceed in the manner of the reflective tradition, that is, that we look for this subjectivity in its intention, endeavor, and works. Neither is there a physics without physicists, that is, without trial and error, groping in the dark, abandonments, and unparalleled discoveries. Kant's Copernican revolution did not consist in the apotheosis of the subjectivity of scientists but rather in the discovery of that subjectivity which is the reason there are objects. To reflect on the historian's subjectivity is, in the same way, to search out the subjectivity which the historian's craft calls into play.

But if there is a problem peculiar to the historian, this depends upon certain features of objectivity which we have not yet discussed. These features make historical objectivity an incomplete objectivity by comparison with that which is attained, or at least approached, in the other sciences. In presenting these features I shall try not to mitigate the obvious contrasts between this new stage of reflection and the preceding one.

1. The first feature refers to the notion of historical choice, a notion whose meaning we have by no means exhausted in saying that the historian emphasizes the rationality of history. This choice for rationality implies another choice within the historian's work itself; this other kind of choice stems from what could be called the *judgment of importance* in that it presides over the selection of events and factors. History, as it comes through the historian, retains, analyzes, and connects only the important events. Unlike the physicist's subjectivity, the historian's subjectivity intervenes here in an original way as a set of interpretative schemata. The quality of the interrogator therefore becomes essential to the very selection of the documents interrogated. Or, in other words, the judgment of importance, by getting rid of the accessory, creates continuity: that which actually took place is disconnected and torn by insignificance; the narrative is connected and meaningful because of its continuity. Thus the rationality of history depends upon this judgment of importance—a judgment which lacks, however, a sure criterion. On this point we must agree with Raymond Aron when he says that "theory precedes history."

2. Secondly, history is dependent in varying degrees upon a *popular conception of causality.* According to this conception, cause sometimes designates "the phenomenon which is last in the order of occurrence, which is the least permanent and most exceptional in the general order of the world" (Marc Bloch), or it may designate a configuration of slowly evolving forces, and sometimes a permanent structure. In this respect, the work of Braudel (*La Méditerranée et le monde méditerranéen à l'époque de Philippe II*) marks an important date, from the point of view of methodology, owing to its effort to unravel and put these causalities into order. First, Braudel posits the permanent influence of the mediterranean setting; next, the particular but relatively constant forces of the latter half of the sixteenth century; and lastly, the flow of events. This effort to distinguish different tiers of causality is certainly in line with the endeavor of historical objectivity. But this ordering will always remain precarious, for to arrange in a composite whole various causalities which are scarcely homogeneous and which have themselves been established and properly constituted by analysis raises a practically insoluble problem. In

any event, among the component causalities must be included psychological motivations, and these are always tainted by a common sense psychology.

The very meaning of the causality which the historian makes use of often remains naive and pre-critical, wavering between determinism and probability. History is condemned to *use* several schemes of explanation concurrently, without having carefully considered them or even, perhaps, distinguished them: conditions which are not determinations, motivations which are not causations, causations which are only fields of influence, opportunities, etc.

In short, the historian "practices" ways of explanation which go beyond his reflection. This is natural, because explanation is brought about and effected before being possessed reflectively.

3. An additional feature of this incomplete objectivity stems from what could be called the phenomenon of "historical distance." To understand rationally is to attempt to recognize or identify (Kant called intellectual synthesis the synthesis of recognition in a concept). Now, history's task is to specify what has changed, what has been done away with, what was *other*. The ancient dialectic of the *same* and the *other* crops up here again, and the professional historian encounters it in the very concrete form of the difficulties related to historical language, particularly those of nomenclature. For example, how can we designate and make discarded institutions and situations understood in contemporary language—in the actual national language—if not by using functional likenesses which will be corrected later through differentiation? We have only to recall the difficulties that accompany the words *tyranny, serfdom, feudalism, State,* etc. Each of these words illustrates the historian's struggle to find a nomenclature that will allow him both to identify and to specify; this is why historical language is necessarily *equivocal.* Historical time here sets its own dissimulating work, its disparity, against the assimilative quality of the understanding. The historian cannot elude the nature of time wherein we have recognized, since the time of Plotinus, the irreducible phenomenon of self-alienation, of drawing out, of distension, in a word, of original "otherness."

At this point we are confronted with one of the sources of the inexact and non-rigorous characteristic of history. The historian is never in the position of the mathematician who denominates and, by denominating, determines the very structure of a notion: "I call line the intersection of two surfaces . . ."

On the other hand, that which takes the place of this primordial activity of denomination, by which an exact science puts itself in direct contact with its object, is a certain ability the historian has of withdrawing from his customary environment and projecting himself hypothetically into another present. He considers the epoch that he studies as the present of reference, the center of temporal perspectives. Such a present has a future made up of the expectations, the ignorance, the forecasts and fears of men of that time, and not of the things which we know happened. That present also has a past, which is the memory of past men and not of what we *know* of their past. Now, this projection into another present, which belongs to the type of objectivity proper to history, is a kind of *imagination,* a temporal imagination, as it were, since another present is re-presented, and re-placed in the background of "temporal distance" which is "past times." It is certain that this imagination marks the appearance of a subjectivity which is never approached by the sciences of space, matter, and life. It is even a rare gift to be able to make the historical past come *closer* to us, while at the same time restoring historical *distance,* or, in other words, while establishing in the reader's mind a consciousness of remoteness and temporal depth.

4. The last decisive feature, which is not least important, is that what history ultimately tries to explain and understand are *men.* The past from which we are removed is the human past. In addition to temporal distance, therefore, there is that specific distance which stems from the fact that the other is a different man.

Here again we meet up with the problem of the integral past. For what the historian attempts to restore through the whole network of causal relations is precisely what other men have experienced. The inexhaustible human character of the past therefore necessitates the work of integral comprehension. An attempt is made to reachieve the absolute reality of past human experience in an ever more unified reconstruction and in increasingly differentiated and ordered analytic syntheses.

Now we said that this integral history of past men is an *idea,* the limit of an intellectual approximation. It should also be said that it is the term anticipated by a sympathetic effort which is not merely an imaginative projection into another present but a real projection into another human life. This sympathy lies at the beginning and at the end of the intellectual approximation just mentioned; it initiates the work of the historian as a first immediacy, then it works as a predisposing affinity for the object studied, and springs up again as a last immediacy, as a supplementary compensation at the end of a long analysis. Reasoned analysis is a kind of methodical step between an uncultivated and an educated sympathy.

History is therefore animated by a will for *encounter* as much as by a will for *explanation*. The historian goes to the men of the past with his own human experience. The historian's subjectivity takes on a striking prominence at the moment when, over and above all critical chronology, history makes the values of past men surge forth. This calling up of values, which is ultimately the only way of evoking man that is open to us since we are unable to relive what they lived, is not possible unless the historian is vitally "interested" in those values and has a deep affinity for the task. Not that the historian should share the faith of his heroes; in that case he would seldom write history but rather apologetics or hagiography. He must, however, be capable of granting their faith hypothetically, which is a way of entering into the problematic of that faith while at the same time "suspending" or "neutralizing" it and not looking upon it as an actually professed faith.

The suspended and neutralized adoption of the beliefs of past men is the sympathy proper to the historian; it adds the crowning touch to what was called earlier the imagination of another present by means of temporal projection. Accordingly, this temporal projection is also an extension into another subjectivity which is adopted as a center of perspective. The necessity for this springs from the historian's radical situation: he is a part of history not only in the trite sense that the past is the past of his present, but also in the sense that the men of the past are part of the same humanity. History is therefore one of the ways by which men "repeat" their belonging to the same humanity; it is a sector of the communication of minds which is divided by the methodological stage of traces and documents; therefore it is distinct from the dialogue wherein the other *answers*, but is not a sector wholly cut off from full intersubjectivity which always remains open and in process.

Here we reach that other frontier where the objectivity of history brings out the latent subjectivity of history and no longer just the historian's subjectivity. Before taking this step, let us turn back upon our path to get our bearings. Do these considerations destroy our first cycle of analyses concerning historical objectivity? Does the intrusion of the historian's subjectivity signify, as some claim, the "disintegration of the object"? By no means; we have only specified the kind of objectivity that arises from the historian's craft, the historical objectivity among all the objectivities. In short, we have elucidated the *constitution* of historical objectivity as being the correlate of the subjectivity proper to the historian.

The foregoing, then, explains why the subjectivity brought into play is not just *any* subjectivity, but precisely the subjectivity *of* the historian. The judgment of importance, the network of schemes of causality, the projection into a different and imagined present, the sympathy for other men and other values, and lastly, that ability to meet another from a different epoch—all of these bestow on the historian's subjectivity a greater wealth of harmonics than, for example, is entailed by the physicist's subjectivity. But the historian's subjectivity is not, for all that, a subjectivity *adrift*.

It is meaningless to say that history is relative to the historian. For *who* is the historian? Just as the perceived object is relative to what Husserl calls the ortho-aesthetic body, that is to say, relative to a normal sensibility, so too the scientific object is always relative to an ordered mind. This relativity has nothing to do with just any relativism, with a subjectivism of will to live, will to power, or what have you. Like every scientific subjectivity, the historian's subjectivity represents the triumph of a good subjectivity over a bad one.

After the voluminous work of philosophical criticism which reached its climax with Raymond Aron's book, perhaps we should now ask the following question: what is *good* and what is *bad* subjectivity? As Henri Marrou acknowledges, even though he is generally sympathetic to the critical school, we find at a higher level, at the level of that "broadened and deepened history" which Marc Bloch and Lucien Febvre call for, the values that positivism had a scanty but authentic sense of. "Progress (in scientific method) is made by going beyond facts and not by reacting upon them. Our challenge of the validity of the axioms of the positivist method is only on the surface; they remain valid at their level, but the discussion is moved one step forward—we are on a different peak." [4] Positivism does not go beyond the level of documentary criticism; moreover, the physical model it used was deficient and had little connection with the physics of physicists. But over and above its fetishism of facts—by now regarded as false in physics where self-evident facts are not to be found either—positivism reminds us that neither the judgment of importance, nor theory, nor temporal imagination, nor above all sympathy, hand history

4. "De la logique à l'éthique en histoire," in *Revue de métaphysique et de morale*, no. 3–4 (1949), 257. I here express my substantial agreement with H. I. Marrou's book, *De la connaissance historique* (Editions du Seuil, 1954).

over to some subjective madness. These subjective dispositions are dimensions of historical objectivity itself.

After having observed and insisted that history *reflects* the subjectivity of the historian, we must say that the historian's craft *educates* his subjectivity. History makes the historian as much as the historian makes history. Or, to be more precise, the historian's craft makes history *and* the historian. Feeling and imagination used to be opposed to reason; today we put them back, in a certain way, into rationality. But in return, the rationality that the historian has chosen is of such a nature that the cleavage moves into the very heart of feeling and imagination, separating what I shall call an *investigative* ego from a *pathetic* ego, that is to say, the resentful, hateful, reproaching ego. Let us listen one last time to Marc Bloch: "To understand is not to judge." The old saying, *sine ira nec studio,* is not valid only at the level of documentary criticism; its meaning merely becomes more subtle and valuable at the level of the highest synthesis. Nor should we neglect to note that this pathetic ego is not necessarily one which thunders forth; it may also be the apparent "apathy" of hypercriticism which disparages every reputed splendor and belittles every value which it encounters. This intellectual churlishness flows from what I call the pathetic ego in the same way as political passion which has turned away from contemporary political struggles to focus its attention on the past.

There is no history, therefore, without an ἐποχή [epoché] of everyday subjectivity, without the establishment of this investigative ego from which history draws its excellent name. For ἱστορία [historia] is precisely the "availability" and "submission to the unexpected," that "openness to others" whereby bad subjectivity is overcome.

And so ends this first cycle of reflections. At first objectivity appeared to us as the *scientific* intention of history. It now marks the difference between a good and a bad subjectivity of the historian. Whereas the definition of objectivity was "logical," it has now become "ethical."

[3] HISTORY AND PHILOSOPHICAL SUBJECTIVITY

Is A REFLECTION on subjectivity in history exhausted by these considerations on the subjectivity of the *historian,* by this division in the historian himself between an investigative subjectivity and a passional subjectivity?

Let us recall our point of departure and the manifold "interests" involved in history. We still expect history to uncover a subjectivity other than that of the historian who makes history, a subjectivity which would be history's very own, which would be history itself.

But perhaps this subjectivity no longer concerns the historian's craft but rather the work of the *reader* of history, the lover of history that we all are, something which the philosopher has very particular reasons to be. For the historian's history is a *written* or professed work which, like every such work, only finds its completion in the reader, the student and the public. This *"recovering"* of the historian's history by the philosopher-reader raises the problems which we are now going to examine.

I shall leave aside altogether the use of history as a diversion, as a "delight in hearing and reading extraordinary things," in short, as an exotic adventure in time. Nevertheless, we have seen that this movement of self-estrangement belongs to the historical consciousness and so is the necessary step toward a more philosophical use. For if history did not withdraw us from our customary surroundings, how could it enable us to find a subjectivity that is less egoistic, more mediate, and, in a word, more human? I shall speak even less of history as a source of precepts. For although the self-discovery [*prise de conscience*] of which we shall speak is a recovery [*reprise*] of the values manifested in history and in a way is useful for our instruction, nevertheless we shall not reduce the main use of history to this didactic concern. The instruction that we derive from history is something extra thrown into the bargain when we go back to it as we should. For the moment, therefore, I shall consider only the use that the *philosopher* may make of the historian's history. The philosopher has a specific way of fulfilling in himself the historian's work. This consists in making his *own* "self-discovery" coincide with a "recovery" of history.

I do not hide the fact that this reflection does not agree with all conceptions of philosophy. Yet I think it applies to the whole group of philosophies which we may broadly call reflective, whether they take their starting point from Socrates, Descartes, Kant, or Husserl. All these philosophies are in search of the *authentic* subjectivity, of the *authentic* act of consciousness. What we have to constantly discover and rediscover is that this itinerary from the *ego* to the *I*,[5] which we shall call self-discovery, involves a certain meditation on history, and that this detour of reflection through

5. To the *I* and to the *We*. But it is the same thing, for it concerns the *first* person in the singular and in the plural.

history is one of the ways, the philosophical way, of completing the historian's work in the reader.

This completion of the historian's history in the philosophical act may be pursued in two directions—by way of a "logic of philosophy" which looks for a coherent meaning throughout history, or by way of a "dialogue" with philosophers and particular philosophies, a dialogue which is always unique and exclusive.

1. History as the "Advent" of Meaning

LET US FOLLOW the first path, that of Comte, Hegel, Brunschvicg, the later Husserl, and Eric Weil. In spite of the great differences which separate their interpretations of reason and history, all these thinkers have the same conviction in common: the clarity I am seeking about myself involves a history of consciousness. The "direct" path of self-knowledge and the "indirect" path of the history of consciousness coincide. I have need of history in order to get out of my private subjectivity and to experience in and beyond myself the *being-man*, the *Menschsein*. In this respect, Husserl, with whom I am best acquainted, presents a striking example: this thinker, pre-eminently subjective, was called by events to interpret himself historically. It took the Nazi indictment of all Socratic and transcendental philosophy to make the Freiburg professor look for support in the great tradition of reflective philosophy and recognize there the *meaning* of the Occident.

There is the great word: *meaning* [*sens*]. Through history I attempt to justify the *meaning* of the history of "the" consciousness. But let us not be too quick to look for the difficulties which stand in the way of such a claim. Let us first try to get a good understanding of what the philosopher *expects* from such a step and what he *supposes* to be true in order to undertake it.

The philosopher expects that a certain coincidence of the "direct" path of self-knowledge and the "indirect" path of history *justifies* this claim. Hence, the philosopher calls on history because he is threatened, shaken, and even humiliated to his very depths. Distrusting himself, he tries to regain possession of his own meaning by recovering the meaning of the history lying beyond his own consciousness. The philosopher therefore writes history also; he makes history, the history of the transcendental motive, the history of the *Cogito*. Thus the philosopher expects a justification from this history of consciousness.

Let us now show what this expectation presupposes: it presupposes that the coincidence of the meaning of my consciousness and the meaning of history is possible. The philosopher believes in a certain teleology of history. In other words, history as a flux of *events* ought to be such that through this flux man arises, an *advent* of man is mediated.

We see, then, that this supposition is twofold: there is the element of reason and the element of history. With respect to the first, the philosopher supposes that reason develops a history because it is of the order of necessity, of a task, of what ought to be, of the regulative idea—and tasks are only realized in a history. With respect to the second element, the philosopher supposes that history is endowed with its properly human quality through the emergence and promotion of values which the philosopher can go back to and understand as a development of consciousness. Such is the twofold supposition of the philosopher. It is a twofold trust that the philosopher places in the historicity of reason on the one hand, and in the significance of history on the other. The birth and development of philosophy in Greece and in the Occident are for him the proof and pledge that this twofold trust is not given in vain. The history of philosophy appears to him to be the bond between the historicity of reason and the significance of history.

That is what the philosopher—at least the Socratic, transcendental, reflective philosopher—expects from history and what he presupposes in his expectation. No doubt the professional historian considers such an undertaking with a good deal of suspicion; his reservations should help us to measure the scope and limits of a philosophical use of history.

In the first place, the professional historian will flatly refuse to identify history with the history of philosophy, even less so with the history of consciousness, and least of all with any advent whatsoever. He will undoubtedly say that the meaning and teleology of history totally escapes him, that this is not a true question for a "professional historian," and that the supposition of some meaning or other is not even required by an "apology for history." Longing for the enlargement and thorough exploration of history, he looks for them not in a rational meaning but rather in the complexity and wealth of connections between the geographical, economic, social, and cultural factors. He believes that mankind is infinitely varied in its factual reality, much more than it is unified in its theoretical meaning. On the whole, the historian will distrust philosophy, above all the philosophy of history. He fears that the latter will crush history with its system-building mentality, will destroy its characteristic of *historia*. And so the historian will oppose the objectivity he conquers by means of his subjectivity as a historian to the philosophical subjectivity in which the philosopher would like to engulf both the historian's objectivity and his subjectivity.

The historian's reservations and refusals are quite legitimate and show us the real meaning of a history of consciousness. The philosopher does not have to ask the historian for such a history, and, if he should, the historian ought to reject his request. For a history of consciousness is a work of the philosopher, of the historian of philosophy, if you like. The history of philosophy, however, is an undertaking for the philosopher.

The reason for this is that the philosopher is the one who composes the history of philosophy. He does so by means of a second degree operation whereby he comes back upon history in order to "recover" meaning. The philosopher has asked history (the historian's history) a certain type of question which discloses the "choice of the philosopher" (in the sense in which we spoke above of the "historian's choice"). These questions have to do with the emergence of values dealing with knowledge, action, life, and existence—values which emerge through the temporal span of human societies. Once he has chosen to privilege this interpretation, he faithfully follows out the execution of his project. And since he too has a limited subjectivity and approaches the meaning of history with a preconception of what is to be looked for (but whoever looks for nothing finds nothing), the philosopher rediscovers in history the meaning he had suspected was there. Shall we say it is a vicious circle? Not at all, for this meaning remains presentiment until history intervenes in order to raise this presentiment of meaning to a definite, articulated, and true understanding. We may always criticize the various histories of consciousness, be it Comte's *Course of Positive Philosophy,* Hegel's *Phenomenology of Spirit,* Brunschvicg's *Le Progrès de la conscience dans la philosophie Occidentale,* Husserl's *Krisis der europäischen Wissenschaften,* or Eric Weil's *Logique de la philosophie.* The only legitimate way to criticize them, however, is to write another and better history of consciousness, that is, one which is both more comprehensive and more coherent. But once it is understood that this sort of history is a second degree *composition,* an act of philosophical responsibility and not a datum of the historian's history, still less an absolute reality or a history in itself, we cannot see what objection the professional historian can still have to such an undertaking. In the words of Eric Weil, the historian's history brings human "attitudes" into the open; the philosopher, through his specific act of recovery, raises the "attitudes" to the status of "categories" and looks for a coherent order of the categories in a "coherent discourse." But then this history of spirit becomes a "logic of philosophy" and no longer remains an historian's history.

It seems to me that the above clarification considerably lessens the enormity and scandal that the historian finds in the philosopher's pretension to treat history as the advent of meaning. Since meaning appears through a specific act of "recovery," the difference between *event* and *advent* therefore remains. The historian's history is not swallowed up in this meaningful history. On the contrary, it is always presupposed as the great matrix of the attitudes which the philosopher recovers. Moreover, not content with nourishing the history of philosophy, the historian's history is a permanent warning against the risks of such an undertaking; it reminds the rationalist philosopher of the importance of what he leaves out of consideration, of what he refuses to thematize because of his rationalist "philosopher's choice." The historian's history reminds the philosopher of the nonsense from which every sense is taken. And yet the philosopher will not be disturbed by the display of greed, follies, and failures which history unfolds, for he knows that his history is not discovered, but rediscovered within the tasks of reason.

Furthermore, this history of consciousness not only abandons the non-meaningful (at least from the point of view of philosophical reason), but it also abandons the individual, the non-systematizable, and the exceptional. But is not the singularity and incomparability of each philosophy just as important an aspect of history as the rationality of the movement of the whole?

2. History as a Sector of Intersubjectivity

WE ARE THEREFORE led back to the other philosophical interpretation of history. Instead of looking for breadth and system, the philosopher-historian may look for depth and singularity. He may turn toward a particular philosophy and try to determine how the whole problematic of an epoch and all the influences of the past are contained therein. Instead of putting that philosophy back into the movement of history, he will look upon the whole history of that philosophy as the motivation that it undergoes and embodies. In a word, history, instead of unfolding as a cohesive movement, will weave itself into persons and works; the philosopher-historian will then try to approach the question that the other philosopher is alone in having encountered and asked, the living question with which the thinker becomes identified. This long frequentation of an author, or of a small number of authors, tends toward the kind of close, exclusive relation that a man may have with his friends. The depth of the relationship does not allow him to extend this sort of communication to all philosophers, to all thinkers, to all men.

This philosophical way of viewing history is no more shocking for the professional historian than the previous one. Moreover, the historian who reflects on his own situation within the whole sphere of mankind is led to look upon the history he practices as included in the over-all communication of minds. The sector that history cuts out of this intersubjective totality is only defined methodologically by the conditions of a knowledge through traces, therefore by the initial role of the document. This explains why the encounter with history is never a dialogue, for the first condition of dialogue is that the other *answer;* history is this sector of communication without reciprocity. But granting this limitation, it is a kind of unilateral friendship, like unrequited love.

Will the choice of great philosophers as the topic of concern offend the historian? But the historian of philosophy does not claim that history culminates in a few philosophical geniuses; he and the professional historian have only made different choices. The choice for unusual individuals and their work, insofar as their work is singular and irreducible to generalities and familiar types (realism, empiricism, rationalism, etc.), implies that the economic, social, and political factors are considered *only* as influences, situations, and opportunities with respect to the appearance of some creative thinker or some outstanding work. The creator and the work become the center of gravity, the receptacle, the unique carrier of all influences, whether they be passively received or actively exercised. History is then understood as a series of disconnected appearances, each of which requires a new and total encounter.

I have deliberately presented these two ways by which philosophers interpret history parallel to one another. The historian's history is such that it can and should be "recovered" by philosophy in these two different styles, which are two different ways of bringing out the subjectivity of history. This subjectivity first appears as a unique human consciousness whose meaning is in progress as a continuous series of logical moments; it appears a second time as a multiple emergence—as a disconnected series of upheavals, each of which has a particular meaning. The most Hegelian philosopher, the one most determined to read history as coming to the self from the mind, cannot explain away the emergence of great men. The appearance of a Descartes, a Hume, or a Kant remains an event which is irreducible to the advent of reason through the partial discourse that each of these men constitutes in the whole of discourse.

This twofold possibility of philosophical interpretation may be instructive for the professional historian, for it brings out a latent paradox in all history, although the paradox only comes into view by this recovery of general history in a history of consciousness, be it collective or individual. The latent paradox is this: we say history, *history in the singular,* because we expect this unique history of mankind to be unified and made reasonable by a human meaning. The rationalist philosopher who writes a history of consciousness tries to elucidate this implicit wager. But we also say men, *men in the plural,* and we define history as the science of past men because we find persons who emerge as radically manifold centers of mankind. The existentialist philosopher brings this idea out into the open by devoting himself to the outstanding works in which the cosmos is reorganized around an exceptional center of existence and thought.

History, for men like ourselves, is virtually continuous and discontinuous, continuous as a unique meaning in progress and discontinuous as a configuration of persons. And so the virtual rationality and virtual historicity of history come to the surface in the philosophical discovery of history. We could easily show that this division affects not only our representation of time, whose structure leads to antinomies at the level of the philosophical discovery of history, but also our representation of truth. For the antinomy of historical time is not the antinomy of sense and nonsense, as if meaning were only one alternative, but is rather the antinomy of the meaning of history itself. The notion of meaning is not exhausted by that of development or sequence, for the episodic events of history cannot be viewed as sources of irrationality but must be seen as organizing centers of significance. Contrary to the first interpretation, we may say, in the words of P. Thévenaz, that "the most genuine event is one which most forces itself upon consciousness as an organizing center of historical becoming. Its irruptive force comes from its radiating power which orders history and gives it significance. Indeed, the events themselves make the reality of history; they support its rationality and give it meaning. The significance of history does not lie outside of the events; if history has a meaning it is because one or several central events (which, of course, always overlap within a consciousness of historicity) give it a meaning, because the event is the meaning itself." [6] History may therefore be looked upon as an extensive development of meaning and as an irradiation of meanings from a multiplicity of organizing centers. No man who is immersed in history, however, can arrange the total meaning of those radiated meanings. Every "narrative" shares in the two aspects of meaning; as a composite unity it counts on the whole order in which the events become unified; as a dramatized narration it runs from episode to episode, from climax to climax.

Lastly, this antinomy of historical time is the reason for our hesitation between the two fundamental "attitudes" which men take toward their own history. Whereas the interpretation of history as an advent of consciousness leans toward an optimistic ideal, the interpretation of history which takes account of the sudden appearance of individual centers of consciousness leads rather to a tragic vision of the ambiguity of man who always begins anew and who may always defect.

Perhaps it is of the essence of all history to lend itself to this twofold interpretation and to this fundamental hesitation. But only the recovery of history as the philosophical history of *subjectivity* makes the latent divorce come to a head and display itself. At least this divorce, at the level of a reflection on history, throws light on the past and justifies the historian's quandaries, caught as he is between the event-filled aspect and the structural aspect of history, between the great personages who make their appearance and the slowly progressing forces, or even the stable forms of the geographical environment. The historian has to tackle everything at once, for he works prior to the division between two histories of subjectivity. Indeed, what he writes is not at all a history of subjectivity but rather a history of men under all their aspects: economic, social, political, and cultural. The philosophical cleavages are consequent upon the philosopher's choice. But in looking back, we can see that the necessity of these cleavages explains how the historian's methodological quandaries are *founded* and that, in spite of his scruples, he must tackle an event-filled history and a structural history at the same time.

Perhaps that is not the only benefit the historian may draw from the philosophical recovery of his own work; not only is he enlightened after the events on the inherent ambiguities in his

---

6. P. Thévenaz, "Evenement et historicité" in *L'Homme et l'histoire*, pp. 223–24.

undertaking, but also on his fundamental intention. In point of fact, the philosophical act has made man appear as consciousness, as subjectivity; this act is valuable as a reminder and perhaps at times awakens the historian. It reminds the historian that the justification of his enterprise is man—man and the values he discovers or develops in his civilizations. And this reminder sometimes rings as an awakening when the historian is tempted to repudiate his fundamental intention and yield to the *fascination for a false objectivity*—that of a history in which there would no longer be men and human values but only structures, forces, and institutions. Thus, the philosophical act brings in view, *in extremis,* the cleavage between a true and a false objectivity, I would readily say between objectivity and the objectivism which omits man.

The historian's profession has seemed to us to be sufficient to distinguish between the good and bad subjectivity of the historian. Perhaps the responsibility of philosophical reflection would be to distinguish between the good and the bad objectivity of history. For reflection constantly assures us that the *object* of history is the human *subject* itself.

The History of Philosophy
and the Unity of Truth

Quo magis res singulares intelligimus eo magis Deum intelligimus.
SPINOZA

WHOEVER TEACHES the history of philosophy or studies it as a branch of philosophical training runs up against the
problem of its *philosophical significance*. The problem concerns
the *meaning* of the work of the historian of philosophy. It also
concerns the original philosopher who does research at his own
risks for his own benefit and without troubling to explain the past.
For he is well aware that if philosophy goes on it is because there
are philosophers and because the history of philosophy continues
to make them present and to place us within their particular frame
of mind. The most self-taught philosopher cannot pass over
Socrates, Plato, Descartes, or Kant. For history ought to have some
meaning for the pursuit of truth.

Does this mean that philosophy exists and continues to exist
only by means of a history which *philosophers* make and is
accessible to us only through a history which the historians of
philosophy relate? I shall not try to construct a systematic answer
to this question by starting with a dogmatic principle. Rather, I
shall proceed by a series of *approximations* wherein the solution
reached at one level will be rectified by bringing the initial problem back into question.

[41]

[1]

Our point of departure will be an *aporia* or difficulty whose meaning we shall penetrate gradually by attempting to resolve it. We find this difficulty as soon as we relate the historical situation of philosophy to the idea of truth which initially confronts us as a first approximation. In its most unrefined form, truth appears as a regulative idea, as the task of unifying knowledge both from the side of the object and from the side of the subject. It is the task of imposing unity on the diversity of our field of knowledge and of resolving differences of opinion. This idea of truth gives us an uneasy feeling within our historical condition—makes it seem disturbing and deceptive while making us long for a fullness of knowledge in the unity of immutability. I think it is good to start with this difficulty, even with its roughest form, using it as a first approximation of our problem. On the one hand, we have a series of philosophies which contradict and destroy each other, each of them manifesting a changing truth; the history of philosophy then becomes a lesson in scepticism. On the other hand, we are seeking a truth whose sign, if not the criterion, would be an agreement of minds. If all history engenders a degree of skepticism, every claim to truth fosters a degree of dogmatism. From this point of view, history would only be a history of errors and truth would be the suspension of history.

It seems to me that we must take this first approximation of the problem seriously and not attempt to get rid of it too quickly. There is no historian of philosophy who, in a moment of dejection, has not been tormented by this vertigo of variation. Likewise, there is no philosopher who, in a moment of exaltation, has not been tempted by this imperialism of truth. For when it is discovered, the idea of truth does away with history. And so Descartes and Husserl thought they were putting an end to the wanderings of history, they cast history aside and viewed it as that from which truth had extracted them. History had foundered under the great subversion of doubt.

Certainly we must take this first approximation of the problem seriously, but we must also shield the problems of history and truth against premature solutions. The most mediocre is that of eclecticism, the most enticing that of an immanent logic of history. Eclecticism does not deserve a very detailed examination, although it is a tempting way out and an economic solution—that of philosophical chattering. Eclecticism proclaims that all great systems ultimately say the same thing, at least if one knows how to distinguish the essential from the accessory. Truth is then the adding together of scattered and harmonious truths. In actual fact, the history of philosophy, according to eclecticism, is saved by a shameful philosophy; eclecticism goes to history to search out the scattered members of a philosophy without genius. The geniuses converge toward eclectic talent. But in this vulgar form we may recognize the vice of all histories of philosophy which pretend to be the unacknowledged philosophies of history: one philosophy (the historian's personal philosophy) is privileged and placed at the end of history as the goal toward which all past efforts were aspiring. History marches toward me; I am the end of history. The law governing the construction of the history of philosophy is the very meaning of *my* philosophy.

This quite patent vice in eclecticism is that of Hegelianism. According to it, there is an internal history of philosophy inasmuch as a unity of intention manifests itself in a development. Consequently, it is possible, it maintains, to find the law of this internal progress and to consider the departures and apparent impasses of philosophical reflection as a kind of "dodge" of reason or as a purely mental pedagogy.

This solution is quite tempting because it allows us to reconcile history and reason by endowing history with a meaning and reason with a goal. At the same time, it appears to be the only thing capable of giving meaning to the idea of *history of philosophy*, the unique philosophy appearing as the unique movement that traverses all philosophies. Moreover, within the social flux of thinking and acting, it gives its autonomy to the manifold series of philosophies: in linking each phase of the history of philosophy to the preceding one, the philosophy of history detaches the ensemble of philosophies from the several other series (economic, religious, linguistic, etc.). And this is why this solution is very tempting. I believe it is necessary, however, to have the courage to deprive ourselves of it and *to do the history of philosophy without doing the philosophy of history*. If, in effect, we save philosophy as a unique development, we then lose the multiplicity of philosophies, and this for two reasons. First, what is sacrificed is ultimately the profound originality, the incomparable intention, and the unique vision of the real that a philosophy proposes to us. According to the above theory, each philosopher must occupy a certain rank, continue the work of his predecessors, and pave the way for his successors. The absolute center of thought that each philosopher is must become a relative moment within a dialectic, the transitory seat of a development, like those individual organisms which Bergson says are the places where the stream of life passes. Secondly, and this is perhaps the more serious reason, the philosopher who imposes a single interpretation on the history of philosophy exercises on all authors a kind of imperialism which is the contrary of the historian's attitude. The latter, it would seem, agrees at the outset to "uproot" himself, to put himself under the law of another, and to conduct his investigation as an exercise in communication and, I might add, in charity. But the philosophers who do the history of philosophy as philosophers of history not only do not respect the distinct and incomparable intentions of the great philosophers, but also require all history to end in them. The grandiose philosophies of history are tormented by the same evil as are the wretched eclecticisms: they end history with the last philosopher of history.

The difficulty, therefore, remains intact: there is a huge gulf separating the task of establishing a single truth and the history of divergent philosophies.

[2]

BUT PERHAPS we must bring the terms of the contradiction back into question so as to raise it from the level of a *mortal dilemma* to that of a *living paradox*. We shall approach a second approximation of the difficulty by deepening our understanding of the history of philosophy. Then we shall move on to a third approximation by symmetrically correcting our idea of truth.

The history of philosophy becomes a lesson in skepticism only if it is looked upon as a series of varying solutions to unchanging problems, those that are called the eternal problems (freedom, reason, reality, soul, God, etc.). If the problems remain constant while the solutions to them vary, the contradiction of systems results from the common element of an identical problem. This first supposition is linked to a second one. The varying answers to fixed problems are typical answers: realism, idealism, materialism, spiritualism. Now we must question this interpretation of philosophies as being typical answers to anonymous and abstract problems which are passed on from hand to hand. Hence we must first consider a preliminary question: *what is it to understand a philosophy?*

I shall begin with some remarks made by E. Bréhier in the first two chapters of his book *La Philosophie et son passé*, chiefly in the chapter on "Causality in the history of philosophy." E. Bréhier distinguishes three levels of work which are proper to the historian of philosophy. First, external history sees in a philosophy only a cultural fact, a network of representations susceptible of being explained by sociology, psychology, or even by psychoanalysis or economics. From this point of view, a philosophy is merely one social or psychological effect among others. The bond between philosophy and the philosopher is weakened to the benefit of the historical context. In this sense, philosophy is nothing more than a symptom. This point of view is valid within the framework of an *objective* investigation of societies and the psychism. Yet it lacks the core of the philosophical intention. As seen by a non-philosopher, the history of philosophy rests upon a history of ideas or upon a sociology of knowledge. But as we shall see, the history of philosophy is, in certain respects, a philosophical activity (we shall come back to this presently in correcting our idea of truth).

At the second level is found critical history, and this level is closer to the intention of the philosopher himself. It looks for *sources*. Let us note this word: not the causes, but the sources, that is to say, the influences which have not only been experienced passively but also assumed and in certain respects chosen. Now, this critical history, which must always be done and which is the element of erudition in the historian of philosophy, is not sufficient of itself alone. For in so far as we look for the origin of such and such a theory we dismantle the system so as to reconstruct its fragments from all corners of the past; we reduce the unity of intention to the plurality of sources. The more we *explain* by sources the less we *understand* the system (according to this method, there would no longer be any philosophy at all, since each system would have to undergo this same process of decomposition: what would remain would simply be fibers of thoughts which come together and disband without any original creativity ever being achieved). I maintain that this critical history is not sufficient of itself alone, for it cannot explain the organic unity or the directive principle which makes up the coherence of a philosophy. The true historian puts trust in his author and wagers on coherence all the way: to understand is to understand in virtue of unity. Understanding therefore opposes a centripetal movement, which marches toward the central intuition, against the centrifugal movement of explanation by sources. In the words of E. Bréhier, the problem of the history of philosophy is the concentration of influences in "these personal intuitions which are the absolutes of the history of philosophy." [1] In this way we are led to search out the "direct and incomparable intuitions" [2] within different philosophies. The similarity between these views and those of Bergson (in *Philosophical Intuition*) and Karl Jaspers (whom Bréhier cites several times) is quite obvious.

Here, now, is the way in which we may extend these views so as to transform our initial problem of history and truth. Skepticism, we said, was linked: 1) to the reduction of philosophies to *typical* solutions (the famous textbook *isms*); and 2) to the comparison of these typical solutions to unchanging questions. Let us consider these two points in succession.

1. To understand a philosophy is to grasp either its central intuition, the ways in which it develops, its organic interconnections, or its systematic organization. *Typology* remains at the level of systematist thinking. Undoubtedly it has a pedagogical function in the sense that it orients the beginner's mind toward a sphere of problems and solutions; it creates an expectation directed toward a certain meaning, in accordance with the outlines of a more or less impersonal and anonymous *Weltanschauung*. In short, it serves to identify a philosophy as a first approximation by situating it within a familiar group (rationalism, empiricism, etc.). True historical comprehension, however, begins precisely at the point where this indentification is ended. It remains to move from the rationalist and realist types to a singular philosophy. The unity of a philosophy is a singular unity. In the words of Spinoza, it is not a *common species* but a *singular essence*. Now, this passage from the type or the species to the singular essence effects a true revolution in understanding. When one finds Plato breaking away from the realism and idealism of ordinary classifications, or when Berkeley shatters their neat, capsule formulae, but in a different way that is wholly original, it is at this moment that one approaches the singularity of their philosophies. Not that the most singular philosophies do not in any way lend themselves to such methods of classification: it is indeed inevitable that they should fall into them because of the common and anonymous thought-structures which lingered on in the consciousness of their epoch. It is unfortunate because they have only reiterated these anonymous thought-structures without transposing them integrally into their own singularity. Thus, the schema of the three hypostases was, for the whole of Alexandrian philosophy, a *Selbstverständlichkeit*, a com-

1. *La Philosophie et son passé*, p. 109.
2. *Ibid.*, p. 105.

mon way of classifying beings which is found in other Neo-Platonic authors besides Plotinus.

Every philosophy is therefore susceptible of typology in virtue of this "anonymity" that it bears. To which we must add that a polemic relation to other philosophies accelerates a process of sclerosis which initiates a lapse into the type. A philosophy not only takes on a certain amount of "anonymity" but engenders it as well. That is so true that the majority of the words of typology have come to be ignominious categories whereby adversaries attempt to contain each other, as in an abstract enclosure wherein they should die of starvation. Typology is therefore not merely an innocent pedagogical method which prepares for the encounter of a philosophy by orienting it toward the region or the vague spot where one could nail it down definitively. It also wanders into the realm of those deadly abstractions with which history is filled: instead of singular philosophies it knows only their empty shell, their socialized wrappings.

It is necessary, moreover, to have a proper understanding of these philosophical *singularities*. It would be entirely wrong to reduce them to the subjectivity of the philosophers themselves. For this would be to fall into literary explanation, psychography, or the psychoanalysis of philosophies. The important thing in the history of philosophy is that Plato's or Spinoza's subjectivity was raised to the status of a *work*, a network of significations where the author's biography is expressed or masked but where it is nevertheless suppressed in favor of a *meaning*. The singularity in question is that of the meaning of the work and not that of the author's peculiar experience. Even if it remains true that the *Ethics* is Spinoza's existential project, what is alone important to the historian of philosophy is the fact that Spinoza the man realized his project in the *Ethics* otherwise than in his life. This is the meaning of his work, the "philosopheme" of Spinoza which is the *singular essence* the historian aspires to attain.

2. We may now attack the idea of eternal and immutable problems. If we consider a philosophy in its concrete totality, the problem or problems that it raises, even if the author takes them over from an ancient tradition, share in his singularity; like him they become unique and part of his incomparable situation. Moreover, a great philosopher is above all one who upsets the anterior problematic, who recasts the principal questions in accordance with a new design. More radical than the man who answers, he is the man who questions. The great philosopher is one who, for the

first time, becomes astonished at a way of being in the world, and this astonishment inaugurates a new way of philosophizing—a question that *is* someone. Philosophical reason in him is primarily the elaboration in universal form of his fundamental question: the Cartesian problem of certitude, the Kantian problem of *a priori* synthetic judgments. If a new philosophy is approached by its questions rather than by its answers, one has the opportunity to approach the core where influences are concentrated. Previous philosophies here are no longer objective causes but aspects of its fundamental situation, aspects of a "philosophical motivation," of a totally motivating *Umwelt*. A philosophy is no longer the *effect* of a set of causes but rather that which encompasses everything else, and, up to a certain point, the choosing of its own historical motives.

Once we arrive at this point, our initial skepticism becomes dissipated, unless, as we shall see, it has not become transformed. When the typology of systems has been surpassed and philosophies have been singularized, and when solutions have been reduced to problems, then *philosophies become incommensurable*. Two problematics which are understood in terms of their most radical elements are incomparable; there is a radical discontinuity from one philosopher to another, over and above the continuity of influences, themes, and terminology. One is then tempted to say that each philosophy is *true* in so far as it provides an integral answer to the group of problems it has raised. The adequation of thought to reality—which is the classic definition of truth—here takes on the form of the adequation of answers to questions, of solutions to problems. And the great philosopher is the one who revives a problematic and offers a solution for it. In effect, he attempts to give the most coherent and comprehensive solution to the problem he raises. To be more precise, if one passes from truth-adequation to truth-discovery, then the truth of a great philosophy is more than the internal agreement of its answers to its questions, it is the discovery of the meaning of its situation, such as it appears to it problematically in the form of a question.

Let us stop at this level: we have delineated a skepticism of the first order, one that is based on the comparison of solutions which in turn are proportioned to eternal problems. This skepticism has been undermined along with its presuppositions. Is there a more subtle brand of skepticism which is its successor?

First, there are *many* philosophies. But is there *one* history of philosophy? We are faced with a discontinuous series of singular totalities, and in order to move from one to another, one has to make a leap. Bergson said that had Spinoza been born in a different epoch he would not have written one line of what he wrote, but there would have been a Spinozism identical to the one that we know. And Bréhier, who cites him without criticism, tends to make each philosophy an essence: "the philosopher certainly has a history," he says, "but not philosophy." [3] There is one history only because previous philosophies are part of the memory and situation of the new philosopher. In his own way, each philosopher encompasses the history of the past within himself in a historic moment that is a kind of absolute.

When we void the idea of history as a coherent series or as a logical development, we also void the idea of a unique truth. Philosophies are neither true nor false, but *other*. The otherness is, so to speak, beyond the true and the false. The great historian of philosophy, such as Delbos was, renders invulnerable or irrefutable the author that he reconstructs on the basis of that author's central point. Henceforth he *is*, Spinoza *is*, Kant *is*. And what we are here saying is not theoretical but quite accurately describes the temperament of the true historian. For him, the movement from one philosopher to another presupposes an effort of sympathy, a philosophical imagination that constitutes a kind of *suspension,* of ἐποχή [epoché], of truth.

Our initial dilemma between varying history and the idea of immutable truth henceforth takes on a more subtle form: a *neutral* sympathy becomes attached to history; *engagement* and the risk of being mistaken become associated with the search for truth. We know very well, moreover, that this opposition refers to a real situation: once one has taken on the task of understanding Spinoza in himself, one no longer asks whether what he said is true or false; one has, through the historian's craft, entered into the cycle of a truth which is granted by hypothesis, a truth that does not necessarily involve belief. In this way history may always become a kind of evasion of the search for truth. It is always possible to hide behind history so as to affirm nothing on one's own account. The true philosopher, however, plunges himself so completely into his own philosophy that he becomes almost incapable of reading other philosophers. It is known how the great philosophers held their predecessors and contemporaries in contempt; at a certain point some of them no longer read other philosophers and became encysted as it were within their own system. The progress of a philosopher within his own system

3. *Ibid.,* p. 115.

gradually makes him blind to history and unavailable to others. This incompatibility between the philosopher-historian of philosophy and the systematic philosopher has something in it that is both derisory and dramatic. Ultimately, the "skeptical" historian would no longer search for anything, and the "dogmatic" philosopher would have nothing but enemies or students but not friends.

[3]

IT MIGHT SEEM that we are confronted with a new impasse. Yet if we now bring back into question the other term of the antithesis, perhaps the preceding development will not have been useless.

We have considered the idea of truth as an abstraction that is both timeless and impersonal. Such is, as our first approximation, the idea of truth. But it takes on this abstract meaning only because it is the correlative idea of a task which is proposed to individual persons. It is the horizon, the final, abstract, timeless, and impersonal meaning of a concrete, temporal, and personal task. The idea of truth is sustained only by the *duty of thinking*. Henceforth, the other term which pairs off with history is not the idea of truth but *my* personal search whose idea of truth is on the horizon as my intended goal.

What is it therefore to search for truth? Perhaps the answer to this question will allow us to encompass the history of philosophy no longer as the antithetical term of truth, but to encompass it as its complement and its privileged road.

The search for truth, it seems, is characterized by being stretched, so to speak, between two poles: a personal situation, and a certain intention with respect to being. On the one hand, I have something to discover personally, something that no other except myself has the task of discovering. If my existence has a meaning, if it is not empty, I have a place within being which invites me to raise a question that no one else can raise in my place. The narrowness of my condition, my information, my encounters, my reading, already outline the finished perspectives of my calling to truth. And yet, on the other hand, to search for truth means that I aspire to express something that is valid for all, that stands out on the background of my situation as something universal. I do not want to invent or to say whatever I like, but what *is*. From the very roots of my situation I aspire to be bound by being. Let being be thought in me—such is my wish for truth. And so the search for truth is itself torn between the "finitude" of my questioning and the "openness" of being.

It is here that we discover the history of philosophy as the memory of great and singular philosophies: for on the road that ascends from my situation toward the truth, there is only one way of moving beyond myself, and this is *communication*. I have only one means of emerging from myself: I must be able to live within another. Communication is a structure of true knowledge. Thanks to it, the history of philosophy is not reduced to an irrational parade of scattered monographs, for it shows me the "meaning" of this historical chaos. This history is no longer the "imaginary museum" of philosophical works but the road of the philosopher who travels, as it were, from self to self. The history of philosophy is a philosophical work with multiple detours all heading toward self-clarification. There is no inherent meaning in this sympathy and ἐποχή [epoché], in this suspension of engagement, or in this philosophical imagination. Historical understanding does not have any *meaning* proper to itself. On the contrary, it acquires meaning when it becomes the motivating principle of philosophical searching which is actually ventured and engaged in.

Thus, the task of understanding the history of philosophy and the task of philosophizing in an original and creative manner appear as the two sides of one unique search for being. By being in contact with acts of contemporary creativity, past history is freed of its self-sufficiency and, at the same time, the personal search for truth escapes its narrow limitations and its fanaticism. The pure historian who looks for nothing turns out to be a non-existent abstraction, comparable to this other abstraction: the pure autodidact, the one who learns nothing from others, the one who has no tradition or philosophical memory.

At this level of our reflection, the mortal dilemma has certainly turned into a living paradox: we should reject any definition of truth which is, as it were, *monadic*, wherein truth would be for each person the adequation of *his* answer to *his* problematic. On the contrary, we now approach an intersubjective definition of truth according to which each one "explains himself" and unfolds his perception of the world in "combat" with another; it is the "*liebender Kampf*" of Karl Jaspers. Truth expresses the being-in-common of philosophers. *Philosophia perennis* would then signify that there is a community of research, a "*symphilosophieren*," a philosophizing-in-common wherein all philosophers are in a collective debate through the instrumentality of a witnessing consciousness, he who *searches* anew, *hic et nunc*. In this debate, the philosophers of the past are constantly changing their meanings: the communication that saves them from oblivion and death brings out the intentions and possibilities of response that their contemporaries had not seen. That is so true that the philosophies which have pretended to be eternal have not succeeded in eluding this law: they have at least the history of their readers. Like Platonism, Thomism is equally subject to this exigency of living on only through the history of Neo-Thomisms, just as history records a series of Neo-Platonisms. These renovating interpretations constantly shift the pivotal point of the initial doctrine.

In this way, a reciprocity is established between history and contemporary research. It is precisely because of this reciprocity that philosophies are able to elude not only the classifications of typology, but also the immobility of singular essences. The shifting relationship of Plato with a present-day reader tears him away from any systematic history that would attempt to fix him in the immutable role of a "moment" of "absolute Knowledge." In virtue of his singularity, but also by means of dialogue which kindles his meaning anew, the philosophy of Plato has become ἄτοπος, unplaceable.

[4]

IF IT SHOULD BE THOUGHT that we are at the end of our investigation, one might be tempted to call *truth* this endless process of researching coupled with the understanding of the past, and to move from "monadic" truth to the truth of monadology by a kind of mental addition of all perspectives.

It is necessary to become aware of the new deception created by this new approximation of the initial difficulty: we may not call truth this regime of disconnected truths. There are several reasons for this.

First, it is unusual for the philosophies which I study as an historian to enter into a dialogue that I am able to guide. "Encounters" which are worthy of the name are very rare. There is a whole history of philosophy that I make professionally, as it were, without my being able to see how it shares in my own research: it is a history without dialogue which leaves the *mortal dilemma* of history and truth standing intact behind the *living paradox* of research and communication.

Moreover, when I actually succeed in effecting in myself a debate with the author I am studying, the two attitudes of the historian and the philosopher always remain somewhat disparate: when I read Plato or Spinoza I indulge in a to-and-fro movement; in succession I suspend my own questions and my own answers so as to make myself *other* and submit myself to the author studied; then I reassume my responsibility by bringing the critique to this more profound level to which the ἐποχή [epoché] led me, and, again, putting trust in my author, I allow myself to be won over by him. The "skeptical" moment and the "dogmatic" moment cannot perfectly blend.

Lastly, and above all, between the problems of diverse philosophies there is still an invincible disparity which is such that any comparison between philosophies remains in certain respects a misconstruction. Here is the most serious deception. This misconstruction or disparity between problematics, which in the last analysis are incomparable, is such that there can be no *totality* of communication. *Communication would be truth if it were total.*

I am therefore led to attempt a last approximation of the problem of history and truth. We have constantly maintained, on the horizon of this vast debate between philosophers and philosophies, what we have called the idea of Truth. We have considered it as a regulative idea in the Kantian sense, that is, as a rational structure which requires the unity of the domain of affirmation. Perhaps a new reflection on this structure of the horizon of truth will help us to extract ourselves from this impasse. Certainly we have by no means done justice to it by considering it as the goal of our duty to think; we have taken the "task" of truth by its subjective, noetic side. This was sufficient at a certain stage of our reflection in order to understand the dialectic of *research* (philosophical questioning) which in turn listens to history and inaugurates a new question.

Now it is necessary to question the correlative term, the noematic side of the "task" of truth, namely, this *One* which has been pestering us and driving us from position to position since the beginning of our investigation.

We have the feeling that this *One* is what unifies the various philosophical singularities into *one* history and makes this unique history *philosophia perennis*. And yet we have no other access to this *One* than the debate of one philosophy with another. What is in question in every question, what gives rise to the question—the *Being* preliminary to the questioning—is also the *One* of history; but this *One* is neither a particular philosophy that is allegedly eternal, nor the source of philosophies, nor the identity of what they affirm, nor becoming as an immanent law of philosophical "moments," nor the "absolute knowledge" of this becoming. What is it, then, if it is none of the above?

Perhaps in a roundabout way one may concretely elucidate the relation of the history of philosophy (as a collective dialogue) with the *Unity* of Truth. This detour is the relation between the duty of thought and a kind of ontological hope. I am thinking of an expression such as "I hope I am within the bounds of Truth." The exegesis of this expression should lead us to the relation of history with its perenniality.

What is meant by this formula: "I hope I am *within* the bounds of Truth"? The preposition "within" brings out a new relation which is not exactly the one suggested by other prepositions such as: in sight of the truth, or in the direction of the truth. Here truth is not merely a term or an horizon but a milieu such as the atmosphere or light, the latter being an expression common to Gabriel Marcel and Martin Heidegger. I hope that what I call my philosophy and my thought "bathes in" a certain milieu constituted by its non-resistance to mediations and even by its power of establishing all mediations—like the way in which light, according to the *Timeus,* mediates between the fire of the eye and the fire of the object.

This metaphor of the preposition "within," while leading us to this other metaphor, that of truth as milieu or light, leads us to a theme which we earlier encountered: that of being as *"openness."* We had opposed openness to our situation as "narrowness" (or finitude). Earlier it had been masked by the idea of "task" as research pointing toward an horizon. But what does this idea of "openness" signify? It signifies that the many philosophical singularities (Plato, Descartes, Spinoza, etc.) are *a priori accessible* to each other, that all dialogue is possible *a priori,* because being is *that* act which, preceding and founding all possibility of questioning, grounds the mutuality of the most singular philosophical intentions. It is this openness, this clearing, this *lumen naturale,* that the naive imagination projects in the Elysian Fields where dialogues among the dead are possible. In the Elysian Fields all philosophers are contemporaneous and all communications reversible: Plato may *answer* Descartes, his junior; the Elysian Fields represent the *openness* prior to history and make possible all dialogue in time. Plurality is therefore not the final reality, nor is misunderstanding the ultimate possibility of communication. The being of every question originally opens everyone to everyone else and grounds the historic and polemic truth of communication.

But here we must be on our guard against separating the "within" ("within the bounds of truth") from the "I hope" ("I hope I am within the bounds of truth"). I cannot express, articulate, or enunciate this unity rationally, for there is no Logos within this unity. I cannot compress within a coherent discourse the "openness" that founds in unity all questions. Otherwise I should not say "I hope *I am within* the bounds of truth" but "*I have* the truth." This possessive relationship to truth is perhaps the reason for the pretension and the aggressiveness characteristic of all rebellious thought that is hidden in all eclecticism and in all systematic philosophy of history. For it is still necessary to have the truth in order to reflect the immanent becoming of history in an absolute Knowledge. No, this hope does not give us the power to master history or to order it rationally. And yet this "openness" is not absolutely dissimulated; ontological hope has its *signs* and its *guarantees:* the deeper the knowledge one has of a philosophy, the more one is inclined to allow oneself to be seduced by it (and consequently, one better understands the irreducibility of this philosophy to types). The more one affirms its autonomy in relation to the influences it has experienced, the more one accentuates its *otherness* in comparison to every other philosophy. Consequently, one is proportionately rewarded with the joy of hitting the essential, as if by plunging oneself into the denseness of a philosophy, along with its difficulties, its intentions and its refusals, one thereby experienced its inexpressible consonance with every other philosophy. In this way, one may reach the conviction that Plato, Descartes, and Kant are animated by the same being. This is how I understand the profound saying of Spinoza: "the more we understand individual objects, the more we understand God." But this consonance cannot become systematized or thematized. That is why it is rather of the nature of Promise or of Reminiscence (which should be the same thing). I hope that all great philosophers are within the same truth, that they have the same pre-ontological understanding of their relationship to being. I think, then, that the function of this hope lies in always keeping the dialogue open and in introducing a fraternal intention into the most bitter of debates. In this sense, hope is the vital milieu of communication, the "light" of all our debates. History remains polemic but illuminated, as it were, by this ἔσχατον [eschaton] which unifies and eternalizes history without being able to be coordinate to history. I maintain that the unity of truth is a timeless task only because it is at first an eschatological hope. This is what supports not only my deception before the history of philosophy but also the courage to make the history of philosophy without doing the philosophy of history.

Our initial skepticism has been driven from several successive positions; but it has also unseated us. At the outset, it is conquered in the One; but I do not *know* this One. Consequently, skepticism remains existentially the temptation *par excellence* of the historian's craft. History remains the place of the abolished, of the distant, and of the "other." No one may write the *philosophia perennis*.

This *ambiguous* status of the history of philosophy is that of communication which modulates on the Same and the Other, on the One and the Many. It is ultimately the ambiguous status of *mankind,* for the history of philosophy, in the last analysis, is one of the privileged roads on which mankind struggles for its unity and its perenniality.

Note on the History of Philosophy
and the Sociology of Knowledge

THE HISTORY OF PHILOSOPHY is a philosophical discipline. From the outset, it presupposes living philosophical questioning which takes place in the present. For it is by situating himself within other problematics that the living philosopher conquers his own narrowness and begins to universalize the questions which he raises. The ultimate meaning of this detour through the vast memory of history remains the recapturing of history by present philosophy. But between this initial act of philosophizing and that ultimate recapturing, the history of philosophy may be viewed as a relatively independent discipline which becomes constituted mediately through a "suspension" or a certain ἐποχή [epoché] of the problematic peculiar to the philosopher-historian: the latter allows for the existence of other philosophies, for what is *other* than his philosophy.

At this point one discovers the unstable status of the history of philosophy. It appears condemned to waver between two extremes and thereby tends to lose its proper characteristics as a philosophical or historical task. On the one hand, it tends to become confused with a sociology of knowledge which is not a philosophical but a scientific undertaking. On the other hand, it tends to become confused with a philosophy of history which is a philosophical undertaking, but not an historical discipline in the strict sense of the historian's craft.

Careful reflection on the history of philosophy should show us how the history of philosophy is situated between a sociology of knowledge and a philosophy of history. The goal of this short essay is to explore the first of these two frontiers.

A critique of the sociology of knowledge is today an essential task of the historian of philosophy. This relatively new science provides an opportunity to acquire an awareness of the properly philosophical aspects of the history of philosophy. Let us say at the outset that this critique bears not on the validity but on the scope of such a science. In fact, by reflecting on the limits of the sociology of knowledge, one both reinforces its rightful presence within these limits and, secondly, brings out the specific character of a philosophical history of philosophy.

The limits which interest us here are not those related to the working hypotheses of the different sociologies of knowledge—those hypotheses of P. Sorokin, Max Scheler, Karl Marx, Lukacs, Mannheim, etc.[1] (We shall later come back to the necessary multiplicity of these working hypotheses.) The limits which do interest us here are those which manifest the belonging of these working hypotheses to a single sociology of knowledge.

[1] THE LEGITIMACY OF A SOCIOLOGY OF KNOWLEDGE

THE SOCIOLOGY OF KNOWLEDGE wishes to be a science: straightway it seems to answer the questions left unanswered by the history of philosophy. The latter leaves them unanswered to the extent that it is merely a collection of "monographs" on the "great" philosophers. What is the criterion of the "great" philosopher? What is his significance once he is isolated from the streams of thought and traditions maintained by thinkers of lesser scope? What is the connection between philosophies?

The sociology of knowledge rejects an immanent history of ideas which would be governed only by the structure of problems and their philosophical solutions. It attempts to replace the would-be history of ideas within the total dynamics of societies. One could not object to the philosophical origin of such a project, particularly

---

1. In addition to the standard bibliographies on Marxism, cf. G. Lukacs, *Geschichte und Klassenbewusstsein* (1923); Max Scheler, *Die Wissensformen und die Gesellschaft* (1926); Karl Mannheim, *Ideologie und Utopie* (1929; the English translation includes the important article "Wissenssoziologie" from the *Handwörterbuch der Soziologie*, by Wierkandt, 1931); Pitirim Sorokin, *Social and Cultural Dynamics*, II: *Fluctuation of Systems of Truth, Ethics and Law* (New York: American Book Co., 1937); Robert Merton, "Sociologie de la connaissance" in *Sociologie au XXe siècle*, by Gurvitch and Moore (1947); Jacques Maquet, *Sociologie de la connaissance* (1949).

its *geschichtsphilosophisch* presuppositions (e.g., the polemical reversal of the Hegelian philosophy of Consciousness and Spirit, a rejection which, for the less dialectical of Marxists, leads to an extreme theory of "consciousness-reflection"; the "economist" craze for industrial work wherein man appears as the producer of his social existence; the schematic representation of history within the class struggle; the theory of "alienation"; the Nietzschean interpretation of "points of view" by means of "instincts," and the theory of *"vital lies"*; the theory of cultural types and the recurrence of great cultural systems, etc.).

If one were to argue against the project of a science which proposes to investigate the economic, social, and cultural conditionings of thought, one could not dispute the philosophical origin of the project, not if one decides to treat these implicit philosophies as working hypotheses and theories, as in the sense of "physical theory." Unlike natural sciences, sociology does not find the spontaneous connections of its object in ordinary knowledge or in the first degrees of scientific knowledge. "Theory" plays a role as early as the search for facts, which presupposes at the outset a certain preconception of the connections to be established between thought and historic and social existence. If the connection were purely functional, the search would have no other guide than the probability of the relationship between the variables in question; and the immense complexity of interhuman relationships would always forbid us to begin the enterprise. But the sociologist does not look only for functional relationships, but also for *meaningful* relationships understood in terms of certain well-chosen examples. For example, prior to any inductive research, he takes for granted that an interpretation of the world may reply to the instincts of an individual, a group, or a class. This "patent" motivation coming from the *Falsches Bewusstsein* is an example of the "latent" relationships for which systematic pursuit is legitimate. These meaningful relationships are what the sociology of knowledge anticipates at the start of its search into a "theory."

Thus there is no discredit in the fact that the field of investigation of this relatively new science is from the outset divided between conflicting working hypotheses. Representative of this diversity of "theories" are such outstanding works as those of Max Scheler, Karl Mannheim, P. A. Sorokin, etc.

Henceforth the interesting stage of the sociology of knowledge is the method of verification that it applies to the correlations between "knowledge" and social or cultural situations. Whether it is a question of class in the Marxist sense or of any other social affiliation, or even the fact of belonging to the "cultural mentalities" propounded by Sorokin, the main question is whether the sociology of knowledge is capable of transforming its working hypotheses into empirical laws by means of a methodical investigation of correlations. If it were successful, the relationship between a system of thought and social existence would not only be a meaningful relationship, understood through sympathy, but also a functional relationship between a dependent variable and an independent variable. This relationship would be governed by a logic of probability.

In this respect, we should be thankful for Sorokin's introduction of the idea of "mass study" into the sociology of knowledge. It is perfectly legitimate to try to weigh, on the basis of objective criteria, the influence of a thinker, a school of thought, or a philosophical, literary, or cultural movement, and thus to determine the value of streams of thought quantitatively. The sociology of knowledge is here on solid ground, and such tentatives show what the sociology of knowledge may and may not do.

[2] LIMITATIONS OF THE SOCIOLOGY OF KNOWLEDGE

OUR REFLECTION on the limitations of the sociology of knowledge concerns the concept of understanding in the history of philosophy.

1. It is striking that conflicting working hypotheses, such as those of Marx, Mannheim, and Lukacs on the one hand, and of Sorokin on the other, restrict explanation to "typical" modes of thought. For Marx, as well as for Mannheim, ideology is *anonymous*. What is amenable to ideological explanation is mechanistic rationalism or romanticism considered as "types." Anabaptist anarchism, liberalism, conservatism, and communistic socialism characterize the Mannheimian history of utopia. The same holds true for Sorokin: in effect, what are the "streams of thought" which he ultimately relates to the three great cultural systems, which, according to him, alternate throughout history (sensual, ideational, and idealistic systems)? They are those solemn abstractions which afflict the history of philosophy: empiricism, rationalism, skepticism, etc. By its very nature, the sociology of knowledge can encounter only "common types" and not "singular essences." It is here that the history of philosophy outruns the sociology of knowledge; understanding requires the philosopher-historian to

abandon all "typology" and to reject the panoramic views on "streams of thought." It requires him to communicate with a singularized essence. This does not mean that he must communicate with the author's subjectivity (in which case we should escape from the sociology of knowledge only to fall back into psychology), but to communicate with the meaning of the work in accordance with its internal coherence. For the historian of philosophy, the meaning of a work, along with its own development, constitutes a singular essence. But the common types mask the singular essences.

2. This first limitation leads to the following one: before a philosophy is an attitude or a vision of the world or, in short, an answer, a philosophy is the historic emergence of an original problematic. The great philosopher is the one who opens up a new way of questioning. Now the singularity that transcends all typology is primarily the singularity of the problematics themselves.

The sociology of knowledge is, in principle, short of the *radicality* of the philosophical problematic, and in consequence, short of the singularity of great philosophers. Its most general hypothesis is that "all supra-organic phenomena are socio-cultural" (Sorokin). At the outset, philosophy undergoes a *sociological reduction* that takes on a different form depending on the school in question. Thus, the great cultural constants, of which Sorokin establishes the recurrence, are like answers without *questioning;* we then arrive at this paradox, that all cultural systems are attached to perfectly anonymous and "eternal problems" or to *questions in themselves.* The task of the history of philosophy is to reachieve the philosophical posing of these questions. For Marx and kindred sociologists, thought is looked upon merely *as* a factor of domination; the radical power of questioning is sacrificed to its social "weight." It is projected on the level where man is productive through work. Henceforth there are no longer any specific problems concerning human discourse, neither as speech establishing significations nor as universal *logos* taking possession of man's speech. The initial sociological reduction makes for a good sociology of knowledge, particularly at the level where ideas are inherently reducible to ideology. It runs aground, however, at the threshold of the great philosophies enrooted in the least industrial possibilities of human speech. By its power of signifying universally, the word goes beyond work and contains in an embryonic form the *irony* of the thinker with respect to his own social motivation.

The history of philosophy is the understanding of philosophy by itself on the basis of this primordial "irony." It remains to know whether this recapturing by the history of philosophy of the most fundamental possibilities of questioning and of signifying can be satisfied with a philosophy of history.

The History of Philosophy
and Historicity

THE FOLLOWING REFLECTIONS take their point of departure within the craft of the historian of philosophy. The question which I raise is this: are not the difficulties which the historian of philosophy encounters and actually resolves revealing of the difficulties inherent in history in general?

My working hypothesis is that the history of philosophy reveals certain aspects of history which would not appear without it. The history of philosophy has a hidden power of literally manifesting historical characteristics of history. It does this to the extent that history becomes reflected in the history of philosophy and becomes aware of itself in the form of the history of philosophy. My procedure will be regressive. I shall start, in the first part, with certain contradictions that result from the very nature of the history of philosophy. In the second part, I shall try to elucidate the general law of the relationship between the history of philosophy and history proper. In the third part, and in light of this general law, I shall try to illuminate the historicity of all history by means of the structures of the history of philosophy.

[1] THE "APORIAS" OF UNDERSTANDING IN THE HISTORY OF PHILOSOPHY

THE PROBLEMS OF METHODOLOGY within the history of philosophy and the type of understanding peculiar to the history of philosophy may be grouped around two themes. First, the

[63]

history of philosophy is not capable of being unified in one single style; in this domain there are two models of understanding. The first of these models is the *system* and according to it, the sum total of philosophies would only form one single philosophy in which historical philosophies would be particular moments. A large part of the historian's work falls under the sway of this Hegelian model. To the extent that one tries to achieve understanding in the history of philosophy, one is bound to set up sequences. These sequences may be short or partial, but the type of intelligibility brought into play will already be a type which in the broad sense may be called Hegelian; from this standpoint, a philosophy will be understood to the extent that it is placed within a certain line of development. All historians of philosophy, even those who have a bias against the "system," practice this kind of understanding. For example, the sequence formed by Descartes, Spinoza, Leibnitz, and Kant is classic in the history of French philosophy. With the Germans (after all, Hegel himself initiated this schema and we shall soon see that there is something rather malevolent in the operation), we have the following sequence: Kant, Fichte, Schelling, Hegel. To understand in this sense is to understand by means of the movement of the whole or the totality. For example, how does Hegel in his *Lectures on the History of Philosophy* understand Spinoza? According to Hegel, Spinoza provides us with a philosophy of substance without subjectivity. Since substance is deprived of the moment of reflection, subjectivity thus "falls" outside of substance; this is what makes it possible for philosophy to be an Ethics. Consequently, to understand consists in reading Spinoza from cover to cover in terms of a philosophy which integrates subjectivity into substance. In this way each new philosophy throws light on its immediate predecessor and thus endows it with intelligibility. Such is the first model of understanding in the history of philosophy, the *system*.

There is, however, another type of understanding which consists in always understanding a philosophy as unique or *singular*. According to this second model, each unique philosophy will be understood so much the better if one has thoroughly penetrated its singularity. Spinoza will no longer be a variety of pantheism or rationalism, for there will no longer be an "ism" with which to designate him; he will be only himself, thanks to philosophical understanding. To understand Spinoza will therefore consist of relating all his answers to all his questions; Spinoza's system will no longer be a set of answers to questions in general. Spinoza's position among and in contrast with other philosophers will not be determined in relation to anonymous problems. But Spinozism will proceed from a question which he was alone in asking. Consequently, his incomparable truth will consist of the adequation of his answer to his question. The philosophy under consideration then becomes a singular essence (instead of philosophy, it would be better to speak of philosopheme, that is to say the sense of the work and no longer its author's individual subjectivity; it is rather a matter of the work being taken as a cultural object, holding its meaning in itself—secreted by itself, so to speak). From this point of view, singular philosophies are radically isolated from one another; each one constitutes a total world into which it is necessary to penetrate slowly by means of a kind of familiarity which is never totally achieved. It might be compared to the attempt to understand a friend without ever confusing him with another. Naturally, there is no system in which I could classify my friends; each of them is my friend in a unique and incomparable way.

These "types" of interpretation run up against a twofold limitation. On the one hand, it is difficult to embrace the system in any total fashion. But for that matter, perhaps all is not system, even for Hegel. On the other hand, it is equally difficult to penetrate singularity; the historian always stops with a type of intermediate understanding; he achieves the level of common types but does not attain the singular essence. These common types are quite familiar to us, they are called realism, idealism, spiritualism, materialism, etc. Lacking the ability to penetrate singularity, one stops at the level of typology. It is of course true that typology is one way of understanding, whose irreducible role, moreover, we shall soon see. But if one pushes beyond the common types, then there is only one way of designating Spinoza's philosophy: it is Spinozism. Obviously this "ism" must be constructed, as we have seen, in a special way. And so instead of concentrating on breadth and system, I shall rather emphasize depth and singularity.

It would seem that when a philosophy is thus isolated, it is no longer in history or a moment of history. But on the contrary, one may say that all history is in it. Previous history becomes contracted in it, concentrated in its sources and its origins. All future developments, moreover, are adumbrated within it. It has its past and its future which are implied in a kind of absolute present which truly makes of it an eternal essence.

Such is the first remark with which I wished to start. Historical understanding refers to two models, both of which, as we shall presently see, do away with history: the system and the singular essence.

My second remark is that these two interpretations of the history of philosophy correspond to two requirements or expectations, and ultimately to two models of truth, both of which refer to each other. Indeed, what do I expect from the first interpretation of the history of philosophy? We have presently employed the word "totality." But why is it that I try to understand through the totality? It might be said that the totality is the "great detour" of self-consciousness. According to Plato, in order to be understood, the individual must be studied first on a larger scale in terms of the State or Community. Likewise, we may better understand self-consciousness in terms of the larger scale of the history of philosophy. It is here that I discover all the possibilities of self-consciousness, possibilities which are accomplished, however, in the works of what Hegel called the Spirit. Through this movement, self-consciousness becomes Spirit instead of remaining the poor, anecdotic singularity of one's own life. On the other hand, one may say that history becomes self-consciousness, because the order of history coincides with the introduction of the radical teleology of self-consciousness. History becomes human and receives its human qualification by lending itself to this interpretation. It becomes perfectly meaningful by coinciding with the succession of philosophical ideas and in tending toward system. What is striking is that *my* consciousness becomes thought at the same time as history. And it is the system which effectuates this twofold promotion: human consciousness raising itself to the clarity of philosophic discourse, history approaching its rationality. What I expect from this absorption of history into the history of philosophy, and from the absorption of the latter into the system, is the appearance of meaning.

It must be admitted, however, that the appearance of meaning is a Pyrrhic victory. The triumph of the system or the triumph of coherence and rationality leaves a gigantic loss in its wake: *this loss is precisely history*. There are several reasons for this. First, there is the pulp of man's lived history which, by contrast to the system, seems senseless. Violence, madness, power, desire: none of this can pass into the history of philosophy. It is true that when I am faced with violence, in the sense of violence used by Eric Weil, I am called upon to choose between sense and nonsense. I am a philosopher and I choose sense; so much the worse for the nonsense which remains. But what is truly unfortunate is that I have not only left out nonsense but "another sense" or another way of achieving meaning. That is why one cannot be Hegelian; for the two possibilities have an equal value but are different and irreducible to any synthesis. Indeed, one does violence to philosophies by forcing them to enter this species of Procrustean bed; the system requires that Spinoza's philosophy be only the philosophy of substance without subjectivity. But whoever has frequented Spinoza knows that this is not true. If there is a progression from the first to the fifth book of the *Ethics*, it is because self-consciousness is present in a certain way, although it is not present in the dialectical form of Hegelianism. It is necessary, then, to admit that everything is in each philosophy, that each philosophy is in its own way the totality, or in Leibnitz's words, a total part or a partial totality. I do not have the right to say that a philosophy is only a "moment." If I reduce it or congeal it into a moment or stage which only acquires meaning by reference to other moments, I then do violence to it. The type of understanding which I earlier called amiable, and which would practice "truth in charity," would penetrate to the internal coherence and to the perfect sufficiency of singularity. In other words, the other way of understanding in which I am also interested is the one which would bear on a monad or a person, on a wholly personalized essence which would no longer have meaning outside of itself. This singular essence requires the type of understanding which consists of projecting oneself into another, exactly as I encounter in each of my friends the totality of human experience from a certain point of view.

This exigency counterbalances that of totality. It is the exigency of communication. Communication rules out any pretension to encompass or reduce the other to a part of my total discourse. According to the system, each philosophy takes its place as a moment of a single philosophy. I exercise a sovereign domination over philosophies by understanding them as moments; but from the perspective of communication, the philosopher whom I try to understand is really my partner. From this standpoint he is not simply a partial discourse but a complete personality. Obviously, I am here invoking another model of truth, a truth which is such that it excludes all "Summation." One might say that truth, in this sense, would be complete if communication could be achieved; but it remains open. Truth, as Jaspers says, is nothing else than "philosophizing-in-common." I can understand someone only if I, myself am someone and if I engage in debate. Consequently, there can be no privileged position for interpreting the system, for truth is radically intersubjective.

I shall pause here in order to qualify the word "communication." In certain respects it is improper to use it here since communication in the historical mode differs fundamentally from communication with a friend. In the latter case, the other replies; in the former, by definition, the other cannot reply. What characterizes historical communication is the fact that it is unilateral; history is that segment of intersubjectivity wherein reciprocity is impossible, because I do not have the presence of the men of the past, only their traces. Simiand, it will be recalled, referred to history as a knowledge through traces: in the history of philosophy, the traces are works of philosophy. As an historian, I question a work which does not reply. There is, then, unilateralness in the relation: nevertheless, I may speak of communication, in the broad sense of the word, in that I, who read and understand the other philosopher, am part of the same history as his. It is within the total movement of consciousnesses that a consciousness understands others who do not answer.

[2] PHILOSOPHIC DISCOURSE AND ACTUAL HISTORY

FROM THE ABOVE ANALYSIS I shall retain the following ideas: in the history of philosophy, understanding tends toward two extremes which represent two models of truth. How can this division of understanding and of truth in the history of philosophy serve as a source of revelation with respect to history in general? In order to reply to this question we must undertake an intermediate analysis which bears upon the relationship between philosophic discourse, understood in one or another sense, and the actual history which embodies this discourse. It is here that my problem encounters and extends the one which is necessarily posed by a philosophy of history when it tries to integrate the economic, political, and cultural factors into one single history. How does the history of philosophy fit into general history? And is it a question of a fitting-in?

Two things may be said here, one negative and the other positive—the latter obviously being more important. The negative remark is that we must regard all relationships of the reality-reflection type as naive and narrow. The same holds true for all the varieties of cause-effect relationships. To be more precise, this kind of explanation has a restricted validity which it is important to delimit clearly in order to see the point beyond which it is no longer usable. The theory of the "reflection" is valid only as long as it is merely a question of explaining the social import of a philosophy, its social selection, its success or efficacity. It is not valid when it is a question of explaining the radical origin of a philosophy. One may say that a given epoch calls for a certain type of philosophy, and calls for it in diverse ways: not only as a justification, as a weapon, as a direct expression of self, but also as an expression of refusal. In this sense, one may say that the thought of an epoch is the reflection of that epoch *and* its effect, but only on the condition that one leaves entirely aside the radical problem of the birth of a philosophical problematic and restricts oneself merely to measuring the historical success of a doctrine. The second limitation of this type of sociological explanation of the history of philosophy is that one must restrict oneself to explaining types, not singularities. For example, one may legitimately show that in its ascending phase the French bourgeoisie had need of something like Cartesianism. But a different rationalism could have taken care of the matter just as well. As Goldmann has demonstrated, in a period of self-doubt the same class may call on something like a tragic philosophy. It seems to me that, granting these limitations, it is legitimate to have recourse to a sociological explanation which establishes correlations between socio-economic classes and types of thought or ways of seeing the world.

But what we have justified by this means is not the history of philosophy but the sociology of knowledge, which is perfectly legitimate as science. But to the extent that the sociology of knowledge is a scientific activity, the history of philosophy is a philosophical activity. It is the philosopher who, in order to philosophize, tries to understand himself through his historical memory; and it is a philosophical act to engage in the history of philosophy. What eludes the sociology of knowledge, however, and what can only be recaptured in a philosophical history of philosophy is precisely the origin of the system, that is to say the constitution of a certain discourse on the basis of a certain number of fundamental questions. It is quite obvious that there is a hiatus between that which is mere social effectiveness, (what I was formerly calling the social import of a doctrine) and, on the other hand, the constitution of a problematic. For it is in a field other than an operative, utilitarian, and pragmatic field that a philosophy springs up in the world of discourse. It springs from an inherent philosophic *intention* to express what is as it is. The appearance in Greek philosophy of the verb *to be* is a witness to this philosophic intention. This type of question goes beyond every kind of social causality. It is also this type of question which can appear only in singularities, and not in types. Types suppose abstract forms of general questions which are raised by no one. Only questions which are "in the air" are amenable to a sociology of knowledge.

The birth of a philosophic *problem* in a *singular* philosophy is not.

If we reject this cause-effect relationship, or the reality-reflection relationship—relationships which supposedly exist between an environment and a philosophy—then in what does the positive relationship consist, the relationship which as we know exists between thought and an epoch? It would be absurd to say that a philosophy such as Plato's or Spinoza's has no connection with its time. But what is this relationship? I believe that we should be oriented toward a solution in maintaining that a philosophy *appears* in a certain situation. The word "situation" may direct us toward something rather different than the cause-effect or reality-reflection relationship. For how can I obtain access to the meaning of a situation, to the situation of an artist, a thinker, or for that matter, any creative individual? It is quite obvious that I cannot know "his" situation outside of his work or prior to the examination of his work, but, as it were, only "in" and "through" his work.

When a certain philosophy surges up it acquires a situation. And because it rises up within a given epoch and entrenches itself, it thereafter has causes and a reality for which it will in the future be the reflection. Thus there is a relationship which is more primary than the cause-effect or reality-reflection relationship. Once a given work is born, one can find a situation for it from that moment onward. Here we encounter something which is altogether paradoxical, something which should give us pause: the situation is not an ensemble of conditions which would have been the same if the philosopher had been different, which would mechanically produce their cultural effect and allow us, in consequence, to move from the social to the ideological. On the contrary, I must place myself within the work in order to grasp its situation as well as the very thing which it brought to the surface and exhibited. Sartre brought this out quite clearly in his article in *Les Temps Modernes* entitled "Questions of Method." There he maintains that one must always start with the artist himself in order to discover the nature of the situation that he has made his own in bringing out a certain work.

We shall be able to make the argument more concise if we consider the philosopher rather than the artist. How does the philosopher manifest his situation? It is quite noteworthy that the social and political situation of a great philosophy by no means appears plainly in its *text*; it is not named or expressed anywhere, yet it is *manifested*, although very indirectly, through the *problems* that the philosopher raises. In other words, his situation undergoes a kind of transmutation or transvaluation; from a lived situation it turns into an expressed and enunciated problem. What is the significance of this? Let us take notice of a fact which at first sight seems quite harmless but which in reality is altogether decisive: it is in discourse and only in discourse that the philosopher may evince his epoch. The work of the philosopher is a work which by its very nature is linked to words, so much so that our problem presents the most extreme and perhaps the clearest aspect of the relationship which may exist between actual history and discourse—between the history that men effectuate and the discourse which they constitute. It is quite obvious that philosophy is speech, but this fact is of sufficient weight to elude the cause-effect and reality-reflection relationships. No discourse as such can be a reflection. The word has meaning but the reflection is of a thing or object, as is the reflection in a mirror. We know of no reflections which are discourses. There is something quite specific in the relationship between a situation and a discourse, and this relationship is simply signified. In this sense, the case of the philosopher is more enlightening than any other, for the discourse to which he lays claim requires that he ask universal questions. This brings us back to the center of the difficulty and the paradox. For when a singular philosophy is born, it manifests its epoch by expressing it in the form of the universal. In asking the question, "What is an *a priori* synthetic judgment?" Kant inaugurates his philosophy, and the question that he raises is a universal question. Kant manifests the narrowness of his singular situation within this universal question.

The philosophic work gives form to the question which animates it. But the universal form of the question is the problem. The philosopher expresses by posing universally, in the form of a problem, the difficulty which is peculiar to him and which is constitutive of him. He expresses by giving form.

Straightway we see how difficult it is to find a direct relationship between a philosophy and a socio-economic, political situation. It is necessary, we were saying, to rediscover that situation within the work itself; but the characteristic feature of the philosophic work is to transpose all those very singular problems which the philosopher experiences into a universal question. It is sometimes said that the philosophic work dissimulates its social and political situation. But dissimulation is not the equivalent of insincerity. This dissimulation would be a false consciousness only if it pretended to express its situation. It "dissimulates" because it does not wish to say in which epoch it is born, which social milieu it expresses; it wishes to express something different. It asks: What is real? What is *physis*? What is an idea? What is transcendence? In this the philosopher is silent as to his situation, and it is the silence of the philosopher with respect to his own situation (be it his class situation or another) which causes the disinterestedness of his question. It is because his situation has been transmuted, so to speak, into a disinterested question that his question dissimulates his situation. It dissimulates because it surpasses and transcends.

From this we see that it is always in an indirect way that one may establish the relationship which links a philosophic work to its epoch. For this relationship can be looked for only within the work itself, and the most perfect work is the one which dissimulates the most. If there is a problem of the *false consciousness,* in the sense in which Marx and Lukacs use this term, it is because a deceitful relationship can be inserted into the fundamental relationship that exists between every work of speech and situations, because a work of speech overspills its situation and dissimulates it by going beyond it. This primitive dissimulation may turn into false consciousness, untruth, or a refusal to recognize the situation. The philosopher falls into the untruth of his epoch when he adorns himself with universal discourse and denies all adherence to a class. He may then pretend to have made short work of the movement of history, emancipation, and liberation, whereas it is only in intention that he transcends his situation. Nevertheless, it remains true that in virtue of his manner of questioning, he really transcends his situation although this may be in intention only.

This relationship between an historical epoch and a philosophic work—the relationship of manifestation-dissimulation—is the extreme form of the status of language in the world. The language which wishes to be most universal reveals what happens to all speech and discourse in society. As soon as an epoch represents itself by its works, it has already broken through the narrow confines of its own situation. This is indeed the reason why one may never reduce literary works, and in general any work, to a mere layer of appearances which would be as the fringe of foam of the waves beating against the shore. Every work is a new reality with its own history—the history of discourse. It calls for a peculiar type of understanding, for it is connected to its situation only by transcending it. In this sense, the signification of speech always exceeds the function of merely reflecting a situation. Let us recall the Moslems' dream of Constantinople, which was discussed recently. One can only see a political ambition in that dream. But since this dream was "said" in a myth, it passed beyond Constantinople and took on the form of an eschatological symbol. That is so true that this theme of the taking of a city is found again in Christian mysticism, in the "castle" of St. Theresa as well as in Kafka's *The Castle*. We find in the theme of the Grail, or in the quest for "treasure," the same wealth of mythical and mystical harmonics. Thus there is a surplus of signification in works or myths which exceeds their historical foundations, although one may always discern such historical, social, and economic foundations. But as soon as they are "said," they undergo a transformation into the element of Logos, and this speech will be able to be recaptured and understood in terms of other historical situations.

[3] THE CONTRADICTION OF ALL HISTORICITY

LET US GO BACK over our path. In the first part, I tried to show that the history of philosophy involved a strange type of understanding since it proposed two models of truth, one tending toward system and the other involving individual works. Next, my problem was to determine what this contradiction teaches us about history in general. In order to resolve it, I introduced an intermediate question: how is the history of philosophy related to history? As we have seen, it is not related to it in the manner of an effect or a reflection, but by way of constituting a meaningful universe which always transcends its specific historical causality.

Because there is something "more" in philosophic discourse, the history of philosophy may reveal aspects of history which do not otherwise appear.

1. In the first place, our twofold interpretation of the history of philosophy reveals two aspects which are virtually present in all history. All history may be understood as the advent and progress of a unique meaning and as the emergence of singularities. These singularities are either events, works, or persons. History wavers between a structural type and an "event" type of understanding. But it is only by means of the clarifying function of philosophic discourse that these two possibilities are separated and manifested.

In what sense does history include this twofold possibility? On the one hand, we speak of history in the singular and thus testify to a single history, a single mankind: "The whole of mankind," writes Pascal in the *Traité du vide,* "should be looked upon as one man who continues to exist and constantly learns." We have the conviction that wherever we encounter a human sign it may be referred *a priori* to a single field of humanity. Before I ever start doing history, I am aware of this by a kind of antepredicative understanding of the historical field. But the historian cannot explain this understanding. For him it remains "pre-judged," in the literal sense of the word. This prejudgment of the historian is justified only by the philosopher's attempt to recapture the partial discourses within a single discourse. Without being Hegelians, and even without being philosophers at all, we have the feeling that all that philosophers have said, always and everywhere, *must* be such so as to constitute an undivided and harmonious whole. What gives rise to this feeling is human speech, discourse, or Logos. One may say, then, that the system, or the ultimate possibility of the system, reveals that history is potentially one. (Presently, I shall come back to the word "potential.")

There is another conviction before us which the first one cannot eradicate. Even though we may speak of "history" in the singular, history is also the history of the plurality of men, that is to say not only of individuals, but also of communities and civilizations. Thus, a certain pluralism is inherent in the preconception of the drama of history and historical work. Not only do I put men in the plural, but I also put events in the plural. History is necessarily manifold and multiple: there is this and then that. It is the "and then," "and then," "and then again" which make up history. If there are no ruptures and innovations, there would be no history at all. Where, then, is this other latent aspect of history, its "event" aspect, made perfectly manifest? Our answer is within the singularity of works. It is here that the historian proves what might be called his "granular" or "quantic" characteristic. We know the mind only in the works of the mind, in cultural works, each of which demand our friendship. And the more we advance in this friendship for works, the more we leave behind the generalities which mask it and progress toward the singular and the unique.

From this standpoint, in so far as philosophic discourse is not the mere reflecting of meaning but the very constituting of meaning, it manifests the twofold characteristic of all history, which is to be both structural and event-filled, the unity of history, and the multiplicity of events, works, and men. Such is our first conclusion: the history of philosophy shows the latent duality of all history. In dividing itself into two models of intelligibility, it displays what was internal to history.

2. This first conclusion calls forth another. The understanding of works, especially philosophic works, inclines history toward one or the other of the two interpretations we have set forth. When this occurs, the result is somehow a destruction of history. This conclusion is perhaps still more paradoxical than the first one. Yet it is this twofold destruction of history which reveals history as history.

It is to be noted that the two ultimate models of understanding in the history of philosophy (the system and singularity) represent a certain suppression of history. First, as soon as one grants the system, there is no more history. In the *Phenomenology of Spirit* one still finds a certain history, but it is, however, "ideal." This history is made up of the "forms" of the Spirit. But when we move on to Hegel's *Logic*, we no longer find "forms" but "categories"; there is no more history at all. The ultimate goal of historical understanding involves, therefore, the suppression of history in the system. One may find the same thing in the work of Eric Weil, a work for which I have great admiration: attitudes are still in history, the categories no longer compose a history, but a *Logic of Philosophy*. The passage from history to logic signifies the death of history. On the other hand, history is destroyed just as much when we take the second direction. When we engage in the history of philosophy following the second method, we end up in a kind of schizophrenia—we live in one philosopher, then in another one without there being any path from one to the other. One might say that these philosophers no longer belong to any epoch; they are singularities who hover outside of history—singular and timeless essences. Their work has become a kind of absolute which contains its own past, but a past which has become essentialized. Spinoza's work has a certain past, but that past becomes essence, and the essence itself is not in any moment. From this standpoint, one may say of that singular work that it *is* and that it is *such* and, on that score, irrefutable. As Nietzsche said, "A sound cannot be refuted," no more than can words, thus absolutized.

We may see, then, that the history of philosophy discloses the fundamental characteristic of all history, showing it to be both a matter of structure and multiple events, only through its peculiar work which destroys historicity. Perhaps this is the only meaning that can be given to the notion of an end of history. In a sense, every philosophy is the end of history. The system is the end of history because history becomes nullified in Logic; singularity too is the end of history since all history is repudiated in it. Thus we come to this paradoxical result: it is always either at the frontier of history or at the end of history that the general features of historicity are understood.

3. I come now to my last conclusion: if history is revealed as history in so far as it is surpassed and moves toward discourse or toward the singular work, it is necessary to say that history is history only to the extent that it has reached neither absolute discourse nor absolute singularity—to the extent that the meaning of it remains confused and entangled. Lived history is all that which happens prior to its decomposition and suppression by the system and singularity. Prior to its decomposition, history is essentially equivocal in the sense that it is virtually a matter of events and virtually structural. In point of fact, history is the realm of the inexact. This discovery does not discredit the historian's craft but actually justifies him. For it accounts for all his difficulties and shows that historical method can only be an inexact method. We have understood this necessity on the basis of a viewpoint from which all these difficulties would be surpassed, but as we have seen, from this viewpoint there would no longer be any history. All difficulties of historical method are justified when we realize the limitations of philosophic discourse. History wishes to be objective but it cannot. It wishes to relive the past but it can only reconstruct. It wishes to make past events contemporary but it must at the same time restore the distance and depth of historical remoteness. Lastly, this reflection tends to justify all the difficulties of the historian's craft, those which Marc Bloch noted in his defense of history and the historian's craft. These difficulties do not result from faulty methods but are well founded ambiguities.

I shall conclude with a few corollaries. If history is that which happens prior to the clarification through philosophic discourse, we must then maintain that universal history does not *exist*. If it did exist, it would be the system and no longer history. This is why the idea of universal history can only be a task or an idea of reason. This task keeps the historian from believing in incommunicable isles; as soon as there are two isles, I think of them together in one and the same cosmos. Hence it will always be a task to search out all the relationships between all the partial totalities.

Lastly, if universal history does not exist, neither do absolute singularities exist; they could exist only in works which would be completely singularized. But history also includes forces, tendencies, currents, the anonymous, the collective. It is only in perfect and rare works that singularity is at least approached, if not attained. There are few beings, however, who are personal, really personal. For personality is a limitation of existence. If we are to follow the idea of clarification to its utmost point, either in the sense of system or in the sense of singularity, then the historical is precisely that which cannot occur. Thus the ambiguity of history is also its imperfection, and this will always hold it a little short of that which would complete it: short of the goal of the unity of meaning or the goal of singular works. And since that which would complete it would also be that which would abolish it, perhaps we should say—although the expression is a bit too Hegelian—only that which abolishes is also that which manifests.

2 / Theological Perspectives

Christianity and the Meaning of History

[1] PROGRESS, AMBIGUITY, HOPE

IN OUR TIMES it would indeed be pretentious to advance a complete answer to the problem of the meaning of history, requiring, as it would, the abilities of the historian, the sociologist, and the theologian. The purpose of this study is to clarify the problem by showing that there are several ways to view history and that, in consequence, there may also be several levels of replies to the question of the meaning of history. Perhaps a Christian interpretation of the mystery of history is called upon to provide, so to speak, the underpinnings for other interpretations which remain true at their level.

The very kind of false problem which confronts us at the outset is the clash between Christian eschatology and the concept of progress. Religious polemics has too often strayed into this impasse. Certainly it is true that the subject of the natural and uninterrupted progress of mankind is the aftermath of a secularization and, to put it briefly, of a rationalist corruption of Christian eschatology. Yet nothing is more misleading than to oppose progress and hope or progress and mystery. By showing that history lends itself to several levels of interpretation, we shall show that progress and mystery do not meet at the same level. The subject of progress only comes up if one decides to see in history merely what can be considered as the *accumulation of acquirements*. (As we shall see, this first level concerns tools in the broadest sense of the term: material or cultural tools, tools of knowledge, and even tools of consciousness and of the spirit.) But at this level there is no drama; and there is no drama because man has been left out of consideration so as to consider only the anonymous proliferation of tools. (All this will be clearer, I hope, when we consider it more fully; for the moment, it is only a question of indicating the main divisions of the problem.)

There is, however, a second level of interpretation in which history takes on a dramatic character with its decisions, crises, growths, and declines. Here we pass from an *abstract* history, where only the works of man and the accumulation of his vestiges are considered, to a *concrete* history in which *events* take place. This whole analysis will attempt to show that this second interpretation of history, and not the first, begins to link up with a Christian view of history. The principal difficulty will be to determine in what sense the Christian is justified in recognizing a total meaning in a history involving decisions and events; in short, how he can relate Christian hope to this open, uncertain, and ambiguous adventure which is life.

We have used three words which will serve as guides for our inquiry: progress, ambiguity, and hope. They stand for three stages in the flux of history, three ways of understanding and recovering meaning, and three levels of interpretation: the abstract level of progress, the existential level of ambiguity, and the mysterious level of hope.

[2] THE LEVEL OF PROGRESS

PERHAPS WE MAY TAKE the problem of progress out of its routine setting by asking a preliminary question: What is capable of progress?

If man stands out in such sharp contrast to nature and the unending repetition of animal habits, if man has a history, it is primarily because he *works* and because he works with *tools*. With tools and the works produced from them we touch upon the striking phenomenon that the tool and its products are preserved and accumulate. (The conservation of tools, according to the Paleontologist, is one of the unequivocal signs of man.) Thus we have here a phenomenon which is truly irreversible. Whereas each man in himself is transitory, his tools and works endure. The tool leaves a vestige which gives to human time—to the time of the arts—a continuing foundation, the time of works.

It is within this time of works that progress may take place. But before examining in what sense the tool involves growth as well as progress, we must first take notice of the entire sweep of the notion of "equipment."

The technical world of material tools and their extension into machines is not the whole of man's *instrumental world*. Knowledge is also a tool or instrument. Everything man has learned and all that he knows,—everything he can think, say, feel, and do—all that is "acquired." Knowledge becomes stratified, deposits of knowledge accumulate like tools and the works which result from them. Concretely, it is writing and especially printing which have permitted knowledge to accumulate and leave traces. Knowledge is in books and libraries as an accessible thing, as a part of the instrumental world (moreover, machines themselves are at the intersection of the world of tools and the world of solidified signs). On the basis of this sedimentation, the quest for knowledge, like the technical pursuit, is irreversible. For all new thought uses the thought of the past as a tool or instrument and in this way carries history forward.

In the *Fragment d'un traité du vide,* Pascal said that "The whole succession of mankind ought to be considered as one and the same man who continues to exist and learn." The history of technics and inventions constitutes one single history which is the result of varying national and individual geniuses who come to be forgotten and merge with that history. The uniqueness of this history indeed appears more distinctly if we consider the fact that the personality of the inventor is obliterated by the invention at the time that it becomes a part of common history. The very history of the discovery, the unparalleled drama which each invention meant to some individual is, so to speak, "bracketed" so that the anonymous flow of human power and knowledge might be established. And should the histories of technics, science, and general knowledge preserve the recollection of the crises in methods and solutions, their purpose is not to shed lustre on the *existence* of the men who actually wrestled with the problems. These crises are not preserved under their existential aspect but only in so far as their methodological features exemplify how previous knowledge was recast and reorganized in terms of a new hypothesis which assimilated the previously known. From this standpoint, there is no radical loss or fruitless efforts, and therefore no real drama.

Furthermore, in addition to the pursuit of knowledge, the searchings of *consciousness* also enter into the range of the category of instruments. Moral reflection, self-knowledge, and the understanding of human nature accumulate in the form of instruments for living. There is a moral and spiritual "experience" of mankind which is put aside like a treasure. Works of art, monuments, liturgies, books on culture, spirituality, and ethics form a "world" within the world and provide us with stepping-stones similar to objects or things outside ourselves. Of course it is very important to distinguish here between the schema of decisions, events, and *acts,* in which man always starts over from scratch, where individuals, by dying, take their experience with them, where civilizations starve to death next to their spiritual nutriments, and the schema of traces, of works left behind, and of *tradition.* In abstracting from decisions, events, and acts, we isolate the movement of tradition so that it is viewed as a constantly enlarging historical motivation, as a cumulative phenomenon. The momentum can be broken only by great cosmic or historic catastrophes—earthquakes or invasions—which destroy the real basis of this experience. This is why we cannot "repeat" Socrates, Descartes, or da Vinci; we know much more than they did; our knowledge of mankind is more elaborate, that is to say both more comprehensive and more subtle. (What we do with it existentially is quite another question.)

We had to begin, therefore, by presenting a rather broad view of history as the accumulation of traces and the deposit of human works detached from their authors, something analogous to liquid assets. This provisional analysis gives an immense role to progress and at the same time shows its limitations: an immense role because the instrumental world is much more extensive than what we ordinarily call the technical world, which also includes our knowledge and our cultural and spiritual past; limitations because progress only concerns an anonymous mind cut off from human life and the dynamics of man's achievements, torn from the concrete drama of suffering, striving individuals, and the rise and fall of civilizations.

The foregoing explains why at this level there is no decisive meeting between the "Christian meaning of history" and that anonymous proliferation. Christianity made a violent entry into the Hellenic world by introducing a concept of time containing events, crises, and decisions. Christian Revelation scandalized the Greeks through the narration of those "sacred" events: creation, fall, covenant, prophetic utterances, and, more fundamentally, "Christian" events such as incarnation, cross, empty tomb, and the birth of the Church at Pentecost. In light of these exceptional events, man was made aware of those aspects of his own experience which he did not know how to interpret. His own life was also made up of events and decisions and marked off by important alternatives: to rise up in rebellion or to be converted, to lose his life or to gain it. At that moment history acquired meaning, but it was concrete history in which something happens, in which people themselves have a personality which may also be lost or won.

Owing to its abstract and anonymous nature, a reflection on progress is therefore still removed from the level where a confrontation is possible with the "Christian meaning of history." This does not mean, however, that no comparison is yet possible at this level. For we have left out one feature of this anonymous history, this epic of human works without man. This feature is the one which permits us to call it progress and not simply evolution, change, or development. For to say that the growth of tools, knowledge, and consciousness is progress is to say that *more* is an *improvement*. Consequently, it is to ascribe a *value* to this anonymous and faceless history.

What is the significance of the above idea of value? What bearing does the "Christian meaning of history" have on that assertion? It would seem that the value found at this level is the conviction that man fulfills his *destiny* through this technical, intellectual, cultural, and spiritual experience; yes, that man fulfills his role as a creature when he breaks away from the repetition of nature and makes his history, integrating nature itself into his history and pursuing the vast enterprise of the humanization of nature. It would not be difficult to show in detail how technical progress, in the narrowest and most material sense, realizes this goal of man: it has allowed us to lighten the workingman's load, to broaden human relationships, and initiate man's dominion over the whole of creation. And that is *good*.

What does Christianity have to say here? Unlike Greek wisdom, it does not condemn Prometheus: according to the Greeks, the "sin" of Prometheus lies in having stolen fire, the fire of technics and arts, the fire of knowledge and consciousness. The "sin" of Adam, however, was not the same. Adam's disobedience was not in being a technical and knowing man, but in having broken the vital bond with the divine in his experience as man. Thus the first expression of that sin is the crime of Cain, the sin against his brother and not the one against nature, the sin against love and not the sin against unhistorical animal existence.

But if Christianity does not condemn Prometheus and even recognizes in him the expression of a creative intention, it is not fundamentally *interested* in the anonymous and abstract aspect of the histories of technics, the arts, knowledge, and consciousness. It is interested in what the individual does with them for his ruin or preservation. In the last analysis, the value of progress remains an abstract value like progress itself. Christianity addresses itself to the whole man, to a complete behavior and a total existence. This is why discussions on progress are ultimately rather sterile. On the one hand, we are wrong to condemn evolution; but in return, little is gained by praising it.

Actually, if we consider the destiny of man and the fulfillment of the human species as a whole, we find a positive value in this collective epic; but it becomes much more ambiguous when we relate it to man in the concrete. In each age our knowledge and capabilities are at once a blessing and a danger. The same mechanism which lightens man's burden, which broadens human relationships, and which bears witness to man's dominion over things also inaugurates new evils: specialization, consumer slavery, total war, the impersonal justice of bureaucracy, etc. We would find a like ambiguity attached to what we called earlier the progress of knowledge or consciousness.

This ambiguity therefore forces us to pass from one level to another, from the level of anonymous progress to the historical adventure of man in the concrete. At this level, Christianity actually comes to grips with our interpretation of history.

[3] THE LEVEL OF AMBIGUITY

ONE MIGHT BE TEMPTED to think that by leaving the level of anonymous progress, we forsake all historical considerations and immerse ourselves in the solitude of the individual person. Such is not the case. We also have a concrete history, that is to say a comprehensive and meaningful pattern worked out by the mutual actions and reactions of men.

Let us now search out some of the manifestations of this concrete history so as to determine the authentic categories of history (by categories of history, I mean notions like crisis, apogee, decline, period, epoch, etc., which enable us to think historically).

A first sign of this new historical dimension is the fact that there are *several* civilizations. From the point of view of progress, mankind is one; from the point of view of the history of civilizations, mankind is multiple. These two interpretations do not exclude each other but are, as it were, superimposed upon one another.

We may look upon each of the "varieties" of mankind as a historico-geographical complex which covers a certain domain and which, although it may not be rigidly defined, has its own peculiar vital cores and zones of influence. A certain cultural affinity and unity of purpose bring men together in time and define their belonging to the same "space" of civilization. Thus the core of a civilization is a global will-to-live, a way of living; and this will-to-live is animated by judgments and values. Naturally we have to beware of reducing these concrete judgments to a list of abstract values (as when we say that the eighteenth century bequeathed us the idea of tolerance or equality before the law, etc.). Here it is a matter of values which are actually experienced and acted upon, and which must be seized in concrete tasks, in the manner of living and working, of owning and distributing goods, and of being bored and having a good time. (An extraordinary example of this type of historical comprehension is given by Huizinga in *The Waning of the Middle Ages*.)

What best proves the inadequacy of knowing about the equipment (even in the broadest sense) of a civilization in order to understand it, is the fact that the significance of this equipment does not lie within the equipment itself; it depends upon the fundamental attitudes taken by the men of a given civilization in respect to their own technical possibilities. There are groups who feel repugnance to industrialization—for instance, the peasants, the artisans, and the lower middle classes which resist modernization. In 1830–1832 we witnessed the anti-technocracy reactions in the working class (in this respect, see the views of Schuhl in *Philosophy and the Mechanical Age*). Thus, the tool is not even useful unless it is valued, and this shows that there is a more basic schema than the history of technics which, after all, is only a history of means. A concrete history would be a history of ends and of means, a history of the complete intentions of man. For a civilization is a temporal manner of projecting a concrete style of existence, of *willing* man.

Now, with this first aspect of concrete history (which we may call "civilizing styles"), we discover historical categories which were concealed by the concept of progress. The first blunt fact is this: civilizations rise and fall. Mankind endures in the midst of the rise and fall of civilizations. Thus it is possible to hold to a cyclical conception of historical *periods* and also to a linear conception of progress. These two conceptions are on unequal levels: one is on a more "ethical" level while the other is on a more "technical" level. We see at once that whereas the phenomenon of progress was linked to the fact of the accumulation of traces and to the "sedimentation" of what has been acquired, the life and death of civilizations is linked to the notion of "crisis." This point was brought out quite well by Toynbee in *A Study of History* (it is not by accident that a historian of civilizations has been brought in to reorganize our views on history around categories which are irreducible to the technical schema, and which are more closely connected to the life of consciousness and willing). For Toynbee, each civilization appears to be characterized by *situations* which are challenges for it (coldness, the continental immensity, overpopulation, religious disunion, linguistic separation, class conflict, etc.). Each challenge is like the question of the sphinx: answer, or you shall be eaten. A civilization is the whole of the answers to these challenges. As long as there are creative nuclei which "answer," the civilization lives on; when it repeats its old answers and no longer invents adjustments to new difficulties, it dies. From this standpoint, the destiny of a civilization always remains uncertain; it may or may not invent the answers which will make it survive, or it may stagnate; it may cast off its outdated values or fall into decadence. And so there are suspensions of consciousness and awakenings, declines and renaissances, restorations and resistances, inventions and survivals.

At one time or another, every historian uses the majority of these words. He almost never criticizes them; he only uses them. Yet as soon as we explain their meaning, it becomes obvious that they do not belong to the same class as the notions of progress. Here the worst is always an imminent possibility. A history thus understood is singularly closer to the type of history, with its decisions and crises, which is presupposed by Christianity.

We should now correct this oversimplified conception: a civilization does not advance *en masse* nor does it stagnate in every respect. It has several schemata which may be followed, as it were, longitudinally: a schema of industrial equipment, a schema of social integration, a schema of public power and authority, a schema of the arts and sciences (of such and such arts and such and such sciences), etc. In the midst of these schemata appear crises, growths, regressions, etc., which do not necessarily coincide. The tide does not rise at the same time on all the shores of a nation's life.

Furthermore, we should indicate what crisis, decline, and invention signify for each of these structures of history. We speak of a "crisis" in mathematics, of an economic "crisis," of a ministerial "crisis." The word does not have the same meaning in every case. What is striking is that the "crises" of a social or cultural compartment have their peculiar motivation and their specific solution. Thus the crisis in mathematics during the Pythagorean era was largely independent of the general history of the time; it was a challenge internal to mathematics (namely, the irrationality of the diagonal in relation to the side of the square); [1] and this crisis found its solution in a purely mathematical procedure. The subsequent stagnation of this science, from Euclid to the Renaissance algebraists, has no decisive relationship with other historical developments. Likewise, an era may be progressionist in political matters and, at the same time, regressive in artistic affairs as was the French Revolution, or progressionist in art and stagnant in things political as was the Second Empire. A "great century" or era is such a period when almost everything comes to maturity at the same time, as in the century of Pericles or in the thirteenth and seventeenth centuries.

These remarks tend to show that history, which is *one* through the progress of instruments, has many ways of being *multiple*. It is not only divided into civilizations and periods, in space and time, but also into certain streams of thought and tendencies which pave the way for specific problems, particular crises, and inventions.

The over-all result would be "integral" history, but this eludes us. In a few privileged instances we perceive trains of causalities which are not too entangled. Thereupon systematic man arrives with his heavy-handed classifications and the thought succession of "dialectics." But the longitudinal motivations peculiar to each series and the transversal interferences from one series to another form such a closely woven tissue that they go beyond the ordinary "dialectics" to which one might want to confine them. For example, it is true in one sense that the state of technics "commands" the whole social process, but this depends on the sciences and particularly on mathematics which has historically been connected to the great metaphysical systems—Pythagorean, Platonic, Neo-Platonic (to the Renaissance). And so different histories involve each other to such an extent and in every sense that any explanatory system would appear naive and premature. The consciousness of an era is the confused and massive synthesis of this entanglement; it is sensitive to the existence of zones of stagnation and zones of vitality, of intermittent "challenges" which it does not experience as a theoretical system of problems but as disparate "unrests" (in

1. What the author apparently refers to is the irrationality of the numerical value of the hypotenuse of an isosceles right triangle to the numerical value of its sides.—Trans.

the sense in which we speak of school unrest or of colonial unrest); it is sensitive to localized advances in certain sectors of collective life. The net effect is therefore more like a vague feeling than a vivid awareness, and this is why it is ordinarily very difficult to tell where a civilization is headed.

A new indication of this concrete life in history is the indomitable character of the historic, significant *events* and *personalities*.

We know that the old historical method inflated history excessively with battles, dynasties, marriages, successions, and partitions. History was absorbed in the arbitrary, fortuitous, and irrational. Certainly it is beneficial to view history from a higher level, in sweeping geographical classifications (Braudel's recent book on the *Méditerranée au temps de Philippe II* marks the triumph of this method of understanding) as well as in technics, in social forces, and in all-inclusive movements. But on the other hand, we cannot follow this tendency to its logical conclusion, although this would seem to be the only way to explain by causes and to understand through intentions. For in becoming intelligible, history would ultimately cease to be historical. We would eliminate the actors who make it; we would have a history wherein nothing happens, a history without events.

History is historical because there are unparalleled actions which count and others which do not count; men who carry weight and others who do not; a lost battle, a leader who dies too soon (or too late!), the result being a changed destiny. To be sure, consistent with its popular Nietzscheanism and its radical irrationalism, Fascism has abused this "dramatic" vision of history. Yet this abuse should not conceal the importance of the events of history; for in the last analysis, they are what constitute the history of man himself. It is through this history that man is "in process." Moreover, phrases such as "the country in danger" and "the public welfare," words which are embedded in the very core of our Jacobin history, bear witness to the existential character of fate, or more appropriately, of *destiny*, which is attached to the concrete history of man.

A new feature of this concrete history is the prominent place of the "political" aspects of history. Our preceding remarks on the role of historic events and historic men lead naturally to this new point of view, for there is a close connection between the "event" aspect and the political aspect of history.

Now it is necessary to have a proper understanding of the word political. This word designates the sum total of man's relations in connection with *power:* conquest of power, exercise of power, preservation of power, etc. Power is the central question of politics: Who commands? For whom? Within what limits and under what restrictions? It is in activities which concern power, either from the side of those who possess it or from the side of those who come under its sway, challenge it, or court it—it is in all these activities that the *destiny* of a nation is created or doomed. "Great men" act directly or indirectly upon the course of events through their exercise of power. The events themselves may be largely accidents of power, such as revolutions and defeats. (We saw in 1944–1945 that the entire Nazi way of life was only brought into question by the overthrow of the State wherein the will of this regime was concentrated.) Finally, if we connect these last remarks to our first analysis of the movement of the rise and fall of civilizations, one sees again that it is within the political sphere of these civilizations that the challenges, crises, and great options are reflected.

Naturally, one must be careful not to go too far with this identification of the "dramatic," "event" aspect of history with its political aspect. As we pointed out earlier, while the manifold movements of a given civilization may have certain interrelationships, their critical or creative periods do not necessarily coincide. The arts and sciences have a destiny which only rarely coincides with the great historic events coming from the political sphere. Thus, history is always richer than our philosophies of history show.

Yet the privilege of political "crises" is twofold. First, they concern the *physical destiny* of civilizations as well as their intentions. They are of the nature of life and death, like the illnesses of individuals in comparison to their intellectual evolution or their religious conversions. For this reason, these crises have at least a radical, if not a total character. Secondly, they cause a fundamental trait of man to make its appearance within the core of history. This trait is *guilt*. The most deadly passions proliferate around power: pride, hate, fear. This sinister trilogy shows that wheresoever is man's greatness is also his fault. The grandeur of empires is also their fault, and this is why their collapse may always be understood as their punishment.

It is here that this analysis and portrayal of history as events, decisions, and the occurrence of dramatic "crises," opens up into a theology of history. This is achieved primarily but not exclusively by means of the concept of guilt. Let us re-read the Prophets of Israel and the psalms: we shall find the themes of national pride, hatred of the wicked, fear of the common people. The great neighboring powers of Egypt and Assyria were witness to the historical guilt of Israel, guilty to the extent that it wished to imitate their dreams of grandeur. Mary extols in the *Magnificat*: "He has scattered the schemes that the proud were forming in their hearts. He has thrown the powerful from their thrones and He has exalted the humble." [2]

I think that one of the tasks of the theology of history would be to go back to this Biblical critique of power in light of our modern experience of the State and the concentrationary world. We would also be equipped with the resources of a psychology and a psycho-analysis of the passions. Yet the greatest danger would be to allow the bond between greatness and guilt to escape, a bond which is as a second manifestation of the ambiguity of history. We must recognize that wherever there is guilt there is also greatness.

One may easily understand how essential it is to restore the dimension of history as a project of man, as a network of decisions and crises, in order to initiate this theology. Guilt only appears where history is the possibility for projects of greatness. The schema of progress remains attached to instruments. The instrument is not guilty; on the contrary, to the extent that it expresses the *purpose* of man in creation, it is good. Hence there is a justifiable optimism attached to a reflection on progress.

But if it is necessary to have rediscovered history as crisis in order to give any meaning whatsoever to the notion of fault, we must say, inversely, that a theology of guilt can put us on the alert, sensitize us to this dramatic aspect of history which involves a meditation on fault. Fault does not originate in the universe of the event; only an ambiguous history, a history which may always be lost or gained, an open, uncertain history wherein the chances and risks are linked together, may be guilty. A natural being cannot be guilty; only a historical being can become guilty.

We now approach one of those points where the existential and theological aspects of things come together. A dramatic vision of history has much more affinity with Christian theology than the rationalism of the "Enlightenment" which destroyed the very ground upon which a theology may be propagated—the ground of ambiguity.

2. *Luke* 1:46–55.

[4] THE LEVEL OF HOPE

THE CHRISTIAN MEANING of history is not exhausted by the notions of decision and crises, of greatness and guilt mingled together. In the first place, sin is not the center of the Christian Credo: it is not even an article of the Christian faith. We do not *believe* in sin, but in salvation.

How does the hope for salvation fall in with our understanding of history, with our thoroughly human way of living history? What new dimension does it add to our vision of history?

The few comments which I shall make on this last level of reflection may be summarized in two words: meaning and mystery. These two words in some way nullify each other but are nevertheless the contrasted language of hope. Meaning: there is a unity of meaning; it is the fundamental source of the courage to live in history. Mystery: but this meaning is hidden; no one can *say* it, rely upon it, or draw an assurance from it which would be a counter-assurance against the dangers of history. One must risk it on signs. Yet this mysterious meaning of history does not nullify the ambiguity which we discovered at the second level, nor is it to be confused with the rational meaning which was discovered at the first level.

What authorizes the Christian to speak of meaning when he takes shelter in mystery? What authorizes him to transcend this schema of ambiguity in which history may turn for the worse or for the better, in which rising and falling civilizations may weave their way into the fabric of progress? Does all of this have a *total* meaning?

For the Christian, faith in the Lordship of God dominates his entire vision of history. If God is the Lord of individual lives he is also Lord of history: God directs this uncertain, noble, and guilty history toward Himself. To be more precise, I think that this Lordship constitutes a "meaning" and not a supreme farce, a prodigious caprice, or a last "absurdity," because the great events that I recognize as Revelation have a certain pattern, constitute a global form, and are not given as pure discontinuity. *Revelation* has a kind of bearing which is not an absurdity for us, for we may discern in it a certain *pedagogical* plan in going from the Old Testament to the New Testament. The great Christian events— death and resurrection—constitute an order open to what St. Paul calls "the understanding of faith."

Thus, what allows the Christian to go beyond the disconnectedness of lived history and to transcend the apparent ambiguity of this history, which very often resembles "a tale told by an idiot," is the fact that this history is imbued with another history whose meaning is not inaccessible to him and which may be *understood*.

Hence the Christian is the man who lives in the ambiguity of secular history but with the invaluable treasure of a sacred history whose "meaning" he perceives. Likewise, his life accumulates the suggestions of a personal history wherein he discerns the link between guilt and redemption.

The Christian meaning of history is therefore the hope that secular history is also a part of that meaning which sacred history sets forth, that in the end there is only *one* history, that all history is ultimately sacred.

This meaning of history, however, remains an object of faith. If progress is the rational part of history, and if ambiguity represents the irrational part, then the meaning of history for hope is a surrational meaning—as when we say surrealist. The Christian says that this meaning is eschatological, meaning thereby that his life unfolds in the time of progress and ambiguity without his seeing this higher meaning, without his being able to discern the relation between the two histories, the secular and the sacred, or, in the words of St. Augustine, the relation between the "Two Cities." He hopes that the *oneness of meaning* will become clear on the "last day," that he will understand how everything is "in Christ," how the histories of empires, of wars and revolutions, of inventions, of the arts, of moralities and philosophies—through greatness and guilt—are "recapitulated in Christ."

In conclusion, I would like to indicate the attitudes that such a faith inaugurates: we may relate them to these two words, *meaning*, but a *hidden* meaning.

First, the Christian would be the man for whom the ambiguity and dangers of history are not a source of fear and despair. "Fear not!" is the biblical saying which confronts history. Despair, more than fear, is exorcized here; for the true contrary of hope is not progress; the contrary at the same level is hopelessness, "unhope"; this unhope is epitomized in the blasphemous title *The Twenty-fifth Hour*. ("The Twenty-fifth Hour, the moment when every attempt at rescue becomes useless. Even the coming of a Messiah would not change anything. The precise time of Western society. It is the present hour, right now.") [3]

3. C. Virgil Gheorghiu, *La Vingt-cinquième heure* (Paris, 1949).

Christian hope, which is hope *for* history, is primarily the exorcism of this false prophetism. I should like to insist upon the current implications of this denunciation. Gheorghiu's book is largely responsible for all the "catastrophism" in France, perhaps even for the latent defeatism of a public opinion weary of war and in search of alibis for its flight from the problems of the modern world. What is in question is the *antecedent* trust or distrust that we place in this history; yes, *antecedent,* for in advance of the whole of history, we cannot draw up the balance-sheet; we would have to be out of plays to make the final tally; the game would have to be finished in the eyes of an alien spectator. Hence the meaning which history may have as a whole is an object of faith. It is not an object of reason, as is instrumental progress, because what is in question is the global meaning which this form may take on in the process of being delineated by the actions of man. This meaning cannot be established or concluded; one can only wait for it with a powerful grace capable of directing the dreadful and the vain to the glory of God.

On the basis of this faith, life presents itself in the form of a task. One is led to believe that there will always be tasks to be performed and opportunities to grasp. The theoretical consequences are of no less importance than the practical consequences. Hope speaks from the depths of the descent into the absurd, it takes hold of the ambiguity and manifest incertitude of history and says to me: look for a meaning, try to understand! It is here that Christianity branches off from existentialism. Ambiguity is the last word for existentialism; for Christianity it is real, it is lived, but it is the next to last word. This is why the Christian, in the very name of this confidence in a hidden meaning, is encouraged by his faith to *attempt* to construct comprehensive schemata, to embrace the terms of a philosophy of history at least as an hypothesis. In this respect, Christianity is closer to the Marxist than to the existentialist temper, at least if Marxism manages to remain a method of investigation without falling into dogmatism.

We must now show the other aspect of this hope in research and action. Hope tells me that there is a meaning and that I should seek it. But it also tells me that this meaning is hidden; after having encountered the absurd, it now faces the system. Christianity has an instinctive distrust of systematic philosophies of history which would like to provide us with the key to intelligibility. One has to choose between system or mystery. The mystery of history puts me on guard against the theoretical, practical, intellectual, and political fanaticisms.

The applications are easy to see. From the methodological point of view, this sense of mystery encourages the desire to multiply our outlooks on history, to correct one interpretation with another in order to defend ourselves from pronouncing the last word. It seems to me that this is where the Christian feels distrust for the dogmatic employment of the Marxist method: Do all historical phenomena fall under its elementary dialectic? Does the historical experience of the proletariat alone elaborate the meaning of history? Is not history richer and more complex?

In order to guard against fanaticism, it is helpful not only to multiply explanatory outlooks, but also to maintain, from a practical point of view, the sense of the discontinuity of problems. It is not certain that the difficulties and "challenges" of the modern world form a system, and, by way of consequence, that they are amenable to political strategy. The American "ultras" and the communists would perhaps like to enclose us within their dualism; but on the contrary, are we not forced to say that things are much more complicated and confused? The Manichaeism in history is foolish and wicked.

Lastly, it is essential to maintain, under the heading of mystery, the consciousness of the plurality of the historical callings of civilizations as well as of persons. One does not have to be in a hurry, for example, to give a visible effectiveness to art and literature. Let the artist be more concerned with understanding the problems internal to his art than with "serving society." He will serve society without knowing whether he is himself faithful to his tradition. For the total significance of an epoch has more profound roots than social or political utilitarianism will ever suspect. It may be that the so-called "uncommitted" literature will have better expressed (because more secretly and more radically) man's needs in a given epoch than a literature anxious to have a "message" immediately understood and eager to exercise an immediate influence on its time. Perhaps it will have expressed only the most superficial, trite, and hackneyed aspect of the consciousness of an epoch.

Faith in meaning, but in a meaning hidden from history, is thus both the *courage* to believe in a profound significance of the most tragic history (and therefore a feeling of confidence and resignation in the very heart of conflict) and a certain rejection of system and fanaticism, a sense of the *open*.

But in return, it is essential that hope always remains in direct contact with the dramatic, disquieting aspect of history. It is precisely when hope is no longer the hidden meaning of an apparent nonsense, when it has freed itself from all ambiguity, that it comes back to rational and reassuring progress and heads toward stagnant abstractions. Thus it is necessary to remain attentive to this existential schema of historical ambiguity, situated between the rational schema of progress and the suprarational schema of hope.

The Socius and the Neighbor

IF WE DEFINE SOCIOLOGY as the science of human relationships within organized groups, then it would seem that there is no sociology of the neighbor. This study flows from the astonishment engendered by such a statement. It is important for reflection to seize upon this surprise and deepen it into a positive meditation situated between a sociology of human relationships and a theology of charity. If there is no sociology of the neighbor, perhaps a sociology which has recognized its limits, in confrontation with a theology of charity, becomes changed in its project, that is to say in its intention and pretension. If there is no sociology of the neighbor, perhaps there is a sociology which starts out from the frontier of the neighbor.

[1] THE LEVEL OF ASTONISHMENT

FIRST, LET US RENEW our astonishment by immersing our reflection once more in the freshness of *parable* and *prophecy*:

"A certain man went down from Jerusalem to Jericho, and fell among thieves, who also stripped and wounded him. . . . And it happened that a priest went down the same way. . . . In like manner a Levite also passed by. . . . But a certain Samaritan being on his journey came near him; and seeing him, was moved with compassion. . . . Which of these three men, in thy opinion, was neighbor to him that fell among the thieves?" [1]

A unique narrative and a question at the end. Such is the Biblical nutriment of reflection and meditation.

1. *Luke* 10:30–37.

What is at first surprising is that Jesus answers a question with a question, but with a question that has become inverted by means of the corrective virtue of the narrative. The visitor asked: Who is my neighbor? How is my brother related to me? Jesus returns the question in these terms: Which of these men has acted like a neighbor?

The visitor was making a sociological inquiry concerning a certain social object, a possible sociological category susceptible of definition, observation, and explanation. Jesus answered that the neighbor is not a social object but a behavior in the first person. Being a neighbor lies in the habit of making oneself available. This is why the neighbor is the subject of the story: once upon a time there was a man who became the neighbor of a stranger beaten by thieves. The story relates a series of *events:* a chain of unsuccessful encounters and a successful encounter. And the story of the successful encounter turns into a command: "Go and do likewise." The parable has turned the story into a pattern for action.

Thus there is no sociology of the neighbor. The science of the neighbor is thwarted by the praxis of the neighbor. One does not *have* a neighbor; I make myself someone's neighbor.

There is still another source for our astonishment: the point of the parable is that the event of the encounter makes one person present to another. It is striking that the two men who do not stop are defined by their social category: the priest and the Levite. They are themselves a living parable: the parable of man as a social function, of man absorbed by his role. They show that the social function *occupies* them to the point of making them unavailable for the surprise of an encounter. In them, the institution (the ecclesiastical institution, to be precise) bars their access to the event. In a way the Samaritan is also a category; but here he is a category for the others. For the pious Jew he is the category of the Stranger; he does not form part of a group. He is the man without a past or authentic traditions; impure in race and in piety; less than a gentile; a relapse. He is the category of the non-category. He is neither occupied nor preoccupied by dint of being occupied: he is travelling and is not encumbered by his social responsibility, ready to change his itinerary and invent an unforeseen behavior, available for encounter and the presence of others. The conduct that he invents is the direct relationship of "man to man." His conduct is of the nature of an event, for it takes place without the mediation of an institution. Just as the Samaritan is a person through his capacity for encounter, all his "compassion" is a gesture over and above roles, personages, and functions. It innovates a hyper-sociological mutuality between one person and another.

Astonishment is born of parable and is reborn of prophecy:

And the Son of man shall come in his glory . . . And he shall set the sheep on his right and the goats on his left. Then the King shall say to them that shall be on his right: *Come, ye blessed of my Father. . . . For I was hungry, and you gave me to eat; I was thirsty, and you gave me to drink. . . .* Then shall the just answer him, saying: *Lord, when did we see thee hungry, and fed thee; thirsty, and gave thee drink?* . . . . And the King, answering, shall say to them: *Amen I say to you, as long as you did it to one of the least of my brethren, you did it to me.* Then he shall say to them that shall be on his left. . . .[2]

The parable related an encounter in the present, the prophecy relates an event at the end of history which, in retrospect, unfolds the meaning of all the encounters in history. For prophecy bears upon and unveils the meaning of encounters, encounters similar to those of the Samaritan and the stranger overpowered by thieves: to give to eat and to drink, to take in the stranger, to clothe the naked, care for the sick, and visit those in prison, these are so many basic and simple gestures that are feebly formulated by the social institution; therein man is shown to be tormented by limiting situations, socially stripped, reduced to the distress of the mere human condition. The object of this primordial behavior is called one of the "least," the man who has no leading role in history. He is merely the supernumerary providing the amount of suffering necessary to the grandeur of the true "historic" events. He is the anonymous bearer of the caravan, without whom the *great* alpinist would fail to achieve fame. He is the private first class without whom the *great* generals would miss their strokes of genius as well as their tragic errors. He is the laborer doing monotonous and repetitive work without which the *great* powers could not construct modern industrial equipment. He is the "displaced person," a pure victim of *great* conflicts and *great* revolutions. The meaning of history, at least such as it is deciphered by the actors themselves, comes through the important events and men. The "least" are all those who are not captured within this meaning of history. But there is another meaning that reassembles all the minute encounters left unaccounted for by the history of the greats; there is another history, a history of acts, events, personal compassions, woven into the history of structures, advents, and institutions. But this meaning and this history are *hidden*. That is the point of the

2. *Matthew* 25:31–42.

prophecy: the "least" were representative of Christ, and neither the just nor the unjust knew it; the last day astonishes them: *Lord, when did we see thee hungry and thirsty?*

Thus the compassion of the Samaritan has a profound, transcendent meaning. The *practical* intention of the parable—"Go and do likewise"—is suddenly illuminated by the theological or rather *Christological* intention of the prophecy. The meaning of compassion in the present is inhabited by a transcendent, eschatological meaning.

It may be seen in what sense, indeed, in what twofold sense, a sociology of the neighbor is shut out. First, in the sense that the neighbor is the personal way in which I encounter another, *over and above all social mediation.* Secondly, in the sense that the significance of this encounter does not depend on *any criterion immanent to history* and cannot be definitely recognized by the actors themselves but will be discovered on the last day, like the manner in which I shall have encountered Christ without knowing it.

[2] THE LEVEL OF REFLECTION

HAVING REACHED THIS POINT, where, so it seems, the veracity of biblical theology ought to lead us, we shall turn back and ask ourselves *what this means* for us, here and now, in a world where the differentiation and organization of social groups constantly increases. It would seem that we do not live in the world of the "neighbor" but in that of the "socius." The *socius* is the person I attain through his social function; the relation to the *socius* is a mediate relation; it attains man in this or that capacity. . . . Roman law, the evolution of modern political institutions, the administrative experience of large states, and the social organization of work, not to mention the experience of several world wars, have gradually forged a type of human relationship which is always becoming more extensive, complex, and abstract. It is only natural that such be the case; for the essence of man lies in breaking away from nature and entering into the "civil" state, which was propounded in the eighteenth century. There is nothing new or harmful in that. With the appearance of man comes language, tools, and institutions. From this standpoint there is no question of an essential difference between a so-called natural social existence and an artificial social existence, but only questions of a difference in degree. We have merely become more sensitive to the progress of social "mediations" because it has accelerated. Further, the sudden appearance of the masses in history has provoked a demand for goods, comfort, security, and culture which, given the present state of affairs, requires rigid planning and a social technology. Naturally, this may often remind us of the anonymous and inhuman organization of an army out in the field.

Contemporary man also asks: who is my neighbor? Is it not necessary for us to come back from astonishment to critical doubt and to conclude that the immediate encounter of a man, an encounter which would make me the neighbor of this concrete man, is a myth in comparison to life in society? Is it not the dream of a mode of human relationship *other* than the real mode?

Such a myth concerning social relationships is what gives rise to the two contrary attitudes which we are now going to examine and which it will be necessary to set side by side.

On the one hand, the theme of the neighbor may nourish a radically anti-modern attitude: the Gospel would totally condemn the modern world; it would denounce it as a world without the neighbor, the dehumanized world of abstract, anonymous, and distant relationships. According to a certain form of Christian eschatologism, the world of the *"socius"* manifests itself only in the monstrous associations found in factories, military camps, prisons, and concentration camps. From this point of view the dream of the neighbor must seek its representations on the fringes of history, fall back on small, non-technical, and "prophetic" communities, and await the self-destruction of this world whose own suicide will incur the wrath of God.

One must choose between the neighbor and the *socius*. This choice also pertains, although in an inverse sense, to those men who have chosen the role of the *socius* and who merely see in the parable of the good Samaritan, and in the prophecy of the Last Judgment, manifestations of a backward mentality. They regard the category of the neighbor as outdated. The insignificant dramas of the parable would sufficiently show this: it takes its point of departure from a society in disorder, a society full of plundering. The rabbi who relates the fable does not rise to the standard of a socio-economic analysis of the causes of the disorder; he sticks to the particular and the fortuitous; the colorful story has a thought-content which remains at the prescientific stage. Consequently, the moral of the story leads the compassionate action of just men astray and into a dispersed order which perpetuates human exploitation. The perpetuation of beggars is not only the effect, but perhaps also the first presupposition of the Gospel morality of individual compassion. For if there were no beggars what would become of charity? But we men of today are marching toward the day when mankind, in emerging from its prehistory, will no longer know hunger, thirst, captivity, and perhaps not even the misfortune of death. From this point of view, the parable and the prophecy will have lost all meaning, for the men of the future will no longer understand the *images* upon which parable and prophecy are based.

These two interpretations agree on one essential point: the *socius* is the man of history, the neighbor the man of regret, of dreams, and myths.

[3] The Level of Meditation

The phenomenon of astonishment was linked to an isolated significance: the encounter, the event of the encountering of the neighbor. By taking hold of this isolated significance, reflection has undertaken an *ideological* work on it wherein the Event has become a theory of the event, and the encounter a warhorse against historical and social factors. And since the analysis of the *socius* has been carried out in the same systematic spirit, we have arrived at the false alternative between the *socius* and the neighbor. Our meditation must now reconsider in depth the whole interplay of oppositions and interconnections and thereby attempt to comprehend the *socius* and the neighbor together as the two dimensions of the same history, the two faces of the same charity. It is with the same emotion that I love my children and take an active interest in juvenile delinquency. The first love is intimate and subjective albeit exclusive; the second is abstract but has a wider scope. I am not discharged of all responsibility to other children by simply loving my own. I cannot escape others, for although I do not love them as my own or as individuals, still I love them in a certain collective and statistical manner.

The principal task of elaborating a "theology of the neighbor," which is the ultimate goal of this preparatory study on the *socius* and the neighbor, lies in attempting from the very beginning to become aware of its full scope. By this problem of scope or range, I understand the concern to rediscover, or at least constantly to seek out the *unity of intention* underlying the diversity of my relations to others. It is the same charity which gives meaning to the social institution *and* to the event of the encounter. The brutal opposition between community and society, between personal and administrative or institutional relationships, can only be one stage of reflection. Soon we shall have to determine why this stage is necessary, indispensable, and never done away with in our human history. But first we must show to what extent this stage is deceptive when it is privileged and *cut off from the total dialectic of the Kingdom of God.*

When I reduce the theology of the neighbor to a theology of the encounter, I miss the fundamental meaning of the Lordship of God over *history*. It is this theological theme which gives to the theme of charity all the *extension* and *breadth* of which it is capable. We shall presently see that, in return, the theme of charity gives to the theme of the Lordship of God over history its *intensity* and its *intention*. For the moment, however, we must reachieve this extension that destroys a reflection fascinated by oppositions, dilemmas, and impasses.

The Gospel prepares us in many ways for this recapturing of the scope of the theme of charity. It does this by means of a meditation on history: besides the representation of the Person, embodied in the good Samaritan, it also gives us the representation of "Nations," that of the "magistrate," of "Caesar," which refer to the State. The episode involving the coin bearing the image of Caesar: "Render to Caesar what is Caesar's and to God what is God's," and the episode of Jesus before Pilate: "You would have no power over me if it were not given to you from above," allow us to perceive this other form of the love of God in the institution, and by means of this special prestige of the institution that is "authority." For authority, even when it comes from below, as a result of elective processes or otherwise, is in another sense still moved by charity under the form of justice: "For the magistrate is God's minister for thy Good . . . ruling justly . . . when he faithfully fulfills his duty." [3] This text does not advocate the spirit of subordination but primarily the recognition that the relation of "authority" to "fear" is one of the dimensions of charity, the dimension which St. Paul calls *justice*. Justice is the dynamism of order, and order the form of justice. This dialectic of justice and order enters in turn into the great dialectic of history which is moved by the charity of God.

It is of the nature of this great dialectic to appear broken. The figure of the neighbor as person and the figure of the neighbor as magistrate (for Caesar is also my neighbor) are two partial and one-sided representations of the government of history by charity.

Hence, the growth of the Kingdom of God develops amid the

3. *Romans* 13:1–7.

suffering of contradictions: in our individual and collective lives, there is a perpetual debate between "direct" or person-to-person relationships and "indirect" relationships within the context of institutions. This debate is one aspect of this historical suffering.

This is what is not understood by the "reactionary" interpretation of the relationships between the *socius* and the neighbor. When the theme of the neighbor is cut off from the social context wherein it finds its historical impact, it turns to sterile regret and becomes the victim of some frightful propensity for avenging disaster. It is much more necessary to remain attentive to the historical scope of charity and to discern the whole wealth of the dialectic of the *socius* and the neighbor. At times the personal relationship to the neighbor passes *through* the relationship to the *socius;* sometimes it is elaborated on the *fringes* of it; and at other times it rises up *against* the relationship to the *socius.*

Indeed, very often the indirect route via the institution is the normal process of friendship; letters, means of transportation, and all the techniques used in human relationships bring men together. In a broader sense, distributive justice with all its juris-dictional organs and administrative apparatus is the privileged way of charity: the event of the encounter is fleeting and fragile. As soon as it is consolidated into a lasting and stable relationship, it is already an institution. There are very few pure events, and they cannot be retained nor even forecast and organized without a minimum degree of institutionalization. We must take our analysis one step further. The object of charity quite often appears only when I attain, in the other man, a common condition which takes on the form of a collective misfortune: wages, colonial exploitation, racial discrimination. Then my neighbor is concrete in the plural and abstract in the singular: charity reaches its object only by embracing a certain suffering body. This is something that the Greek Fathers had often recognized. St. Gregory, in particular, looks upon men as a "we" and humanity as a "pleroma." Therefore it is not necessary to enclose oneself within the letter of the parable of the good Samaritan, nor to impose upon it a personalist anarchism. The parable does not relieve me of the responsibility of answering this question: what does the concept of "neighbor" mean in the present situation? This may be to justify an institution, amend an institution, or criticize an institution.

At other times, it is true, the relationship to the neighbor is worked out only marginally, that is to say in the interstices of the relationships to the *socius.* This is largely the meaning of the "private" as opposed to the "public" or the "social," as well as the meaning of "leisure" as opposed to "work." It is also true that in a world where work is more and more divided, and in this sense more abstract, we are forced to look outside of the context of work and social obligations for the warmth and intimacy of authentic personal exchanges and real encounters. Hence, we look to the private realm for what we cannot find in the social realm. This is true. But the connection between the private and the public realms all the better stresses the relationship between the neighbor and the *socius*. Indeed, there is no private life unless it is protected by a public order. The family home has no intimacy unless shielded by legality, a state of peacefulness based on law and force, and in possession of a minimum of comfort which is assured by the division of labor, commercial exchanges, social justice, and civic rights. The abstract is what protects the concrete, the social establishes the private. Thus, it is illusory to try to change all human relationships into a kind of communion. Love and friendship are rare relationships which spring up within the context of more abstract and anonymous relationships. These relationships are more extensive than intensive and constitute in some way the social fabric of the more intimate exchanges of private life.

The opposition of the neighbor to the *socius* is therefore only one of the possibilities of the historical dialectic of charity. It may be the most spectacular and dramatic possibility, but it is not the most meaningful one.

It is now possible to speak of the irreplaceable significance of all these *divisive situations* which "eschatologism" isolates and which "progressivism" misunderstands.

There is an inherent evil in the institution, taking this word in its most general sense and understanding thereby all the organized social forms which are the proper object of sociology. It is the evil of "objectification" found in all forms of organization. Within the division of labor it takes the subtle form of the sadness and boredom which gradually work their way into the most "fragmented" and monotonous tasks of industrial labor when it is very specialized. One might say that the arduous labor which in past times was associated with physical conveyance and with dangerous and unhealthy work is now found in a psychic frustration which is more insidious than physical pain. On the other hand, the complex machinery of distributive justice and of social security are often imbued with an inhumane mentality because of their anonymity, as if the vast administering of things to men were stamped with a foreign and cancerous passion, the passion of an abstract administration. Lastly, every institution tends to develop the passions for power in men who dispose of some form of equipment (material or social). Whenever an oligarchy is established, be it technocratical, political, military, or ecclesiastical, it tends to make this equipment a means of domination and not one of service. We see these passions spring up every day right under our eyes, and there is no need to list the great perversions of powerful oligarchies. Within the center of the most peaceful and harmless institutions lies the beast, obstinacy, the tendency to tyrannize the public, and the abstract justice of bureaucracy.

The theme of the neighbor is primarily an appeal to the awakening of consciousness. It would be absurd to condemn machines, technocracy, administrative apparatus, social security, etc. Technical procedures and, in general, all "technicity," have the innocence of the instrument. The concept of the neighbor is an invitation to situate evil within the specific passions that are connected to the human employment of instruments. It is an invitation to break away from the old philosophies of nature and to initiate a purely internal critique of man's "artificial" existence. The vice of the social existence of modern man does not lie in being against nature; what is lacking is not naturalness, but charity. Consequently, criticism goes completely astray when it attacks the gigantism of industrial, social, or political machinery, as if there were a "human scale" inscribed within man's nature. This was the illusion of the Greeks who attached the stigma of culpability to the rape of nature (Xerxes spanning a bridge across the Bosporus, imposing "a yoke on the sea" and piercing Mount Athos, as is witnessed in Aeschylus' *Persians*). We are in need of a critique other than this idea of Greek "measure" which opposes the great planning researches of modern social life. Man's technical, social, and political experience cannot be limited in its extension, for the theme of the neighbor does not condemn any horizontal extravagance or growth in these areas. If a particular organization has overextended itself, this is an error and not a fault within the ethical realm. In this instance, what is called for is a purely pragmatic critique of the advantages and disadvantages of gigantism. The optimum dimension of an enterprise, of a complex industry, a sector of state planning, a political entity, etc., has to do with purely "technical" criteria, not "ethical" standards. The theme of the neighbor rather condemns a vertical extravagance, that is, the tendency of social organisms to absorb and exhaust at their particular level the whole problematic of human relationships. The extravagance of the social realm as such lies in what we earlier called "the objectification" of man within the abstract and anonymous relationships of economic, social, and political life. The social realm tends to block access to the personal and to *hide* the mystery of interhuman relationships, to dissimulate the movement of charity behind which stands the Son of Man.

Thus the depth of human relationships often appears only through the failures within the social realm: there is a technocratic or institutional slumber, in the sense in which Kant spoke of a dogmatic slumber, from which man is awakened only when he is socially stripped, be it by war, revolution, or great historical disasters. When these occur, there arises the unsettling presence of man to man. Indeed, the glory of such ruptures lies in their giving rise to new types of institutions. Thus the meditations of the Stoic sage, and those of the first Christians on man as a citizen of the world have been both the effect of a certain incohesiveness of the political consciousness after the failure of the Greek city, and the cause of a broadening of historical perspective: the opposition between the citizen and the slave, between the Hellene and the barbarian, the city and the tribe, is upset by Christian brotherhood and the worldly citizenship of Stoicism. And this upsetting permits a new revolution of the social bond and its stabilization at a new level in medieval Christendom.

The theme of the neighbor therefore effects the permanent critique of the social bond: in comparison to love of neighbor, the social bond is never as profound or as comprehensive. It is never as profound because social mediations will never become the equivalent of encounter or immediate presence. It is never as comprehensive because the group only asserts itself against another group and shuts itself off from others. The neighbor fulfills the twofold requirement of nearness and distance. Such was the Samaritan: near because he approached, distant because he remained the non-Judaean who one day picked up an injured stranger along the highway.

We must never lose sight, however, of the fact that personal relationships are also the victim of passions, perhaps the most fierce, dissimulated, and perfidious of all passions. After all, what have three centuries of bourgeois civilization made of the concept of charity? Charity may be nothing more than an alibi for justice. And so the protest of the "private" against the "social" is never entirely innocent. The "private" has its own peculiar evil when it opposes itself to the "social" and condemns its abstraction and anonymity. True charity is often scoffed at doubly by inhumane "justice" and by hypocritical "charity." The dialectic of the neighbor and the *socius* is all the more perverted in so far as relationships to others, under one form or another, are themselves more corrupted. Thus, all that we really possess are the shattered pieces of true charity.

Has our meditation retained something of our initial state of astonishment? I believe so. The neighbor, we said, is characterized by the personal manner in which he encounters another independently of any *social mediation*. The meaning of the encounter does not come from *any criterion immanent to history*. This was our starting point and now we shall return to it.

The *ultimate* meaning of institutions is the service which they render to persons. If no one draws profit from them they are useless. But this ultimate meaning remains hidden. No one can evaluate the personal benefits produced by institutions; charity is not necessarily present wherever it is exhibited; it is also hidden in the humble, abstract services performed by post offices and social security officials; quite often it is the hidden meaning of the social realm. It seems to me that the eschatological Judgment means that we "shall be judged" on what we have done to persons, even without knowing it, by acting through the media of the most abstract institutions, and that it is ultimately the impact of our love on individual persons which will be judged. That is what remains *astonishing*. For we do not know when we influence persons. We may think we have exercised this immediate love within direct relationships between man and man, whereas our charity was often only a form of exhibitionism. Likewise, we may think we have no influence on persons in the indirect relationships of work, politics, etc., and perhaps here too we are deluded. The criterion of human relationships consists in knowing whether we influence people. But we have neither the right nor the power to apply this criterion. In particular, we do not have the right to employ the eschatological criterion as a process enabling us to privilege direct relationships at the expense of indirect and abstract relationships. For in reality, through them we also exercise a kind of charity with regard to persons. But we are not necessarily aware of this. Thus, so long as the sociological veil has not fallen, we remain within history, that is, within the debate between the *socius* and the neighbor, without knowing whether charity is here or there.

We must, therefore, say that history, with its dialectic of the neighbor and the *socius*, supports the *scope* of charity. But in the last analysis, it is charity which governs the relationship to the *socius* and the relationship to the neighbor, giving them a common *intention*. For the theology of charity could not have less extension than the theology of history.

The Image of God
and the Epic of Man

To F. and J.–P.—August 2, 1960

[1] Toward an "Epical" Theology

WHEN THE THEOLOGIANS of the sacerdotal school elaborated the doctrine of man that is summarized in the startling expression of the first chapter of Genesis—"Let us make man in our image and likeness"—they certainly did not master at once all its implicit wealth of meaning. Each century has the task of elaborating its thought ever anew on the basis of that indestructible symbol which henceforth belongs to the unchanging treasury of the Biblical canon. I should like to begin, therefore, with the consideration of the most grandiose interpretation given to it by some of the Greek and Latin fathers even before Origen and Augustine: it will immediately upset the flimsy representation that we are prone to give to it when we follow the most facile direction of the metaphor.

We readily believe that the image of God is simply an imprint like the worker's trademark; we then discuss among ourselves in order to know whether, in the economy of sin, this mark has worn away and to what degree, and whether only lightly or totally. But what should happen if we should invert the metaphor, if we should see the image of God not as an imposed mark but as the striking power of human creativity; if we treat it not as the residual trace of a craftsman who has abandoned his work to the ravages of time, but as a continuous act in the creative movement of history and duration?

Another question: where are we most prone to seek out this imprint left in us? In the very depths of the individual, in its subjectivity. The image of God, we believe, is the very personal and solitary power to think and to choose; it is interiority. According to such an atomistic interpretation of the image of God, I am an image of God and you are an image of God, but the facts of history cannot be coordinated with this divine stamp which is passive, immutable, and subjective.

Now let us listen to the Fathers of the Church. For them, the image of God is man, indivisibly collective and individual; it is man drawn forward by a progressive expansion of his horizons and oriented toward the vision of God, even to the manifestation of the figure of the Son. Listen to Irenaeus:

> It was first necessary that man should be, then, once existing, that he should grow; having been created, it was necessary for him to become an adult; having become an adult, that he should multiply, acquire strength, and be glorified; and having been glorified that he should see the Lord.

And again:

> It was first necessary that nature should appear, and that what was mortal should be vanquished and absorbed by what was immortal, and that man should become as the image and likeness of God, having acquired the knowledge of good and evil.

Let us think about the scope of the revolution in the history of thought that this text represents in relation to that Neo-Platonism in which reality is a progressive *withdrawal,* an ineluctable beclouding that increases as we descend from the One, which is formless, to the Mind, which is bodiless, to the World Soul, and to souls which are plunged in matter, which itself is absolute darkness. Are we sensitive to the distance between this text and any notion of salvation conceived as an individual recruiting of isolated members of the elect who are torn from an evil or indifferent history, but who, on the other hand, are not familiar with the idea of the coming of the image of God?

Here we have, in the face of the ancients as well as that of men of modern times, the primordial Christian philosophy of the image of God: that of a creation in time that advances by the birth of a personal and communal being, scarcely inferior to a God.

Naturally, I am aware of all the qualifications needed to give balance and measure to this vision of historical creation, if it is to rightly account for the gravity of evil and for the height, breadth, and depth of grace. But I should like it to be understood clearly that evil is not something to be cut away from and grace something to be added to the historical creation of man, but that creation continues in the midst of evil and by means of grace. It is just this that the Fathers understood: that creation is not inert, finished, and closed: "My Father," Jesus says, "is at work even to this hour." Evil is not to be cut away from nor grace added to creation. Rather, our idea of creation must be expanded until it can encompass both the willful character of evil and the gratuitousness of grace. The grandiose divine pedagogy of the Fathers consists in drawing forth a god from a sinner. In the words of Irenaeus: "How could man have known the good if he had been ignorant of the contrary of the good? And how shall that man be god who has not yet been man?" If Irenaeus and Tertullian included evil and grace in a vision of creation, it is because Christ was for them the path, in the creation of man, from evil to grace, the restarting of creation, the renewal of the image of God. Let us listen one last time to Irenaeus: "Because of his immense love he became what we are so that he might make us become what he is himself."

Such is the panoramic fresco that I wished to place before you in order to give tone, measure, and proportion to our reflection. It opens us neither to an active pessimism nor to a tragic optimism—which in the last analysis is the same thing—but rather to an *epical* sense of our personal existence situated again within the perspective of a vaster epic of mankind and creation.

Now we must ask how this reflection on "the image of God" can help us to orient ourselves in all our "encounters" with our fellow man. There is a possible avenue of approach. In the preceding article on "The *Socius* and the Neighbor," I compared the "direct" relations between man and man (the relations with one's neighbor) to the "indirect" relations experienced in institutions and by means of social devices (the relations with the *Socius*). Our reflection on the image of God allows us to take as a point of departure what was at that time our conclusion, namely, the deep and mysterious unity of all these relationships which fall under the heading of a theology of love that would at the same time be a theology of history.

The Fathers knew that Man is one and many, the individual and the collectivity: man is each man and all mankind. Some of them were aware that Adam meant Man, *Anthropos*, not an old, individual gentleman, all alone with his wife in a garden, who would transmit his quite individual and personal propensity for evil to his descendants by means of physical generation. They were capable of conceiving a *singular-collective*, an individual who had the value of an entire nation, a collectivity convertible into individual thoughts, volitions, and feelings. They always understood this paradox because they had retained the historical and cosmic dimensions of the image of God.

How could we not stand in wonder, we men of today, we who are threatened as never before with seeing our humanity broken in two, on the one hand, between the direct relationships of friendship, of the couple, of our private lives, and on the other hand, the indirect relationships of economic, social, and political life? This dichotomy between man's private and public life, which makes madness of both, is the very antithesis of an anthropology which starts with a meditation on the image of God.

In order to acquire a fuller understanding of what is false in the contemporary opposition of the individual and the "big animal,"—in the words of Simone Weil—I shall give a simple example: that of language. It is a good example since the Lord allows himself to be called the Logos and since, according to Scripture, creation proceeds by the Word. Now, how do we experience the fact of language? Language is not a wholly individualized human reality; no one invents language; its sources of diffusion and evolution are not individualized; and yet, what is more human than language? Man is human because he speaks: on the one hand, language exists only because each man speaks; but language also exists as an institution within which we are born and die. Is this not a sign that Man is not wholly individuated, but is both individual and collective?

If we follow this path, which has been opened to us through our initial reflection on the image of God, we must try to avoid the dichotomy between the neighbor and the *socius*, between direct and indirect relationships. Certainly our daily experience seems to drift only too easily toward such a dichotomy. But rather than allow ourselves to be taken in by this dichotomy, we shall strive to traverse those spheres of human relations which can be experienced in a very personal or a very anonymous manner.

I propose to follow a convenient and instructive method of presentation which is at the same time allied with the most natural and enduring manifestations of man's reality and history: we shall distinguish between the relationships within the spheres of having, power, and value [*avoir, pouvoir, valoir*]. This division is suggested to me by Kant's *Anthropology from a Pragmatic Point of View,* which has the advantage of situating us at the very core of highly individualized feelings and passions: the passions of possession, domination, and ostentation (*Habsucht, Herrschsucht, Ehrsucht*). It also places us within three very important institutionalized spheres concerning the relations of man to man: the economic sphere of having, the political sphere of power, and the cultural sphere of mutual recognition.

The first of these institutionalized spheres is determined by the relation between work and ownership; the second by the relation between commanding and obeying (or, if you will, between the governing and the governed, the political relation *par excellence*). The third sphere also has an objective reference in morals, codes, monuments, works of art, and culture. In virtue of their twofold participation in the emotional life of the individual and the institutional world of the collectivity, the spheres of having, power, and value escape the conflict between the neighbor and the *socius* as well as the dichotomy between direct and indirect relationships: the same situations are experienced on an interpersonal plane *and* within the setting of economic, political, and cultural institutions and organizations.

I should now like to suggest what the epic of the image of God might be when it is unfolded within the three registers of having, power, and value. Naturally, it is understood that the incessant interferences of the private and public worlds must be taken into account. I propose to elucidate a quite general sketch that is divided into two panels. On the first, we shall perceive the downfall of having, power, and value. On the second, we shall perceive the work of redemption, the divine pedagogy working within the economic, political, and cultural spheres, strengthening individual attitudes and the life of groups with their structures and institutions.

[2] THE DOWNFALL OF HAVING, POWER, AND VALUE

OUR INITIAL EXAMPLE of language suggests to us that evil passes both through the individual and the collectivity. The story of Babel illustrates the destruction of language as an instrument of communication. Language as an individual power is attacked in many ways: by the lie, gossip, flattery, and enticement. As a cultural institution, speech is stricken by the scattering of languages and by misunderstanding on the various levels of cultural groupings, nations, social classes, and environments. Here we have an example that inspires us to analyze the spheres of having, power, and value, without worrying over the evident antinomy between individual and collective sin: man is evil not only in his "heart" but also in the non-personalized part of his humanity, in the diverse collectivities which are like the essential fabric of his humanity.

Let us begin with the *evil of having*. In itself, having is not evil. It is the relation of the primordial Adam with the land he culti-vates, the familiar relation of appropriation by which the "I" is extended into the "mine" on which it depends, humanizes, and by which it establishes its realm of belonging. But although having is innocent in itself, it is nevertheless one of the greatest pitfalls of human existence.

There is a curse attached to possession that we may catch sight of on both the individual and collective levels. The moralists have repeatedly said that in identifying myself with what I have, I am possessed by my possessions and lose my autonomy. That is why the rich young man must sell all his possessions in order to follow Jesus. "Woe to the rich" thunders the Christ of the Gospels. The evil attached to the hard-hearted person lies in an obstacle to com-munication. "Mine" excludes all third parties, and thus individuals expropriate themselves by appropriating things to themselves. This is the origin of our way of representing human lives as isolated from each other. But in their essence, they are united by a thousand bonds of similarity and communication, by mutual in-volvement in tasks and all that is suggested in the word "We." What causes division among men are their private realms of possession.

But this personal and interpersonal misfortune also has a communal form of expression. The phenomenon of possession, in fact, only exists within the context of a regime of property. It is here that we may draw upon Marx, quite apart from any concern for Marxist orthodoxy. When the Protestant Revival was forgetting social structures and instead concentrating on individual conver-sion, Marx's peculiar greatness was in not being a moralist. Any effort to make him one would only result in our losing the fruits of his analysis. His greatness is in having attempted to describe and explain alienation—that is, a retrogression of human nature to the inhuman—on the level of social structures. The book he wrote was not entitled The Capitalist, but *Capital*.

Certainly capital entails a certain destruction of humanity, wherein man is made into a thing. Capital is the great fetish by which man becomes dehumanized. In this sense, Marxism is true. In a world dominated by the category of money, thought and speech are merely variations of the great fetish. Materialism is the truth of a world without truth. False as a dogmatism—first there was matter, then came life, then man, and finally communist man will emerge—this materialism is true as a phenomenology of the untrue. Whatever one might think of the rest of Marxism, of its theory of classes, of the proletariat as the universal class, of the dictatorship of the proletariat, the flower of its crown will always be the theory of alienation. The practical value of this theory has restored to us a vision of evil, not on the level of the moral or immoral individual, but rather on the level of institutionalized forms of possession. In this way, we may rediscover the historical dimension of sin, known so well by the prophets, and realize that no one is individually responsible for sin but rather that all of us perpetuate it and are involved in it without having to invent it anew. In being born, I enter into relationships of possession that are corrupt within the context of the collectivity, although their degree of corruption may always be intensified by individual acts of appropriation and exploitation that are morally scandalous.

What we have just said about *having* may also be applied to the realm of *power*. Power is the fundamental structure of the political order. It introduces the whole network of relations between the governing and the governed. Even in the exceptional case of a self-governing community that operates without the interposition or delegation of power, a distinction would still exist between commanding and obeying. It is by passing through the necessary stage of unlimited power, wherein there are no bounds to compulsion and physical constraint, that a historical community becomes organized as a State and acquires the power of decision.

Now, what relationship is more fragile than this one? Power establishes between men an unequal, non-reciprocal, hierarchical, and non-fraternal form of communication. And yet this relationship is fundamental and constitutes the very foundation of human history. It is through the employment of power that history is made. Accordingly, it is the same relationship which, in the literal sense of the word, establishes man and has always led him astray as well. We are familiar with the complaints of the wise against the great and the mighty. The Old Testament abounds in violent criticisms of kings; the *Magnificat* foretells the humbling of the great and the exaltation of the meek. Jesus himself states that "the rulers of nations enslave them." The Greek tragedians were aware of the same problem: Oedipus, Creon, and Agamemnon exemplify haughty grandeur brought to ruin. Socrates draws the portrait of the tyrant and in him epitomizes anti-philosophy before falling victim of the unjust city. Alain sums this up: "Power renders man mad."

Now the passion for power has this remarkable characteristic: it does not strive for personal satisfaction but, on the contrary, has an ascetical character about it. For he who worships power, it is worth the sacrifice of personal satisfaction.

Is this to say that a reflection on power is limited to a purely moral meditation on the passions of power and how they may be corrected or even eradicated? Anyone can perceive that thought would reach an impasse if it allowed itself to be restricted to the consideration of how individuals use power. The problem of the "tyrant" is only a subjective projection of the problem of "power." There is a pathological aspect of power which cannot be reduced to the base intentions of individuals, such as the Prince's violent nature, and the cowardice of his subjects. The violence of one man and the cowardice of all conspire within one single vicious symbol, within one guilty form which they engender and maintain, but which, in return, molds the tyrant and his humiliated neighbor.

This symbol of power, this alienated form, can be considered in a special and autonomous reflection. Thus St. Paul speaks, in a mythical sense, of "authorities" as demoniacal powers; and so does St. John with his "beast" of the Apocalypse. Mythical language is the most faithful way to express power which is without bounds, unshared, and without control or orderly procedure, or to give expression to the seductive enticements with which it clothes its violence. Mythical language best preserves the revealing power contained within the *imago dei*. It makes manifest the fact that man's nature has been degraded not only in the individual, but also in the collectivity. There are infamous and criminal laws. Corrupt legislation is always the necessary outgrowth of the evil passions of an individual, a group, or the class in power. For example, it is quite useless to assume a moralistic attitude and condemn the tortures occasioned by the Algerian war—as if one could make a dirty war decent—if we do not at the same time condemn the special interests, the introduction of *ad hoc* laws, and lastly the war itself in so far as it has grown into a sort of national institution destined to perpetuate colonialism.

In this respect, the Christian has everything to learn from the critique of power elaborated by classical "liberal" thought from Locke to Montesquieu, by the "anarchist" thought of Bakunin, by those who supported the *Commune,* and by the non-Stalinist

Marxists. I am thinking in particular of the group *Socialisme ou Barbarie* which has taken up the analysis and elucidation of the structure of power in planned societies of the twentieth century. It has also posed in precise terms the problem of management by workers themselves, direct democracy in small economic unities, and the structuring of political power from bottom to top and not just from top to bottom as in the authoritarian democracies of the East, and even in the West.

These examples suggest the idea of continuity between a theological anthropology inspired by the patristic interpretation of the "*imago dei*," and a concrete critique of power, adjusted to the realities of our time. Owing to its scope, this theological vision of the image of God ought to be able to reintegrate the scattered parts of a critique of historical and political man that traditional Christendom has left to be developed outside its own narrow and individualistic conceptions.

Will the encounter between man and man in the third cycle of relationships be more exclusively personalized than in the two preceding ones? Such would seem to be the case. What is at issue here concerns that quest which each of us is pursuing, the quest for the esteem of others which is so essential to the consolidation of our personal existence. For we exist to some degree in virtue of the recognition that others give us, others who bestow value upon us, approve or disapprove of us, and who reflect our own personal worth. The constitution of a human person is a mutual activity which employs opinion, esteem, and recognition. Others give meaning to me by throwing back to me the trembling image of myself.

Now, what is more fragile than this reflected existence? This relationship of mutual recognition is quickly encroached upon by all the passions of vanity, pretense, and jealousy. The moralist, the novelist, and the dramatist are here valuable witnesses to man's struggles for the reflected "image" of himself. Here we find an interpersonal relationship of prime importance, massacred by evils and vices which cut into the very heart and soul of individual men.

This is true. But this same struggle for recognition is pursued by means of cultural realities which undoubtedly do not have the consistency of economic apparatuses and political institutions, but which, nevertheless, form an objective reality, in the sense provided by Hegel when speaking of objective spirit. This quest for mutual esteem is pursued through *images* of man; and these images of man constitute the reality that is culture. By this I understand customs, morals, law, literature, and the arts. And these manifold images of man which are conveyed by culture are embodied in monuments, various styles, and works of art. When I attend a Van Gogh exhibition, I am face to face with a vision of the world that has solidified into a thing, a work of art, the vehicle of communication. And even when it is not a human figure which is represented, what is conveyed is still a representation of man. For the image of man is not just the portrait of a man, but also the sum total of the ways in which man projects his vision on things. In this sense, a still-life is an image of man.

Now all of these images of man are embodied in our interpersonal relationships. They are silent forms of mediation which steal in and insert themselves between the looks which two human beings exchange. Each of us sees himself in the images of man. Thus culture, with its manifold meanings, comes to ballast the relationships which we believe the most direct and immediate.

If our encounters are truly mediated by the images of man which are embodied in cultural works, interhuman relationships can be lowered to the level of these mediating images. This is what happens when an aesthetic or literary movement destroys or perverts the fundamental representations that man makes of himself, whether it be in the realms of sexuality, work, or leisure. It might even be said that we have here a fundamental source of discord in interhuman relations. For perhaps literature and the arts have a permanent function of scandalizing. By readily and insistently representing evil, the artist destroys the conventional and hypocritical image which the righteous are inclined to assume; and so the artist is always accused of perverting man by distorting the image of man. Naturally, his role must remain an ambiguous one, as he is both a master of truth and a master of seduction. But you can see at once that a meditation on the fallen aspects of interhuman relations cannot neglect this drama and crisis which is being played out on the level of cultural representations, collective phantasms, and aesthetic media. Man always makes and unmakes himself not only in the heart of another, but also through the media of all those "objects" which sustain the relationship of man with man, from the economic object to the cultural object, passing through the political object.

[3] THE ÉLAN OF REDEMPTION

LET US NOW CONSIDER the second panel of the diptych on which is inscribed in letters of fire and joy the word "redemption." The Greek Fathers interpreted this as divinization. Let us first note that this second panel is not simply the rejoinder to the first. Several years ago, in commenting on *Romans* 5:12–21, Karl Barth stressed a decisive expression of St. Paul: "If the sin of a single man brought death to all, *by all the more reason* the grace of God and the gift of this grace coming from one man—Christ Jesus—has abounded unto many." And later we read: "If by one man's fault and through his deed alone death has reigned, *how much the more* they, who receive through the deed of Jesus Christ alone grace and the gift of justice in their full abundance, shall reign in life." *By all the more reason, how much the more.*[1] That is the divine measure, the divine transcendence of all measure. If sin abounds, grace superabounds.

Do we measure up to this understanding? Do we know how to seek out the *superabundance* of grace which is God's answer to the *abundance* of evil? Yes, of course, we know the orthodox answer: this superabundance is Jesus Christ, but what *signs* of this do we detect in this vast world? We do not dare look for the signs of this "superabundance" except in the interior experience of an overflowing of joy, peace, and conviction. We believe that sin abounds in the external world, but that grace superabounds only in the interior of man. Are there to be no *signs* of the superabundance of grace outside of the interior life, or only in a few small and isolated communities? No signs of this on the great stage of the world? Certainly it is true that from Augustine onwards, the division was already made: the dominant school of theology maintained that sin was perhaps collective, but grace was surely private and interior. The city of God is recruited within the ranks of the *massa perdita*, the *massa iniquitatis, irae, mortis, perditionis, damnationis, offensionis,—massa tota vitiata, damnabilis, damnata.* From this united mass of the damned, only the Church emerges and survives as a "Body" of salvation.

I am quite aware that there is some difficulty in speaking of salvation for a collective reality and *I wish to attack it immediately without disguising the difficulty of the enterprise.* It may be said that salvation comes to us through the remission of sins, but can the remission of sins be announced to an anonymous reality and could this reality recognize it? Obviously the question is rather ambitious and I, for one, am hesitant to approach it. Yet by feeling my way and with the sense of embarking on a new adventure, I shall attempt to advance our reflection.

1. πολλῷ μᾶλλον.

Let us ask ourselves the following questions: Do we have a proper understanding of the full scope of the remission of sins? Have we not limited our understanding of it because of our atomistic idea of salvation? The Greek Fathers had a grandiose vision of the growth of mankind which God orients, in the very midst of evil and by means of grace toward divinization. Should this not inspire us to break away from our individualistic conception of the remission of sins, parallel with our conception of sin itself?

Let us try to recognize the signs of this remission of sins in a non-moralistic sense of the word, that is, in a sense I would prefer to call architechtonic and which would befit the *imago dei* taken in its fullness. I shall not follow the previous order of economic, political, and cultural, but rather start with the political sphere. Indeed, we have here the opportunity to base ourselves on the Pauline doctrine on government. With this as a basis, perhaps we may also say something about the other spheres of human relations.

In *Romans* 13, St. Paul develops a theory of government of which one aspect is relevant here: through its *institutional* and not its *personal* character, authority is said to come from God.

All authority is "constituted," [2] is instituted by God: to resist authority is to resist the order established by God. "The ruler is the minister of God for thy good." [3] Our respect is given to their "function." All these words—institution, order, good, function— are found on that level which we earlier called the human collectivity. What does this mean? Does it mean that Genghis Khan, Napoleon, Hitler, and Stalin have been personally invested with divine right by some kind of election? No, it means, I believe, that wherever the State is the State, in the midst of and in spite of the evil of the titular authority, something is functioning for the good of man. I look upon this good credited to the State as a wager. It is the wager that, in the last analysis, in the midst of and even in spite of the evil of the individuals in power, the State is good.

It must be admitted that St. Paul has won his wager. In spite of their violent nature, empires have been influential in advancing law, knowledge, culture, the well-being of man, and the arts. Mankind has not only survived, it has grown, it has become more mature, more adult, and more responsible in a way that is somehow mysterious and will remain so until, in the heavenly Jerusa-

2. τεταγμέναι εἰσίν.

3. τῇ ἐξουσίᾳ τῇ τοῦ Θεοῦ διαταγῇ.

lem, the violent pedagogy of the sword-bearing ruler becomes co-ordinated with the pedagogy of brotherly love. It should not be forgotten that Chapter 13 is inserted between two hymns dedicated to reciprocal love; this proves that St. Paul is not troubled by the distinction between personal and public relationships: "Do not render evil for evil to anyone," he says in the preceding chapter. After the paragraph on the State he returns to this theme: "Love wishes no harm to the neighbor, love is therefore the fulfillment of the law." Thus his theory of government is inserted between two appeals to fraternal love. There is a paradox here. For the ruler, contrary to the commandment of love, renders evil when he punishes. How are we to understand that it is the same economy of redemption which is unfolded throughout these two pedagogies? We live in the very cleavage between these two pedagogies.

It may be objected that the Pauline doctrine on government scarcely incites one to search out the signs of redemption on the level of historic communities, since authority does not bear the mark of fraternal love. Has not the theology of the reformed churches more often preferred to speak of the political sphere as the order of conservation rather than the order of redemption? But what is gained by this distinction? Mankind is not only preserved through the medium of the political sphere, but is also established, elevated, and educated by it. If this education falls outside of the order of redemption, then what does it have to do with the Gospel and why does St. Paul speak of it? And if redemption does not include the actual history of men, which is, in part, political, does it not become abstract and unreal?

Three observations will permit us perhaps to attenuate the disparity between redemption, in so far as it is symbolized in brotherly love, and that type of human pedagogy which the Apostle says was instituted by God for our good. We are reluctant to speak of redemption at the level of the political development of mankind, because we have lost one of the fundamental meanings of the redemption, namely, the growth of humanity, its coming to maturity, its state of adulthood. "One must be made man in order to be made god," said Ireneaus. Now, the most secular institution and the least ecclesiastical authority, if it is *just* and if it conforms to its function, as St. Paul says, cooperates in this growth. In this sense, it is one of the paths of the corporate redemption of men. Kant himself was still aware of something which the post-Augustinian theologian rarely understands: "the means which nature employs to bring about the development of all the capacities implanted in man, is their mutual antagonism in society, but only as far as this antagonism becomes at length the cause of an order among them that is regulated by law." [4]

Is not this "unsocial sociability," which becomes the instrument of civil society, the secularized expression of the theology of the Fathers? And is it not *right* that this expression be secularized, if it is true that the redemption takes the tortuous path of the authorities instituted by God, not when they are clerical but rather when they are just?

My second observation is the following: the violent pedagogy which pertains to authority is attached to the *ordo amoris*, the fraternal order of love, by means of the tenuous thread of the concept of Utopia. The idea of Utopia indeed has great theological import: it is one of the indirect paths of hope, one of the roundabout paths on which the humanization of man is pursued in view of an eventual divinization. The notion of Utopia can be of value to us today when society has many means and few ends. I am thinking in particular of that brand of Utopia for which the State withers away, common among the great liberals, those who supported the *Commune,* and the Lenin of *Revolution and the State.* Indeed, it is by means of a Utopian notion of the ending of the State—at least of the repressive state such as we know it today—that we dream of the reconciliation between politics and love. To be sure, we are dreaming of a State which would only be the administrator of affairs and the educator of men toward the possession of freedom.

This Utopian ideal is vital for the very destiny of the political order. It gives the political sphere its aim, its tension and, if I may use the term, its hope. I recognize my Gospel in the "anarchist" who advocates the dissolution of the police State. It is my Gospel which has fallen from my hands and has been taken up by a man who does not know that he is confessing Jesus Christ. Is it not under the sign of Utopia that we must read St. Paul himself? "The ruler," he says, "is the minister of God for thy good." But what State can minister to my good before the coming of the universal, peaceful, and educative State? No existing State fulfills the ideal of Utopia, but it gives meaning and direction to all of them.

My third observation: the chasm between the violent pedagogy of the State and the pedagogy of fraternal love is not only diminished by means of Utopia, which in effect carries the sign of reconciliation beyond history, but also by the presence of those

4. Kant, *Idea of a Universal Cosmopolitical History,* fifth Proposition. [The English translation is from W. Hastie's *Kant's Principles of Politics* (Edinburgh, 1891), p. 9.]

who in advocating non-violence have marked our own times with its sign. I am thinking expressly of Gandhi, of non-violent forms of action taken by American Negroes, and of the various expressions of non-violent resistance in Europe. What does the non-violent person do? At first sight, it would seem that he excludes himself from the political sphere, since he disobeys authority; but in reality and at bottom, he saves the State by reminding it why it exists: to lead men to freedom and to equality. Non-violence is the hope of the State, whether it comes about in season or out of season. It is "untimely" hope, in the literal sense of the word. Indeed, the means used by the non-violent man are the very means granted in advance to the ends of every state, including the State which employs violence. It is by these means that the non-violent man announces to this state its participation in the redemption, that is, its establishment for the good of men.

These are a few observations which perhaps will enable us to understand in what sense human rulers are organs of redemption, of the great redemption which is pursued not only by way of fraternal love but also by the path of the "big animal."

I had proposed to speak of redemption in the three spheres of having, power, and value. I have not, however, followed this order. I have attempted a breakthrough on the political level and I have outlined the theme of corporate redemption through the media of institutions which, taking St. Paul for our authority, have been instituted by God.

Can we not find an analogous form of *institutional redemption* in the economic order and in the cultural order, which in some way form a basis for the political order? There is a need, therefore, to enlarge and generalize this notion of institutions in such a way as to have it encompass the whole field of stable and enduring mediations, from tools to works of art, by which men communicate among themselves.

Extending our reflections from the political to the economic sphere is relatively easy: we have already stated that the relation between man and his possessions has no existence outside of a system of ownership and an organization of economic power. Scripture itself attaches a significant value to the full mastery of nature:

> When I look up at the heavens which thy hands have made, at the moon and the stars which thou hast set in their places;
> What is man that thou art mindful of him?
> What is the son of man that thou shouldst care for him?
> Thou hast placed him only a little below the angels and crowned

him with glory and honor, and bidding him rule over the works of thy hands.

Thou hast put them all under his dominion, sheep and oxen, and even the wild beasts of the field; the birds of the air, the fishes of the sea, everything that travels by the paths of the deep.

(Psalms 8: 4–9)

Dominion over things is thus one of the ways of access to maturity, to the adult stage of man, and, in that respect, one of the expressions of the *imago Dei.* We know today that this dominion is established by the organization of labor, economic planning, and all the "constituted" forms of economic power. It is therefore not only the personal relationship between an individual and his possessions, but also the sum total of economic institutions which is summoned to redemption. Accordingly, it is to this established whole that we must try to apply our earlier observations, which were then restricted to the sphere of political authority.

First, we must note that the full significance of the notion of *civil authority* only appears when it is extracted from its purely repressive and penal function. Today we are more aware of the fact that the function of authority manifests order only as "established order," which is also "established disorder." An institution is a sign of the Kingdom only in so far as it builds the human community and constructs the City. Punishment only serves to preserve an already established order. It is, in a sense, the force of the institution, its reaction against the "evil-doers," who are to some extent the vehicles of the more just and more fraternal institutions of the future. This is why, in broadening the notion of institutions to the dimensions of the social and the economic, we elucidate not only the human significance of justice but also the theological meaning of the institution. The development of the modern State is, in this respect, like a living and concrete exegesis of the Pauline concept of institution.[5]

On the other hand, what we have said of the function of the concept of Utopia as a purely human, reasonable, and civil expression of hope finds here not only an essential application but also a very concrete foundation. The purely political, Utopian notion of the gradual disappearance of the repressive State is an abstract

5. "When the State ceases to be a purely repressive power preserving an order established by the chance contingencies of history, an order which can hardly conceal the fundamental disorder of individual and collective passions and interests, at that precise moment its function takes on its meaning in accordance with God's plan. It can then participate, within the domain proper to it, in the edification of those signs which, for faith, herald the kingdom to come."—R. Mehl, *Explication de la confession de foi de La Rochelle,* p. 162,

Utopia, so long as it is not co-ordinated with a Utopia wherein work no longer has an alienated character. This is perhaps the Utopia *par excellence,* the one which answers to the curse of "having" and the greed which divides man against man. For it is in terms of wealth, material, intellectual, and spiritual wealth, that all curses are expressed: "Woe to the rich!" All blessings ought, therefore, to find their projection in the same register. What can be the meaning of this, if not a revolution which overthrows the relationships of expropriation and mutual exclusion established by property? The reappropriation of man's essence, which is lost in "having," or what amounts to the same thing, the reconciliation of men divided by their possessions, is, along with the Utopian concept of the disappearance of the State, the Utopia which governs all economic thought anxious to display the signs of the Kingdom to come.

If we are to continue the parallel with redemption by means of authority, should we not say that non-violence on the political level has its counterpart in Franciscan poverty? Does not Franciscan poverty announce in an untimely way—certainly untimely with respect to any reasonable and ordered economy—the end of the curse which is attached to the private and selfish appropriation that generates callousness and solitude? Does not a wide and generous vision of the redemption teach us to read some signs of the Kingdom to come in the most foolish endeavors associated with the disintegration of the Monster that is Capital and the Beast that is the State?

I am proceeding timidly on hazardous pathways, and I would ask you whether it is hope which calls us onward or the seductive influence of the world . . . . Perhaps some few pearls of hope have been mistakenly placed in the straw of false hopes.

It is not very common to speak of "institutions" in respect to *culture,* such as with regard to political, social, or economic life. Yet the profound meaning of the institution appears only when it is extended to the images of man in culture, literature, and the arts. These images have indeed been constituted or established. They have stability and an internal history which transcend the chance happenings of the individual. Their structure may be subjected to a psychoanalysis of the imagination which would analyze the pervasive theme of these images of man, their lines of force, and their evolution. It is in this sense that culture is established at the level of the tradition of the imaginary. Accordingly, it is at this level that we must search out the signs of the Kingdom to come.

The imagination has a metaphysical function which cannot be reduced to a simple projection of vital, unconscious, or repressed desires. The imagination has a prospective and explorative function in regard to the inherent possibilities of man. It is, *par excellence,* the instituting and the constituting of what is humanly possible. In imagining his possibilities, man acts as a prophet of his own existence. We can then begin to understand in what sense we may speak of a *redemption through imagination:* by means of dreams of innocence and reconciliation, hope works to the fullest human capacity. In the broad sense of the word, these images of reconciliation are *myths,* not in the positivistic sense of legend or fable, but in the phenomenological sense of religion, in the sense of a meaningful story of the destiny of the whole human race. *Mythos* means word or speech. The imagination, in so far as it has a mytho-poetic function, is also the seat of profound workings which govern the decisive changes in our visions of the world. Every *real* conversion is first a revolution at the level of our directive images. By changing his imagination, man alters his existence.

A few examples drawn from literature and the arts will enable us to understand these revolutions more thoroughly. Earlier, I said that man can be perverted in virtue of the images he creates of himself. At that time, I stressed the function of scandal in literature and, at times, in the plastic arts, and also the ambiguity which seduces and which yet pretends to express truth. Let it be said now that the signs of redemption need not always be sought in the contrary to scandal. To be sure, quite often it is through scandal that salvation is announced. For even under the most destructive appearances the image may be "edifying." There are mockeries which purify just as there are apologies which betray. Like the ruler, literature punishes by the sword—the sword of denunciation and scandal.

But in itself, scandal is only the other half of the Utopian function of culture. The imagination, in so far as it seeks out the most impossible potentialities of man, is the advanced outpost of mankind marching toward greater lucidity and maturity, in brief, toward the stature of adulthood. The artist, then, is to the cultural sphere what the non-violent man is to the political sphere; he is the "untimely" man. He takes the greatest risks, for he never knows whether he is constructive or destructive, whether he is destroying while thinking he is constructing, or whether he is constructing while thinking he is actually destroying. He does not know whether he is planting when it is time to uproot, or uprooting when it is time to plant.

Should we, therefore, be frightened by the enormous risk of being a man? Perhaps we should relate this dangerous schooling of man through good and evil to the generosity of God and trust in his generosity.

I shall conclude where I began, since the bulk of this essay hinges on the interpretation which the Fathers gave to the image of God. Let us then come back to the Fathers of the Church one last time. When the Gnostics tried to embarrass them with the problem of evil, the Fathers did not hesitate to include in the grandeur of creation the creativity of a free man capable of disobeying. For them, the risk of evil was thus included in the coming to maturity of the whole of creation. As Irenaeus declares:

> God manifests his generosity and thereby man has known both the good of obedience and the evil of disobedience, in order that the eye of his intelligence, in receiving the experience of both one and the other, should make a choice for the better things with sound judgment and never be lazy or negligent in what concerns the precept of God.

For Tertullian, also, man is an image of God in virtue of his free commitment:

> It was necessary that the image and likeness of God be made free and autonomous in its will, since the image and likeness of God is defined by this freedom . . . . Through freedom man ceases to be a slave of nature. He comes into his own good and assures his own excellence, not as a child who receives but as a man who consents.

Perhaps it is necessary to believe that God Himself, wishing to be known and loved freely, ran this risk which is named Man.

PART II
Truth in Historical Action

3 / Personalism

Emmanuel Mounier:
A Personalist Philosopher

OUR FRIEND Emmanuel Mounier will no longer answer our questions. One of the cruelties of death is to alter profoundly the meaning of a literary work in progress. Not only does the work no longer involve a continuation since it is finished in every sense of the word, but it is also torn away from the dialogue of questions and answers which situated its author among the living. It will forever remain a *written* work and that is all. The break with its author is final; henceforth it enters into the only history which is possible for it—that of its readers and the men whom it will inspire. In a sense, a work attains the truth of its literary existence when its author is dead: every publication and every edition begins the inexorable relationship of living men with the book of a man who is virtually dead.

Surely, those who are least prepared to enter into this relationship are those who have known and loved the man, the living man . . . and each reading revives in them and somehow hallows the death of their friend.

I have not been able to reread Mounier's books as books should be read, as the books of a dead person. Consequently, within these pages one should not expect to find a strict historical study but rather something of the nature of a hybrid which embarks upon an interpretation and vainly strives to continue the forbidden dialogue. . . .

At the outset, and as a counterpoint so to speak, I reread Emmanuel Mounier's articles which appeared in *Esprit* between October of 1932 and December of 1934 (published as a collection in *Révolution personnaliste et communautaire* [1]) and the short and excellent *vade mecum* of the personalist philosophy entitled *Le Personnalisme*.[2] Roughly speaking, these are the two focal points of Mounier's work: 1932 and 1950. It became surprisingly obvious that the writings of 1932 endow his whole philosophical endeavor with its true perspective and hide under their youthful and iconoclastic form the intentions of his subsequent work.

This collection clearly shows that Emmanuel Mounier's thought is marked negatively by his departure from the university—by his rupture with teaching—and positively by his assumption of responsibility for a movement which was embodied in a Review. This first observation is of more importance than it might seem: the works of Bergson, Brunschvicg, Blondel, and Maritain, which were contemporary with the beginnings of the review *Esprit*, were characterized by a didactic style and form that was geared to a public composed of students, professors and, in general, adult education. Up to the pre-war period, French philosophy was obviously a part of the teaching function in the broadest sense. That teaching function points up rather well the strength and weakness of university philosophy. Its weakness was in situating its problems on the fringes of life and history and in giving itself a life and history which, strictly speaking, were unrealistic. Its strength, however, was its ability to deal with problems of method and fundamental questions, the quest for a "point of departure" and the "first truth," and, naturally, the orderly command of discourse.

In founding *Esprit*, Mounier tried his luck with a non-university philosophy. By detaching himself from the university —because teaching is in a way a commitment—his good fortune then was not to fall into idle leisure but rather to serve a movement by creating it. Mounier's first commitment was the *Esprit* movement; and it is precisely here that our friend's style, manner, and philosophical purpose acquired form.

His great strength is in having, in 1932, linked his way of philosophizing to the awareness of a crisis in civilization and in having dared to envisage, over and above all academic philosophy, a new civilization in its totality. The scope of that initial plan is not

---

1. *Révolution personnaliste et communautaire*, *Esprit* series (Paris: Aubier, 1935) (*Oeuvres*, I, Editions du Seuil).

2. *Le Personnalisme*, collection *Que sais-je?* (Paris: P.U.F., 1950) (*Oeuvres*, III, Editions du Seuil).

sensed if one begins with the *Traité du caractère* or with *Le Personnalisme;* in that case, one indulges in the fruitless and minute comparison of Mounier's "philosophy" with the existentialist or Marxist "philosophies." It is fruitless because these three "philosophies" are not different solutions to an identical group of problems; they are not even different problematics located on an identical *theoretical* level; they are divergent ways of sketching the relations of theory and practice, of reflection and action.

We shall have to come back to this comparison later, especially to the conditions for this comparison. This may be done, however, only after we have rediscovered the initial aim of personalism, the vision of a *civilization*. It is well worth noting that the adjective "personalist" designates first a civilization, a civilizing task.[3] The *Personnalisme* of 1950 reminds us that in 1930 the term was intended "to designate the first investigations of the review *Esprit* and of some allied groups concerned with the political and spiritual crisis which was then breaking out in Europe."[4]

That awareness of the times, that grasping of our epoch as a developing crisis of the civilization which sprang up at the Renaissance, is the first provocation assumed by personalism. Yet that awareness of crisis was far from being at the heart of the official thought in France in 1932. Certainly it did not play any decisive role in university philosophy and was even less in a position to orient a philosophical vocation in any radical way. Therefore it is a methodical doubt with historical and cultural features which starts all of Mounier's reflections. His answer is not despair, a prophecy of decadence, or a descriptive attitude, but rather a plan for a new Renaissance: "Remake the Renaissance." That is the title of the first editorial of *Esprit,* signed Mounier.

This slogan, which links a task to the awareness of crisis, suggests the broad dimensions of the personalism of 1932. In its origin, it was not a question of analyzing notions or describing structures but of bearing on history by a certain type of combative thought.

This intention goes beyond what we ordinarily understand by a "philosophy." I would venture to say that Emmanuel Mounier, like Péguy, was the *pedagogue* and *educator* of a generation. Naturally we should have to draw from these two words their twofold

3. *Manifeste au service du personnalisme, Esprit* series (Paris: Aubier, 1936), p. 9 (*Oeuvres,* I, Editions du Seuil).
4. *Le Personnalisme,* p. 115.

kinship: their reference to childhood that one proposes to lead to adulthood, and their connection with a teaching function, to an already differentiated social body (as we say, "National Education"). Or again, I would say that Mounier preached a *revival*, if it were possible to transplant this expression common to religious communities into the larger perspective of a civilization taken as a whole.

Personalism: in the beginning a pedagogy concerning communal life linked to an awakening of the person.

In 1932–1934, that intention was more and less than a "philosophy." It was more than a philosophy in the sense that the plan for a new historical epoch implied a "philosophy" and perhaps several "philosophies" in the academic sense of the word, something which Mounier stressed by saying that personalism includes personalisms. It placed itself above a philosophical problematic, in the strict sense, above questions concerning a starting-point, methods, and order. Its main contribution to contemporary thought has been to offer a *philosophical matrix* to professional philosophers, to propose tonalities to them, theoretical and practical holding notes containing one or several philosophies, pregnant with one or several philosophical systematizations. For many of us, this is our true debt to our friend.

Yet in 1932–1934 that revival and that pedagogy were less than a philosophy in the sense that the theories of value, history, knowledge, and being, which they presupposed, remained implicit. However, as we shall soon see, the books of the post-war period inclined his research in a more philosophical direction by interpreting personalism as one of the *philosophies of existence*. In 1949, Mounier wrote: "Personalism is a philosophy and not merely an attitude. . . . It is a philosophy and not a system. Personalism is a philosophy and not merely an attitude because it specifies structures. . . . But since its central affirmation is the existence of free and creative persons, it introduces into the heart of these structures a principle of unforseeableness which shatters any hope for definitive systematization." [5]

From 1932 to 1950, Emmanuel Mounier's thought therefore seems to be a movement which starts with a project for a "personalist" *civilization* and aims toward a "personalist" interpretation of philosophies of existence. The meaning of this shift in accent will be made more explicit in the course of this study.

5. *Ibid.*, p. 6.

[1] Personal Awakening and Communal Pedagogy

CERTAINLY TO PLAN a civilization presupposes that a civilization is, at least in part—a decisive part—the work of men. The making, unmaking, and remaking of the Renaissance is man's goal. Personalism looked upon itself as "the sum total of the first assents capable of grounding a civilization dedicated to the human person." [6]

1. *Remaking the Renaissance*

THIS ENTERPRISE could well be called *ethical* if Mounier had not rejected with horror the mind of the moralist. The moralist always seemed to him to be lost in generalities and rhetoric, restricted to the dimensions of the individual without a foothold on history, and tainted with hypocrisy. The criticism of moralism is itself one of the elements of the permanent criticism of idealism which we shall constantly encounter along the way.

But through his criticism of "the doctrinaire or moralist error," Emmanuel Mounier has helped to restore the reputation of ethics, making it traverse the whole sphere of technics, social structures, and ideas, and undermining the force of determinisms and ideological apathy. He has made ethics real and truthful. In effect, the long progress of ethical concerns through the flesh and blood of societies only makes the basic affirmation of the personalist and communal revolution more striking. A civilization is "primarily a metaphysical reply to a metaphysical calling, an adventure of an eternal character, proposed to each man in the solitude of his choice and responsibility. . . . Every age realizes a nearly human achievement only if it has first listened to the superhuman call of history. . . . Our long-range goal is still the one which we gave ourselves in 1932: after four centuries of mistakes to remake patiently and collectively the Renaissance." [7]

This fundamental conviction that a civilization is founded upon options and assents which are lived and "acted" more than reflected upon, or upon working values, is what Mounier called the "primacy of the spiritual," violently opposing this to the spiritualism which banishes the mind to another world. Yet Mounier did not treat this conviction as a fundamental sociological problem or

6. *Manifeste* . . . , p. 8.
7. *Ibid.*, pp. 11, 15.

as a speculative question which takes the form: what are the dialectical relations between man's choices and the economic, political, and ideological forces? He risked and manifested his conviction both in his interpretation of events and in his plan for the task to be undertaken. In this sense, it has more the character of "praxis" than "theory," and this is the way in which every awakening, every pedagogy, and all Reform is initiated.

The same practical style is seen in the elucidation of the personalist theme: from the outset, Emmanuel Mounier shuns starting with abstract definitions; he takes his bearings from a certain sense of the concrete in the midst of the forms of civilization, exercising a kind of "discrimination of minds." This sense proceeds at first on a critical mode: all the personalist researches of the pre-war period begin either with "the critical study of forms of civilization which complete their cycle, or with those which, from their first orientations, postulate their succession." [8] The achievement peculiar to Emmanuel Mounier is to recapture those types of civilization in "pure forms" or "ultimate doctrines" which are not so much "theories" as kinds of life and ways of being, or, in his words, "ultimate profiles," and "directions of experience." [9]

The bourgeois is the fundamental "figure" who serves as a contrast; here the genius of Socrates says no. The key to all of Mounier's remarks on the world of the bourgeois is to understand it globally as something which is by nature self-destructive. The bourgeois is a descending style: from the hero to the bourgeois; from values of conquest and creativity to values of comfort. This intuition of the *negative* aspect in the bourgeois paves the way for all of Mounier's reflections on the opposition between the individual and the person. The individual is primarily a pole of civilization, or more exactly, a counterpole. By this term, Mounier meant the combination of several tendencies which on the surface are disparate, but among which circulates the same descending current: the disconnectedness of superficial images, of varying personages between which the interiorless man is divided; the complacency with these images; the fundamental greed of a person lacking generosity; the security in which he encloses himself; and lastly the cold, rationalist, and legal assertion with which he shields himself. Thus a "world" of the individual coagulates, and this is at once the world of pretense and moral standing, the world of money, the world of the impersonal, and the world of legalism.

8. *Ibid.*, p. 15.
9. *Révolution personnaliste* . . . , p. 75.

If the world of the bourgeois, for which the individual is the ultimate profile, is a world of "less" (loving less and being less) the fascist's world is a world of the "pseudo": his enthusiasm is a pseudo-generosity, his nationalism a pseudo-universal, his racism a pseudo-concrete, his aggressiveness a pseudo-strength. Such was the great deception of the years from 1933 to 1939: Buchenwald finally exposed the imposture of it all. And so the world of the person recovers its loss and eludes its caricature: the individual.

2. *The World of the Person*

THE PERSON IS STILL ANTICIPATED in a positive form as the "world of" the person. Indeed, as early as 1932 we find formulae which tend toward a definition of structure, just as we shall find them more frequently in the post-war period: thus the person is opposed to the individual as the vital unity which transcends personages, as "the invisible center where everything is connected," as the "unique figure" which would be a "presence in me." [10] It feels repugnance toward the values of evasion and refuge in spiritualism, and aspires to transform its body and history. Above all, it turns its back to the individual's greed; it exacts and restrains; it gives and gives of itself; the person is generosity.

But these formulae are not unrelated to the movement by which man proceeds toward a "world" to be promoted. They are less definitions of the person than signs indicating a civilization to be made. Thus, vocation has meaning only for a world of "meditation," incarnation only for a world of "engagement," communion only for a world of personal "renunciation." The words meditation, engagement, and renunciation describe a society which would be a "person of persons"—a community. The person is the ultimate pattern of the true community, just as the individual is the model for the bourgeois non-civilization, and the partisan that of the fascist pseudo-civilization.

It is in this sense that Mounier insisted on the *And* of the expression "personalist *and* communal Revolution": the *And* points up the single intention turned toward the I and the We ("Without the misery of language it would be superfluous to speak of personalist *and* communal philosophy").[11] The awakening of the person is identical with the pedagogy of the community.

Hence, one should not separate the formulae relative to the person from the outline of a "communal ascesis" [12] which is found

10. *Ibid.,* p. 69.
11. *Ibid.,* p. 91.
12. *Ibid.,* p. 96.

in different forms in the writings of the pre-war period and whose whole meaning, furthermore, is in being an "initiation to the person." I shall only evoke the principal stages of this "communal ascesis" since my purpose here is not to summarize the work of Emmanuel Mounier but rather to bring out his intentions and the methods which he employed.

As early as 1932, he used the word "One," like Heidegger, to designate the ultimate form of massive depersonalization which is epitomized by the "insipid insensibility of *Paris-Soir* readers." [13] Then he passed to the level of societies formed by "we others," partially realized by the groupings of "partisans" and based on camaraderie and trade-unions. Their abnegation and heroism puts them above "vital societies" governed by values of comfort and happiness, but they are in a state of regression because they destroy individual initiative and spontaneity in mutual relations. Above them come "rational societies" which waver between two levels of impersonality, that of a "society of minds" which holds, for example, a scientific congress, and that of a "juridical, contractual society" toward which democratic juridicalism tends.

We see that these societal types are less representative of objective sociological categories, in the way of Durkheimian or Bergsonian distinctions, than of stages of an "ascesis" directed toward the ultimate model of a "person of persons." These stages are more comparable to those of Kierkegaard, in a different register, or to the "degrees of science" expounded by Plato and Spinoza. Obviously, some of these stages were suggested by Max Scheler. But in any event, it is not a question of empirical types which result from observation, but of possible forms of living in common, marking out the way of each and of all toward perfection. In short, it is a question of *pedagogical* stages.[14]

13. *Ibid.*, p. 80.
14. Within the limitations of a study on *Emmanuel Mounier: A Personalist Philosopher*, I cannot show how a pedagogy encompasses a politics, or rather, how it implies one while situating it within a larger perspective. Here again, it is the typical figure of the bourgeois which makes the problem of money the key to all of Mounier's sociological analyses: *Argent et vie privée, Anticapitalisme, Note sur la propriété*, etc. (*Révolution personnaliste . . .*, pp. 147 ff.); *De la propriété capitaliste à la propriété humaine* (Aubier, 1934; republished in *Liberté sous conditions*, 1949). It remains to be seen how Mounier's pedagogy is linked to his "ethic of needs" which governs his views on property and socialism. But above all, a philosophical study must not neglect the constant battle waged by Mounier against the antitechnicist prejudice: "Personalism is not an inclosed garden where the civilized take shelter from civilization, but rather the principle which should impel every civilization to reinvent itself" (*Révolution personnaliste . . .*, p. 152).

3. *Personalism and Christianity*

HERE IS WHERE we may rightfully raise the question concerning the relations between Mounier's pedagogy and Christianity, on the one hand, and Marxism on the other. The "conversion" of the one and the "praxis" of the other are obviously brought into play by this awakening and this ascesis.

It is undeniable that Mounier's pedagogy is directly inspired by the Christian theme of "sanctification": the figure of the "saint" attracts the personalist community, just as the figure of the "hero" attracts the fascist society.[15]

The theological virtue of charity is the paradigm for the person's generosity, and the "Communion of Saints," confessed in the Christian *Credo*, is that of the mutuality of persons. A short essay written during the winter of 1939, entitled *Personnalisme et Christianisme*,[16] makes a tangible connection between Christian preaching, as distinguished from the naturalist and impersonal modes of thought of the Greeks, and access to the world of the person. "Divine exuberance" gives rise to centers of personal responsibility, beings capable of saying "Adsum!", present![17] The same Christian influence which calls to renunciation also invites to self-respect: "It gives tone to the person and makes it virile, but it disarms it. It calms its volitions so as to open it to abandon."[18] I shall leave it to others to determine in what way Emmanuel Mounier's Christianity was specifically Catholic, not only on the point of the Catholic doctrine of authority (pp. 54–60), but also concerning the doctrine of sin (against Luther, pp. 50, 58, 67) and especially his conception of "nature" (principal pages: 69–72).[19] On the whole, Mounier follows an essential Thomism whose hu-

15. *Révolution personnaliste* . . . , p. 75; *Manifeste* . . . , p. 79.

16. *Liberté sous conditions*. Three essays: *Personnalisme et Christianisme* (1939); *De la propriété capitaliste à la propriété humaine* (1934); *Anarchie et personnalisme* (1937); (Paris: Editions du Seuil, 1946) (*Oeuvres*, I, Editions du Seuil).

17. *Personnalisme et Christianisme*, pp. 20, 25.

18. *Ibid.*, p. 31.

19. "What the Church will always retain of the 'naturalism' of St. Thomas is, first of all, the affirmation of Christian humanism which is its very soul" (against Luther, orthodoxy, and the pessimism of realist politicians). Secondly, ". . . the idea that the most adventurous constructions of man must be grounded upon a primal substructure, on the natural . . ." (against rationalist anthropology and its idea of an inventing of man by man without structure or foundation). ". . . it is in this sense that a catholic politics will always remind evangelic or rationalist utopias of the value of bonds, the weight of duration and the limitations of the dream." (*Personnalisme et Christianisme*, p. 71).

manism seemed to him to be a crestline between Lutheran pessimism and the optimism of the Enlightenment. But his own function, in comparison to that essential Thomism, is in having elucidated the notion of "nature" in the sense of historical invention, of boldness and risk: this is why he prefers to speak of the "human condition" rather than of "human nature." [20]

Does this mean to say that personalism is Christian (and Catholic) *par excellence?* In that case, does not the community run the risk of becoming a temporal and secularized projection of the "Kingdom of God," just like the "Kingdom of ends" in Kantianism or communism's classless society? The question not only is an affair of Christian orthodoxy but also concerns the possibility of collaboration among Christians (of different faiths) and non-Christians in the center of *one* relatively coherent personalism. Mounier always maintained that this collaboration was possible in principle.

It seems to me that in this respect, Gabriel Marcel's position on the relations between philosophic inquiry and the Christian faith is very illuminating: the theme of the person springs up and takes on meaning in a "peri-Christian" zone of the ethical conscience, in a zone of sensitization which receives Christian preaching vertically and the life-giving influences of the most authentic Christian conduct horizontally, but which, through this twofold impregnation, unfolds its *own possibilities.* Through Christianity, the ethical man, the man capable of civilization, is open to his *own* anticipations. If such is the case, personalism can neither be viewed as an amalgamation of various Christian tenets nor as an eclecticism of non-Christian sources.

It would seem that this is the sense in which Emmanuel Mounier speaks of "values," of a "scale of values" (material, vital, rational, spiritual). In much the same way as Max Scheler and his disciple Paul Landsberg,[21] whose friend Mounier was until Landsberg's tragic death by deportation, Mounier understands values as permanent exigencies which, however, are incongruous outside of the history written by persons. Personalism therefore implies a concrete ethics which is relatively independent of Christian faith, independent as to its *significances,* dependent as to its *factual*

20. *Ibid.,* p. 72.
21. Cf. Landsberg's articles in *Esprit:* "L'Anarchiste contre Dieu" (April, 1937); "Réflexion sur l'engagement personnel" (November, 1937); "Introduction à une critique du mythe" (January, 1938); "Kafka et la métamorphose" (September, 1938); "Le Sens de l'action" (October, 1938); "Notes sur la philosophie du mariage" (April, 1939); "Réflexion pour une philosophie de guerre" (October, 1939).— *Problèmes du personnalisme* (Editions du Seuil, 1952).

manifestation in such or such a consciousness. Again, it is in this perspective that Mounier, who before 1939 anticipated his future debate with existentialism, evokes the existence of a "human nature," of a "basic truth" for which he seeks a new "historical outlet." [22] If he was accustomed to insisting on the continuity between his Christian faith and his personalist studies, that is natural if one takes into consideration that his studies were more concerned with *pedagogy* than criteriology. The pedagogue in Mounier is by temperament more sensitive to the continuity of his inspiration than to the discontinuity of notions. But whenever the problem of the collaboration with a non-Christian came to the fore, it is this autonomy of concrete ethics that he called upon.

And here there is no mention that the Christian alone has a fecundating role in the task of discovering with others the world of the person. In the past it has happened that professed Christians or established Christian sects have blocked certain historical outlets of the faith. Hence, a given heresy or a dechristianized form of thought is often in a better position to open up a realm of value which Christian confessions have neglected or even screened. Thus if personalism is a pedagogy, the Christian is not necessarily the pedagogue of the agnostic. For the Christian constantly learns from the non-Christian the nature of this civilizing power of the ethical man to which he is all too frequently desensitized by *de facto* Christendom. And so we see that the Christian is often very much in arrears by comparison to the non-Christian, for example, in the realm of the understanding of history, of the social and political dynamism.[23]

4. *Personalism and Marxism*

AT THIS POINT we may validly introduce Mounier's debate with Marxism. After the war, Mounier's personalism was interpreted as one of the philosophies of existence. Now, just as his personalism lends itself to a debate with what has come to be called, in the strict sense, existentialism, so too does his early plan for a civilization lend itself to a comparison with Marxism. His keen sense of determinisms to be understood and to be orientated places him on the fringes of "socialist realism." "Because Marxism has the confidence of the world which is in misery," [24] it cannot be treated in the same way as the bourgeois world with its negative

---

22. *Manifeste* . . . , pp. 8, 13–14.
23. *Révolution personnaliste* . . . , pp. 103, 115, 121–31, 140–43.
24. *Manifeste* . . . , p. 43.

values and the fascists with their pseudo-values. Further, over and above any academic comparison of notions and theories, it is the total mentality of the personalist "pedagogy" which must be compared to the total mentality of communist "praxis."

What personalism objects to in Marxism is the fact that Marxism is less than an awakening and less than a pedagogy. At the time of the *Manifeste au service du personnalisme*, his critique retained an idealistic aspect. It was directed in particular against the "scientist" mentality of Marxism whose enslavement to positivism makes it "the last philosophy of an historic era which has lived under the dominating influence of the physico-mathematical sciences, the result of which is a narrow rationalism and an inhumane, centralized form of industry which embodies, at least provisionally, the technical applications of these sciences." [25] But behind this theoretical process, what is in question is the meaning of revolutionary action. The real question is the following: what is ultimately the actual basis for the Marxist's new man? The answer is that they base themselves on the *future* effect of economic and political changes, *not* on the attraction exercised *here and now* by personal values over revolutionary men. Only a material revolution enrooted in a personalist awakening would have meaning and chance for success. Marxism is not an education but a training.[26] This explains why it is "an optimism of collective man covering a radical pessimism of the person." [27]

Here is the core of the debate: the conviction of personalism is that one does not progress *toward* the person if the person is not *in the beginning* what demands, what presses on in the midst of the revolt of the famished and afflicted. The danger in a revolution which does not take its own end as its source and proper means is to debase man under the pretext of liberating him, and merely to alter the form of his alienations. This fundamental reproach contains the germinal elements of all the others, both with respect to historical explanation and revolutionary tactics as well as to world strategy in our time. One overcomes this danger only by going back to Mounier's educative intention which transcends all personalist "theory." The dichotomy between Mounier's pedagogy and communist praxis is witnessed especially in his refusal to consider the history written by the communist party as normative: his pedagogy is also open to the possibilities of man which are

25. *Ibid.*, p. 52.
26. *Ibid.*, p. 60.
27. *Ibid.*

excluded from the narrow confines of recorded history. The meaning of a concrete ethics, with all its revolutionary exigencies, is
precisely to overspill the thin thread of actual history and not to
"entrust the spiritual treasure of mankind to this canton of party in
this canton of duration!" [28]

[2] FROM THE EDUCATOR TO THE PHILOSOPHER

THE POPULAR FRONT, the war of Spain, Munich, the
World War, the Resistance, the politics of national fronts . . .
Could the personalist "philosophy" remain unchanged after experiencing all those events, none of which was simply a brute
fact to be experienced and explained, but each of which constituted a question and the occasion for a choice? I shall leave
it to others to comment on those choices as well as the freedom
and coherence of them.

With the appearance of these events, the thought of Emmanuel Mounier developed in three directions. On the one hand his
personalism, in viewing itself critically, took guard against puris-
tic, idealistic, and anarchistic temptations and made the greatest
effort to learn from the movement of history. On this level are
situated *Qu'est-ce que le personnalisme?* [29] and *La Petite Peur du
XXe siècle.*[30] But while he rejected a "personalism of purity,"
Mounier deepened and purified the Christian motive of his personalism. One should not isolate the antipurism of the two preceding
books from the evangelical purification expressed in *L'Affrontement chrétien.*[31] It is on the basis of these two lines of thought that
one must appraise the "philosophical" effort to situate personalism
in relation to the human sciences on the one hand, and in relation
to the philosophies of existence on the other. The great *Traité du
caractère* [32] (great by virtue of its length, the breadth of its scope,
and the wealth of questions it considers), *Introduction aux
existentialismes* [33] and *Le Personnalisme* of 1950 are linked to
this third line of thought which is strictly philosophical. Here the

28. *Révolution personnaliste* . . . , p. 140.
29. *Qu'est-ce que le personnalisme?* (Editions du Seuil, 1947) (*Oeuvres*, III).
30. *La Petite Peur du XXe siècle* (Cahiers du Rhône, Editions de la Baconnière
and Editions du Seuil, 1948) (*Oeuvres*, III).
31. *L'Affrontement chrétien* (Cahiers du Rhône, Editions de la Baconnière,
Neuchâtel, 1944) (*Oeuvres*, III).
32. *Traité du caractère* (Editions du Seuil, 1946) (*Oeuvres*, II).
33. *Introduction aux existentialismes* (Denoël, 1946) (*Oeuvres*, III).

accent is moved from problems of civilization and revolution to more theoretical problems of the structure and the existential status of the person.

1. *"Anti-Purism" and "Tragic Optimism"*

QU'EST-CE QUE LE PERSONNALISME? is a re-interpretation of the *Manifeste* of 1936 after ten years of history. The basic thought-structures are the same but the point of the argument is shifted. If the specific danger in the Marxist revolution is its contempt for man, the personalist ethics has its own inherent risk which calls forth a self-critique from Mounier:

> A certain preoccupation with purity tended to be the principal fea-ture of our attitude: purity of values, purity of means. Our intellec-tual formation inclined us to look for this purification first in a purification of concepts; and the individualism of the times, which we were against, did not fail to have an effect upon us and to dis-tract us from this doctrinal revision and lead us to a too exclusive concern for our individual lives.[34]

Against "the demon of purity," [35] it is necessary to strive to experience more fully the *weight of situations* which we have not created and which we can only partially understand and master, as well as to realize that this servitude is not a misfortune: it bullies the Narcissus which lingers in us. "We are free only to the extent that we are not entirely free." [36] Here we find the broad outlines of the type of philosophy of existence that personalism privileges: according to it, freedom is not gratuitous, but is understood neces-sity and exercised responsibility. At this point, the sketch of "free-dom under conditions" turns to a critique of the Utopian frame of mind which attempts to elaborate the plan for a society and rules for action based on principles, but without ever incorporating into its research the interpretation of events or the exegesis of historical forces. Its error is in the failure to understand the meaning of a concrete ethics: value does not appear to a timeless conscience alien to the struggles of the century, but to a combatant who is oriented in the crisis, who discerns so as to act and who acts so as to discern. "A personalism may be affirmed only within the core of a concrete historical judgment." [37]

34. *Qu'est-ce que le personnalisme?*, p. 16.
35. *Ibid.*, p. 20.
36. *Ibid.*, p. 26.
37. *Ibid.*, p. 44.

The *Manifeste* and *Révolution personnaliste et communautaire* already contained such formulae on the personalist affirmation which is, as it were, "at the crossroads of a judgment of value and a judgment of fact, . . . of a precise metaphysical direction and . . . clearly defined historical judgments." [38]

Thus *Qu'est-ce que le personnalisme?* tends to link up with a flexible interpretation of Marxist dialectics freed of its scientist encumberance. Mounier's hope was to help Marxism remove this encumberance and to work within the heart of the revolutionary movement as a leaven, all the while purging himself of any anarchic temptation following the bitter lessons of collective efficacity. His formula was not: "Beyond Marxism," but: "To the heart of materialism, collectivism, and spiritualism." [39] After the war, Emmanuel Mounier sensed the convergence of an "open Marxism" and a "personalist realism." [40] I shall not comment on the immediate political import of these formulae. For the philosopher, this hope of eventually "personalizing collectivism," although preserving it from the "infantile illnesses of personalism," [41] rests on the more profound conviction concerning the "solid relationship" between the meaning of the eternal and a certain meaning of "matter." In the short space between heaven and earth, we bypass the lingering and hollow eloquence of moralists, the ruminating of the scrupulous, and the sloth of eclectics. But for Mounier this praise of "matter" in the vicinity of the "spiritual" (which is found in *Le Personnalisme* of 1950) is not purely speculative: the intuition of the carnal-spiritual, of the historical-eternal, has a philosophical side only because it has a practical side; it paves the way for a critique of existentialist pessimism only because it communicates with this civilizing volition formulated in Mounier's first labors:

> In order to entrench personalism into the historic drama of our time, it is not sufficient to speak of person, community, and the total man, etc. One must also speak of the end of Western bourgeois society, the introduction of socialist structures, and the initiatory function of the proletariat. Year in and year out we must further advance the analysis of forces and possibilities. Failing this, personalism will turn into an all-accommodating ideology. And if it is blunted of its revolutionary edge, it will only serve to strengthen

38. *Révolution personnaliste* . . . , p. 120.
39. *Qu'est-ce que le personnalisme?*, p. 81.
40. *Ibid.*, p. 79.
41. *Ibid.*, p. 85.

conservative or reformist apathies. A sworded-philosophy, as it has been called, then becomes a masked-philosophy, in the literal sense of the word, a mystification.[42]

La Petite Peur du XXe siècle continues this exorcism of "the misinterpretations grafted directly onto the personalist inspiration" and undertakes to "demystify" the catastrophism professed by so many "spiritualists" of our time. In particular, the second lecture brings a sort of social psychoanalysis to bear on the block of fears expressed in the anti-technicist reaction. Mounier here detects a primitive fear which is truly a fear of self, a fear of the demiurge which we are by destiny: "The dread of a collective disaster of the modern world is primarily an infantile reaction of incompetent and panic-stricken travellers." [43] It is "the instinct toward self-preservation" which arouses panic over "the long drifting away from ports." [44] "We are collectively frightened in face of the machine." [45] Formerly in fear of unconquerable nature, today man is afraid of the human world: to which he replies with "a frustrated, childish reaction." [46] Mounier's method is therefore to explain first, and in this way to reduce the antitechnicist myth so as to clarify the real dangers, the dangers of a specifically human world which do not merely flow from machines but from all abstract apparatus, from all the "mediations" that man invents and places between himself and things, or between himself and other men (Laws, States, Institutions, Sciences, Languages, etc.): "Wherever there is mediation, alienation lies in wait." [47]

This last remark suggests that the idea of progress, even if it is corrected, does not exclude from history an indomitable ambiguity, a twofold possibility of either petrification or emancipation. The situations that man has invented and which subsequently block his route as enigmas to be deciphered, are a complex of chances and risks. But the task of man is to take his chances. The tendency toward the artifical results from the very condition of man in so far as he has a "history" and not only a "nature." From this standpoint, Mounier comes very close to Marx: "Nature is not merely the matrix of humanity; it presents itself for man to recreate. . . . Today man finds himself called upon to become the demiurge of the world and of his own condition." [48]

42. *Ibid.*, p. 95.
43. *La Petite Peur du XXe siècle*, p. 27.
44. *Ibid.*, p. 32.
45. *Ibid.*, p. 51.
46. *Ibid.*, p. 83.
47. *Ibid.*, p. 91.
48. *Ibid.*, p. 75.

Here reflection arrives at its decisive point: does this history which is constitutive of a whole destiny have any meaning? And is this meaning oriented toward a better one? And does this better meaning move along the privileged road of the sciences and technics? And lastly, is the meaning of this ascent for man "the glorious mission of being the author of his own ascent"? [49] This complex of questions constitutes the problem of progress. Emmanuel Mounier approaches it by putting trust in a fundamental optimism, although not without critical reserves, rather than by starting with a predetermined pessimism. The whole of this book tends, in the mind of the reader, to substitute for the emotional regime of "active pessimism" the contrary mood of "tragic optimism," that is, the mode of confidence, corrected by the experience of indecisive combat and overshadowed by the possibility of failure. One should not accuse Mounier of having systematized his apology for progress: his most lucid pages serve to distinguish Christian eschatology from the concept of progress as interpreted by the rationalism of the eighteenth century or by Marxist dialectics. In particular, the usage which is made of the *Apocalypse*, in the first and third lectures, serves to privilege optimism, but with a thousand reservations which one may not neglect to take into consideration. In point of fact, the "mood" which Mounier designates by the name "tragic optimism" is more complex than it appears at first glance: it conceals two tendencies which are on the verge of dissociating. One of them remains in the foreground and tends toward optimism as the final result of the drama; but the other, which is more discreet, tends toward the feeling that history is ambiguous, pregnant with the best and the worst. Emmanuel Mounier has obviously initiated a debate involving historians, sociologists, philosophers, and theologians. The question which he leaves open is at the crossroads of a biblical theology and a secular philosophy of history, at the crossroads between optimism as a positive balance sheet of human views, and hope as the firm assurance of a hidden meaning. But you see at once that his proper function is to put us on guard against a speculative treatment of the problem, detached from the critique of the contemporary world and isolated from the central problem of the Revolution of the twentieth century.

2. *Toward a Christianity of the Strong*

So MUCH PROXIMITY to the movement of history might lead one to divinize man. But the more Mounier accentuated

49. *Ibid.,* p. 104.

his relationship with Marxist dialectics, the more he became equalized by an abrupt and forceful sense of Christian transcendence. Hence, one should not read *La Petite Peur du XXe siècle* apart from *L'Affrontement chrétien*. The latter was written at Dieulefit during the winter of 1943–1944, a winter which represented so much material poverty and interior denial. I shall leave it to others to speak of the Christian in Emmanuel Mounier; for the ordinary Christian, this book is extremely difficult and exacting; however, I shall confine my remarks to its philosophical aspects. It may be said that it is entirely a meditation on the virtue of strength, which St. Thomas treated following the Fathers. It is not by chance that this book is haunted by the shadow of Nietzsche, as is the *Petite Peur* haunted by that of Marx. For only the Christian who has the wherewithal to reply to Nietzsche is a Christian strong enough to resist being subdued by that part of Marxism that Nietzsche embraces. Here is the connection between the first two groups of meditations published after the war. Nietzsche asks the Christian a question which, in the last analysis, hits him closer to the heart than does Marxism. For the anti-Christian argument of Marxism still remains too sociological to be truly damaging: some have answered all too quickly that Marx was only familiar with a mere caricature of Christendom, only a decadent Christianity which was anxious to camouflage the privileges of the bourgeoisie by a corrupt Gospel of resignation. But behind the sociological collapse of Christianity, Nietzsche pretends to discover an original collapse or failure which he links to Christianity as such: "Is it therefore true that Christianity, which characteristically casts a quiet light on ancient civilizations and the lives of people approaching the end of their days, is actually poison for young bodies, an enemy of manly force and natural grace . . . ? Has Christianity borne in itself an initial defect whose effects are finally coming to light after having been delayed by the slowness and complexity of history?" [50]

Emmanuel Mounier undertakes to use the "atheist awakening" as a provocation for a "Christian awakening." [51]

The first act of the Christian, in the form of the "knight dressed in black," is to acquire the quality of the tragic Christian who is worthy of dialogue with Nietzsche: tragedy of transcendence, tragedy of sin, tragedy of paradox—since it is necessary to die in the world and to engage oneself in it, to be grieved at sin and to

---

50. *L'Affrontement chrétien*, pp. 11, 14.
51. *Ibid.*, pp. 23–24.

rejoice over the new man. But what decadence there is in moving from these tragic feelings to the "parvenu assurance" of the ordinary Christian, to the "dull and almost stupid sadness" of the contrite, to the "unfortunate state of the disgraced or the anemics of spiritual combat," to the "spiritual cowardice" and to the "dreary and sterile purity" of the virtuous!

The second step is to discover within the heart of authentic Christianity this moment which outruns the tragic and which in the last analysis distinguishes it from despair: "Within the heart of Christianity and beyond the asceticism of paradox, anguish, and annihilation, there is an asceticism of simplicity, of availability, patience, constant humility, gentleness and even weakness, supernatural weakness." [52] According to Mounier, in this movement from the tragic to "weakness" there is the trap of insipidity and pallidness, of cowardice and all the forms of resignation.

"There is color and vivid force in the instant which *actually* becomes lost before being rediscovered at the end of spiritual freedom. There is a primary and real impoverishment of our humanity by Faith." [53]

Thus it is still necessary for the Christian to deepen the meaning of his humility and unrelentingly dissociate it from the servile attitude which takes on so many contemptible forms: moralism and legalism, the proclivity for spiritual directions which free one from the burden of choice, and that submissiveness to events which Marx categorically denounced. . . . The true Christian is the proud and free man who only bows before God and in no way slackens on the road "from abasement to confrontation." [54]

3. *Person and Character*

ONE COULD NOT APPROACH the more "philosophical" books such as the *Traité du caractère*, the *Introduction aux existentialismes*, and *Le Personnalisme* [55] without being aware of the civilizing intention of Mounier's first studies and without linking to them the twofold self-critique which comes from Mounier's encounter with Marx and Nietzsche.

Personalism has clarified its philosophical scope in two ways: on the one hand by relating itself to the *human sciences* and

52. *Ibid.*, p. 37.
53. *Ibid.*
54. *Ibid.*, p. 81.
55. References for these works were given previously.—Trans.

objective procedures so as to elucidate the person, and on the other hand by situating itself in relation to the *philosophies of existence.* As we shall see, the two endeavors coincide in many respects.

One must give precedence to the *Traité du caractère* over the other two small books, if only because of its copiousness. Furthermore, in many respects, it is comparable to books ordinarily written by philosophers. This may be attributed in part to the circumstances under which it was written; the forced leisure of imprisonment and the long retreat at Dieulefit put Emmanuel Mounier into a frame of mind similar to that of psychologists and philosophers. The work which resulted from these extraordinary circumstances shows what the theoretical work of Mounier might have been had he not sacrificed it to the *Esprit* movement. On the other hand, the point of view of this work places it between objective knowledge and existential understanding, between science and "personal mystery." The countless references to psychophysiology, psychopathology, psychoanalysis, characterology, social psychology, etc., make this *traité* a vast synthesis wherein several objective disciplines are integrated under the direction of the personalist theme.

The purpose of this book is, therefore, to test the comprehensive capacity of the notion of person from the side of *objective knowledge.* Thus it would be wrong to confine personalism to a confrontation with existentialism. Its significance is not primarily polemic but rather integrative. Certainly the concept of the person transcends objective data, but first one must integrate and summarize the objective aspects of the person.

Thus the concept of person coincides partially with the notion of "structure" which psychologists, psychiatrists, and present-day characterologists rank higher than the notion of components or elements. But when Mounier takes up his studies, the "personal mystery" provides material to initiate a critique of the reduction of structures to types or purely statistical realities. The "type" would rather express the exterior outline of a limitation, the failure of the personality rather than the idea of an internal plastic force: "We are typical only in the measure that we fail to be fully personal." [56] Further, while coinciding partially with the synthetic schemata of pathologists, the theme of the person proves resistant to the imperialism of the clinic: "It is no longer the generative disorder but the generative theme of an individual psychism which we take as the ultimate goal of characterology." [57]

56. *Traité du caractère,* p. 41.
57. *Ibid.,* p. 44.

Furthermore, Mounier refuses to allow character to be confined to *data* and tries to show how the affirming "I" takes possession of its own character, at times by assuming its moods and propensities, at times by compensating for its weaknesses, but always by achieving its meaning by an act of valorization. Thus, this open characterology borders on an ethics: if character is something which is at once given and willed, then a merely objective science of it is no longer possible. What is necessary for it is an intuition which sympathizes and a will which projects. In this respect, the most Bergsonian notations (for example, the parallel between the characterologist and the novelist rather than the naturalist; [58] understanding viewed as a personal interpretation of a personal signification,[59]) are inseparable not only from the structural analyses which they have undergone, but also from the whole pedagogy of personalism: "There is no knowledge of man except within a will for humanism which is in conformity to the essence of man." [60] "Only those who view man with respect to the future are qualified to decipher the mysteries of man here and now." [61]

Thus, by virtue of this discreet intention, this scientific book is related to personalism. While it is to be feared that the sheer weight of the branches of knowledge drawn upon may overtax the momentum of this long book, still it is good to plunge into its density. Step by step its peculiar rhythm compensates for the long ramblings in which his analysis lingers, and it appears that these long detours were required by the nature of the subject matter. It was first necessary to start from the lowest and most external aspects—from social and organic "surroundings"—in order to exhibit an environed and enrooted man who only masters a milieu to which he "belongs" (this is the leitmotiv of the psychophysiology of character, as well as of the psychology of geographical, social, professional, and cultural environments). But it was also necessary to multiply the psychological intermediaries between the low and the high, between the exterior and the interior, so as to combat from all corners the ever-recurring dualism. Thus he first considers in detail the primary movements of emotivity, which represent "psychological perturbation at its roots." He then considers the modalities of psychological force and all the "primary attitudes taken at the vital level" which express *vital reception*, that is, the outline of the person's responses to provocations coming from the

---

58. *Ibid.*, p. 42.
59. *Ibid.*, p. 45.
60. *Ibid.*, p. 58.
61. *Ibid.*, preface.

milieu which yet conspire with the powers of perturbation (see the excellent pages devoted to the concept of generosity-greed, pp. 332–336, which are quite representative of our friend's style: for we find there one of the master intuitions governing his ethico-economic studies on money and property as well as his metaphysical reflections on creation). Then and only then can we understand the *battle for the real,* not in the strict sense of a theory of knowledge, but in accordance with the full scope of our debate with our diverse spheres of behavior, without excepting this "real which is more real than the real" and which only the imagination probes.

It is well worth noting that Mounier did not accentuate the voluntary stage within the sum total of our replies to the provocations of the environment. He considers the will only as impatience with an obstacle facing our action: "The will is nothing other than the person considered under his offensive aspect, rather than under his creative aspect." [62] In short, this treatise is as little voluntarist as possible, and on that score is in agreement with the major tenets of a thought concerned with nourishing the power of self-affirmation from below, from the side of vital impulses, from above by creative grace, and laterally by provocations from others. Thus, the book does not end with the evaluation of the "splendors and miseries of the will," [63] but takes account of two fundamental ventures of character: that which is offered to it by others, and that which is provided to it by space and all the things to be possessed. And so the "drama of others" and "having" add new aspects to this multidimensional understanding of character.

Other aspects come to light within the orders of valorization, intellect, and religious life. But what is noteworthy is that within this treatise on total man, the various perspectives are not added to one another but implicate each other in a reciprocity which is always reversible: thus the "original character" is at work as early as the most obscure choices of initial provocations by the living person himself, whereas on the other hand vocation comes through the "roads and limits" which sketch the invincible figure of character. Such is the inward necessity of this complex work.

At the same time, we see in what sense the person is character: character is another name for person when it is brought before the sciences of man and demonstrates its power to both reorganize and transcend all the dimensions of anthropological knowledge.

62. *Ibid.*, p. 472.
63. *Ibid.*, pp. 467–77.

4. *Person and Existence*

To REORGANIZE and transcend the object: such is precisely the meaning of existence for a critique of knowledge and for an ontology. It will suffice, therefore, to bring about this critique and this ontology in order to inaugurate a confrontation with the philosophies of existence.

But then personalism carries over to this new frame of reference everything it has maintained prior to the eruption of existentialisms in France, in particular its experience of a fundamental liaison between thought and action.

In this respect the *Introduction aux existentialismes* is especially relevant to doctrinal research. Besides being excellent as an historical introduction, this small book may be used, in accordance with its broadest perspectives, to support the open horizons of existentialisms and thus avert the tendency to identify existentialism with Jean-Paul Sartre.[64] Accordingly, personalism fits into a vast existentialist tradition: "In general, one may characterize this trend of thought as a reaction of the philosophy of man against the excesses of philosophies concerned with ideas and things." [65]

It is interesting to see Emmanuel Mounier, who was so anxious to effect a rupture with past civilization, intent upon stressing the philosophical continuity of the tradition upon which he bases himself. This should not be surprising. As early as 1932, Emmanuel Mounier had stressed that it was upon a foundation of permanent values that the "personalist and communal Revolution" emerged, that this revolution should provide a new historical outlet for an ancient exigency. Moreover, this intention to evince the present scope and the traditional coherence of existentialisms is not foreign to the guiding preoccupations of the *Esprit* movement: by comparing Christian personalism with one of the great existentialist traditions and by showing that there is a common source for all existentialist traditions, a common manner of raising problems and common themes, Mounier continues to work out a grouping which respects philosophical pluralism while conserving a central intention.

This design is served by an original method. Instead of writing a series of monographs devoted to the different existentialisms, each of which would have required an exhaustive critique of sources, influences, and relationships, Mounier preferred to eluci-

64. *Introduction aux existentialismes,* p. 8.
65. *Ibid.*

date certain common "directive themes" which are consonant with the diverse traditions.

If we examine these "directive themes," two points become quite clear: first, personalism becomes integrated with the philosophies of existence only by means of a rupture with traditional philosophy, particularly university philosophy. The end of the privileged status of the theory of knowledge is a clear indication of this rupture. The problematic of knowledge may be expressed thus: how can something be an object for a subject? In an idealistic context, the question is: what is that in the subject which renders possible the appearing of an object for him? A problematic of knowledge, then, certainly deals with man, but it confines itself to that aspect which makes possible an order on the side of things. Thus, in the last analysis, it is the coherence of a world which is known and explained that is the chief concern of a theory of knowledge, even when it is a question only of the subject and its possibilities as a subject. The philosophies of existence all strive to replace knowing within existing, the subject within man. The omission of existence is here the "original philosophical sin." [66] This reintegration of the classical problematic of knowing within the core of a vaster problematic brings to the fore the question concerning the human condition as a whole. Priority is given to the *drama* wherein freedom and the body, death and fault, passion and habit, history and private life are the principal challenges for reflection. Personalism is by no means foreign to this renovation since it has contributed to it. Hence, the "directive themes" of the *Introduction aux existentialismes* are very much related to the themes of the *Traité du caractère* and *Le Personnalisme*. The "personalist awakening," in accordance with the expression of 1936, rings as the "philosophical awakening" of existentialism.[67]

Yet in spite of this relationship, some differences still exist in the *initial intention*. Even when the existentialisms subordinate a problematic of knowledge to an exegesis of the human condition, they conserve a speculative and theoretical turn which continues to ally them with the tradition of classical philosophies. The critique of the "system" and "objectivity" demonstrates the permanence of the problem of the relations between the knower and the world. In many senses existentialism is a classical philosophy: by its reflection on the limitations of knowledge revealed by the situation of the human existent; the importance of its discussion

66. *Ibid.*, p. 17.
67. *Ibid.*, pp. 13, 154–55.

on the universal and the particular, essence and existence, the concept of the "existentials," and on mystery and problem. Hence, the important problem remains that of truth—even though one speaks of the truth of the existing person, of subjective truth. Or in different terms, the problem remains that of reason (Karl Jaspers says that the *philosophia perennis* is entirely a hymn to reason)—even when one makes a sharp dichotomy between the "reason of the englobing" and anonymous and analytic understanding. The existentialist philosophy attempts a new possession of objectivity, the elaboration of a new form of intelligence, and sometimes it goes as far as to use the phrase "a new philosophical logic."

It would therefore seem that the active and prospective character of personalism continues to distinguish it from the critical character of existentialism. In the last analysis, its tendency to promote action makes it prevail over the tendency to elucidate significations.

Furthermore, existentialism is related to classical philosophy by its search for a new ontology which saves it from being mere idle concern and false pathos. Its fundamental question is this: What does being mean for me, being for others, being for the world; what is the being of everything which is, of being in general? Heidegger has shown that this question has by no means been exhausted, but merely prepared for by the exegesis of the human condition, which is what is implied when one elucidates the status of man as contingent, being-there in such and such a way. The very idea of nothingness is still within the ontological register, as well as are "ciphers" (Jaspers) and "mystery" (Marcel).

Emmanuel Mounier's encounter with existentialist ontology would seem to be the following: the educative intention of his work goes beyond a strictly philosophic problematic—a critique and an ontology—but following the expression proposed earlier, it has value as a philosophic matrix; it is capable of a philosophy, and we shall now turn to the elucidation of this.

The intention which inspires his work introduces into philosophy a tact, or to be more precise, a discernment, when it is projected onto the level of a critique and an ontology.

It is no longer only within the *Introduction aux existentialismes* that one may see this discernment at work, but also in the *Traité du caractère* and in *Le Personnalisme*. It orients one toward the proper usage of the "existentialist drama," the themes of anguish, of irrationalism, of experience, and the presence of nothingness in being.

1. First, more than any of the existentialists, Mounier stresses the liaison and tension between person and nature, or, as he often said, matter. Remaining faithful to his first analyses of the pair "person-individual," he continues to represent, by these two notions, two directions rather than two plans: a direction of emergence or of transcendence and a direction of immerging or of incorporation, and he continues to locate this twofold movement in attitudes of civilization. Yet after more than fifteen years, the ontological perspective has become more important: personalism "specifies structures" [68] and seeks with the name person "the properly human mode of existence." [69] The terms nature and matter are henceforth more comprehensive than the term individual and suggest a broader dialectic which Mounier, in a note in *Esprit,* called anthropocosmic.[70] The tragic optimism of the *Petite Peur* is included therein [71] as well as all the reflections on the unity of the destiny and vocation of mankind.[72]

2. The "theme of the other," which occupies such an important place among all existentialisms, is likewise found in personalism: but the fundamental feeling of the bond between personal and communal life here operates also as a critical detector in the labyrinth of existentialist analyses. It is not by chance that the originality of the person is first expressed in communion and not in solitude.[73] What is more important, then, is to find the ontological implication of the "original acts" by which the self becomes open to the other and advances from self-concern to availability, from greed to giving.

But just when Emmanuel Mounier is so close to Gabriel Marcel, once again he turns against all "spiritual anti-collectivism" and looks within the technical and abstract apparatus of social relationships for the fundamental channel of communal relationships. It is to be noted that Mounier's last book is more concerned than any of the others with the "rational." "If thought does not

68. *Le Personnalisme,* p. 6.

69. *Ibid.,* p. 9.

70. *L'Homme et l'univers* (book review, May, 1949), pp. 746–47; man, recapitulation and verb of the universe: "He humanizes it and integrates it to the divinization of the entire universe . . . , he continues, as it were, the primordial thrust of creation." Yet Mounier is still mindful of the threats which bear upon this adventure from the fact of the fall. It is this anthropocosmic perspective that is opened at the end of *La Petite peur du XXe siècle.*

71. *Le Personnalisme,* pp. 30–32.

72. *Ibid.,* pp. 47–50, 101.

73. *Ibid.,* p. 35 ff.

become communicable, therefore remaining impersonal under one aspect, it is not thought but delirium. Objective knowledge and reasoning are the indispensable supports for intersubjectivity. Likewise, law is a necessary medium." [74] It is in the same spirit that this book accentuates the idea of a spatio-temporal unity of the human race, understood at least as a "movement toward the unification of the personal universe."

This explains Mounier's resistance to the analyses of Sartre: those concerning the "gaze," for example. Another's gaze congeals me into an object only in the measure of my own unavailability; absorbed in myself, I experience the actions of others as encroachments, but then "it is through a previous design of unavailability and not through my freedom as subject that I grasp the other as object; it is in the same disposition that I compel myself to receive him as an intruder." [75]

3. Henceforth it is with much moderation, and as a "complementary pulsation" of personal life, that Mounier introduces the themes of self-communion, privacy, singularity, and rupture. The previous critique of private life, of the world of money and having, is still implicitly contained here and manifests these essential categories as mutilated by isolation: the existentialist themes "are unaware of the dispositions of relaxation, openness and giving, which are also constitutive of our being."

Thus *Le Personnalisme* no more stresses the theme of freedom than did the *Traité du caractère* set up a monopoly of the will. To replace freedom in "the total structure of the person," [76] is not only to join it to its conditions—*freedom under conditions,* says one chapter, in memory of the book written during the war—but also to recognize the values which make it "the eminent dignity" [77]: "My freedom does not merely gush forth aimlessly, it is ordered, or better, 'summoned' "; [78] my freedom is that of a "situated" but "valorized" person. At this point, Mounier is close to Scheler, Buber, Hartmann, and Gabriel Marcel—but in his own way: the critique of the bourgeois, of happiness, and of "the communal ascesis," advanced before the war, continues to form the concrete substance of this philosophy of values.

4. Lastly, for Mounier freedom "is not the being of the person but the way in which the person is all that it is more fully than by

74. *Ibid.,* p. 46.
75. *Introduction aux existentialismes,* p. 105.
76. *Le Personnalisme,* p. 72.
77. *Ibid.,* p. 83.
78. *Ibid.,* p. 79.

necessity. . . . The person is not being; it is the movement of being toward being and it is stable only in relation to the being toward which it aims." [79] Values are precisely the meaning of action which stake out the path of this movement toward being.

Certainly it is here that Mounier breaks with Sartre. Mounier takes Sartre to task for his method which admits as exemplary and canonical, in the exegesis of the human condition, the authentic experiences of "despair" which Sartre has systematically analyzed. "Would not this rage against being merely betray resentment over having failed to achieve what Gabriel Marcel calls 'the nuptial bond of man with life'?" [80] But underlying this clash in method is a real metaphysical opposition: "Philosophical absurdism involves a sort of logical blackmail. Judging from the way in which it sometimes argues, it seems that reason or being can be sought in the world only through a sort of cowardice or philosophical infantilism, that a position is defensible only when it is untenable. Let us cut short these intimidations. It takes no more courage to deny everything than to deny less." [81] Here we encounter again the notation of *L'Affrontement chrétien:* discernment is a fine line separating the tragic from despair. Fundamentally, for Mounier, Sartrian existentialism would be better characterized as "unexistential" since it has failed to recognize and greet generosity, the superabundance which attests at the core of the person that its existence is paradoxically given to it in the inwardness of its volition. This bestowal of being makes possible a truth *for* the person, a communion *between* persons and even a nature *of* the person which is the permanent style of its inventions and revolutions.

If it were necessary to summarize the fundamental encounters and divergences which are signified by the words *person* and *existence,* we could do so in the following way.

First, person and existence refer primarily to two orders of preoccupation which are not exactly co-extensive: on the one hand, there is an ethico-political concern, a "pedagogical" intention in touch with a crisis of civilization; on the other hand, there is a critical and ontological reflection in contact with classical "philosophical" tradition.

Second, the word person is a way of designating one of the interpretations of existence, once one is situated on the strictly critical and ontological level of the philosophies of existence. Thus,

79. *Ibid.,* pp. 82, 85.
80. *Introduction aux existentialismes,* p. 60.
81. *Ibid.,* p. 62.

the word stresses certain aspects of existence which are contained implicitly in the pedagogical intention of personalism: these are the ones which we earlier emphasized in connection with the material conditions for the realization of human existence, the communal path of this realization, its orientation through values, and its foundation in being which is more internal to it than itself.

We have been led to subordinate all new points of view on the person to the original one: a concrete ethical research in direct contact with "the Revolution of the twentieth century." The confrontation established by the *Traité du caractère* with the objective sciences of man points up another direction for investigation which may not be approached within the framework of the existentialist problematic. Thus person and individual, person and character, and person and existence, are expressions which describe different sectors of research.

Emmanuel Mounier, as no other of those he gathered to his cause, had the pluri-dimensional sense of the theme of the person. But it seems to me that the reason for our attachment to him is something more profound than a many-sided theme—the rare accord between two tonalities of thought and life; what he himself called *strength* [*la force*], following the ancient Christian moralists, or the virtue of *confrontation*, and *generosity* or *abundance* of heart, which rectifies the hardness of the virtue of strength by means of something forgiving and graceful. It is this subtle alliance of a noble "ethical" virtue with a noble "poetic" virtue which made Emmanuel Mounier this man at once indomitable and selfless [*irréductible et offert*].

4 / Speaking and Praxis

Truth and Falsehood

IT WOULD BE DESIRABLE to begin a meditation on truth with a celebration of unity. The truth does not contradict itself, falsehood is legion. The truth brings men together, falsehood scatters them and sets discord among them. But it is not possible to begin in this way. The *One* is too distant a reward; it is an evil temptation. Hence the first part of this study [1] will be devoted to elucidating the various senses of the notion of truth. I would like to show that the effort to multiply the levels or *orders* of truth is not a mere academic exercise, but corresponds to a historical movement of rupture. The Renaissance was the moment *par excellence* of the realization of the pluri-dimensional nature of truth. It is by this historical process that the problem of truth pertains to the very movement of our civilization and lends itself to a sociology of knowledge.

But this process of pluralization is countered by an inverse process of unification, of *totalization.* To this the second part of our study will be devoted. The interpretation of this process is the key to the entire account. I shall try to show that the unification of the true is at once the wish of reason and a first violence, a fault. We shall thus reach a point of ambiguity, a point of greatness and of guilt. Precisely at this point the lie strikes nearest to the quick of

1. This study was originally a *Report* submitted to the discussions of the "Esprit Congress" (Jouy-en-Josas, September, 1951). Nothing has been changed as to its schematic and unilateral character. While it called forth other complementary perspectives, which came up during the ensuing discussion, these perspectives have not been included so as the better to promote discussion and criticism. On the other hand, this report was to introduce two others bearing upon the more precise and concrete features of "Truth and Falsehood in Private Life and in Politics." This study is therefore but an introduction, the positioning, as it were, of the other two reports.

truth. We shall go straight to the aspect of the problem which concerns the interpretation of our civilization. Historically, the temptation to unify the true by violence comes and has come from two quarters, the clerical and the political spheres. More precisely, it can come from two *powers*, the spiritual power and the temporal power. I would like to show that the clerical synthesis of the true comes about through the guilt of the special authority which the believer identifies with revealed truth, just as the political synthesis of the true is due to the culpable action which corrupts the naturally and authentically dominating function of politics in our historical existence. I shall thus be led to outline the sort of authority that theological truth can exercise on the other levels of truth, the "eschatological" and not the "systematic" sense in which it can unify all the orders of truth in the eyes of the believer. Likewise, I shall have to elucidate the limitations of a philosophy of history in its pretension to unify the multiple levels of truth in a single "sense," in a single dialectic of truth.

The cardinal points of my analysis will thus be: the pluralization of the orders of truth in our cultural history; the ambiguous nature of our will to unity, at once the goal of reason and violence; the "eschatological" nature of the theological synthesis; and the merely "probable" character of any synthesis set forth by the philosophy of history.

Perhaps it is already apparent that the spirit of falsehood is inextricably bound up with our search for the truth, like a tunic of Nessus clinging to the human form.

[1] DIFFERENTIATION OF THE ORDERS OF TRUTH

AT FIRST GLANCE, nothing is simpler than the notion of truth. Tradition defines it as an *agreement,* an agreement at the level of our power of judgment (of affirmation and negation), an agreement of speech with reality, and, secondarily, an agreement among ourselves, an agreement of minds. Let us note the features of this definition of truth: it is a manner of disposing ourselves "in conformity with," "in the same way as . . ."

But upon examination, this definition appears purely formal, like the very term "reality" which serves as its reference. There is an extreme case in which the sense is all the clearer as it is of lesser purport. This is the case in which the conformity of our thought is but the simple repetition of an already structured order, in which our speech discovers nothing, invents nothing, contends against nothing: it's raining, the wall is white; yes, that is true, everyone knows it is. But as soon as we leave behind these customary and lazy truths, we see that the movement of *disposing oneself in accordance with . . . , such as the thing is,* is part of a whole labor which consists precisely in formulating the fact as fact, in structuring the real.

Let us set ourselves immediately at the level of experimental science. Here is the best known truth-activity and yet the most difficult and the latest to develop.

Its way of structuring reality establishes a type of truth which is fundamentally linked to its methodological style. But before this could develop, mathematics, which turns its back on visible reality, had to reach a certain maturity and the mind had boldly to posit that only the mathematizable aspect of reality was "objective" and that perceived qualities were only "subjective." This decision of the mind has a history (which has been written by Alexandre Koyré): it dates very exactly from Galileo. It is this cultural event of the birth of experimental science which brought about the destruction of the philosophico-theological synthesis of the true, or at least made its dissolution visible, for as we shall see, this synthesis never existed but as an intention or a pretension.

Does this mean that this level of truth may be regarded as the sole frame of reference for truth and that it is possible to propound a sort of monism of scientific truth? The character of the notion of the scientific "fact," as we have formulated it, is already enough to show that the work which renders true—the work of verification with which experimental truth is identified—is inextricably bound up with the method which governs this work and the mind's decision to define the objective by the mathematizable. (There are no elements of this, its instruments included, which are not, as Duhem showed, detectors of scientific facts and material contractions of previous science and applied theories.) Thus truth appears inseparable from the process of verification, that is to say from possibilities of instrumentation, from the particular methodology of a given science (which determines a fact as physical, chemical, biological, psychological, etc.) and from the experimental method in general.

Thus experimental truth excludes other levels of truth. Yet we can briefly show how it is bound up with them in a sort of "circle."

First, experimental truth presupposes the very thing that it excludes, namely, the power of conviction that emanates from the perceived world via a community of men. The sounds, colors, and concrete forms which make up the fabric of our life's environment (our *Lebenswelt*), are declared subjective; and yet, if we are in the world, it is because there is something which is perceived. This is true for the scientist not only in his extra-scientific life—for him, too, the sun rises, bread and wine announce themselves by their flavor and consistency—but also in his scientific life: for the scientific objects that he frames are determinations of this world that he perceives; it is within the horizon of this perceived "world" that his research is itself directed at the interior of the world. Moreover, it is within this perceived world that are found the cultural objects which comprise the laboratory itself, the cross hairs in the telescope, the fluttering of the indicator, the path of the particle in the Wilson Cloud Chamber.

Thus the tendency in experimentation to resorb what is perceived cannot be pushed to the limit, since what is perceived continues to be the existential reference point of scientific objectivity. Here we witness the first fission of truth into objectivity and perceived existence. This division appears straightway as mutual encompassment, a "circle." This is important for our impending interpretation of the unity of the true: this "circle" cannot be reduced to a "hierarchy," an idea which is much more satisfying to our sense of synthesis.

I began with this example because it is the most striking, but here is something which strikes closer to our ethical and cultural preoccupation.

We said that the advent of experimental science was an event in our cultural history like literature, theology, or politics; we called the laboratory and its instruments cultural objects like houses, books, theaters, languages, or rites. All of these cultural objects are not only enrooted in the incontrovertible presence of this perceived world, but they are also the achievement of a cultural activity, of a cultural life of which science, considered subjectively as human work, is a part.

Now science proceeds to the reduction of the objects of culture at the same time as to that of perceived objects. Moreover, it reduces man to the same measure of objectivity, man who is the bearer of this culture; biology, psychology, and sociology are departments of natural science in which man has, as an object of science, no special privilege whatsoever. And yet this science, which resorbs man as an object, *presupposes* scientific activity and man as a subject, the sustainer and author of these activities. The very reduction of man to the status of an object is only possible within a cultural life which encompasses him in his total praxis. Herein, science is never more than one "praxis" among others, a "theoretical praxis," as Husserl says, constituted by the decision to suspend all affective, utilitarian, political, aesthetic, and religious considerations and to hold as true only that which answers to the criteria of the scientific method in general, and the particular methodology of such and such a discipline.

We thus encounter a new "circle": that of man as the object of science and man as the subject of culture. Straightway a new level of truth emerges which has to do with the coherence of the total praxis of man, the order of his action. It is the level of ethics in the most general sense of the word.

We shall presently come back to the difficult notion of ethical truth; for the moment, however, let us be content with having elicited the various orders of truth one from the other by a double process of exclusion and mutual encompassment. We have thus outlined a more or less triangular dialectic between perception, knowledge, and action. The perceived, with its world-horizon, encompasses knowledge and action as the vastest theater of our existence. Laboratories, the applications of science to work, well-being, and war, give a perceived presence to science which is thus woven into our life and our death.

And yet, in its turn, scientific knowledge encompasses all, since science is precisely science of the perceived and of all biological, psychological, and sociological life. We have been so imbued with a minimum of science that we "almost" perceive the scientist's objects, the immense dimensions of the sky, the vibrations of sound and light, and the hormones of our neighbor.

But we can also say that action encompasses all since knowledge and even perception are cultural achievements. In point of fact, this three-term dialectic is still quite crude. Each attitude in some sense "dialectizes" itself for itself, and not only in calling forth the other attitudes which it excludes and requires. In saying that each term of this triad "dialectizes" itself within, I mean that each one has working within it a twofold and inverse process, a tendency to *dogmatize* itself and a tendency to *problematize* itself. Here we have a more subtle way of making the truth vibrate.

Let us consider the scientific attitude which served us as a first reference point, a first framework of truth. We have seen that it proposes a single and simple style of comportment with regard to the real: the experimental style. But the matter is not quite so simple. This experimental style is in many respects the counterpart of a mathematical style characterized by the denial of the real. But scientific achievement presents itself to man both as the ambition of science and as the work of the sciences. In the course of history, scientific achievement ceaselessly calls forth a labor of assembling, of systematization (sometimes disciplines which have independent origins, or disparate techniques, fuse into a methodology which embraces both); ceaselessly the work of science divides into disciplines, specialities, and different methodologies. The diversified tree of science remains our presupposition, but any dogmatic linking together of the sciences is disrupted by gaps or encroachments which render the very idea of a system of the sciences problematic.

Further, if science has a unique position in the eventual structure of truth, it is because it is for us the touchstone and the model of truth. All truth, we think, ought to be *of* science or at least *like* science. This model of truth has been eminently fulfilled by science as long as the ideal of *Epistêmê*, a result of Greek geometry, has appeared to us without opacity, as an answer which satisfies and totally satiates the question which gave rise to it. The Galilean era, which is now coming to an end, rests on a total faith in the exemplary character of the mathematical knowledge derived from the great Alexandrians; it is upon this foundation of clarity that the mechanistic exploration of the whole empire of the visible has been inaugurated and pursued with such evident success.

Thus, a certain mathematical order was answered, at the other extremity, by an experimental world capable of being mathematized. The more the scientific act showed itself to be the pattern for all other activities (for ethics, law, economics), the less it appeared problematic. And here it is that opacity resurges at the two extremities: reverting to the first crisis of its origin, mathematics discovers acts, decisions, enterprises, there where Plato saw mathematical beings—indeed not absolute *in all respects* since he did distinguish in numbers and figures "beings by position," beings of less dignity than the beings reached by philosophic dialectics. Yet these mathematical beings had at least the power to endow thought with coherence and lead to vision.

We shall never be able to realize just how much our sensitivity to truth has been learned, educated, and, in a word, delighted with the idea that truth is a spectacle for our understanding—a spectacle that the heavenly order unfolds before our human eyes as the ordained beauty in which the mathematical order is embodied. If ethical truth had some dignity for a Kant, it was as the practical reply of that order which "obliges" thought: the starry heavens above us and the moral law within our heart. . . .

This crisis of foundations is answered, at the other pole of the exploration of our world, by the discovery of energy, not a sight like the heavenly order which the Ancients contemplated, but something like the sanctioning of human enterprise; the atomic energy that man is *responsible* for having liberated, with all the possibilities and dangers which it involves, is, so to speak, symmetrical to the act by which man has inaugurated mathematics. The two acts mutually question each other. At once, all the activities leading up to the axioms of mathematics and experiments in nuclear physics, all this scientific activity which springs from Greek geometry and Galileo's mathematical physics suddenly appears as a reassuring activity, clear and dogmatic in comparison to the understanding of the ends of mathematics and the ends of physics, or in comparison to the great problematization of science which is being effected before our very eyes.

We have not finished drawing the consequences of Greek *Epistêmê*. Indeed, we have brought the foundations of this *Epistêmê* into question. On the one hand, everything invites us to dogmatize as men of science and to smash with contempt any procedure which has not traversed the quantitative clarification of a scientific discipline: are we not on the threshold of a stirring mastery of the phenomena of life? Do we even have an inkling of what would be a true science of the higher psychism? On the other hand, besides these developments of science beyond the cycle of mathematico-mechanistic experience, a new phase of theorization is opened, not merely by the proliferation of mathematical disciplines, but by their association with recent symbolic logic on the one hand, and with physical theory on the other. In short, a scientific reason of a different scope than the one known by Descartes and Kant is now taking form before our eyes.[2] This is true: all this invites the scientific mind to dogmatize and to fail to recognize this "circle" in which it is nevertheless included, and in which it is in debate with both the perceptual consciousness of our being-in-the-world and with the ethical consciousness of our responsibility: with existential truth and ethical truth.

But the work of *problematization,* which operates in a direction inverse to the dogmatizing tendencies of the scientific mind, replaces the scientific act in its context of existence and responsibility.

We find that there are theoretical decisions at the beginning of mathematics, and that practical decisions, or even political and military ones, are brought about by the discovery of atomic energy.

2. Cf. D. Dubarle, "Le Christianisme et les progrès de la science." *Esprit* (September, 1951).

Mankind's assimilation of such a discovery no longer raises problems of objectivity or of knowledge, but rather of the management of human affairs. The military, industrial, and economic problems which are consequent upon the discovery of atomic energy are not raised in terms of the truth or falsehood of the atomic theory, but rather in terms of our existence; they are raised in the world such as it appears. They do not come up in the universe such as the physicist represents it to himself, but in the world of perception in which we are *born*, in which we live and die. It is within the world of perception that our instruments, our machines have an ethical significance and bring into play our responsibilities. Thus we are brought back to our "circle." The extension of scientific truth encompasses man as a canton of objects, but the responsibilities which scientific truth brings into play show that the scientific act is encompassed within the sum total of the acts of the responsible man, in the global form of human "praxis."

One could say as much of the conquest of life by science and the eventual conquest of the higher psychism and of human sociality in the strict scientific disciplines. More than all scientific progress, this conquest categorizes man and resorbs him in the classification of things. But on the other hand, more than all scientific progress, it encompasses a *virtual ethical question:* What shall we *do* with such a power over life and man?

The fact that we are able to fear for man, to recognize the dangers which threaten man, *because* the science of man begins and advances—this very fact demonstrates the power of mutual encompassment of knowledge and ethics. These fears for man—which so frequently degenerate among our contemporaries into fright and despair—are beneficial in the measure that they show that ethical truth is man's answer to the progress of his knowledge, that ethical truth is, in short, the very vigilance of man, in the core of his perceived world, among other men.

The way in which scientific truth "dialectizes" itself in itself and thus lends itself to the "circle" of perceiving, knowing, and acting, is found again in the core of ethical truth.

There is nothing more apt to be dogmatized than the ethical conscience; and also nothing more vulnerable to problematization. On the one hand, what gives coherence to a personal code of ethics, such as the stability of a common tradition, lies in *not recommencing* forever to evaluate one's principal options, not to call into question one's fundamental values, but rather to conserve them as solid convictions and to use them as steppingstones so as to approach new situations gradually and without scruple. Thereby an order of values takes form and this allows us to decide quickly and free the path of hesitations which beset daily decisions.

This idea of the sedimentation of our choices constitutes for us an ethical "world," a conception of happiness and of honor which is our personal moral code, more like the treasure of great civilizations. A whole history, both individual and collective, is thus contracted into a stable order. We are able to *support* ourselves upon it; it is in this way that one of the two aspects of ethical truth is constituted for us: true behavior is, in a sense, one which complies with . . . , which disposes itself *in accordance with* this moral order which is not called into question.

But it is enough to have once doubted an old prejudice, a custom, or a conviction in order for everything suddenly to become shaky and for the "ethical world" to manifest its precarious condition. The result is an endless questioning which assails the main supports of our ethical actions; and the vertigo of our ethical condition lays hold of us. Is there a power which can compel us; is there a center of authority which withstands our fancy, the temptation of the gratuitous act? This questioning is the other aspect of the idea of ethical truth: for in this doubt, in this questioning which upsets established order, we seek authentic obligation, we dispose ourselves in accordance with the more authentic and original exigency which is capable both of commanding us and of attracting us. We have the feeling that moral truth ought to be something like the tension between blind obedience to an already established order, which is always close at hand, and the questioning and doubting obedience directed to the essential value which is always more elusive than any already consolidated custom.

Perhaps one could find this movement of dogmatization and of problematization in ethical truth at the source of all the paradoxes of the moral life: a value is recognized only by serving it; a value is authentic—justice, truthfulness, etc.—only in its dialectic with another; the universal is the historical, etc.

This is not the proper place to elucidate a theory of moral truth. After having outlined and situated three great orders of truth in relation to one another, it was necessary to somehow animate from within, or, as we have said, to "dialectize" each of these orders so as to suggest not only that truth entails several orders of truth but to show that each order is shaped by a twofold movement of dogmatization and of problematization.

Thus our modern conscience never ceases to pluralize itself. What would happen if we introduce into this triangular schema the multitude of the other dimensions in which a comportment of "conformity"—that is to say a comportment of truth—may intervene?

Art itself involves truth. There is the truth of respect and the truth of doubt. There is no architecture without respect for the exigencies of materials: the art of the stone may not imitate wood; the art of reinforced cement may not repeat the art of the stone; columns may not give the outward appearance of supporting a vault. Even the imagination has its truth with which the novelist is very familiar as well as is the reader: a character is true when its internal coherence, its complete presence in the imagination, dominates its creator and convinces the reader.

But this truth of submission is also a truth of doubt and questioning. The true artist only experiences the motivation which is proper to his art and does not yield to any commands exterior to his art: to court the tyrant, to give renown to the Revolution. Even when he portrays the society of his times, even when he foretells the future, the artist is true if he does not plagiarize a sociological analysis which has *already* been done or a claim which has *already* found a non-aesthetical expression. On the contrary, he will create something new, something which is socially and politically valid, only if he is faithful to the power of analysis which flows from the authenticity of his sensitivity as well as from the maturity of the means of expression which he has inherited. We shall have to come back to this when we deal with the "political synthesis of the true." True art, in conformity with its proper motivation, is engaged when it has not deliberately willed it, when it has agreed not to know the principle of its integration within the total setting of a civilization.

Whatever the case may be with this political situation of aesthetic truth, it introduces into our cultural life a new dividing line and rupture point. A purely aesthetic existence is possible; and all other men benefit from the artist's adventure. What would the stirring spectacle of this perceived world, the matrix of our existence, be if the artist did not convey to us the joy of it, even if he should resort to the artifical means of abstract art? By preserving color, sound, and the flavor of the word, the artist, without willing it explicitly, revives the most primitive truth of the world of our life which the scientist shrouds. By creating figures and myths, the artist interprets the world and establishes a permanent, ethical judgement on our existence, even if he does not moralize, and especially if he does not moralize. *Poetry is a criticism of life.* . . . Thus all the orders of truth are mutually contested and reinstated in an endless "circle."

It is necessary to give yet another dimension to this coded and supra-coded message of our cultural history: the *critical* dimension, the one which is opened up by our Western philosophy of the Socratic, Cartesian, and Kantian type, and which consists of moving the previous question: how is it possible that there is a "meaning" for me or a meaning in itself? Western philosophy has introduced into the range of truth a power, both corrosive and constructive, of *questioning,* which transforms the very problem of truth which individual disciplines have encountered as a problem of external concordance and internal coherence. It constitutes the problem of *foundation.* This is also a part of our cultural tradition. As the sciences cut themselves off from philosophy, conceived as a Universal Science, philosophy re-emerged as an inquiry concerning the limitations and foundations of all science. Thereby it gave birth to a second-degree history, the history of philosophical subjectivity which doubts and questions the foundation. This history is not useless, for a critique of life is already a new life, a new type of human relationship: the genre of philosophical life. This history, which has repercussions in the sciences, law, and ethics—and even, as we shall see, in theology—is pursued in a discontinuous fashion through empires and wars, striding over long periods of silence and suddenly joining up with new works.

[2] Unity as Goal and as Fault: The Clerical Synthesis

WE NOW ARRIVE at the critical point of this whole reflection. The cultural development resulting from Greek thought is therefore a process of the pluralization of human existence, which has become capable of innumerable counterpoints.

And yet we are dedicated to unity. Our wish is that truth be in the singular, not merely in its formal definition but also in the works of truth. We would like for there to be a total meaning which would be as the meaningful form totalizing all our cultural activity. What is the meaning of this intention concerning the unity of truths?

It seems to me that this wish is very ambiguous. On the one hand, it represents an exigency, that is to say an authentic goal: an absolute pluralism is unthinkable. This is the profound significance of "reason," in the sense in which Kant distinguishes it from the understanding: the understanding applies itself to objects, embodies itself in the works of thought, it is already in dispersion. Reason is the supreme goal of unifying thoughts and works, unifying mankind, unifying our conception of virtue and happiness.

Unity is the goal of feeling just as much as the goal of reason. By the word feeling I mean this confused pre-possession, on the mode of desire, of sadness and joy, of the unity sought, lost, or foreseen; unity is loved. Without conceiving it, we understand affectively that the joy of mathematics should be the *same* as that of the arts or that of friendship. Each time we sense deep affinities between realities, points of view, or disparate personages, we are happy. The happiness of unity shows that there is a level of *Living* which is more profound than the dispersion of our culture. Yes, Life ought ultimately to signify unity, as if there were first brute life, the undivided will to live, then the powerful cultural explosion of our existence in accordance with all the dimensions of truth, and beyond this dispersion, another unity which would be Reason and Life. . . .

Whatever may be the case in respect to this wish for unity,[3] it is at the beginning and at the end of truths. But as soon as the exigency for a single truth enters into history as a goal of civilization, it is immediately affected with a mark of violence. For one always wishes to tie the knot too early. The *realized* unity of the true is precisely the initial lie.

Now this culpability which is linked to the unity of the truth—this lie of *the* truth—appears when the goal of unifying coincides with the sociological phenomenon of *authority*. Not, indeed, that authority is vicious in principle; on the contrary, it is an indispensable function. It is unthinkable, perhaps, that the government of persons, in all its forms, should disintegrate into the mere administration of things. There will always be situations in which man will command man, even by delegation of power. Authority is not culpable in itself. But yet it is the occasion of the passions of power. It is by means of the passions of power that certain men exercise a unifying function. In this way, violence feigns the highest goal of reason and the most persistent expectation of feeling. Certainly it is a good example of ambiguity where, as always, fault is indistinguishable from greatness. . . .

The first historical manifestation of this violent unification of the truth—at least the first which we shall consider, for there is no question here of exhausting the problem of power—is linked to theology, to its authority, to the clerical power over the true

3. Cf. the appendix at the end of this essay: *Note on the Wish and Endeavor for Unity.*

(hereafter I shall use "clerical" in the pejorative sense which is opposed to "ecclesial").

Henceforth I shall place myself within a Christian perspective which is theological and ecclesial. I should add that if my position is strongly marked in a "reformed" sense, I hope it is essentially compatible, with the exception of a few accents, with that of my Catholic companions.

For the Christian, theology introduces into his cultural life a dimension of truth which it is imperative to situate in relation to the preceding ones. But theology is not a simple reality: from the point of view of our inquiry on truth, theology is a complex of levels of truths. Before it turns into the temptation toward violence, with which we are concerned, it is a subordinated, submissive reality; its self-transcending reference is the Truth which *is* and which is *shown* as a Person. This is the way in which it presents itself, and the agnostic sociologist can at the very least understand it phenomenologically such as it presents itself. This Truth is not theology, but rather the mistress of theology, to which theology does not have direct access; for this Truth which has shown itself does not reach us but by a series of witnesses and testimonies. To the Truth which is corresponds truth as testimony: the finger which points. This first testimony is Scripture; the truth of preaching is subordinated to and is measured by the truth of Scripture. Through the forms and acts of worship, preaching transmits and explains to the community of today the primary testimony (Scripture). Thus if there is a truth to preaching it must lie in its conformity to the testimony concerning the Truth-Person. But as preaching is always an act which takes place in the present, it already introduces the dialectical characters of human truth; it too dialectizes itself between the two mortal poles of anachronistic repetition and hazardous adaptation of the Word to the present needs of the community of the faithful. The truth of preaching is therefore always in search of a fidelity which would be creative.

It is to this truth of preaching, which is always in process, that the possible truth of theology and the profession of "doctor" which supports this possible truth is connected. Now theology is of necessity a cultural act which interferes with the whole cultural life of a nation or a civilization.

In effect, theology is an effort to *understand*, not in the sense that it would attempt to make Revelation believable, but in a double sense: first, it is a critique of preaching the content of which it measures against the Word of God; thus it judges preaching. Secondly, this critical function presupposes a function of totalization. For theology, understanding is to understand the stages of Revelation as a whole; to understand is always to grasp a totality. The themes of preaching refer to scattered events which occur throughout the course of the year, but theology wishes to make of them a combined whole. Thereby, it is a cultural reality comparable to others. It searches for implications and sequences, it establishes order: order among the themes of life for the believer (sinning, justification, sanctification, hope for the end), order among the themes of life and absolute events (Incarnation, Cross, Resurrection, Parousia), in short, order among a totality of experience and a totality of events. However dialectical, however streaked with antitheses this order is—distended between incarnation and redemption, between individual conversion and communal life, between present life and eternal life, between historical effort and last ends—it is yet a way of understanding. As such, it uses languages, notional apparatuses of philosophy, of law, of the surrounding social life, and thus mixes in with the whole of culture.

Theology intermingles with culture not only by *integrating* cultural elements, but also by *opposing* itself functionally to this other tentative so as to recapture the whole of our existence, that is to say by opposing itself to philosophy. Theological truth is constituted by this very polarity: there may be preaching which is indifferent to philosophy, but there can be no theology without philosophical reference, and this reference cannot fail to be a nascent opposition, at least one of a methodological type. Indeed, if theological understanding is a critique of preaching, and if, in this quality, it is always in harmony with a community of the faithful, then philosophy is a critique of the understanding and of knowledge. Its base of reference is the ideal of rational knowledge, and, to be more precise, contemporary science such as it fashions the structure of the understanding at a given moment. The will to understand universally is necessarily in tension with the theological will to understand by absolute events and by an experience centered on these absolute events. This polarity is now going to acquire its dramatic form as we take up the elucidation of the violent and authoritarian synthesis of truth.

Theology affects culture not only by its manner of understanding, but also by its character of authority. Authority is not a superadded social accident in theology; it is a fundamental aspect of the Revelation and the truth which the believer confesses. The events of Revelation are capable of changing *my* life; but they are likewise promotive of a new communal existence. In this sense, these events have authority over *my* life and over *our* community. The word of God is authority by virtue of its meaning for me and for us. Authority is a fundamental phenomenon of the religious sphere: God wills something for me and for us. As Cullmann has demonstrated, this is the primary meaning of the term *dogma*, which is more radical and more vast than the term *doctrina* which only explicates the dogma's theoretical dimension: the *dogma* is an order for me coming from an absolute event, and which, as such, contains implicitly a *doctrina*. It is through this roundabout way that Truth is authority; the sequence presents itself thus: authority of the Word, authority of scriptural testimony, authority of faithful preaching, authority of theology.

Frightful trust—and frightful temptation for the "authorities" of the Christian community to exercise this authority of the Word! For here we have an authority of man over man—the authority of the priest, of the leader of the Church—which the authority of the Word of God with respect to man seems to authenticate and support. The ambiguity of a special sociological authority and of the authority of the Truth is inscribed in the very ambiguity of the ecclesial reality.

This ambiguity is the privileged trap for the clerical passion. For there is a clerical "pathos" which is at one and the same time *rabies theologica* and passion for power. More often than not, it coincides with the despotic spirit and the narrowness of the field of consciousness that comes with age. This passion is all the more treacherous for it believes itself to be serving the truth. It accompanies the history of the Church and the history of Churches as an ever-present shadow.

With this fundamental situation of clerical authority as a basis, we must now attempt to understand the endemic pretension of Churches in order to recapitulate all the levels of truth within one *present* system which would be both a *doctrina* and a civilization. It is not a pure historical accident that during the Middle Ages there was an attempt to link the Word to a system of the world, to an astronomy, a physics, to a social system. This endeavor has its roots in the passional deviation of ecclesiastical authority into clerical power. The whole conception of Christianity would have to be thought out anew on the basis of a critique of the passions of unity. This grandiose endeavor would express both the grandeur of man seeking unity and the culpability of clerical violence.

It is here that falsehood is most contiguous with the truth: what is really called for is a complete exegesis of the falsehood which results from clerical motivations. How many ruses there are in order to remain "conformed," as if nothing were more like the conformity of the truth than the conformism of the false! Whoever introduces changes in astronomy or in physics will try to hide, from others or even from himself, the breach with the clerical synthesis that his discovery entails. The day of these maneuvers, of these adjustments and ways of saying without saying, of insinuating and backing out, is not over. Possibly cosmology no longer raises such problems today—at least not in the same terms as used during the Renaissance—but more recently biology, and, today and in the future, the sciences of man create and will continue to create the same type of alternative which almost cost Galileo his life. The clerical passion is capable of engendering all the fundamental forms of falsehood which are reinvented by political totalitarianism: from the commonplace untruth, dissimulation, and trickery, to the art of deception which is the soul of propaganda and which consists in congealing a set of beliefs, customs, notions, and symbols into an undivided mass which presents a sort of glossy, steely surface, impervious to the dissolving action of reflection and criticism. In its turn, this active falsehood of clerical propaganda, which has often lost the threads of its own plots, serves as a cover for "the most cunning of the beasts of the garden"—imposture—imposture or bad faith consolidated into faith.

It seems to me that at this point, the phenomenon of the sundering of truth, which we have identified, in general, with the spirit of the Renaissance, takes on an entirely new sense. We described this phenomenon as a process of methodological differentiation. This process may now be reinterpreted in light of our reflections on the clerical synthesis.

1. It appears that this sundering of truth has been first and foremost the rupture of the clerical unity of truth.

2. The autonomy of science is the privileged point of this rupture: in this regard the incident involving Galileo has a symbolic significance: "And yet it turns. . . ." This affair is not an historical accident; it sums up a permanent drama: the drama of the authoritarian truth of Revelation and the libertarian truth of science. But this autonomy of science, in its turn, always risks swinging toward a new dogmatism, a pretentious self-sufficiency which has its own "pathos" in face of that of the theologian.

3. If science is the locale of the rupture, philosophy, with its power of questioning endlessly, is the nerve of the revolt. It is here that we again encounter our reflections on the polarity of theology and philosophy; but now it is necessary to complete them. For this

methodological polarity between two manners of understanding, of thinking by totality, now splits into a passional polarity, and a culpable polarity. For if there is a theological "pathos," there is also a philosophical "pathos." Confronting this "pathos" of authority is the "pathos" of freedom as defiance; and that is something which is not easily admitted by the philosopher. When freedom becomes mad, it no longer tolerates the authority of the Word, and, "throwing the baby out with the bath," expels the ecclesial along with the clerical and rejects the "obedience of the faith," of which St. Paul speaks, along with clerical obedience. Thus, philosophy and theology encounter each other throughout the course of Western history by means of their peculiar passional expressions. The philosopher denounces the Inquisition and intercedes in behalf of Galileo against clerical violence. The theologian denounces the *hybris* of towering philosophical systems, even if and especially if these systems pretend to be the system of God. The philosopher and the theologian both evince something essential, the one the audacity of truth and the other the obedience to the Truth. But perhaps it is not the case that they are cured of their vice to such an extent that they may declare the truth which would prove their position. Perhaps it is not possible for the theologian to declare, without a spirit of annexation and bitter satisfaction, the frightful word: "I shall destroy the wisdom of the wise, and I shall dumbfound the intelligence of the clever." Perhaps it is not possible for the philosopher to make use of the glorious and overwhelming freedom of Socratic doubt without arrogance.

4. For the Christian, the rupturing of this violent unity of truth is desirable. On the one hand, it indicates the conscious awareness of all the possibilities of truth and the range of man. On the other, it signifies the purification of the truth of the Word. The Word of creation and of re-creation is not a language of science, is neither a cosmology nor even an ethics or an aesthetics. It is of another order. This division can only be, in our passional economy, but a cruel apprenticeship of the rupture, a harsh schooling in deception in which the actual breach is the only possible solution for reparation. This rude process is still going on in the sciences of man, history, the social sciences, psychology, and politics.

What, then, is the unity of truth for the Christian? It is an eschatological representation, the representation of the "last day." The "recapitulation of all things in Christ," in the words of the Epistle to the Colossians, signifies both that unity will be "manifested at the last day" and that unity is not to be found in history. In the meantime, we do not *know* what it means that there is a mathematical truth *and* the Truth which is Someone. At the very most, we sometimes perceive a few invaluable, congruent adumbrations which are as the "pledges of the Spirit," beyond all the violent syntheses and all the cultural dissociations of clerical unity.

Thus the idea of an "integral humanism," in which all the various levels of truth would be harmoniously situated, is an illusion. The ultimate meaning of man's perilous adventures and the values which they unfold is condemned to remain *ambiguous:* time remains the time of debate, discernment, and patience.

[3] THE POLITICAL SYNTHESIS OF TRUTH

WHAT WE HAVE JUST SAID of the "clerical" synthesis facilitates the approach to the second temptation of the unification of truth: by the *political* conscience.

Here we have a new set of relationships to be taken into consideration. In effect, politics has a fundamental vocation and capacity of grouping together the interests and goals of human existence. It is in political power that the destiny of a geohistorical group is secured: city, nation, or a block of nations. For each of us, life in the State is not one sector like the others of our existence: herein something is brought into play which concerns work and leisure, welfare and education, technics and the arts, and ultimately life and death, as war reminds us. Certainly this is why life in the State is an encompassing totality with respect to the sciences, the arts, and customs. Naturally this is evident from the fact that the sciences, the arts, and customs are realities which have a "public" character. The State, as a central, "public" will, has a minimum of responsibilities with respect to these activities of common interest. This holds true even for the most liberal State. Thus we have obviously reached the crossroads of the political sphere and the manifold orders of truth. In the last analysis, there is no problem which is politically neutral, that is to say without some bearing upon the life of the State.

I have intentionally stressed the Hegelian aspect of these notations so as to outline in a few words the irruption of the political sphere into the range of the concept of truth. The State is certainly one of the points in which the diverse filaments which we complacently unraveled in the first part are focalized.

Now the formation of a political conscience, especially since the French Revolution, coincides at once with the moment when the complexity of the levels of existence and truth reaches a high point of virulence, and with the moment when the dechristianization of our society leaves no place for the theological function of assembling: at the end of the triumph of the Renaissance, the stage is set for the transition from clerical violence to political violence.

How may the State exercise this hegemonic function, particularly over scientific research, over the aesthetic and even ethical parts of our lives? The Church exercised it by means of a doctrine, a doctrine having authority: theology. From the point of view of a sociology of knowledge, this mediating function between the power of the State and the different levels of human research has been adhered to by the philosophy of history for the past century.

All philosophies of history, of course, are not fitted for this function. Violence does not creep in through this door but upon two conditions. First, it is necessary for the philosophy of history to look upon itself as a search for a *unity of meanings*. This does not hold true for all philosophies of history. Secondly, as soon as the philosopher of history puts into perspective all the levels of truth, all cultural activities in relation to a guiding motive of history, he begins to exercise a virtual violence upon the diverging tendencies of history, even if his intention is only to understand and not to transform history. He says: "a single truth is in process and shall be: all contradictions will culminate in a higher synthesis." And indeed, he no longer tries to understand what does not come under his law of construction; he strikes it off and mentally destroys it.

The second condition for this type of actual violence is the identification, by the philosophy of history, of the sole law of construction (whether it is dialectical or non-dialectical) with a social force, with a "man of history." The tyranny of fascisms was so grotesque because their man of history was restricted to one nation and one race. Their philosophy of history was nothing but a provincialism without an over-all perspective on mankind, or else the subjection to the master race. This is why totalitarianism materialized in an almost pure state. The case of Marxism is uncommonly complex for in many respects, it is *the* philosophy of history *par excellence*: not only does it provide a formula for the dialectics of social forces—under the name of historical materialism—but it also sees in the proletarian class the reality which is at once universal and concrete and which, although it be oppressed today, will constitute the unity of history in the future. From this standpoint, the proletarian perspective furnishes both a theoretical meaning *of* history and a practical goal *for* history, a principle of explication and a line of action. Proletarian universalism is, in principle and fundamentally, liberating in comparison to fascist provincialism. But the capturing of power, in some province of the earth, by men of the dialectic causes the resurgence of all the authoritarian consequences of a philosophy of history which lays claim to the monopoly of orthodoxy.

Here is a State which looks upon itself at once as the humble instrument and the proud interpreter of the philosophy of history. All research and hypotheses, even scientific ones, are henceforth placed into perspective, oriented and carved out by this State; there are no more autonomous truths or detached scientific "objectivity." The liberal era opened at the Renaissance is closed. One can see, then, that from this standpoint, a debate in biology or in linguistics may be settled by reference to a political criterion.

Thus a universalist doctrine, through the prism of authority and power, may be just as tyrannical as a racist doctrine, if it understands its duty of unifying in the same way. Similarly, although more puerile, the *American way of life,* by refusing to be brought into question by the history of the rest of the world and professing to have a good conscience, is just as susceptible of inheriting Naziism as "democratic centralism." Whenever there is attempted the premature synthesis of the levels of existence and of truth, the same violent processes are repeated with the same banality.

I do not believe the sociological importance of the appearance of philosophies of history is understood if one does not first have a clear awareness of the course of cultural dispersion from which they encounter resistance. Nor do I believe this is understood if one is not aware of the historical role of the clerical synthesis. The philosophy of history is the crux of the political synthesis just as theology is the crux of the clerical synthesis. The functional parallelism between the integrating function of the philosophy of history and that of medieval theology is striking. The philosophy of history—whether it be dialectical or not—also cumulates a goal and a fault. On the one hand, the philosophy of history is one of the concrete manifestations of this will for unity in which we had recognized the grandeur of reason and of feeling; on the other, it testifies to that original violence which corrupts every claim to "system." Greatness and guilt attached to the political unity of truth. . . .

The functional parallelism between the clerical unity and the political unity of truth, or more precisely, the similarity between the instruments or organs of unity, between the theology and the philosophy of history, are expressed by a strange resemblance within the kingdom of falsehood. The clerical and political origins of falsehood have a striking affinity: clever submissiveness and cunning disobedience; propaganda adept at playing on all the psychological strings; censuring of opposing opinions and the placement of books and films on the index; the art of "make believe," coagulating all aspects of a civilization into a mentality impervious to external criticism; vicious transformation of Socratic doubt into self-criticism which merely restores the momentarily disturbed orthodoxy.

It may be objected, and rightly so, that the philosophy of history, and singularly the Marxist philosophy of history, is the only means of ordering the swelling of the past. Moreover, it would seem that it alone can provide a rational politics which is capable of encompassing both the interests of the proletarians and of colored people, and of formulating a long-range world politics. In short, Marxist universalism, by its nature and *par excellence,* rids us of the romantic violence of a "Führer" and a "Duce."

This is certainly true and it is for this reason that there is a problem. For that matter, our critique of the theological synthesis of truth was not totally negative either. For we have insisted on the *eschatological* character of unity. Now we must lay stress on the fruitfulness of philosophies of history in general and of the Marxist dialectics in particular as a *working hypothesis,* that is to say both as a *method* for researchers and as a *probable* rule for politicians.

We are in search of and in need of order: within the medley of historical fibers, every hypothesis justifies itself by its power of discovery and of comprehensive simplification. In this regard, the socio-economic schema has an obvious superiority over the arbitrary recital of battles, successions, and divisions in ancient military and dynastic history. Further, the interpretative function of a Marxist "great hypothesis" is doubly potent in its political fruitfulness in that it serves not only to explain but to orient the actual liberating movements of the proletariat and of colored people. But history is extraordinarily rich; it allows for many other interpretations and it is necessary for us to keep in mind the *limiting action* of other possible schemata so as to shield ourselves against the fanaticism which springs up with all premature unity.

This *limiting action* exercised by other great hypotheses seems to play the same role as the eschatological idea in face of the clerical temptation. Consequently, it merits our attention. Without attempting to outline these other working hypotheses, I would like to show the principal reasons why a plurality of systems of interpretation is possible. For this I shall refer the plurality to the very core of the growing movement of history. The history which we write, retrospective history (*die Historie*) is made possible by the history which is made (*die Geschichte*). If there are several possible interpretations of history, perhaps it is because there are several entangled movements of "historization," if I may use the expression.

We carry on several histories simultaneously, in times whose periods, crises, and pauses do not coincide. We enchain, abandon, and resume several histories, much as a chess player who plays several games at once, renewing now with one, now with another.

If it were necessary to extend the elucidation of this major illusion of the unicity of history, I would not hesitate to say that a stubborn illusion as to the nature of time is concealed therein. We presuppose that there is a continuous trajectory, a single duration, which synchronizes history, whether this be the one of the two cities of St. Augustine, the history of the sciences and empires, or the history of philosophy or art.

Actually, we are drawing upon certain intuitions of mechanics for the model of the uniform and continuous movement after which all durations are patterned. Thus our wish is that all the events of history mark a single, undifferentiated, and continuous flux which would be the flow *of* time.

One may suspect that Bachelard's reflection on temporal superpositions,[4] if transferred to the core of the philosophy of history, would there work havoc and undermine the basic postulate of a unified flow of history. The great "symphony of history" of which St. Augustine wrote—and upon which Marrou reflected recently—is structured by innumerable axes which have their own way of linking together and enduring, and they permit us to see that global interpretations are premature.

Thus there is a history of the sciences which structures a time of discoveries, spanning huge lacunae and joining together a discontinuous series of creations. These inventions, detached from their inventors, accumulate and are stratified in a single history of knowledge whose line traverses the socio-economic dialectics, the rise and fall of empires. Naturally, one could describe many other histories which have their own peculiar type of sequence.

Technical discoveries have a somewhat similar way of linking

---

4. *La Dialectique de la durée* (Paris: P.U.F., 1950).

together by cumulation and of enduring by capitalization. Thus a time of progress is constituted which is by no means the sole temporal axis of our existence but which traverses all histories as a projectile of becoming. Here nothing is lost, everything accumulates: Chinese powder, Semitic hand-writing, the English steam engine, etc. All histories which have this same cumulative style—the history of scientific discoveries, of instrumental inventions, industrial techniques, of comfort and war—all these histories are easy to apply to the same axis of duration, which we are prone to confuse with the time of mechanics, patterned on the movement of the stars. Here is the occasion for illusion; a single historical rhythm, in collusion with the time of mechanics, furnishes the canvas of dates, that is, coincidences and rendezvous, like the measures on a symphonic score.

But other historical rhythms are jumbled together which are not exactly linked to the axis of the progress of sciences and technics. Civilizing cycles open and close, powers rise and consolidate; time here requires categories other than those of sedimentation and progress: notions of crisis, apogee, renaissance, survival, and revolution; a time of bulges and sags (in a sense, this time is more related to the periodic structure of the phenomena of microphysics than to the linear structure of the time of kinematics and pure mechanics).

Moreover, a new civilization does not have one massive tempo: it does not advance as a whole nor does it stagnate in all respects. In it there are several lines which may be followed longitudinally. The tide neither rises nor goes out at the same time on all the shores of a nation's life. The crises of a particular social or cultural behavior have their peculiar motivations and rightful solutions. Thus the crisis in mathematics during the Pythagorean era was for the most part independent of the general history of the time; it was a challenge internal to the mathematics (the irrationality of the diagonal in relation to the side of the square) [5] which gave rise to it: as the result of a strictly mathematical procedure, this crisis had a strictly mathematical solution.

The history of music would give support to reflections of the same order, although with a higher degree of complexity. In a sense, one can consider the history of music as a relatively autonomous sequence of stages in the technique of musical composition. The development of music, however, also expresses the lateral

5. What the author apparently refers to is the irrationality of the numerical value of the hypotenuse of an isosceles right triangle to the numerical value of its sides.—Trans.

suggestions of the other arts and of sensitivity in general; it manifests the expectations of a public, or even the dictates of benefactors or the State. The history of music, with its, so to speak, longitudinal motivation, is constituted as a technical series by itself; but it is also a series of inventive explosions linked to great creators. And lastly, with its transversal relationships to other manifestations of culture and life, it is constituted as one aspect of the epoch.

Thus the same history, which is one by the progress of material and intellectual equipment, has many ways of being multiple. Not only is it divided into successive periods (which already raises many problems), but also into longitudinal fibers which do not have the same mode of linking together and do not propose the same temporal problematic. The idea of "integral history" is therefore a limiting idea; any dialectic is oversimplified and overburdened with the criss-crossing of the longitudinal motivations proper to each series and with the transversal interferences from one series to another. It would require the simultaneous reading of the counterpoints established, as it were, by the rhythmic horizontal movements and by the harmonious vertical movements. Everything leads us back to the *circular* character of the most manifest dialectics which we can uncover. One example: in a sense, the progress of technics and machinery sweeps along with it the whole social process as well as ideological super-structures. But in their turn, technics depends on the sciences and principally upon mathematics, which flourished under the influence of the great metaphysical systems such as those of the Pythagorean, Platonic, and Renaissance Neo-Platonic eras. Without these idealist metaphysical systems, the very idea of a mathematization of nature would have been unthinkable.

Thus there is a "naïveté" in dialectics which endeavors to establish a unique and sole meaning unto itself. Many histories may be written—of technics and of work, of classes and of civilizations, of law, of political power, and of ideas—without taking into account this history of the calling into question of history by Socratic, Cartesian, and Kantian subjectivity, which is the second-level history of philosophical reflection.

It appeared necessary to go to the root of the problem in order to initiate the internal critique of all the claims which pretend to have resolved, by history, the problem of the unity of the orders of truth. It is imperative to keep this reflection on the alert against every justification of the passions of power which would support itself by means of a dogmatic philosophy of history.

I shall conclude by stressing the significance of these reflections for an investigation of falsehood in the modern world. As long as one remains on a banal level of truth and concerns oneself with the idle thoughts of daily propositions (such as: "it's raining"), the problem of falsehood merely relates to *saying* (what is said is a distortion of the very thing which is known or believed not to be true; one does not say what is known or believed to be true). This falsehood, which thus presupposes the truth as known, has veracity for its contrary, while the contrary of truth is error. The two pairs of contraries (falsehood-veracity, error-truth) therefore seem unrelated.

However, in the measure that we rise toward the truths which it is necessary to form and fashion, truth enters into the range of *oeuvres*, principally into the realm of the achievements of civilization. In view of this, falsehood may well concern the act or work of searching for the truth. The falsehood which most "dissimulates" need not necessarily be one pertaining to the expression of known truth, but rather the one which perverts the search for truth. It would appear that we have touched upon a point where the spirit of falsehood—which is prior to falsehoods—borders on the spirit of truth which is itself prior to enunciated truths. This point is the one in which the question of truth culminates in the problem of the total unity of truths and the levels of truth. The spirit of falsehood essentially contaminates the search for truth inasmuch as it requires unity. *It is the erroneous movement from the total to the totalitarian.* This movement takes place historically when a sociological *power* inclines toward, and more or less completely succeeds in regrouping all orders of truth and in forcing men to the violence of unity. This sociological power takes two typical forms: clerical power and political power. It so happens, in fact, that both have an authentic function of consolidation; the religious totality and the political totality are genuine totalities of our existence. This is why they are the two greatest temptations for the spirit of falsehood, the lapse from the total to the totalitarian. Power, and *par excellence* clerical and political power, is the occasion of lapse and virtual culpability.

On the basis of these remarks on the interconnection between totality, falsehood, and power, the tasks for a spirit of truth would be the following:

1. Within the context of the concrete life of a civilization, the spirit of truth is to respect the complexity of the various orders of truth; it is the recognition of plurality. It may even be said that this recognition enables one to discern certain *circles* among these

orders of truth, and this would counter our tendency to establish *hierarchies* prematurely. (I have pointed out one of these circles between the world as an horizon of my existence, the scientific objectification of nature, and the moral, aesthetic, and utilitarian evaluations of my cultural life.) *The "circle" is a representation of failure for premature unity.*

2. The autonomy of scientific research is one of the criteria of the spirit of truth of a society. Man has run the risk of objectification and objectivity; it is a venture which may not be limited in its own pursuit but merely categorized as one of the aspects of total "praxis," as a theoretical "praxis." This is why the spirit of truth will not criticize the dehumanization of man by scientific objectivity; the tyrant also uses this language.

3. Another criterion of the spirit of truth is the repugnance of art and literature for the clerical and political apologetic: one must not hasten to enjoin an immediate effectiveness for the arts; falsehood enters through this passion for usefulness or edification. An artist, however, will serve his epoch more surely—and unknowingly—if his first concern is to understand the internal problematic of his art and of expressing himself in the most exacting way. Perhaps an "engaged" literature will have ultimately expressed only the most trivial aspects of the conscience of its time. And perhaps a "disengaged" literature will have penetrated to a depth of feeling and human desire which is more pregnant with the future. In short, the artist and the scientist need never fear of overstating the ancient Socratic critique of the useful in their quest for the truth of their particular domain.

4. A reflection on the connection between totalitarian power and falsehood should initiate a useful critique of the political conscience. From the point of view of our subject, two important aspects of this critique are to be retained: the idea of politics as *science* must be exposed as false. The level of this fundamental political function remains "opinion" in the Platonic sense, or better, the *probable,* as Aristotle viewed it; there is never but a political "probabilism." On the other hand, the idea of a *unique and exhaustive* dialectical understanding of the social dynamic must be exposed as false; dialectics is a method and a working hypothesis; it is excellent when it is limited by other possible systems of interpretation . . . , and when it is not in power.

5. Lastly, Christians must rediscover the *eschatological* sense of the unity of truth, the significance of the "Last Day" which "will come like a thief" and fulfill "history," "recapitulating all things in Christ." An important task of present-day Christian theology is to

reflect jointly on an eschatology of truth and an eschatology of history. It seems to me that this reflection should dominate all thinking on the concept of Church authority whose splendors and deadly trappings 1 have emphasized. Eschatology is the cure for clericalism. And if such is the case, perhaps the Christian could then live among the extremest multiplicity of the orders of truth with the hope of "one day" comprehending unity just as he would be comprehended by it.

Note on the Wish and
Endeavor for Unity

EVERY APOLOGETIC tends to show that all truths ultimately agree and that religious truth fulfills and comprehends them all. We have rejected this point of view and have rather stressed the *diversity* and *difference* of "attitudes."

Yet can we abide by this decision and portion out into three or four different directions the "attitudes" which divide our life? Is the endeavor of apologetics to found the ultimate unity of all truth on "the Truth of God, of Christ, and the Holy Spirit," totally absurd? Does it not betray an exigency which is more fundamental than our *distinction* of attitudes?

One cannot profess multiplicity without denying oneself. There is some reason why the spirit inevitably searches within objects for the unity which it sees, knows, wishes, and believes in. In any case, plurality cannot be the absence of relations.

1. A primary unity is indispensable, but it is an entirely "formal" unity; it is the very one which is associated with the idea of truth. Ultimately, truth cannot be multiple without repudiating itself. The True and the One are two interchangeable notions. It is falsehood which is legion, error which is multiple. In searching for the One we look for the True. The most radical exigency of reason—it is to be noted that I am speaking of reason and not of scientific understanding—is that the whole of our attitudes, their methods and objects, constitute one single totality.

It is this exigency for the unity of truth which deceives us when we find that we possess but the scattered fragments of a great integrated culture. It is this exigency which impels us to stitch together the various domains of science, ethics, the fine arts, and faith into an elaborate and self-same tapestry. The intention is good but it is empty, for we have no way of offsetting the methodological cleavages by a super-knowledge which would encompass everything. We do not know the unity; we merely require it and this is why we call this unity "formal." For it only prescribes the task of unifying all the domains of existence—of human thought, action, and experience—without giving us the *intuition* which would fulfill this empty form.

2. Lacking the intuition which would show "materially" that the truth of a mathematical theorem is the *same* as the truth of an heroic action, the *same* as the truth of forgiveness and sacrifice, the *same* as the truth of creation and of salvation, our life as men in consequence involves two types of *concrete* unity.

The first is represented by the idea of "world." We have often said that diverse "attitudes" were different ways of living and of realizing our relationship to the "world." The same word "world" serves as a reference-point for all attitudes: cosmology is the science of the "world." Art history attempts to discover the perception of the "world" which was peculiar to the Gothic or Romantic man. Every philosophical attitude flows from a *Weltanschauung,* from a certain vision of the "world." The Bible records that "sin came into the *world"* and that the "Lamb of God takes away the sins of the *world.*"

Herein the world is no longer the unity of an abstract goal, of a form of reason, but *the most concrete horizon* of our existence. This may be made tangible in a very elementary way: it is at the level of perception that this unique horizon of our life as men stands out. Perception is the common source of all "attitudes." It is within the perceived world, in the world which involves my flesh and blood existence, that are encountered laboratories and the computations of the scientist, houses, libraries, museums, and churches. The "objects" of science are in the "things" of the world: atoms and electrons are structures which explain this world-lived-by-me-mind-and-flesh. The scientist himself locates them only by virtue of the instruments which he sees, touches, hears, *just as* he sees the sun rise and set, as he hears an explosion, as he touches a flower or a fruit. Everything takes place within this world. It is also within my life-world that a statue is beautiful, that a death is heroic, that a prayer is humble. It is my life-world and not the world of science which is transfigured into creation in the eyes of the psalmist: it is the trees which "clap their hands" and not the electrons and neutrons. The doctrine of creation which the Jews developed based upon their faith in the Master of history, based upon their experience of the Covenant, is a recapturing of the world of perception and not of the world of science; it is the world in which the sun rises and sets, in which animals yearn for the water of fountains. It is this primordial world which is transfigured into creative Word. It is in this sense that my life-world is the humus of all my acts, the soil of all my attitudes, the primordial stratum prior to all cultural multiplicity.[1]

But what does this *mean*? I am not able to grasp or master this unity, know it, or express it in a coherent discourse. For this primordial stratum of all experience is the always-pre-existing reality; it is always-already-before and I come too late to express it. The world is the word I have on the tip of my tongue which I will never express; it is there, but scarcely have I begun to *say* it when it is already the world of the scientist, the world of the artist and the world *of* such and such an artist: *of* Van Gogh, *of* Cézanne, *of* Matisse, *of* Picasso. It is the world of the believer and the world of such and such a believer: world *of* St. Francis, world *of* the *Imitation*, Jansenist world, and world *of* Claudel.

The unity of the "world" is too prior to be possessed, too lived to be known. It vanishes as soon as it is recognized. This is perhaps why a phenomenology of perception, which would try to furnish us with the philosophy of our being-in-the-world, is a wager akin to the quest for paradise. The unity of the world against which all "attitudes" stand out is merely the *horizon* of all these attitudes.

3. The same thing must be said about the unity which is the *correlate* of the unity of the world: man (me, so and so, such a civilization, such an integrated social group). It is indeed true that it is *the same* man who bears and produces science, art, ethics, and religion.

The same concrete man portions out his use of time as best he can. There is a time for science and a time for prayer, a time for work and a time for the movies, a time for eating and a time for love, a time for reading and a time for trifling. An identical *flux* of existence lays the ground for all attitudes. It is because the same man *lives* in all attitudes that he "suffers" the division of his life, he "suffers" the plurality of his objects, the methods and his attitudes. I remember the story of the deported person who left with a Bible in one pocket and a mathematical treatise in the other: "I don't know how the two go together," he said, "but I do know that I am the one who is carrying them."

1. Husserl called this the *Lebenswelt,* and Heidegger the *ontic* reality, which he opposes to the ontological.

And if man—sometimes man on the scale of a group, of an epoch—suffers this plurality as a *personal conflict,* it is because he lives all his "attitudes" necessarily in accordance with a passional style. Knowledge does not elude the passions; it is even the refuge of the most acute culpability, what the sacred writer called the concupiscence of knowing. There is a *hybris* of culture, of art, of science; one cannot see in fact how these enterprises could originate apart from these exalting passions. Because of these passions, the attitudes which we sagely divide into diverse sectors become telescoped in the same existence, encroach upon each other, confront their pretensions. From the methodological point of view, every intention (intention of objectivity, intention of aesthetic vision, etc.) is experienced as a pretension in the passional order. Intentions may be classified, pretensions tend to be excluded.

If we were to exploit this remark thoroughly, it would lead us back to the core of scientism: its exegesis pertains to the exegesis of passions as well as of methods. Scientism is the methodological intention of science (of the scientific act), but recaptured by a pretension. This pretension is that of giving to science the theological function of salvation.

Thus the intellectual history of the Occident has developed in such a way that the *diverse* attitudes of science, of art, and of theology appear only by means of the passional modes which are encountered. The clash between science and theology receives its mysterious profundity from these passions.

We therefore understand why we are incapable of coinciding with "the flux of existence which lays the ground for all attitudes." First, this unique experience, which is my unique life, is never reflected in its lived simplicity; it is immediately perceived through the diverse cultural realizations which divide it. In this respect, the same holds true for man as for the world, his correlate. Man's unity is too primordial to be understood; but above all, our cultural life is torn by the rivaling passions which have created it and to which religion adds its own: theological rage, pharisaic bad faith, ecclesiastical intolerance. . . .

The unity of the world and the unity of man are too near and yet too distant: near as an horizon which is never reached, distant as a figure seen through an infrangible pane of glass.

4. It is in relation to this triple unity of all our attitudes ("formal" unity, "worldly" unity, "existential" unity) that it is necessary to situate another species of unity. It is the unity which faith proposes to all cultural achievements: "eschatological" unity. Christianity does not propose, as an ultimate model of unity, the

historical realization of a totalitarian "Christendom," of a "Christian civilization" which would embody a Christian art, a Christian science, etc. No, the Christian unity of science and faith is not that of "Christendom." The unity of Christendom is forever a unity in the world, or, if you will, the unity of *a* world among other worlds, the Christian world. If it were to realize itself, this unity would be a violent unity, totalitarian perhaps, but not total.

The ultimate unity which Scripture calls "recapitulation of all things in Christ" is not a term immanent to our history; primarily, it signifies that history is *still* open, that the multiple is *still* in debate. Next, it signifies that the unity of the charity of Christ is *already* the hidden meaning of the multiple and that this unity will be manifested on the Last Day. It is therefore in hope that all things are one, that all truths are in the unique Truth. This is sufficient to enable us to bear patiently with the rifts of modern culture and, among them, the conflicts between science and faith.

Work and the Word

THE NEXUS IN OUR LIFE between speech and work testifies in the most manifest way as to what tensions are maintained by the dynamics of personal existence and the distressing ups and downs of civilizations. This nexus is at once a very primitive and fundamental articulation of our condition and a very rarefied product of the cultures and techniques which history displays. Consequently, one may catch sight of it in a nascent state within a very elementary phenomenological analysis of *saying* and *doing,* as well as capture it at a very high level of complexity in terms of the problems raised in our time by the situation of literature in a technical civilization, by the uneasy feeling in the universities, by the orientation of technical education, by the human problems posed by industrial mechanization, etc. We shall therefore attempt to place ourselves at the two extremities of this reflection: the side of the radical and the side of the present; the side of the roots of work and of speech, and the side of the contemporary tasks of a civilization of work and speech. A meditative interlude on the power of speech will separate the two versants.

But why this theme? For me it is the means of approaching the problem of the unity of civilization from a new angle, a problem which I approach elsewhere by the question of truth and the multiple orders of truth. It had already occurred to me that a civilization advances as much by pluralization and complication of tasks as by the progress of this organic unity which is witnessed in great periods. The primordial dialectic of speech and work leads us to the scene of the same debate. In point of fact, this essay results from deception and anxiety: deception before the contemporary philosophies of work (Marxist, Existentialist, Christian); anxiety in face of the notion of the civilization of work.

The discovery or rediscovery of man as worker is one of the great events of contemporary thought. Our aspiration to establish a civilization of work is in complete accord with the presuppositions of this philosophy of work, and I fully adhere to these philosophical presuppositions and to this socio-economic aspiration. My whole analysis tends to reply to the deception and anxiety which arise within and which are fostered by this adhesion.

My deception is in seeing this rehabilitation of work triumph in a void. Such a reflection starts with a determined form of work: work as a struggle with physical nature in the traditional crafts and in industrial machinery; then, by degrees, the notion of work swells until it encompasses all scientific, moral, and even speculative activities, tending toward the very indeterminate notion of a militant and non-contemplative form of human existence. From this standpoint, work designates the entire human condition of man, since there is nothing that man effects but by a toilsome act; there is nothing human which is not *praxis*. Moreover, if one considers that man's being is identical with his activity, then one must say that man *is* work. And this leads one to ask whether the philosophy of work should not extend itself so as to include the contemplation which is available to man, if it is true that a new realm of becoming and militant activity is yet opened within the core of an eternal life of man. Let it be said, therefore, that human contemplation is work also.

Lastly, by situating work within the continuation of divine creation, can we not see how a theology of work would thus reinforce the foundations and broaden the perspectives of a philosophy of work?

It is precisely this glorification of work which troubles me. A notion which signifies everything no longer signifies anything. Reflection pretends to retain the benefit of the analyses in which the notion of work has a determined meaning—it was expressed extremely well as the rugged virtue of the manual trades "in which one does not play with matter as with words or with a culture based upon words." But at the same time, the notion of work is broadened to the extreme so as to cumulate also the advantages which may be drawn from the indetermination of this notion. One is still thinking of manual work when one bestows upon man the general maxim: make and by making, make oneself [*faire et en faisant se faire*].

And yet there is no deceit in this mode of reflection which

gradually changes the meaning of *doing* from the most material to the most intellectual activity. Resistances become more refined and rebellious nature, with which man the worker battles, takes shelter successively in the obscurity of a world to be understood and, ultimately, in ourselves, in the resistance of a defiant body and in the opacity of our passions. Herein there is no fraud but a dissimulated partiality and, it may be said, a sort of overzealousness.

The problem does not lie in somewhere interrupting this progress of reflection which gradually relates all the sectors of man's activity to his militant condition. The question is rather one of combining with this interpretation of the human condition another interpretation which penetrates it through and through. For step by step, the spoken word also annexes to itself everything human; there is not a kingdom of work and an empire of the spoken word which would set bounds to each other from without, but there is a power of the spoken word which traverses and penetrates everything human, including the machine, the utensil, and the hand.

My deception suddenly takes on meaning: does not this sort of relaxation in the void of the admirable notion of work result from the absence of a contrary which would be proportioned to it and which, by limiting it, would determine it? It is to be noted that amid this glorification of work, one selects for it a contrary which is too remote, too vague, and, in short, one which is visionary and foreign to the human condition: contemplation. This does not mean a human contemplation which is pragmatic, but *pure* contemplation, the gaze which would make itself present to everything in the instant, vision without effort because it is without resistance, possession without duration because it is without effort. To identify existence with work amounts to excluding pure contemplation from the properly human condition. All of which is vain, and in any case scarcely instructive, for such a limiting idea is not a valid counter-pole for reflection. It is a chimera which withdraws from us, it fails to consider the full scope of the human. Is it not more fruitful to discriminate meaningful contrasts within the very core of human finitude, within the heart of man's militant life? Is it not more enlightening to find in work a counter-pole of proper proportions, which heightens the meaning of it while calling into question its sufficiency? For example: should I say that I am working when I go home and rest? Am I working when I read, when I am at the theatre, when I am taking a walk? Am I working in friendship and in love? And am I working when I am tinkering around the house? The splendor of work lies in being in debate with other manners of existing and of thereby limiting them and being limited by them. For us, the spoken word will be this *other*—this other among others which justifies and challenges the glory of work.

[1] DOING AND SAYING

LET IT BE SAID that the spoken word is also human; it too is a mode of finitude. It is not, as is pure contemplation, the transcending of the human condition; it is not the Word of God, the creative word, but the word of man, one aspect of his militant existence; it brings about and makes something within the world. Or to be more precise, speaking man makes something and makes himself, but otherwise than by working.

Let us watch the birth of the word on the brink of the gesture. Let us give the most favorable interpretation to the pragmatist conception of language: let us assume with Pierre Janet that the simplest word was a sort of imperative cry which, at first, accompanied and emotionally facilitated action (the experience called forth has no need of taking place in reality: it stands for an imaginative reconstruction which throws light on the present structure of language). The cry of the leader is detached from action as the initial phase which launches it; and thus the cry is word as soon as it incites to action instead of acting. The imperative cry therefore belongs to the cycle of the gesture: in a certain way it brings about the gesture. The cry is as a first, initiating fragment, then regulative of action. Step by step, every word may thus be brought back to *praxis:* in the simplest case it is only a moment of praxis; this moment becomes a stage of *praxis* as soon as the brief imperative cry takes on the proportions of an anticipating scheme, a Plan, this plan being only the verbal anticipation of *praxis*. Lastly, the whole structure of culture may be considered as the long detour which starts with action and returns to action.

Moment, stage, detour: the spoken word is, in a sense and an authentic sense, an annex of the enterprises of transforming the human milieu by the human agent. This fundamental possibility justifies a Marxist interpretation of culture in which work is seen as the power which reorganizes the full scope of the human.

And yet, from the outset, the spoken word transgresses the bounds of the gesture and bolts forward. For the imperative is now no longer an emotional portion of action in process; in a certain way it already stands for the whole of action. It *"means"* the whole of the gesture; it has an overview of it, it supervises it. (We shall presently find that among the psycho-technicians of industrial work this function of supervision—*Übersichtlichkeit*—contains in an embryonic way the intellectuality capable of redeeming repetitious piecework; thus we are not straying onto the fringes of the concrete problems of civilization, but situating ourselves in advance within the very core of the problems raised, for example, by technical humanism.)

The imperative which presently arose on the confines of the gesture in the act of being performed, allows for the fulfillment of a first level of aloofness, a first reflective withdrawal, which, thanks to the interval, the gap hollowed into the plenum of the gesture in the act of being performed, allows for the projective design of the total gesture.

Taken at the level of the gesture, the spoken word outruns every gesture by *signifying* it. It is the understood meaning of what is to be done. On this basis, it is always possible to look upon the history of work as saturated and carried forward by a history of the spoken word. Garrulous man transforms his utensils by anticipating in language new ways of relating the body to matter. The tool prolongs the body to such an extent that it cannot contain the principles of its own revolution within itself. If the tool is left, so to speak, to itself, then it is of the order of custom and dormancy, as is shown by the permanence and resistance to change of small craft and farm equipment. It is the spoken word which upsets the established form of the gesture and the tool; failure and suffering plunge man into reflection and questioning. At this moment, the interior word takes form: what other way is there? The tool held in suspense, the spoken tool is suddenly penetrated by other forms of action; a disruption of the form, a restructuration of the uses of the body is effected by language; language anticipates, signifies, and assays all transformations within the imagination, within this inventive void opened by failure and interrogation on failure.

But above all, it is the spoken word which effects the passage from the tool to the machine. As Emmanuel Mounier said in *La Petite Peur du XXe siècle*, "the machine is not, as is the tool, a mere material prolongation of our limbs. It is of another order: an annex of our language, an auxiliary language of mathematics to penetrate, stamp out, and reveal the secret of things, their implicit intentions, their untapped possibilities."

It is because man has expressed space in geometry, instead of living and experiencing it in actual measurements, that mathematics has been possible and, through it, mathematical physics and the techniques resulting from successive industrial revolutions. It is striking that Plato contributed to the construction of Euclidian geometry through his work of denominating such concepts as line, surface, equality, and the similarity of figures, etc., which strictly forbade all recourse and all allusion to manipulations, to physical transformations of figures. This asceticism of mathematical language, to which we owe, in the last analysis, all our machines since the dawn of the mechanical age, would have been impossible without the logical heroism of a Parmenides denying the entirety of the world of becoming and of *praxis* in the name of the self-identity of significations. It is to this denial of movement and work that we owe the achievements of Euclid, of Galileo, modern mechanism, and all our devices and apparatus. For within these, all our knowledge is contracted, all the words which at first did not attempt to transform the world. Thanks to this conversion of language into pure thought, the technical world may today appear to us in its entirety as the invasion of the verbal world into the muscular world. This absorption of pragmatic behaviors by the comprehensive behavior is very illuminating: within the very core of productive activity it reveals to us the initial composition of, but also the nascent debate between the spoken word and work. This mutual encroachment is already original contestation: *praxis* annexes the spoken word to itself as a language of planning; but the spoken word is originally reflective aloofness, "consideration of meaning," *theoria* in the nascent state. This primitive and ever-recurring dialectic invites us to reject once and for all every behaviorist and, *a fortiori*, epiphenomenalist interpretation of the so-called cultural superstructures of society. Language is just as much infrastructure as superstructure. The schema of the infrastructure and the superstructure must be rejected resolutely, for here we encounter a strictly circular phenomenon in which the two terms, in turn, implicate each other and transcend each other.

[2] POWER OF THE SPOKEN WORD

THE WORD which is closest to work, the imperative word, is in its nascent state already a *critique* of work in the double sense of a judgment and an imposition of limits. It is a critique of work because it suspends from the outset the concern with living which is the soul of work. It assumes an aloof attitude, it *reflects*. But if it suspends this concern, it returns to it differently; it substitutes a new way of approach which still belongs to the militant condition of man, to human finitude: it returns to this concern on the level of *signs*. Let us linger for a while within the narrow framework of the imperative word which provided us with the means for opening a first breach in the closed preoccupation of action. What new *operation* does the word bring into play within the confines of work?

First, it initiates a specific action upon others, and this pertains to *influence* and not to *production*. Production bears upon nature, be it material or not—upon an "it" in the third person. The influence, in the same imperative form of exigency, already presupposes another, a second person: whether it be urgent or refined, brutal or disguised, the exigency stirs up in others a "sequel" which is no longer an "effect." The relation of exigency-sequel [1] transcends the production-product relationship. The interhuman relationship, born of the word, endows work with both a contrast and a component. A contrast: for influence is something other than this action of non-reciprocal transformation characteristic of production. A component: for the influence at the same time enriches work with the whole gamut of interhuman relations: all labor is collaboration, that is, work which is not only shared but communicated to others. Psycho-sociology is constantly referring to this social and verbal stratum—social *because* verbal—of work. Thus low efficiency and fatigue are influenced by the deterioration of human relations which result not only from the division of work as such, but also from the social organization of work: relations of camaraderie within work-centers, relations of execution between research departments and workshops, relations of social subordination between management and labor, without excluding all the social relations which weave their way into the vast enterprise of business and labor. All these relations which order work (in all the senses of the word order) are found within the universe of the spoken word.

But the imperative word does not only work with respect to others, but also with regard to man who, through the word, becomes a signifying being. Whoever speaks pronounces also upon himself, decides himself; he thus passes judgment upon himself and this elucidates him and breaks up the previous affective confusion. The interior word, which every decision involves, is a striking manifestation of the promotion of mankind represented

1. With respect to this point and certain others in the following pages, I am indebted to the recent book by Walter Porzer, *das Wunder der Sprache*, chap. IX: "Die Leistung der Sprache" (The Achievement of the Word).

by the word: if I say nothing to myself, I do not emerge from the inhuman confusion of the beast. Without the word I am no more ordered than my work.

We shall have to distinguish, behind this work upon others and upon the self—behind the word which influences, behind the word by which I pass judgment upon myself and decide myself—the most dissimulated operation of the word: the operation of the sign itself on meaning, the promotion of meaning achieved by the word. The word, we said, does not "make" anything, at most it incites to action (whether this be by another or by myself treated as another); but if it incites to action this is because it *signifies* what is to be done and because the exigency signified to another is "understood" by him and "followed" by him.

To signify a meaning is, in a very complex way, to operate. It is not possible within the limitations of this essay to give more than a few allusive ideas on this operation which is nevertheless the true counterpart of work, even within work.

To begin with, there is no word without an activity of discrimination by which the verb of action and its agent (and eventually its term, its effect, its means) are distinguished. To this activity of discrimination is connected the great work of denomination, for the two activities are linked together: to distinguish and name objects, the aspects of objects, actions, qualities, etc. To discriminate is the first work, to articulate is the second. The word articulates in phrases, verbs and nouns, adjectives, complements, plurals, etc., and because of this we are able to master our action by a sort of "phrasing" of our gestures. All of our action is thus based upon distinctions and relations. Without this "phrasing" man remains inarticulate and in a state of confusion. The meaning of this phrasing is not a transformation of things or of ourselves, is not a production in the literal sense, but a signification, and every signification designates emptily what work will fulfill in the sense in which one fulfills a plan, a wish, a purpose.

This void of significations is undoubtedly the source of the misery of language and the misery of philosophy; but it is primarily responsible for the splendor of language, for it is through this void of significations, which designate without making something, that the word connects and structures action.

Now this "powerlessness" of the word, compared with the "power" of work, is certainly an operation, an achievement, without the word being, however, a work in the literal sense of the word. To express the same thing more concretely, what we called the "phrasing" of action is a "proposition" (in the sense in which we speak in grammar of a relative proposition or clause). Now, every proposition manifests an act of *setting forth*. The man who speaks *sets forth* a meaning; this is his verbal way of working.

This positional activity is dissimulated within the ordinary word, overworked as it is by use. It comes to the fore in mathematical language in which denomination is always fresh. "We call volume a portion of space limited in every direction. We call surface . . . we call line . . . lastly we call point. . . ." A short time ago, Brice Parain was amazed over this power of setting forth, of *forming* a meaning by naming: "Denomination is the first judgment . . . Our words create beings and . . . are not content to manifest sensations . . . Language is by its nature an abstraction in this sense that it does not manifest reality but signifies it in truth." [2] The responsibility of speaking correctly is surely overwhelming.

1. *The Dubitative Word*

THE WORD is not only imperative; it is time to remove the restrictions which were imposed on our analysis by an entirely pedagogical fiction. Besides, a reflection on the positional work of language already transcended the framework of the imperative.

The word which wishes to express, the word which tries to understand and which aspires to be understood, is also the word as dubitative, as optative, and as poetic.

The imperative incites to action. The dubitative word questions: What? What does that mean? There is questioning only because there is doubt; calling into question and putting into doubt. Just as the tool is characterized by custom and dormancy, the word in its first movement is custom and dormancy: one says that . . . The "one does it thus" is sustained by the "one says." Stagnant civilizations lie dormant upon their treasure of tools and phrases.

Belief, as a spontaneous movement of pre-critical existence, stamps with its everydayness all manners of working and speaking, and preserves gestures and locutions in dead tradition. The word is the awakening of the tool, as we said earlier, only because the word is the awakening of the word: "You think so?"

The dubitative word is directed toward the other, toward me, toward meaning. The dubitative word is *par excellence* the word addressed to another. The other is the man with a response. And in

2. Brice Parain, *Recherches sur la nature et les fonctions du langage* (Paris, 1946).

the response he is wholly second person; he is no longer the "it" characteristic of the factory-produced product but the "thou" who answers. Yet the word does imitate industrial work when it tries to produce a psychological effect after the fashion in which work obtains its effect, that is to say without reciprocity between the product and the producer. Such is the word of propaganda which achieves its psychological effects in the manner in which the machine draws an efficacious form from a wrought material. This word is quite removed from the cycle of question and answer. It produces; it does not call forth. Only doubt converts the word into question and questioning into dialogue, that is to say into a question *in view* of an answer and into an answer *to* a question.

The world of dialogue penetrates and outruns the world of work: it penetrates it because there is no work without a division of work and no division of work without a verbal exchange which portions out tasks and brings out the social meaning of human work. But the world of dialogue also transcends the world of work: the psycho-sociology of repetitious piecework informs us that, oddly enough, workers who are capable of freeing themselves mentally from a work which is the more effectual as it is the more automatic have a better output when they can "talk" while working. Here the word is an aid to work because it compensates it, because it *distracts* it. What shall we say, then, of dialogue as *leisure,* this leisure in which so many men are increasingly seeking their true self-expression, work becoming the necessary social sacrifice for its conquest?

But we shall prolong these diverse bearings of the word on work with respect to the civilization of work.

This appeal to another, turned toward myself, is the essential calling into question which creates the space of reflection and the space of freedom: "I wonder if. . . ." Interior dialogue is reflection itself. I make myself the man of *irony.* Henceforth, the indisputable worm is in the fruit of my own customs, in the tree of work, in the stump of belief. The word is critical and makes every position critical. The end of "naïveté" begins. Naïveté is of the order of the "there is": there are things, there is nature, there is history, there is the law of work, there is the power of those who command. The thing, the act of making and inciting to action is virtually brought into question by the dubitative word: world, work, and tyrants are globally contested by the corrosive power of the word. The great philosophers of the question—and of the "calling into question"—Socrates, Descartes, Hume, Kant, Husserl have elucidated and carried to its extreme point this dubitative genius of the word. In this they are the soul of every culture which rebels against the always premature syntheses proposed and imposed by the civilizations of collective belief, whether the unifying theme of these civilizations be the robe, the sword, or the tool.

Still more radically, the dubitative word effects the decisive revolution within the order of significations: it introduces the dimension of the *possible* into the undivided fabric of the brute fact (in the double sense of being a fact and the reporting of a fact). By creating the realm of the free play of possibility, the word recaptures the meaning of the real—of doing and of the fact—in terms of possible meaning; this is what is done by scientific law, juridical law. It is also this "disengagement" of thought by means of the question which makes possible all "engagement," as a movement subsequent upon reflection, as a responsible act.

If we examine the matter closely, we find that dubitative thought is the true founder of all thought which denies and which affirms, and ultimately of the most simple statements. For the decisive response, the first response, is the one which says *no,* the one which introduces negativity into significations: all that is, is; but the word can express what is not; and in this way what is done may be undone. To deny is to cancel out a possible meaning. It is the unproductive gesture *par excellence;* a gesture which does not work; but a gesture which introduces into spontaneous belief, into the naive positing of meaning, the decisive feature which cancels and deposes the positing, much as a prince is deposed. Hereafter the world of the word is one in which one *denies.* This is why this world is also one in which one affirms: affirmation underscores what negation may cancel or has already cancelled; it validates what negation invalidates. It is in the world of the dubitative word that there are contestations. It is in the world of contestation that there are affirmations.

Consequently, one may say that even statements which on the surface only record facts are conquests of dubitative thought; for a statement is like an answer whose question is left out. There is no narrative which does not answer virtually the question: what happened? How did that take place? And all science is like an answer to the quandaries of perception, erected by philosophy into doubt over the meaning of sensible qualities and into denial of the prestige of appearances.

This doubt and this denial alone have been able to open this realm of possibility in which we have seen appear a law as abstract and as unreal as, for example, the principle of inertia, to which no submissiveness to appearances had been able to lead and from which we have nevertheless derived all thought on mechanism.

2. *Invocation*

IT WOULD NOT BE JUST, however, to enclose the whole of the power of the word within the alternative between the imperative and the critical functions, even when broadening the empire of the dubitative word to affirmation and expression.

Protagoras maintained that the four roots of the word were the command, the wish or request, the question, and the answer. This title—*eukhôlé:* wish, request—opens a vast arena of the word which protects speaking man from the alternative between the imperative, which would ultimately become identified with work, and doubt which, in the last analysis, would destroy man as worker.

Strictly speaking, another empire opens up here: the request which expects everything from another, which offers man to the benevolence of another, is no longer concerned with the self as worker, nor with the ironic self, but, if you will, with the "beseeching" [*orant*] self. It is a human word which is not altogether disenchanted: turned toward God, it *invokes Him* in the language of the chorus of Greek tragedy, in that of the Hebraic psalm, in that of Christian liturgies, in that of the spontaneous prayer of the believer which borders on the everyday modality. Turned toward the world, it attempts to be the *veritable chant* expressing the uncommon meaning, the freshness, the strangeness, the horror, the sweetness, the first upheaval, peace: Hölderlin and Rilke, Ramuz and Claudel demonstrate that the word is not confined to the verbal function of daily living, to techniques and sciences, to codes, politics, politeness, and ordinary conversations.

Turned toward abstract significations, the word which requests is the *optative* of value, the fundamental act of evaluation. It is not by chance that Socrates fought the battle of language over the meaning of the word "virtue," that is to say, the good in man. In opening the field of the possible, the word opens also that of the better. Henceforth the question is posed: what does my work mean, that is to say, what is its value? Work is human work beginning with this question concerning the personal and communal value of work; and this question is a matter for the word.

Turned toward men and toward myself, the word which "entreats" is *par excellence* the language of *exclamation*. If the human condition may be discovered and expressed in its fundamental affective dispositions, it is because the cry has been replaced by the chant, a language similar to that of invocation which has seized the daily expressions of sadness and joy, of anger and fear so as to elevate them to the lyrical level of purified expression. Greek tragedy, the tradegy of Aeschylus, chanted the bitter knowledge which the human heart forges in the rugged school of sorrow, transfigured by the chant and placed under the sign of invocation:

> Zeus, whatever his true name be,
> If this be a name acceptable,
> By this name will I call him.
> When I have reckoned all, only
> Zeus I recognize as capable of
> Removing the burden which weighs
> Me down with Anguish. . . .
> He has shown man the way of
> Wisdom in giving him this maxim:
> 'That man must learn by suffering.'
> In the fullness of sleep, like dropping
> Rain, descend the many memories of pain
> Before the vision of the Spirit.
> —Wisdom thus acquired against the will.
> And this, I believe, is the grace of the
> Gods forced upon us from above.
>   (*Agamemnon*)

Thus the word develops self-awareness and self-expression in multiple directions which we have only outlined in passing: the imperative word by which I come to a decision, bringing judgment upon my affective confusion; the dubitative word by which I question myself and bring myself into question; the indicative word by which I consider, deem, and declare myself to be such; but also the lyrical word by which I chant the fundamental feelings of mankind and of solitude.

At the end of this interlude on the power of the word, the mutual permeation of work and the word becomes evident as well as their latent dissociation.

Perhaps it may be said that there is work whenever man produces a useful effect which answers his needs and that this is done by means of a more or less toilsome effort working against the resistant qualities of nature, whether this latter be outside of us or within us.

In a sense, work encompasses the word, since speaking requires also a more or less laborious effort or even a profession which produces useful effects responding to the demands of a group, even if this were only a stage in the production of things. But the essence of language falls outside of the scope of work: *the word signifies and does not produce.* The end of production is a real effect, that of the word an understood meaning. Moreover, the word is always in some degree *gratuitous;* it is never certain that a word will be useful. Because it searches, it arouses needs, transforms tools; but it may also be sufficient unto itself in axioms; it witnesses, it questions, it invokes. It may also be used so as to say nothing, to gossip, to lie, to deceive and, lastly, to lead to delirium. Consequently, work may easily put to shame the word which, it seems, does not make anything. Hamlet *speaks* of the vanity of speech: *words! words! words!*

But what would the civilization of work be without the splendor and vanity of the word?

[3] Toward a Civilization of Work and the Spoken Word

How DOES THIS DIALECTIC of work and the word help us to become oriented in the present problems of civilization? Essentially in this: that it puts us on guard against a sham resolution of the tensions which support the movement of our civilization.

The present form of this dialectic will pass away, and this is as it should be. But other forms will rise up and pose new problems.

1. *"Alienation" and "Objectification" in Work*

THE PRESENT HISTORICAL FORM of the dialectic of work and the word is dominated by two factors which may not be reduced to each other:

1. Human work is *alienated in the wage-earning classes,* it is contracted for as work detached from the person; it is treated as a thing which is subject to the laws of the market. This *socio-economic* degradation of work is a function of the socio-economic regime of capitalism. One may hope that it disappears along with the conditions of the wage-earner. To this socio-economic degradation of work corresponds the usurped dignity of the word which is all the more arrogant as it does not seem to realize that it too is negotiated on a market of services: there is an arrogance in culture

which is precisely symmetrical with the humiliation in work, both of which must disappear. The roots of this arrogance are deep-seated; they are immersed in Antiquity (Greek, and not Jewish, it should be noted); work being the act of the slave—being *servile*—culture was the deed of the free man, it was *liberal*. The opposition between the servile arts and the liberal arts is therefore greatly dependent upon the social condition assigned to the worker himself within historical societies; and culture evaluates itself, or rather over-evaluates itself, in the measure that it solidifies the regime which devaluates work.

Furthermore, there is a culpability which clings to culture to the extent that it is directly or indirectly a means of exploiting work: those who possess knowledge, the articulate, are the ones who command, who undertake, who run the risks (since a capitalistic economy is one which is based upon calculations and risks). "Intellectuals" are needed to construct the theory of the system, to teach it and justify it in the very eyes of its victims. In short, capitalism has been able to perpetuate itself as an economy only because it has also been a culture, or even an ethic and a religion. Thus the word is culpable for the degradation of work. This is why revolutionary thought kindles an understandable resentment against the whole of classical culture, that is, when this culture is viewed as a bourgeois culture which has paved the way for and kept in power an exploiting class. Every man who thinks and writes, without being hindered in his study or his research by a regime in which his work is negotiated as a merchandise, must perceive that his freedom and joy are corrupt, for they are the counterpart and, whether closely or remotely, the condition and means of work which elsewhere is without freedom and without joy, because he knows himself and feels himself being treated as a thing.

2. But the modern condition of work is not merely defined by the socio-economic conditions of capitalism, but also by the *technological form* given to it by successive industrial revolutions. This form is relatively independent of the regime of capital and work and raises problems which are not solved by revolutions at the level of the social and economic regime of work, even if these revolutions should permit a clearer presentation of the problems and lead to an easier solution of them. The fragmentation of ancient crafts into partial and repetitious tasks which demand less and less professional qualification raises a disturbing problem. The philosopher's and theologian's eulogy of work must not lose itself in the clouds, not at the very moment when an ever-increasing

mass of workers tends to consider its work as a mere social sacrifice which no longer has meaning and joy in itself, but outside of itself: in the enjoyment of the consumer and the pleasures of leisure time won through the shortening of the workday. Today this fragmentation into partial and repetitious tasks reaches not only industrial work, but also office work and is found in different forms in scientific specialization, in medical specialization, and in varying degrees, in all forms of intellectual work.

It is true that this fragmentation and specialization are counterbalanced at all levels by the appearance of new crafts: constructors, regulators, machine repairers; likewise, we are witnessing reorganizations of scientific disciplines, thanks to new theories which encompass and systematize disciplines which up to now have been separate. Later on, we shall have to come back to the measure in which this *polyvalence*, which counterbalances *specialization*, is not the fruit of a theoretical and disinterested culture, a culture with a remote efficacity, which constantly returns to and corrects the technical training of the specialized worker and the specialized scientific researcher.

I am wondering, then, whether the technological condition of modern work does not manifest, over and above social "alienations," a misery of work which pertains to its "objectifying" function. This "objectification," by which man realizes himself, fulfills himself, and reaches his perfection, has certainly been extolled. It has even been looked upon as the philosophical solution of the debates between realism and idealism, subjectivism and materialism, etc., and, in short, the solution to the ancient problems arising from the theory of knowledge and from ontology. The essence of work lies in linking me to a precise and finite task; herein I show what I am by demonstrating what I can do; and I show what I am capable of by doing something limited; it is the "finiteness" of my task which reveals me to others and to myself. This is certainly true; but this same movement which reveals me also dissimulates me; what realizes me depersonalizes me. One can easily see in the evolution of crafts—including that of the intellectual—that there is a limit toward which this movement of objectification is tending: this limit constitutes my destruction in the gesture devoid of meaning, in activity which is literally meaningless because it is without horizon. But to be a man is not only to concern oneself with the finite, but it is also to comprehend the whole and thus to direct oneself toward this other limit, the inverse of the gesture devoid of meaning, toward the horizon of the totality of human existence which I call world or being. By means of this breakthrough proposed to us by modern work, we are suddenly brought back to our remarks on the word as signifying the whole, as a will to understand by the whole.

Perhaps the modern evolution of work therefore only serves to reveal a profound tendency of work which is to absorb us into the finite while fulfilling us. This imperceptible loss of self is betrayed by a sort of *ennui* which gradually replaces the *suffering* connected to the execution of work, as if the labor of objectification became reincarnated more subtly in a sort of psychic illness inherent in the fragmentation and the repetition of modern work.

This tendency is irreducible to "alienation," which in the literal sense is the swallowing up of man not only into another, but also to the profit of another man who exploits him. Alienation raises a social and ultimately *political* problem; objectification raises a *cultural* problem.

Let us ask, therefore, if there is not, in the present-day unrest of culture, something which answers correlatively to the fundamental unrest in contemporary work. Over and above the bourgeois perversion of culture, we find that the arts, literature, and university teaching express man's muffled resistance to adapt himself to the modern world.

This resistance is certainly not unadulterated. It betrays the panic of adolescent man in face of the abrupt mutations of the technical world. It expresses the rupture of an ancient relation of man to a "natural" environment; it attests to the anxiety over a disrupted temporal rhythm. This confusion is also found in a bad conscience, that of Valéry's Socrates who, encountering the architect Eupalinos in Hell, regrets having constructed nothing with his hands and having merely thought, that is, *talked.* And the bad conscience, as always, turns to resentment: for if Socrates finds that he has not left the shadows of the cave for the reality of Ideas, but that he has merely left the reality of machines for the shadows of discourse, then Socrates will hate machines and reality.

Nothing in all of the above is pure or absolutely authentic. Over and above this confusion and this bad conscience, which, oddly enough, come together, culture expresses a legitimate refusal toward adaptation. Culture is also that which unadapts man, keeps him ready for the open, for the remote, for the other, for the all. It is the function of the humanities, of history, and especially of philosophy to offset "objectification" by "reflection," to compensate for the adaptation of man as worker to finite tasks by the interrogation of critical man upon his human condition in its entirety and by the chant of poetic man. *Education,* in the strong sense of the word, is perhaps only the just but difficult equilibrium between the exigency for objectification—that is, adaptation—and the exigency for reflection and unadaptation. It is this taut equilibrium which keeps man standing.[3]

2. Civilization of Work

I CAN NOW EXPRESS the scope and limitations of my adhesion to the notion of civilization of work. I wholly subscribe to the definition proposed by Bartoli: "A civilization in which work is the dominant social and economic category." There is no problem with this definition once one has accepted the critique, which all of us make in other respects, of capitalism in its economic, social, political, and cultural form. This definition is all the more valid as the point of it is not directed against the phantom of contemplation but against the fetish of money. This is what constitutes the superiority of the economist's reflection over that of the philosopher with respect to the question of work.

In the spirit of Bartoli, I shall therefore maintain the following points:

1. A civilization of work is primarily an *economy of work* in which the rational direction of the general plan replaces the laws of the market. From this standpoint, money and price are stripped of their function as the so-called spontaneous regulators of economy; the distribution of goods is carried out at least provisionally in accordance with work and even in accordance with the productivity of work: wages are no longer the cost of work-merchandise, they are the means of dividing the net social product. In this sense, an economy of work is already realized in countries which practice socialist principles; it is only a trend in the modern capitalistic economy, particularly in the form of an organizing law of work, of a transformation of the structure of wages and a politics of full employment.

2. An economy of work does not constitute a civilization of work if it is not an *economy of workers themselves*, that is, if the workers do not actually manage the factories and industries themselves, or if they have not acquired the capacity and the responsibility of management so as to escape a new form of domination, that of administrators and technocrats.

3. An economy of work is false if it is not also a *democracy of work*, that is, if on the constitutional plane, workers do not share in the structuring of the State.

3. "La Parole est mon royaume," *Esprit* (February, 1955).

Hence, does not a civilization of work imply more than the incorporation of unions into the apparatus of the State, but rather a whole network of decentralizations, of divisions, of oppositions of powers, something very different from the structure of the centralizing State which the phase of industrialization imposes upon socialist economies? In this sense, no civilization of work as yet exists, even if an economy of work is already in operation in a part of the world or even present in some degree everywhere in the world.

4. Lastly, let us note that a civilization of work is a civilization in which a *new culture takes form on the basis of work.* The social mixing of professions and functions, which the division into classes considerably checks although without impeding it altogether, cannot fail to have a tremendous *repercussion* in the culture of a nation. When workers have ready access not only to the direction of the economy and of the State, but also to scientific and liberal careers and especially to literary and artistic expression, there necessarily results a profound renewal of culture *independently of an ideological direction of culture.* Modern culture has need of being cured of the unwholesome, of the artificial, of narcissism, by a confrontation and mixing of thinkers and artists in the world of work; it can in this way reachieve fraternal feelings, themes which are at once more vigorous and fresher and thereby free us from Byzantinism. A civilization of work therefore also involves the correction of the miseries of the word by means of the virtues of work.

The theme of the civilization of work mounts up to this repercussion of the world of work in the world of culture by the social mixing of professions and of functions. It mounts legitimately up to this point, but it goes no further. Beyond this point, two serious "mystifications" are to be feared. The first consists in making the whole of culture the celebration of the technician enterprise and, to speak plainly, a factor of industrialization. If the civilization of work consists in propagating a type of man who is efficient, pragmatic, fascinated by the success of techniques, by the collective enterprise of production, and consumed by the daily usage of the products of social work, then this new fetish which is offered for our admiration under the lofty label of civilization of work must be challenged.

The second mystification consists of confusing a culture inspired by work and nourished by workers with a culture directed by *ideology.* This danger is the extreme form of the preceding one; in the phase of instituting a socialist economy, which normally corresponds to a phase of rapid industrialization, the apparatus of the State tries to orient the whole of culture toward the enterprise of collectivization and to impose upon the community the conception of the world which presides over this enterprise.

Hence, the civilization of work is no longer merely the one in which work has a *repercussion* on the word, but one in which the word no longer has but two objects: work itself and the ideology of the State which constructs socialism. Our whole analysis of the dialectics of work and the spoken word warns us that a civilization which fails to maintain this sort of intangible communication between the critical and poetic function of the word and the efficacious function of work is condemned in the end to stagnation. A civilization retains momentum only if it assumes all the risks of the word and establishes a right to error as an indispensable political function. This risk of the word is the price that a civilization of work must pay for the service which the word renders to work.

3. *The Service Rendered to Work by the Word*

THIS SERVICE of the word will outlive the social "alienations" of work in the wage-earner. For this service responds to the more enduring problems posed by the "objectification" of man in a finite work which is increasingly fragmented and monotonous. Nothing could be more baleful than to deny these problems in the name of the more urgent tasks of the "de-alienation" of work: all action and all reflection ought to be staggered in depth in function of urgent dangers but also in function of abiding dangers.

1. A first service of the word within the realm of work may be looked upon as a *corrective* of the division of work. Here we enter upon a whole network of concerns which are being investigated by the social psychology of industrial work. At its lowest degree, this corrective function of the word corresponds to the role of distraction, of chattering in workshops in which jobs are so fragmented and so monotonous that it would be better to carry automation to its logical extreme and openly surrender work to a sort of medullary vigilance so as to occupy the mind of the worker with something else: chatter, informal talks, music, and—why not?—instructive lectures, etc.[4] At a higher degree, this corrective function takes the form of a general perception of the various situations in a factory, of a general apprehension of the sequence of operations which take

4. Georges Friedmann, "Des écouteurs aux oreilles?" in *Où va le travail humain?* (Paris: Gallimard, 1950), pp. 207 ff.

place in an enterprise, even in terms of the various markets scattered throughout the world. This perception and this apprehension of the whole of production are comparable to an "interior word" which situates piecework and endows it with meaning. At a still higher degree, this corrective function becomes identified with a polyvalent professional training which allows for job-interchange and combats against the depersonalization provoked by automation. It may be seen that our dialectic of work and the spoken word leads us also to the very core of the problems raised by technical education which necessarily has two faces, one turned toward specialized professional training and the other toward general culture. It must be said that the most utilitarian training already has a cultural value as soon as it subordinates manual dexterity to theoretical knowledge of a physico-mathematical type. Literature and history conclude the "opening" of professional training upon the world and confirm that technical education is truly a *culture.*

At the highest degree, the *corrective* function of the word consists in endowing work with a social meaning. It is not by chance that books, a book like *Das Kapital,* are at the source of modern revolutions. Ultimately, to speak one's work is to approach the word of the political man. For when he is not in power, the politician, like the preacher, is only armed with the deadly efficacity of the word. This is the element of truth in the profound maxim of Georges Navel which Friedmann gives an account of: "There exists a sadness among the working classes which may be cured only by political participation."

2. The second service of the word is to *compensate* for the division of work by leisure. Leisure will be more and more the great problem of civilization, for the same reason as work.

It is by means of the word—but also by sports, camping, hobbies, etc.—that we may restore and renew the lost contact with nature, with life, with the raw elements. And thereby perhaps one may find a more extensive temporal rhythm, one which is more spontaneous, more relaxed than the exhausting tempo of modern living.

Now, the modern world is a world in which leisures, in the measure that they multiply, become degraded by the invasion of the very techniques which revolutionized production, transportation, and all human relationships. The very meaning of our leisures—won with difficulty through the shortening of the workday—will depend in large measure upon the quality of the human word, upon respect for the human word in politics and in the novel, in the theater and in conversation. For what will a man gain if he earns his living by work only to lose his soul through leisure? Thus, the construction of the socialist state must not degrade the word with the glib rhetoric of propaganda and ideological parlance. In the last analysis, this is why the socialist state must bear the risks of free speech if it wishes to avoid the spiritual destruction of the man it materially constructs.

3. The word has, moreover, a function of *foundation* with respect to all the pragmatic activities of man. It conveys the "theoretical" function in its entirety. There is no technique which is not an applied knowledge, and there is no applied knowledge which is not dependent upon a knowledge which at first repudiated all application. *Praxis* does not give us the whole of man. *Theoria* is its *raison d'être*. This founding *theoria* goes from mathematics to ethics, from physical theory to history, from science to ontology. All radical problems are posed in an attitude which suspends the utilitarian concern and vital impatience. This is why there is no civilization which can survive without some sphere of free play left to disinterested speculation, to research without immediate or apparent applications. Earlier, we called *education* the interplay between adaptation and disadaptation in the formation of man. The University should be *par excellence* the seat of this pulsation. Thus it is legitimate to ask it to answer better than it does to the needs of modern society and also to continue without disgrace the time-honored tradition of the *Universitas*, which more than ever will appear as a privileged means of dominating the tasks of modern work, under the condition that all workers may have access to it.

4. Lastly, in addition to this function of foundation, the word borders upon a function of *creation:* through literature and the arts is pursued the invention and the discovery of a sense of man which no state can systematically plan or arrange, which is the supreme risk for the artist and for the society which produces him. The true creator is not the one who *expresses* the already known needs of his times, the needs which the politician has already enunciated, but the artist whose work is an innovation in relation to the already catalogued and recognized knowledge of human reality. We find here the poetic function of the word with which our meditation on the power of the word ended. We now understand that the word is at the roots of a project of a civilization, even the project of a civilization of work.

Is it possible that the word here touches upon a fundamental creation? Is it possible that a theology of the word coincides in the end with a theology of work? Perhaps. But this means primarily that in human finitude we have need both of work and of the word in order to situate ourselves in the direction of a creative word which we are not.

Hence, every human civilization will be both a civilization of work *and* a civilization of the word.

5 / The Question of Power

Non-violent Man
and His Presence to History

THESE NOTES devoted to violence and to non-violence flow from one central question: under what conditions may the non-violent man be something other than a yogi, in the sense in which Koestler uses this term, or something other than a purist on the fringes of history? The question obviously presupposes the prior conviction [1] that there is some value in non-violence, or, as we shall express it more precisely later on, that there is some value in non-violent forms of resistance. It also presupposes that the true form of non-violence may not be manifest to us from the outset, but that it may be legitimately sought within the caricatures which strangely resemble it: sentimentality, cowardice, lyrical evasion, withdrawal from the world, laissez-faire. I shall not hesitate to say from the outset and as an expression of fair play that this prior conviction for me is an integral part of a more fundamental conviction: that the *Sermon on the Mount* concerns our history and all history inclusive of its political and social structures and not merely private acts without historical import; that it imbues our history with an almost insuperable and *difficult* exigency that places whoever has been gripped by it in a fundamental malaise, in a state of vehemence which often finds no other outlet than

1. I can readily see how one might take exception to the presuppositions of this study which I am formulating on its pre-critical level. But then, who does not begin an analysis without presuppositions or pre-judgments? The problem always concerns where we shall subsequently advance on the road of veracity, up to what point the presuppositions become critically elaborated, incorporated within a common endeavor wherein discussion may arise and thereby make explicit the implicit presuppositions.

inopportune acts which are awkwardly historical; that this malaise, this vehemence, this awkwardness nevertheless imply that the *Sermon on the Mount,* with its non-violence, attempts to enter into history, that its aim is practical, that it summons to incarnation and not to evasion. These prior convictions are what I attempt to elaborate critically in the question: *under what conditions may non-violence concern our history?* For it is history and not the purity of our intentions that counts, what we shall have *done* to others which will fulfill the meaning of what we shall have intended. If non-violence is to be ethically possible it must be put in direct relation to action which is really effectuated, such as follows from all the mutual happenings which form the basis of an elaborated human history.

The first condition which must be fulfilled by an authentic doctrine of non-violence is to have traversed the world of violence in all its density. A non-violent movement always runs the risk of limiting violence to a particular form which it then attacks with obstinacy and narrowness. One must first gauge the length, width, and depth of violence, its movement throughout the course of history, the sweep of its psychological, social, cultural, and spiritual ramifications, its profound enrootment in the very plurality of consciousnesses. The discovery of the forms of violence must be run full length, for it is by this means that violence displays its tragic splendor and appears as the very mainspring of history, the "crisis"—the "critical moment" and the "judgment"—which suddenly changes the configuration of history. Then and only then, at the price of this veracity, the question comes up of whether reflection reveals a *surplus,* a *greater* than history, whether consciousness has sufficient means of asserting itself against history and of regarding itself as belonging to another "order" than the violence which makes history.

But here a second question must be taken up by the non-violent: is he capable of always picturing himself *in* this history which he denies? And can he do so without putting a higher value on the eventual efficacity of his act than upon his alleged purity? *Does non-violence have an efficacity and if so, what is it?* It is clear that this second question is connected to a vaster problem: whether the "prophet" has an historic task and whether this task may insert itself as a wedge between the inefficacity of the "yogi" and the efficacity of the "Commissar."

Third question: is not the contingent efficacity of the nonviolent in necessary tension with the recognized impurity of progressivist violence? In point of fact, if the prophet attacks history with acts which are more on the order of refusals, of disobedience, and therefore discontinuous, circumstantial gestures (linked to the event of a declaration of war, of a riot, etc.), then does not the meaning of his act necessarily culminate in the impulsion which he gives, in the spiritual prophecy which he foretells for a strictly political action, to a continuous, constructive action at the level of structures and institutions?

I shall not conceal the perplexities which are but poorly cleared up by this procedure. We are dealing with truths which are more glimpsed than recognized, more touched upon than possessed.

1. *The Acquisition of the Awareness of Violence*

To SEE THAT VIOLENCE is always and everywhere, one has but to take notice of how empires rise and fall, how personal prestige is established, how religions tear one another to pieces, how the privileges of property and power are perpetuated and interchanged, or even how the authority of intellectuals is consolidated, how the cultural delights of the elite depend upon the massive workings and sufferings of the disinherited.

One's perspective is always somewhat limited when one explores the empire of violence. Thus an *anatomy of war* which credits itself with having discovered three or four key threads which it would be sufficient to sever in order for the military marionettes to fall lifeless on the stage, would condemn pacificism to remain superficial and puerile. An anatomy of war requires the larger task of a *physiology of violence*.

One must look very low and very high for the complicities of human affectivity in tune with the terror recorded by history. The summary psychology of empiricism, which gravitates around pleasure and pain, comfort and happiness, neglects to treat the irascible, the taste for obstacles, the will for expansion, for combat and domination, the death instincts and especially the capacity for destruction, the desire for catastrophe which is the counterpart of all the disciplines which make of man's psychic fabric an unstable and ever *menaced* equilibrium. Let a riot flare up in the streets, let the country be declared in danger, and something in me is touched off and springs loose, something for which neither profession, nor home, nor daily civic duties provide an outlet; something savage, something wholesome and unwholesome, youthful and unformed, a sense of the novel, of adventure, of availability, a flair for rugged brotherhood and for prompt action, without juridical or administrative mediation. It is to be noted that these shrouded depths of consciousness resurge at the highest levels of consciousness: the meaning of terror is also the meaning of ideology; suddenly justice, law, truth take on capital letters in bearing arms and in surrounding themselves with the splendor of morose passions. Languages and cultures are thrown into the blazing mass of pathos; a monstrous totality is equipped for danger and death; God himself is adduced: his name is on swordbelts, in oaths, in the speech of helmeted crusaders.

Such is the fibrous root which historical violence shoots forth into all the strata of consciousness. But a psychology of violence is not yet at the level of history where violence is organized as a structure. Thus it will still be necessary to say something of the structures of the social "forms" to which the assembled forces are ordered, to speak of the structures of terror. In this respect, the Marxist interpretation of history is indispensable for understanding the relation of the psychic to history in the dialectic of class struggle: at this level terror becomes history, while at the same time history, under the sting of the negative, feeds on terror. This is what the pacificists willingly omit, mesmerized as they are by the battlefield; it is easier to bypass the violence of exploitation: this type of violence does not explode into sensational events; battles are events, so are riots; but poverty and the dying poor are not events; they do not consider it an event that under Louis-Philippe the average life span among the working class was twenty-seven months, that in the manufacturing population of Lille there were, during a period of seven years, 20,700 deaths out of 21,000 births.[2] We are still awaiting the awakening of consciousness which would take measures to unmask the violence of law and order. Peace is therefore an immense task if it is to be the crowning-piece of justice: would not the violence of oppression call forth the violence of revolt?

But what a physiology of violence should not neglect to note is that the State is the seat of a concentration and a transmutation of violence: if the instincts are the material of terror and if class struggle is the first social elaboration of it, then it is as a political phenomenon that it penetrates into the zone of power. What is at stake in the political sphere is power in the literal sense of the word. Within the structure of the State it is a question of knowing who commands, who is subordinated, in short, who is sovereign, for whose benefit, under what restrictions, etc. Through the State,

2. Henri Guillemin, *Les Chrétiens et la politique* (Paris: Editions du temps présent, 1948), p. 19.

the government of persons is always more than the administration of things. It is the moment when violence takes the form of war: when two sovereignties of equal distinction meet upon a terrain where only one of them may exist at the same time. Thus, on the one hand, war does not summarize the whole of violence, in the measure in which the battle between States only imperfectly reflects the profound tensions of society; on the other, the State introduces a new dimension into collective violence by raising it to the level of war. It is even in this privileged form that the violence of history better lays hold of an individual who in some manner hastens it and awaits it: it is principally when the group bound by the State is in a catastrophic situation that the depths of the civilized consciousness, rejoining the pathos of abstractions, bursts into the open; it is at the moment when I discover my belonging to a perishable common adventure, to a history broken into several histories, to a strand of history which is threatened by severance, it is at this moment that I am raised to this point of bitter and cruel lyricism symbolized by *La Marseillaise*. This noble historical death, in which my individual death is interwined, elicits the most solemn emotions of existence—1789, 1871, 1914, 1944 . . . and they reverberate as far as the deepest levels of our unconscious. Thus the terror of history and the terror of the psyche mutually precipitate each other.

It would seem, then, that by some maleficence inherent to history, all men are not compatible together: some are *de trop* for others. Let no mistake be made: the intention of violence, the end which it pursues implicitly or explicity, directly or indirectly, is the death of the other—at least his death or something worse than his death. It is thus that Jesus discloses the essence of simple anger: he who gets angry at his brother is the *murderer* of his brother. Premeditated and actual murder is, in this regard, the reference-point of all violence: in the moment of violence the other is marked "to be eliminated." Violence has indeed an endless existence: for man is capable of several deaths of which some, held in suspension, require the dying to be held on the brink of death in order to taste to the dregs the deaths worse than death. The tortured must still be *there* to bear the conscious affliction of degradation and to live his destruction beyond his body to the core of his dignity, his value, his joy. If man is more than his life, violence will attempt to kill it until this *more* retreats; for in the last analysis, it is this "more" which is *de trop*.

It is this terror which makes history: violence makes its

appearance as the privileged mode in accordance with which the form of history changes; it appears as the temporal rhythm of men, as a structure of the plurality of consciousnesses.

But if history is violence, non-violence is now the bad conscience of history, the malaise of existence in history and eventually the hope of the conscience in historical situation. To be authentic, the wish for non-violence must arise on the confines of a meditation on history: it is its first and most basic connection to history, the weight which gives it ballast. To take the violence of history serious is already to transcend it by the judgment. The *ethical* nature of consciousness is essentially opposed to the *historical* course of events. History says: violence. Consciousness rebounds and says: love. Its rebound is a rush of indignation. By means of this rebound it posits an end to history: its suppression as violence. At the same time it posits man as the possible friend of man.

Failing to consider the broadest dimensions of violence, pacifism thinks itself humane and benign. It believes it is already *in* the world, that it has come from the world, the result of the natural goodness of man which is simply masked or hindered by some few evildoers. It is not aware that it is actually very complicated, that it has history against it, that it can only come from *elsewhere*, that it summons history to something other than what is naturally intended by history.

2. *The Efficacity of Non-violence*

IF NON-VIOLENCE comes from elsewhere, how shall it be present to history? How shall the prophet avoid being the yogi? It seems to me that non-violence can be a valid attitude only if one can expect from it some influence—perhaps quite concealed—upon the course of history. What advantage is there for a man to refuse to kill and accept death in order not to soil his hands? For what does his purity matter? Is he pure if all others are unclean? And doesn't his act fall back into history with the deadly effects which he did not intend but which nevertheless fulfill the meaning of his act? Thus the violence which one refuses to embrace turns to the profit of another violence which the former did not prevent or perhaps even encouraged. Hence if non-violence is to have meaning, it must fulfill it within the history which it at first transcends. It must have a secondary efficacity which enters into account with the efficacity of the violence in the world, an efficacity which alters human relationships. Does it have one and if so, what is it?

1. The faith of the non-violent consists in the fact that his non-compliance affords a real presence to values which men of good will only foresee at the end of a long history. Hence his faith is that this concrete and present testimony given to the eventual fellowship of man does not have its efficacy restricted to its inevitable effects in the annals of opposing violences. He hopes that over and above the impurity which he shares with all the acts which light upon history, that his novel act, which is always questionable on the basis of its short-term effects, has a double sense; that it supports the purpose of values and the endeavor of history toward the recognition of man by man.

One would not be able to understand the storm of enthusiasm which flooded a large segment of public opinion, on the occasion of the gesture of Gary Davis, if one did not recognize in him a real efficacy, primarily the power of breaking a *spell*, an enchantment. History falls upon man, who nevertheless makes it, like an alienated fatality: the non-violent reminds us that this fatality is human, since it has once been suspended by a man; at one point the interdict is removed, a future is possible: one man has dared. One cannot say what it will lead to, one cannot know it, for this efficacy is unverifiable in the strict sense of the historical method; it is the plan in which the connection of an act to history is an object of faith. The non-violent believes and hopes that freedom can penetrate the resistance of fate. In this way, he can reinvigorate the projects within the stream of history.

This efficacy alone suffices to situate the non-violent in history: he is not on the fringe of time, he is rather "untimely," unpresent, like an anticipated presence, possible and offered, of another epoch which a long and painful political "mediation" should render historical. He invests capital in a history which remains to be made, to be inscribed in the destiny of institutions and modes of feeling and acting.

In acting not only *in direction* of the humanist ends of history—*in view* of justice and friendship—but also *by means* of the defenseless force of these ends, he prevents history from letting up only to fall back again. He is the counterpart of hope for the contingency of history, of a non-guaranteed history.

2. Under certain favorable circumstances, under the pressure of exceptional personalities, non-violence may take on the dimensions of a movement, of a non-violent resistance with a massive efficacy. Hence it may bring about a veritable historical breakthrough. However inimitable he himself was, however limited his work, Gandhi in our time represents more than a hope or a

demonstration. The most flagrant nonsense which one could say about Gandhi is that he represents the yogi in the sense of Koestler. Gandhi was just as persistently present to India as Lenin was to Russia. Naturally one cannot deny his limits: his distrust of modern techniques, his lack of sympathy for the organized proletariat, his lasting respect for traditional structures responsible for the alienation of the Indian masses which turned to the profit of the Brahmans and the rich.

One should, if need be, reproach him for all that. Yet I do not see how one can, in the last analysis, minimize the exemplary power of his efficacious campaigns of non-compliance in South Africa and in India. Their exemplary significance consists of their bringing into being (once again under favorable circumstances: England was not Naziism) not only the symbolic presence of the goals of humanism, but also their actual reconciliation with the means which resemble them. Hence, far from the non-violent man banishing these goals from history and deserting the scheme of means, leaving them to their impurity, the non-violent attempts to bring them together in an action which is at one and the same time a *spirituality* and a *technique*.

On the one hand, it appears that non-violence was for Gandhi but one fragment in a total spiritual system which included truth, poverty, justice, chastity, patience, intrepidity, contempt for death, meditation, etc. It is to be noted that at the summit of this structure he placed truth, *Satyagraha*, "the indefectible pressure of the truth." "I coined the word *Satyagraha* in South Africa to give utterance to the force which Indians made use of in this country for eight full years. . . . The force of truth is also that of love. . . ." [3] On the other hand, non-violence was for Gandhi a method and even an intricate technique for resistance and non-compliance. We must confess that we are totally lacking and

3. Taken from the *Report of the Indian Congress*, I (1920), translated by L. Massignon in the *Revue du monde musulman* (April–June, 1921). A. P. Cérésole, founder of the *Service civil volontaire international*, questioned Gandhi on the possibility of employing non-violence in the Occident [here is Gandhi's reply]: "Are you sure that the people are ready for it? And do you not think that you are somewhat lacking in leaders? A leader must be the realization of God at every minute, twenty-four hours a day. He must master himself in every way, knowing neither anger nor fear. You must be unmindful of yourselves, not indulging in the pleasures of your appetites and sexuality. Thus purified, you shall have strength, not yours but that of God. What does strength consist of? A boy of fifteen could easily strike me down. I am nothing, but I have been delivered from desire and fear, so that I know the power of God." See the conclusion of Gandhi's autobiography entitled *The Story of My Experiments with Truth* (Washington: Public Affairs Press, 1954).

ignorant of such a technique. It is a mistake not to examine the
calmly premeditated and meticulously executed mechanism of his
campaigns in South Africa and in India. Therein one will note an
acute sense of mass effects, of discipline, of resolution, and especially of the total absence of fear of imprisonment or of death;
here the active character of non-violence blazes forth: for Gandhi,
the true laissez-faire is violence; for by it I surrender myself to a
leader, a chief. Indeed, for Gandhi, non-violence is *force*.

It is this force which, in an exceptional historical experience,
unites and epitomizes the end and the means. Progressivist violence, that which claims to abolish itself while marching toward
the humanist ends of history, is the art of the *detour:* detour of the
ruse, of untruth, of violence. All military and civil powers practice
it: it is the technique of patriotism and revolution. The non-violent
answers the question concerning his efficacity with another question: does not the practice of the "detour" involve the risk of an
endless perpetuation of violence? Does not political action—be it
patriotic or revolutionary—have need, as of a critical presence, of
these symbolic gestures and these partially successful actions in
which the ends *are* the means?

3. *"Non-violent Resistance" and "Progressivist Violence"*

BUT CAN NON-VIOLENCE be everything? Can it be
more than a symbolic gesture, more than a limited and rare
historical success? Can it constitute the total replacement for
violence, can it make history?

Non-violence, even when it is not merely the abstention from
resistance, still involves certain inherent limitations.

1. It is not by chance that its motto is negative: do not kill. Its
career is one of refusal: non-cooperation, no military service, etc.
The very word resistance retains a negative accent: one disobeys
an authority to which one does nothing. I believe in the efficacity of
these refusals as refusals: but doesn't their efficacity flow from
their *connection* to positive, constructive activities? When I move
from "thou shalt not kill" to "thou shalt love," from the refusal to
engage in war to the building of peace, I enter into the cycle of
actions which I determine. Hence I again give birth to oppression; I
enter into the dissociation of ends and means by participating in
endeavors in which human actions are not "compossible," in which
I experience the maleficence of history along with the efficacity of
history.

2. It also seems that non-violence is of the order of discontinuity: circumstantial acts of refusal, campaigns of noncompliance; it is of the order of the *gesture*. These are gestures which bear testimony intermittently to the superhuman exigencies which weigh upon history and summon man to his humanity in a very concrete fashion. But these gestures appear fated to find their complement in long-range actions, in the movements of history, such as the conquest of the modern state over small feudalities, the proletarian movement, the anti-colonialist struggle, etc.

3. Furthermore, non-violence defies concrete situations, State orders which affect me personally; but political action replies to "challenges" (to use the apt expression of Toynbee) which emanate from structures: colonialism, wage-earner and proletarian condition, atomic danger; it therefore operates on the level of the abstract, the customary, the institutional, on the level of anonymous "mediations" between man and man.

It seems to me that today the non-violent ought to be the *prophetic* nucleus of strictly *political* movements, that is to say, movements centered on a technique of revolution, of reform or power. Apart from these institutional tasks, the mystical non-violent runs the risk of heading toward a hopeless catastrophism, as if the reign of disaster and persecution were the last chance for history, as if it were necessary to reconcile our life with a reign in which loyal acts would have no effect, hidden from all, without historical import. This reign *may* come, and with it a regime so inhuman as to allow no other result than the eternal repetition of *no,* unheard outside of prison walls. The reign of inefficacity is always loitering about the doors of history; one must be prepared for the night. But this lurking thought cannot be the thought for the future, for action or construction. Before this reign—if it is to come—and so long as there is light, it is necessary to work in accordance with foresight, planning, projects; there is a political task and this task is in full accord with history.

But then, is it not necessary for prophetic non-violence, resulting from a victory of consciousness over the harsh law of history, to implement history by means of the dramatic relation which it maintains with a residual violence, a progressivist violence, whereas the latter draws its spiritual fortune from the promise and intermittent grace of a non-violent gesture? [4]

But this *comprehension* of a dialectic of prophetic non-violence and progressivist violence, within the very core of efficacity, can

4. Cf. Merleau-Ponty, "Humanisme et terreur," *Esprit* (February, 1949). "Le Yogi, le commissaire et le prophète," *Christianisme Social* (January, 1949).

only be an *outlook* of the historian. For he who lives, who acts, there is neither compromise nor synthesis but *choice*. Intolerance of the mixture is the very soul of non-violence. If faith is not total it repudiates itself. If non-violence is the calling of a few, it must appear to them as the duty of all. For whoever lives it and ceases to watch it from a distance, non-violence wishes to be the whole of action, wishes to make history.

State and Violence

THE GOAL OF THIS LECTURE is not to propound anything whatever resembling a political decision. Besides, it would be highly indiscreet and discourteous to attempt such a thing here on foreign soil.

It is rather a question which precedes any particular politics which I should like to lay before you: what is the meaning of this fact, manifest to whomever considers history and daily life, that man is political? This massive question touches on problems of law, sociology, and history, and I should like to approach it by its most disconcerting aspect: with the State there appears a *certain violence* which has all the characteristics of *legitimacy*. What is the significance of this strange fact, not only for our lives as men, but also for our moral reflection, for our philosophical and religious meditation? The political existence of man is watched over and guided by violence, the violence of the State which has the characteristics of legitimate violence.

Let us first make certain of our point of departure: what is the minimum violence instituted by the State? In its most elementary and at the same time most indomitable form, the violence of the State is the violence of a *penal* character. The State punishes; in the last analysis it is the State which has the monopoly over physical restraint. It has taken from individuals the right to do justice themselves; it has taken upon itself all the diversified forms of violence inherited from the primitive battle of man against man. For all violence, the individual may call upon the State, but the State is the last court of appeal beyond which there is no recourse. By approaching the violence of the State by way of its punitive, penal side, we have directed ourselves to the central problem; for

[234]

the multiple functions of the State, its power to legislate, its power to make rulings and to execute them, its administrative function, its economic function, or its educational function, all these functions are ultimately sanctioned by the power of constraining as the final authority. To say that the State is a *power* and that it is a power of constraining is one and the same thing.

Let us not speak therefore of an evil State, of a totalitarian State, let us merely speak of the State and of what makes the State a State in the midst of different and even opposed regimes and forms of States. Anything which the State adds in the form of illegitimate violence only serves to aggravate the problem. It is enough for us that the State which is reputed to be the most just, the most democratic and liberal, reveals itself as the synthesis of legitimacy and violence, that is to say as a moral power of exacting *and* as a physical power of constraining.

[I]

WHY DOES THIS UNION of law and force within the State constitute a problem? It would not be a problem if life in the State could fully express, integrally realize, and radically exhaust every exigency of the moral consciousness. We would be content if politics could be the fulfillment of ethics for us. But can life in the State quench the thirst for perfection? One might think so if one were to follow certain suggestions of Greek political thought. For the Greeks, the perfection and sufficiency of the *"Polis"* is the goal of individual conduct. It seems, then, that the whole of moral conduct is summed up in the realization of an historical community which is prosperous, strong, and free with a collective freedom. But the same philosophers who look upon the *Polis* as the summit of moral life have refused to amalgamate the "contemplative" ideal of the sage with the "practical" ideal of the Head of State, with the political man, the administrator of an establishment or a municipality. Their morality thus breaks in two and the difficulty of connecting the two models of perfection and happiness together, the philosophical model and the political model, as is found in Plato, Aristotle, and the Stoics, remains insoluble. It may be objected that the ideal of "contemplation" is no longer maintained by us and that Christianity was the first to do away with the distinction between contemplation and action by propounding the "practical" ideal of love of neighbor and by unifying all morality under the sign of "practice."

But Christianity rediscovered by different means and even aggravated the contradiction which the Greeks, political creatures *par excellence*, had not been able to transcend. For Christianity introduced an exigency which, by radicalizing the moral problem, transformed the political problem into an enigma. This radical exigency, as we know, is the interpretation of love of neighbor by Jesus in the *Sermon on the Mount*. Such as it is given, this teaching propounds an entirely sacrificial form of love: "Do not offer resistance to injury . . . , pray for those who persecute you," etc.

Such a command ushers in a more radical rupture than the opposition between contemplation and action. It is "practice" itself which is divided against itself. For as such, politics cannot be pictured within the frame of this ethic of non-resistance and sacrifice.

We have a testimony to this effect in the celebrated thirteenth chapter of the *Epistle to the Romans*. St. Paul is addressing himself to the Christians of the capital, and they, it seems, are tempted to anarchism because of religious motives. He counsels them to be submissive to their lawful authorities not only for fear of punishment, but also in conscience. Perhaps this text is more attractive as a plea for self-discovery than as the resolution of a contradiction, although ordinarily it is commented upon from the latter, dogmatic point of view.

St. Paul was quite aware that by introducing the figure of the "magistrate" and the concepts of authority, sanction, obedience, and fear, he thereby disclosed a dimension of life which is not contained within the direct human relationships susceptible of being transfigured by the fraternal love of which he spoke earlier. Indeed, it is quite striking, as O. Cullmann noted, that St. Paul's political counsels fall into a context in which it is chiefly a question of "love" which all men owe to each other. This love is described, in the manner of the *Sermon on the Mount*, as a love which pardons, which offers no resistance to injury, returns good for evil, and in the end restores or even creates a complete reciprocity between persons. "Love each other with a tender and fraternal affection," says the Apostle.

And suddenly, breaking off with this appeal to mutual love, Paul evokes the figure of the "magistrate." What does the "magistrate" do? He *punishes*. He punishes those who do wrong. Here then is the violence which we were evoking at the outset. It is precisely within the notion of penal action that St. Paul sums up all the functions of the State. To be sure, it is a limited violence, a violence which does not sanction murder and, as we shall see later on, a violence which neither justifies nor institutionalizes war between States. It is a violence which is measured entirely by the very institution of the State. A violence established upon justice which St. Paul calls the "good." There is truth in all of this and it should be brought to the attention of those who see in this text the disgraceful surrender of the Christian before no matter what authority. Authority is that of the "magistrate," that of justice. The "order" which it engenders and maintains could not therefore be separated from justice, even less opposed to justice. But it is precisely this established violence, this violence of justice which constitutes a problem.

For "authority" does not seem able to flow from "love." Under its most measured and legitimate form, justice is already a manner of returning evil for evil. *In its essence, punishment consummates the very first rupture in the ethics of love.* It ignores pardon, it offers resistance to the wrong-doer, it sets up a non-reciprocal relationship. In short, to the direct way, to the "immediacy" of love, it opposes the indirect way, the "mediation" of a coercive education of humankind. The "magistrate" is not my "brother"; this is of the very nature of an "authority" and the reason why he requires "submission." This does not mean that the Christian submits to anything whatsoever; but the relation between the State and the citizen is an asymmetrical, non-reciprocal one, the relation of authority to submission. Even when the authority flows from free elections, even when it is wholly democratic and perfectly legitimate (which perhaps never happens), once it is established it is, in my regard, the power which has a monopoly over sanctions. Thus it is that the State is not my brother and requires my submission.

I have said that for St. Paul, the awareness of the paradox is more important than its resolution. Indeed, it must be admitted that St. Paul leaves us a problem rather than a solution. He merely says that authority is "instituted by God" and that this is "for my good." This leads the Christian to submit out of a motive of conscience and not merely out of a fear of punishment, which would constitute a motive totally foreign to Christian living. Yet the relation of this "institution" to the economy of salvation is merely enunciated and remains for us a source of great perplexity. For this violent pedagogy, which impels history throughout the succession of States, interjects a discordant note into the pedagogy of love, of testimony, of the martyr. St. Paul did not make the attempt to infer political authority from the ethic of love; he finds this power of the State within his examination of human nature;

and he bases himself upon this when he lays claim to his status as a Roman citizen. He knows that the tranquility of order is the condition for Christian preaching. Hence he glimpses the convergence of two pedagogies of humankind, that of love and that of justice, that of non-resistance and that of punishment, that of reciprocity and that of authority and submission, that of affection and that of fear. He glimpses their convergence but he does not see their unity. On the one hand, he glimpses their convergence: this is what he states in the pure and simple affirmation that authority is instituted by God. But on the other hand, he does not see their unity: this is precisely why he uses a word, the word "institution," which has no root in preaching concerning the Cross and the imitation of Jesus Christ.

I know: a systematic bond between the Cross and the "institution," between love and authority has been sought; in fact two have been found. First, the "wrath of God" has been invoked; the wrath of God is mentioned in the context of the State (*Romans* 12). This theme seems to be related to that of the State since the wrath of God is God viewed as one who punishes. Second, it is invoked to deny the individual person the right to avenge himself; one is reminded that vengeance is God's. Hence there is reason to compare the institution of the sanction to the vengeance which is reserved for God. But this comparison between the institution of the State and the wrath of God is less an explanation than the consecration of the enigma. Indeed, who does not see that the duality between love and coercion is merely made more radical since it is taken back to God? Further, if the wrath has been satisfied on the Cross, it must nevertheless be admitted that the history of the State is not the history redeemed by the Cross, but a history which is irreducible to that of salvation, a history which conserves humankind without saving it, which educates it without regenerating it, which corrects it without sanctifying it.

The twofold pedagogy of humankind is thus consolidated by the duality of Wrath and the Cross in God. Yet this reflection on the wrath of God was not in vain; it is, on the contrary, very enlightening, but in the measure that one does not expect from it a fanciful "explication," but merely an indirect "description" of the enigma of the State and its violent pedagogy. The history of the State, swept along by the violence of its successive magistratures, appears therefore as the very movement of mankind toward a judgment of condemnation which has not been entirely taken up or recuperated in the judgment of justification summed up by the Cross of Christ. Perhaps the mystery of the State is indeed to limit evil without curing it, to conserve humankind without saving it. Thus the institution of this State only becomes more enigmatic.

In order to explain the enigma of the State there has also been recourse to Pauline "demonology." From this standpoint, each State is the manifestation of a "power" which dominates its history; St. Paul is supposedly thinking of these powers when he says: "Be submissive to your authorities." [1] The Powers, Thrones, and Dominations would be superhuman majesties whose invisible drama would secretly animate the visible drama of authority. One need not be too hasty in rejecting this demonological interpretation. It has served to clothe a very important intuition: the "powers" which St. Paul, along with popular Judaism admits exist have, with respect to the Cross, this *ambiguous* situation of being *already* conquered, crucified, but *not yet* suppressed. By means of the demonological myth, St. Paul perceived the ambiguity of the State: it belongs to the economy of salvation without belonging to it; it is subject but autonomous; it is traversed by what O. Cullmann calls a "temporal tension" expressed by the words *"already"* but *"not yet."* "Already" conquered but "not yet" suppressed. But by setting forth the at once *real* and *provisory* character of the State in a mythical fashion, by supporting it upon a demonological drama which transcends us, St. Paul has once again *manifested* the enigmatic character of it rather than having *explained* it. To be sure, it is by refusing to make St. Paul's demonological interpretation an "explanation" that we obtain all the instructive value with which it is pregnant.

In any case, it must be recognized that for us there remains nothing of the demonological decor of the Pauline politics (if St. Paul was really interested to such an extent in the status of the State and that a few lines from his letters can represent a politics). It is not enough to initiate an exegetical restoration of St. Paul's beliefs on demons in order to be faithful to his teaching: for once this purely literal restoration is made, one must still ask what these beliefs mean. It is not enough to repeat, one must understand. Now, what do we mean when we posit demoniac powers "behind" States? What does "behind" mean? Does history have a double foundation, one which is inhuman or superhuman, in addition to the absolute one of God? The truth is that the restoration of demonological experience has become impossible because the cul-

---

1. Even if *Romans* 13:1 *has no demonological background* ("Each person must be submissive to the authorities placed above us"), *I Corinthians* 8:2 ("None of the rulers of this world has known the wisdom that we preach to mature men") cannot be understood apart from this demonological context.

tural context which made it comprehensible has been lost; one cannot restore a mythical figure without restoring the totality which supports it. Hence the recourse to "invisible powers" is for us the unintelligible fragment of an outdated explanation. But over and above its explanatory value, we must rediscover its *coded* value. What is important in this conception of the "celestial powers" is their manifestation of the ambiguity of the State, of its "temporal tension" as we earlier expressed it in accord with O. Cullmann. In the midst of demonological language, something comes to the surface which we would not have noticed, perhaps, without it. The "institution" becomes the seat of an internal dialectic; order is not something tranquil and absolutely stable; order vibrates; "order" is a "power." The mythical dimension of power makes the rational dimension of order distressing.[2] Throughout the pretended explication by demons, the State appears as an unstable, dangerous reality: not merely instituted, but destituted-restituted, at once transcended and retained. This is shown mythically by demonology while giving the appearance of explaining. Hence, one must retain the spirit of the myth, that is to say its descriptive intention, at the cost of its letter, that is its explanatory pretension.

[11]

LET US RETRACE the steps of our reflection. Christianity, in a manner unlike that of Greek wisdom, has given rise to a dimension of moral life which shatters the strictly political boundaries of human life: this new dimension is Agape, brotherly love and its vocation of non-resistance, of sacrifice, and of martyrdom. The repercussion of this new ethic upon the political reality consists in making the State appear as a power incapable of maintaining itself at this level of the new ethic; and yet this power is not bad in itself; it is confirmed, but in its rightful place and given a mark of precariousness. The State is no longer the substance of rational history; its coercive pedagogy preserves mankind but it does not save it.

This duality of Christian Agape and the punitive violence of the magistrate foretokens the great conflicts which we must now

2. In this sense, mythical thought is not abolished by rational reflection; the notion of "order" is recaptured within a less mythical, less eschatological theodicy, that of natural law. But from another point of view, this progress is a regression; for the archaic themes of demonology are more in tune with the character of State "power."

consider. Our task was easy as long as we remained within the confines of the problem peculiar to St. Paul, that of a passive citizen in an ordered and relatively just State. The Romans to whom St. Paul addressed himself were little people, "subjects" of Caesar. St. Paul throws a gleam of hope upon their condition as subjugated citizens by showing them a certain divine intention in the source of authority which "comes from above." Thus they may obey not merely for fear of punishment, but in conscience. Limited violence, consubstantial with the State, begins to be problematic as soon as it is a question not only of being subjected to it, but also of making use of it (in reality, to submit oneself interiorly in conscience is already to ratify this violence and to exercise it symbolically by identification with the authority who commands and constrains). Hence the same man who is summoned to brotherly love, which returns good for evil, is the magistrature which punishes wrong-doers. The active citizen, the one who assumes his share of sovereignty, is himself a magistrate. How shall he live under two spiritual regimes, that of love and that of established violence, under two pedagogies, that of sacrifice and that of coercion?

The difficulty grows worse when violence erupts wholly outside of the boundaries of the penal institution: when the citizen is summoned to arms by the imperiled country, when a revolutionary situation places him at the crossroads of two violences—one which defends the established order, the other which forces access to power on behalf of new social strata bearing a message of social justice—or lastly, when a war of liberation joins forces abroad to crush a tyranny.

Step by step, the whole problem of violence in history is coming to light: from the submission of the passive citizen, in an existing State, to the exercise of the magistrature by an active citizen—from this legal violence to the armed defense of the State—and lastly, from the defensive and, so to speak, conservative violence of the State to innovating violence, there is a whole range of gradations which continues to widen the gap between love and violence. At the far end of this divorce, violence appears as the driving force of history. It is violence which brings onto the stage of history forces, new States, dominant civilizations, ruling classes. The history of man then appears to become identified with the history of violent power. In the last analysis, it is no longer the institution which justifies violence, it is violence which engenders the institution by redistributing power among States and classes.

Certainly there is a way of checking this gradual slide from merely punitive violence to innovating violence: this would consist in establishing a precise, manifest, indisputable, and unconditional limit to violence. This limit is immediately found: it is the prohibition of murder; "Thou shalt not kill." This negative commandment, this order in the form of an interdiction, is indeed the only principle of action which is able to hold the two ethics of love and of the magistrate together. Only a punishment which falls short of murder, short of the death penalty, does not contradict love altogether. To be sure, it does not fulfill it, for only "love fulfills the law." But at least it does not repudiate it. In this sense, one may say that if, by its origin and end, the punitive function of the State remains *foreign* to the reign of love, it is nevertheless *compatible* with it as long as it remains within the limits of the prohibition of murder. In the absence of a unity of origin and of end, the two pedagogies, that of sacrifice and that of coercion, may have in common a limit within the order of means. In the last resort, what links politics to ethics, order to charity, is respect for the person in his life and in his dignity. The violence of the magistrate is therefore measured by an ethics of means. It is here that the negative, inhibitive, and prohibitive character of the Decalogue is so valuable. The "Thou shalt not kill" draws the limit which the violence of the State may not transgress under penalty of leaving the sphere of the "good" in which its violence remains in accordance with reason. This interdiction undoubtedly does not show how the ethics of punishment flows from the ethics of charity, but it at least indicates the conditions under which they are practically compatible.

But *can* the State remain within the confines of this ethics of means? I mean to say: can it remain State without transgressing neither the interdiction of murder nor the other commandments of hospitality, respect for speech, filial respect, respect for the welfare of others, etc.?

It is here that the State exposes itself as an alarming magnitude which does not confine itself and never has confined itself within the *limits* of the ethics of means. The State is that reality which up to now has always included murder as the condition of its existence, of its survival, and first of all, of its inception. Such is the bitter truth from which Machiavelli, in *The Prince*, has drawn all the consequences without regard for an ethics of means. He raises the question: how can a new State be founded? On the basis of this question, he implacably describes all the *real* conditions of this foundation: strength of the lion and cunning of the fox. He concludes: if the Prince wishes to succeed, he must be murderous and deceptive. In Biblical language, he must be diabolical. It is easy to challenge Machiavelli's conclusion—"Violence and evil are needed"—on the pretext that murder is forbidden. Machiavelli's *question* stands: "how to found a State?"

War is the test *par excellence,* the limiting situation which puts each individual before the question of Machiavelli. Why does war constitute a problem? The conscientious objector will say: "There is no problem; war is the act by which state violence exceeds the limits and infringes upon the interdiction against murder; therefore, I am released from the duty to obey; through my disobedience, I bear witness to the unity of ethics. The State can have no other ethics but the individual, murder is forbidden to one and all." One must say very plainly and very firmly that the conscientious objector is right when he rejects all the *justifications* for war based upon the violence of the magistrate; the violence of the magistrate is one thing, war is another. The violence of the magistrate is instituted; it is measured by law; it is administered by a court of law distinct from plaintiff and accused. Lastly, it may be maintained within the limits of respect for the life and dignity of the guilty who are punished. In short, the regime of civilized penal law may not contradict love although it does not really fulfill it. Hence, all the hypocritical deductions by which one claims to justify war, based upon the function of the magistrate, must be rejected. One would first have to justify the death penalty and therefore place the magistrate on the terrain of murder. Moreover, one would have to imagine some delegation on the part of a virtual court of law which would instruct a State to punish wrong-doers from the outside and therefore to wage war as a sort of external penal law. The fictitious and hypocritical character of this deduction is obvious. War is and must remain for us a cataclysm, the outbreak of chaos, the return, in the external relations between States, to the struggle for life. This historical unreason must remain unjustified and unjustifiable. The event which hallows the complete disjunction of charity and violence, by destroying the fragile bond (the interdiction of murder) which holds them together, cannot be the object of a moral deduction.

Yet why *does* war constitute a problem? Because it is not merely the institution of murder but, more precisely, the murder of the enemy which coincides with the sacrifice of the individual for the physical survival of his own State. It is at this point that war poses what I would call the problem of an "ethic of distress." If war only posed one problem for me—shall I kill the enemy or not?—then only the fear and idolatry of a deified State could explain my submission to an evil State and these two motives would totally condemn me. My strict duty would consist in being a conscientious objector. But war also poses another problem for me: shall I risk my life in order for my State to survive? War is this limiting situation, this absurd situation which makes murder coincide with sacrifice. For the individual, to wage war is both to kill the other man, the citizen of another State, *and* to throw his life into the scale so that his State might continue to exist.

This problem does not coincide with that of the legitimacy of war for the State. As we have seen, such a moral justification of war as a punitive operation is deceitful. The problem of the physical survival of the State, of its material preservation at the risk of my life and at the price of the life of my enemy, is the monstrous enigma before which the existence of the State places me. It is a fact that up to now—I say up to now because war is perhaps in the process of changing its character so radically that the problem of the physical survival of the State may be on the verge of losing all meaning—States have survived by means of war; this unjustifiable violence has permitted, in the midst of suffering and ruin, the perpetuation not only of a certain majesty, but also of values as well. Furthermore, history proudly points out that the most cruel tyrannies, the most totalitarian regimes were crushed only from the outside, as by a break-in. In short, there are preservative wars, liberating wars, and innovating wars, and yet war as such remains unjustified and unjustifiable.

Precisely because war looms up on the dividing line of two ethics, that of charity and that of coercion, it condemns the individual to an "Ethic of distress." The sole motive for obeying the State when it is up in arms and at war is so *that it may continue to exist and thus preserve the magistrate.* My obedience remains on the non-ethical terrain of the pure and simple existence of my State; it is not groundless, since, without being an act of public authority, without being the exercise of punitive justice, it is the existential condition of all acts of public authority. *Let my State be;* such is the true and unique motivation of the armed and assaulting citizen. Hence I cannot be satisfied with obeying, for my obedience sanctions the fault of my State; its physical survival, in which I cooperate, is its culpability. I contribute to its pure and simple existence only by approving its malice by committing murder.

Shall I disobey? Yes, if I am able to bear the consequences and the meaning of this act. Of course, to bear the consequences, namely the risk of my own death; but I must equally be prepared to assume the meaning of this act, for disobedience is also an ethic of distress. While it bears witness to the hidden unity of the morality of the brother and of the magistrate, my disobedience at the same time puts my State in danger. True, one may say that radical examples of disobedience are quite rare and do not appreciably weaken the State. But this is not enough. I must act with the idea that the maxim of my action might become a universal law. The meaning of my act of disobedience, when extended to all, is therefore a threat to my State whose chances of survival I lessen. This is the "meaning" which I must accept and even assume if I disobey: in the limiting situation of war, the testimony that I bear to the absolute quality of the commandment which forbids murder puts my State in danger and, along with it, my fellow citizens. I do not have the right to bear this testimony if I do not assume, besides the risk involved, the meaning of my action, that is to say the threat to and, in the extreme, the sacrifice of my State.

It may be that in certain extreme cases the sacrifice of my State becomes a *political* duty and not merely an absolute testimony. It was before such a decision that certain anti-Nazis settled in Germany. It may be that I shall one day have to will the defeat of my country, if it simply does not deserve to survive, if it is absolutely incapable of being the State of justice and law, or, in short, if it is simply incapable of being the State. This decision is a dreadful one and it bears a name: the duty of betraying. But this decision, less than another, cannot remain in the register of non-violence. Sooner or later it enters anew into a system of violence. For I cannot will, with a positive and deliberate volition, the death of my State without at the same time willing, through the conjunction of these two major cataclysms, war and revolution, the violent institution of a new State, of a new sovereignty, a new power which in turn will summon my armed and murderous obedience. But the objection of conscience is something different; it refuses to place itself in the perspective of the political defeatism which has its full meaning only in another violence to which defeatism hands over the keys to the city. The objection of conscience wishes to remain a pure testimony. That is all very well, but then its impotency to assume all its *political* consequences, all its bearings on the distribution of forces in the world and primarily on the physical, existential destiny of my State, is its fault. Hence it too is an "ethic of distress."

More often than we may think, we are within one or another of these "ethics of distress." Bertolt Brecht has constantly drawn attention to the bad effects wrought by goodness, to "the terrible temptation of goodness," and to the danger of goodness in an evil world. Hence, ethics is forever wavering between a "testimony" to goodness, incapable of situating itself politically and sometimes harmful in the long run, and a murderous "efficacity" for men and ruin for goodness itself. The split is the ever bitter fruit of political existence driven to madness.

Let us once again retrace our steps. In the first part we considered the primordial discordance between the ethic of love and that of the magistrate. We uncovered a crucial split between love which returns good for evil and punishment which returns evil for evil with an eye to promoting the good of the wrong-doer. This primordial discord would not be a representation of radical evil if the State *could* remain within the boundaries of an ethic of means, which, by forbidding murder, would make coercion compatible with love or at least prevent it from being the absolute contrary of it. But the State is a reality which has not stayed and does not stay within the boundaries of the interdiction of murder. The State is a reality maintained and instituted by murderous violence. Through this connection with the unjustifiable, the State confronts man with a difficult choice, the choice between two "ethics of distress": the one assumes murder in order to assure the physical survival of the State, in order to preserve the magistrate; the other affirms treason in order to bear witness.

This limiting situation, by which ethics splits into two ethics of distress, is undoubtedly not a constant situation, nor even a lasting or frequent one. But like all extreme things, it throws light on the average, normal situations. It attests that until the last day, love and coercion will walk along side by side as the two pedagogies, sometimes converging, sometimes diverging, of mankind.

The end of this duality would be the total "reconciliation" of man with man. But this would also be the end of the State, because this would be the end of history.

The Political Paradox

Like every event worthy of this name, the event of Budapest has an infinite capacity for shocking. It has touched us and stirred us at several levels of our existence: at the level of historical compassion, caught by the unexpected; at the level of ordinary political strategy; at the level of reflection on the abiding political structures of human existence. We must always bear in mind these several powers of the event.

Yet we need not feel regret over having first evoked its power of shock without concern for reconciling tactics. However expected the event was, and there are some who maintain that it was, those few who are never caught unawares, still, the revolt was a surprise precisely because it took place: *the Flames of Budapest. . . .* If we want to be instructed by events, then we must not be in a hurry to solve them.

And then this event, which was left to speak for itself, must be evaluated, it must be reconstituted in the over-all situation. Moreover, we must bring out the unusual meaning contained in it, relating this to the Algerian war, the treason of the Socialist party, the disappearance of the Republican Front, and the resistance of French communists to de-Stalinization. In short, we must pass from absolute emotion to relative consideration.

For my part, the Budapest event, coupled with the October Revolution in Warsaw, has rekindled, confirmed, inflected, and radicalized a reflection on political power. Yet my reflection does not date from this event, since it had already given rise to several studies of which some were delivered at the *Collège philosophique* and others published in *Esprit* and elsewhere. What surprised me in these events is that they reveal the stability, in the very midst of socio-economic revolutions, of the problematic of power. The surprise is that Power has, as it were, no history, that the history of power repeats itself, marks time. The surprise is that there is no real political surprise. Techniques change, human relationships evolve depending upon things, and yet power unveils the same paradox, that of a twofold progress in rationality and in possibilities for perversion.

Many would maintain that the problem of political power in a socialist economy is not fundamentally different from the same problem in a capitalist economy, that it offers comparable if not added possibilities for tyranny, and that it calls for equally if not more strict democratic controls. Yet this is precisely what is rejected by all those who do not subscribe to the relative autonomy of polity in comparison with the socio-economic history of societies.[1]

This autonomy of polity seems to consist of two contrasting features. On the one hand, polity works out a human relationship which is neither reducible to class conflicts, nor to socio-economic tensions of society in general. The State most noted for a ruling class is a State in that it expresses the fundamental will of the nation in its entirety. Hence it is not radically affected, as State, by changes which are nevertheless radical in the economic sphere. By means of this first feature, man's political existence displays a specific type of *rationality* which is irreducible to dialectics based upon economics.

On the other hand, politics fosters specific *evils* which are precisely political evils, evils of political power. These evils are irreducible to others, in particular to economic alienation. Thus, economic exploitation *may* disappear while political evil persists. Moreover, the means which the State employs in order to put an end to economic exploitation may be the occasion for the abuse of power, new in their expression and in their effects, but fundamentally identical in their passional incentive to those of past States.

Specific rationality, specific evil—such is the double and paradoxical originality of polity. It would seem to me that the task of political philosophy is to explicate this originality and to elucidate the paradox of it. For political evil can only be an outgrowth of the specific rationality of polity.

It is necessary to hold out against the temptation to oppose two

1. Throughout this essay, particularly in the second section, the author contrasts polity (*le* politique) with politics (*la* politique). By polity, the author intends the ideal sphere of political organization and historical rationality; by politics, the empirical and concrete manifestations of this ideal sphere, the sum total of the means employed to implement the ideal sphere of polity.—Trans.

styles of political reflection, one which stresses the rationality of polity, drawing upon Aristotle, Rousseau, and Hegel, the other emphasizing the violence and untruth of power, following the Platonic critique of the "tyrant," the Machiavellian apology of the "prince," and the Marxist critique of "political alienation."

This paradox must be retained: that the greatest evil adheres to the greatest rationality, that there is political alienation *because* polity is relatively autonomous. Let us therefore now treat of the autonomy of polity.

[1] THE AUTONOMY OF POLITY

WHAT WILL ALWAYS remain admirable in the political thought of the Greeks is that no philosopher among them—with the possible exception of Epicurus—ever resigned himself to the exclusion of politics from the domain of rationality. All or almost all knew that if politics were declared evil, foreign, and "other," by comparison to reason and philosophical discourse, if politics were literally given over to the devil, then reason itself has capsized. For in that case, reason would no longer be of reality and in reality, at least not to the extent that human reality is political. If nothing is reasonable in man's political existence, then reason is not real, it is floating in the air, and philosophy becomes banished to the world of the Ideal and Duty. No great philosophy ever resigned itself to this, even (and especially) if it begins with the data of everyday existence and at first turns away from the world. Every great philosophy attempts to understand political reality in order to understand itself.

Now, politics discloses its meaning only if its *aim*—its *telos*—can be linked up with the fundamental intention of philosophy itself, with the Good and with Happiness. The Ancients did not understand how a Politics—a political philosophy—could possibly begin with something other than a *teleology* of the State, of the *"res publica,"* itself situated in relation to the final goal of mankind. Aristotle's *Politics* begins thus: "Every State is a society of some kind, and every society, like all forms of association, is instituted with a view to some good; for mankind always acts for an end which is esteemed good. Now if all societies aim at some good, then the State, which is the highest of all societies, and which encompasses all the rest, aims at the highest and most perfect good." The concept of the "good life" mutually implicates politics and ethics.

Henceforth, to reflect on the autonomy of polity is to find in the teleology of the State its irreducible manner of contributing to the humanity of man. The *specific* nature of polity can only be brought to light by means of this teleology. It has the specific nature of an aim, an intention. Through the political good, men pursue a good which they could not otherwise attain and this good is a part of reason and happiness. This pursuit and this *telos* constitute the "nature" of the *Polis*. The nature of the State is its end, just as "the nature of each thing is its end." [2]

From this standpoint, political philosophy is induced to determine how this *meaning*—which is the "end" and "nature" of the State—resides in the State as a *whole*, as an entire body, hence how humanity comes to man by means of the body politic. The fundamental conviction of all political philosophy is that he "who by nature and not by mere accident can exist without a state would be a despicable individual, either above or inferior to man. . . . For whoever has no need of society or is unable to live in society is either a beast or a god. The social instinct is natural to all men." [3] If the destination of man passes through a corporate body, through a whole, through a State defined by its "sufficiency," then it is forbidden to begin with the *opposition* between the State and the citizen. The point of view of philosophy is, on the contrary, that the individual becomes human only within this totality which is the "universality of citizens." The threshold of humanity is the threshold of citizenship, and the citizen is a citizen only through the State. Hence the movement of political philosophy starts with Happiness, which all men pursue, moves to the proper end of the State, then to its nature as a self-sufficient totality, and from there to the citizen. Because the "State is the constant subject of politics and government," the movement of political thought proper proceeds from the State to the citizen and not the inverse: "A citizen is one who, in his own country, has the power to take part in the deliberative or judicial administration of the State." Thus the citizen is characterized by the attribute of power: "For according to our definition, the citizen shares in the government of a state." [4]

In its turn, citizenship fosters the "virtues" peculiar to this participation in public power. These are the "virtues" which govern the relationship of government to free men, virtues of obedience distinct from servility, just as the authority of the State worthy of this name is distinct from despotism. Hence, political thought

2. Aristotle, *Politics*, I, 2 (1252 b 32)—Trans.
3. *Ibid.* (1253 a 2–3, 28–30)—Trans.
4. *Ibid.*, III, 1 (1275 a-b)—Trans.

proceeds from the State, to citizenship, to civism, and not in the reverse order.

Such is the disciplined thought proposed by the ancient model; such also is the disciplined thought which ought to be indispensable for any individual who wishes to gain the right to speak seriously about political evils. A meditation on politics, which would begin with the opposition of the "philosopher" and the "tyrant" and which would reduce the whole exercise of power to the perversion of the will to power, would thereby forever inclose itself within nihilistic moralism. One of the first actions of political reflection should be to push the figure of the "tyrant" off to the side, allowing it to emerge as the frightening possibility which cannot be coped with because men are evil. Still it should not be the object of political science: "It is proper to mention in last place tyranny as the worst of all depravations and the least worthy of the name constitution. For this reason, we have kept it for the end." (Aristotle)

But the automony of polity is something more than this vague, communal destiny of the human animal, something more than the admission of man to humanity by means of citizenship. More precisely, it is the specific nature of the political bond as opposed to the economic bond. This second moment of reflection is basic to what follows; for political evil will be just as specific as this bond and the remedy for the evil as well.

It seems to me that one cannot undertake the critique of the authenticity of political life without having first demarcated the boundaries of the political sphere and acknowledging the validity of the distinction between polity and economics. Every critique presupposes this distinction and can by no means set it aside.

Now, no reflection is a better preparation for this recognition than that of Rousseau. To discover and reiterate within oneself the most profound motivation of the "social contract" is, at the same time, to discover the meaning of polity as such. A return to Rousseau, linking up with the return to the Ancients—to Aristotle's *Politics* in particular—should provide the basis and the background for every critique of power which could not begin, in any case, with the individual.

The great, invincible idea of the *Social Contract* is that the body politic is born of a virtual act, of a consent which is not an historical event, but one which only comes out in reflection. This act is a pact: not a pact of one with another, not a pact of abstention in favor of a non-contracting third party, the sovereign, who, by not being part of the contract would be absolute. No—but it is a pact of each individual with all, a pact which constitutes the people as a people by constituting it as a State. This admirable idea, so criticized and so badly understood, is the basic equation of political philosophy: "To find a form of association that will defend and protect with the whole common force the person and goods of each member, and in which each, while uniting himself with all, may still obey himself alone and remain just as free as before." [5] Not the exchange of savage liberty for security, but the passage to civil existence through law which is given the consent of all.

One may well express dissatisfaction with the abstraction, idealism, and hypocrisy of this pact—and this is true in certain respects. But first one must recognize in this pact the founding act of the Nation. This founding act cannot be engendered by any economic dialectics; it is this founding act which constitutes polity as such.

One might object that this pact has not taken place. Precisely. It is of the nature of political consent, which gives rise to the unity of the human community organized and oriented by the State, to be able to be recovered only in an act which has not taken place, in a contract which has not been contracted, in an implicit and tacit pact which appears only in political awareness, in retrospection, and in reflection.

Hence, untruth can very easily slip into polity; polity is prone to untruth because the political bond has the reality of ideality: this ideality is the equality of each before all others, "for if each individual gives himself absolutely, the condition is equal for all; and, this being the case, then no one should have reason to make it onerous for others." [6] But before being hypocrisy, behind which is hidden the exploitation of man by man, equality before the law, and the ideal equality of each before all, is the *truth* of polity. This is what constitutes the *reality* of the State. Inversely, the reality of the State, irreducible to class conflicts or to the dynamics of economic domination and alienation, is the advent of a legality which will never be completely reducible to the projection of the interests of the ruling class into the sphere of law. As soon as there is a State, a body politic, the organization of an historical community, there exists the reality of this ideality; and herein is contained a point of view of the State which may never completely coincide with the phenomenon of class domination. If the State is reduced to the ideal projection of the interests of the ruling class, then there

5. J. J. Rousseau, *Contrat social* (Paris: Garnier, 1960), p. 243.—Trans.
6. *Ibid.*, pp. 243–44.—Trans.

is no longer a political State but despotic power. But even the most despotic State is still State in that something pertaining to the common good of the vast majority of citizens comes about through tyranny and therefore transcends the interests of one particular group or the dominant groups. Besides, only the original autonomy of polity can explain the hypocritical use of legality as a cloak for economic exploitation; for the ruling class would not experience the need to project its interests into juridical fiction if this juridical fiction were not first the condition of the real existence of the State. In order to become the State, a class must make its interests penetrate into the sphere of the universality of law; this law can mask the relation of force only in the measure that the power of the State itself flows from the ideality of the past.

I am aware of the difficulties related to the notion of general will, of sovereignty in Rousseau's writings. In the Geneva manuscript, Rousseau spoke even then of the "abyss of politics in the constitution of the State" (just as, in the constitution of man, the action of the soul on the body is the abyss of philosophy). These difficulties are not the fault of Rousseau; they pertain to polity as such: a pact which is a virtual act and which founds a real community; an ideality of law which legitimizes the reality of force; a ready-made fiction to clothe the hypocrisy of a ruling class, but which, before giving rise to falsehood, founds the freedom of citizens, a freedom which ignores particular cases, the real differences of power, and the real conditions of persons, but which is nevertheless valuable because of its very abstraction—such is the peculiar labyrinth of polity.

Rousseau, at bottom, is Aristotle. The pact which engenders the body politic is, in voluntarist language and on the level of the virtual pact (of the "as if"), the *Telos* of the State referred to by the Greeks. Where Aristotle speaks of "nature" and "end," Rousseau uses "pact" and "general will"; but it is fundamentally the same thing; in both cases, the specific nature of polity is reflected in philosophical consciousness. Rousseau recognized the artificial *act* of an ideal subjectivity, of a "public person," whereas Aristotle discerned an objective *nature*. But Rousseau's general will is objective and Aristotle's objective nature is that of man aiming toward happiness. The fundamental accord of these formulae comes out in their very reciprocity. In the two cases, with the *Telos* of the State and the generating *pact* of the general will, it is a matter of manifesting the coincidence of an individual and passional will with the objective and political will, in short, of making man's humanity pass through legality and civil restraint.

Rousseau is Aristotle. Perhaps it should be noted that Hegel supports this view. It is important, since Marx, as we shall see, initiated the critique of the bourgeois State and, he thought, of every State, through the instrumentality of Hegel's *Philosophy of Right*. The whole of Western political thought, epitomized in such giants as Aristotle, Rousseau, and Hegel, is supposedly brought together in the Marxist critique.

When Hegel looks upon the State as reason realized in man, he is not thinking about a particular state, nor any state whatever, but rather about the reality which comes into being through empirical States and to which nations obtain access when they pass the threshold of organization as a modern State, along with differentiated organs, a constitution, an administration, etc., and reach the level of historical responsibility within the framework of international relationships. From this standpoint, the State appears as what is desired by individuals so as to realize their freedom: viz., a rational, universal organization of freedom. The most extreme, the most scandalous formulae of Hegel on the State, which Eric Weil recapitulated in his book on *Hegel et l'état*,[7] should be taken as the limiting expression, as the advanced point of a thought determined to situate all its recriminations within the very interior of, and not outside of the fully recognized political reality. It is on the basis of this limiting expression that we must view all that can be said against the State and against the mad *pretension* which lays hold of its rational *intention*.

[2] POWER AND EVIL

THERE IS A SPECIFIC political alienation because polity is autonomous. It is the other side of this paradox which must now be clarified.

The crux of the problem is that the State is Will. One can stress as much as need be the rationality conferred upon history by polity—this is true. But if the State is rational in its intentions, it nevertheless advances through history by means of decisions. It is not possible to exclude from the definition of polity the idea of *decisions of historic import*, that is to say which change in abiding

7. "If, then, society is the foundation, the by no means formless matter of the State, the conscious reason of self is wholly on the side of the State: outside of it there may be concrete morality, tradition, work, abstract right, sentiment, virtue, but there can be no reason. Only the State thinks, only the State can be totally thought"—*Hegel et l'état* (Paris: Vrin, 1950) p. 68. For the definition of the State, cf. p. 45.

fashion the destiny of the human assemblage organized and directed by the State. Polity is rational organization, politics involves decisions: probable analysis of situations, probable projection as to the future. Polity necessarily involves politics.

Polity takes on meaning after the fact, in reflection, in "retrospection." Politics is pursued step by step, in "prospection," in projects, that is to say both in an uncertain deciphering of contemporary events, and in the steadfastness of resolutions. Thus, if the political function, if polity, carries on without interruption, one can say in a sense that politics only exists in great moments, in "crises," in the climactic and turning points of history.

But if it is impossible to define polity without including the voluntary moment of decision, neither is it possible to speak of political decisions without reflecting on power.

From polity to politics, we move from advent to events, from sovereignty to the sovereign, from the State to government, from historical Reason to Power.

It is in this fashion that the specific nature of polity becomes manifest within the specific qualities of the means of which it disposes. Considered from the point of view of politics, the State is the authority which holds a monopoly over lawful physical constraint. The adjective "lawful" attests that the definition of the State, in terms of its specific means, refers to the definition of the same State in terms of its end and its form. But should the State ever manage by chance to become identified with its foundation of legitimacy—for example by becoming the authority of the law—this State would still be a monopoly of constraint; it would still be the power of a few over all; it would still cumulate a legitimacy, that is to say a moral power of exacting, *and* a violence without appeal, that is to say a physical power of constraining.

It is in this way that we reach the idea of the entire sweep of politics. Let us say that politics is the sum total of activities which have for their object the exercise of power, therefore also the conquest and preservation of power. Step by step, politics will encompass every activity whose goal or effect will be to influence the division of power.[8]

It is politics—politics defined by reference to power—which poses the problem of political evil. There is a problem of political evil because there is a specific problem of power. Not that power is evil. But power is one of the splendors of man that is eminently

8. Max Weber calls politics "the sum total of efforts with a view to participating in power, or of influencing the division of power either within the State or between States"—*Politik als Beruf* (Munich, 1926).

prone to evil. Perhaps in history it is the greatest occasion for and the most stupendous display of evil. The reason of course is that power is a very extraordinary phenomenon, since it is the vehicle of the historical rationality of the State. We must never lose sight of this paradox.

This specific evil of power has been recognized by the greatest of political thinkers with a signal unanimity. The prophets of Israel and the Socrates of the *Gorgias* concur unequivocally on this point. Machiavelli's *Prince*, Marx's *Critique of Hegel's Philosophy of Right*, Lenin's *State and Revolution*—and . . . the Khrushchev report, that extraordinary document on the evil in politics—are all in fundamental accord although certainly operating within radically different theoretical and philosophical contexts. This very concurrence attests to the stability of the political problematic throughout history and, thanks to this stability, we *comprehend* these texts as a truth valid for all time.

It is well worth noting that the earliest recorded Biblical prophecy, that of Amos, denounces political crimes and not individual faults.[9] Wherever one might be tempted to recognize a mere survival of the outdated notion of collective sin, previous to the individualization of punishment and fault, one must distinguish the denunciation of political evil as the evil of power. It is man's political existence that confers upon sin its historical dimension, its devastating power and, I would venture to say, its grandeur. The death of Jesus, like that of Socrates, resulted from a political act, a political trial. It was a political authority, the very one which, by its order and tranquillity, assured the historical success of *humanitas* and *universalitas*. It was Roman political power that raised the Cross: "He suffered under Pontius Pilate."

Hence sin manifests itself in power, and power unveils the true nature of sin, which is not pleasure but the pride of domination, the evil of possession and holding sway.

The *Gorgias* is certainly in accord with this. One can even say that the Socratic and Platonic philosophy springs in part from a reflection on the "tyrant," that is to say on power without law and without consent on the part of subjects. How is the tyrant—the inverse of the philosopher—possible? This question cuts to the quick of philosophy, for tyranny is not possible without a falsifica-

---

9. *Amos*, 1:3–15: ". . . since they have crushed Galaad . . . , since they have taken a large number of captives and delivered them to Edom . . . , since they have hunted down their own brother at the sword's point without compassion . . . , since they so coveted Galaad's land that they would rip open the womb of pregnant women, I shall not recall the sentence I have pronounced."

tion of the *word,* that is to say of this power, human *par excellence,* of *expressing* things and of communicating with men. The whole of Plato's argument in the *Gorgias* is based upon the conjunction between the perversion of philosophy, represented by sophistry, and the perversion of politics, represented by tyranny. Tyranny and sophistry form a monstrous pair. Hence Plato ferrets out one aspect of political evil, different from power but intimately linked to it: "flattery," the art of inducing persuasion by means other than the truth. In this way, he brings to light the connection between politics and untruth. The point of his argument is quite important, if it is true that the word is the milieu, the fundamental element of mankind, the *logos* which unifies mankind and founds communication. Thus the lie, flattery, and untruth—political evils *par excellence*—corrupt man's primordial state, which is word, discourse, and reason.

Here, then, we have the elements of a meditation on the pride of power and on untruth, a meditation which shows these two phenomena to be evils linked to the essence of politics. We may rediscover this double meditation within these two great works of political philosophy: Machiavelli's *Prince* and Lenin's *State and Revolution,* both of which attest to the permanence of the problematic of power amid the various forms of governments, amid the evolution of technics and the transformations of social and economic conditionings. The question of power, of its exercise, its conquest, its defense and extension, has an astonishing stability which would make us apt to believe in a certain continuity of human nature.

Much has been said of the evil of "Machiavellism." But should we take the *Prince* seriously, as it must be, then we shall discover that it is by no means easy to evade its problem: how to establish a new power, a new State. The *Prince* evinces the implacable logic of political action: the logic of means, the pure and simple techniques of acquiring and preserving power. The technique is wholly dominated by the essential political relationship between the friend and the enemy: the enemy may be exterior or interior, a nation, nobility, an army, or a counsellor; and every friend may turn into an enemy and vice versa. The technique plays upon a vast keyboard ranging from military power to the sentiments of fear and gratitude, of vengeance and loyalty. The *Prince,* conscious of all the ramifications of power, the immensity, the variety, and the manifold measure of its keyboard, will be equipped with the abilities of the strategist and the psychologist, *lion* and *fox.* And so Machiavelli raised the true problem of political violence, not that of ineffectual violence, of arbitrary or frenetic violence, but that of calculated and limited violence designed to establish a stable state. Of course, one can say that by means of this calculation, inceptive violence places itself under the judgment of established legality; but this established legality, this "republic," is marked from its inception by violence which was successful. All nations, all powers, and all regimes are born in this way. Their violent birth then becomes resorbed in the new legitimacy which they foster and consolidate. But this new legitimacy always retains a note of contingency, something strictly historical which its violent birth never ceases to confer upon it. Machiavelli has therefore elucidated the relationship between politics and violence. Herein lies his probity and his veracity.

Several centuries later, Marx and Lenin returned to a theme which can be called Platonic, the problem of the "false consciousness." It seems to me that what is most worthy of note in the Marxist critique of politics and the Hegelian State is not its explication of the State by means of the power relations among classes, which would therefore be the reduction of political evil to socio-economic evil, but rather the description of this evil as the specific evil of politics. I believe that the great error which assails the whole of Marxism-Leninism and which weighs upon the regimes engendered by Marxism is this reduction of political evil to economic evil. From this springs the illusion that a society liberated from the contradictions of the bourgeois society would also be freed of political alienation. But the essential point of Marx's critique [10] is that the State is not and cannot be what it claims to be. What does it claim to be? If Hegel is right, the State is conciliation, the conciliation, in a higher sphere, of interests and individuals which are irreconcilable at the level of what Hegel calls civil society, which is what we would call the socio-economic level. The incoherent world of private relationships is arbitrated and rationalized by the higher authority of the State. The State is a mediator and therefore reason. And each of us attains his freedom and rights by means of the authority of the State. I am free in so far as I am political. It is in this sense that Hegel maintains that the State is representative: it exists in *representation* and man is represented in it. The essence of Marx's critique lies in exposing the *illusion* in this pretension. The State is not the true world of man but rather another and unreal world; it resolves real contradictions

10. Cf. J. Y. Calvez, *La Pensée de Karl Marx*, in the chapter on political alienation.

only in virtue of a fictive law which is, in turn, in contradiction with the real relationships between men.

It is on the basis of this essential *untruth*, of this discordance between the pretension of the State and the true state of affairs, that Marx meets with the problem of violence. For sovereignty, not being the achievement of the people in its concrete reality, but being another, visionary world, is forced to look for support in a real, concrete, empirical sovereign. The idealism of right is maintained throughout the course of history only by means of the caprice of the prince. Thus the political sphere is divided between the *ideal* of sovereignty and the *reality* of power, between sovereignty and the sovereign, between the constitution and the government, or the police. It matters little that Marx was only familiar with constitutional monarchy, for the split between the constitution and the monarch, between law and caprice, is a contradiction *internal* to all political power. This also holds true in the Republic. Notice how last year our right to referendum was usurped by clever politicians who twisted *de facto* power against the sovereignty of the electoral body. This is of the essence of political evil. No State exists without a government, an administration, a police force; consequently, the phenomenon of political alienation traverses all regimes and is found within all constitutional forms. Political society involves this external contradiction between an ideal sphere of legal relations and a real sphere of communal relations—and this internal contradiction between sovereignty and the sovereign, between the constitution and power or, in the extreme, the police. We aspire to attain a State wherein the radical contradiction which exists between the universality pursued by the State and the particularity and caprice which it evinces in reality would be resolved. The evil is that this aspiration is not within our reach.

Unfortunately, Marx did not perceive the absolute character of this contradiction; he viewed it as a mere superstructure, that is to say the transposition onto a superadded plane of the contradictions pertaining to the inferior plane of capitalist society and, in the last analysis, an effect of class opposition. The State, then, is but the instrument of class violence, even though the State may possibly always envisage a scheme or project transcending disparate class interests. Oddly enough, it would seem that the evil peculiar to the State is its very opposition to this grandiose scheme. When the State is thus conceived of as the organized power of the ruling class for oppressing another, then the illusion of the State being universal conciliation is nothing but a particular instance of the vice of bourgeois societies, showing them unable to offset their own deficiency or to resolve their contradictions except by taking flight into the phantom of Right.

I believe it must be maintained, against Marx and Lenin, that political alienation is not reducible to another, but is constitutive of human existence, and, in this sense, that the political mode of existence entails the breach between the citizen's abstract life and the concrete life of the family and of work. I think too that thereby we retain what is best in the Marxist critique, which interrelates with the Machiavellian, Platonic, and Biblical critique of power.

I should like to adduce the Khrushchev report alone as proof. The fundamental fact would seem to be that the criticism of Stalin has meaning only if the alienation of politics is an absolute alienation, irreducible to that of economic society. If it were not, then how is it possible to censure Stalin while continuing to sanction the socialist form of economy and the Soviet regime? The Khrushchev report is inconceivable without a critique of power and the vices of power. But since Marxism does not allow for an autonomous problematic of power, it falls back upon fable and moralizing criticism. Togliatti was somewhat incautious the day he declared that the explanations of the Khrushchev report did not satisfy him, wondering as he did how the phenomenon of Stalin had been possible in a socialist regime. The reply could not be given to him because it can only flow from a critique of socialist power, something which up to now has not been made and which, perhaps, could not be achieved within the compass of Marxism, *at least in so far as Marxism reduces all alienations to economic and social alienation.*

I should like to make it quite clear once and for all that the theme of political evil, which I have just set forth, by no means constitutes a political "pessimism" and does not warrant any political "defeatism." Besides, the pessimist and optimist labels are to be banned from philosophical reflection; pessimism and optimism are but moods and only concern characterology, which is to say that no use may be made of them here. Yet it is quite important that we should acquire a *lucidity* with respect to the evil of power, for this is something which could not be divorced from a thoroughgoing reflection on polity. This reflection reveals that politics can be the seat of the greatest evil only because of its prominent place within human existence. The enormity of political evil is commensurate with man's political existence. More than any other, a meditation which would parallel political evil with radical evil, making of it the closest approximation of radical evil, ought to remain inseparable from a meditation on the radical significance of politics. Every condemnation of politics as corrupt is itself deceitful, malevolent, and infamous, at least if it neglects to situate this description within the dimension of the political animal. The analysis of polity, as the progress of man's rationality, is not abolished but constantly presupposed by meditation on political evil. On the contrary, political evil is serious only because it is the *evil* of man's rationality, the specific evil of the splendor of man.

In particular, the Marxist critique of the State does not suppress the analysis of sovereignty, from Rousseau to Hegel, but rather presupposes the truth of this analysis. If there is no truth in the general will (Rousseau), if there is no teleology of history amid "unsocial sociability" and by means of this "ruse of reason" which is political rationality (Kant), if the State is not "representative" of man's humanity, then political evil is not grave. It is precisely *because* the State is a certain expression of the rationality of history, a triumph over the passions of the individual man, over "civil" interests, and even over class interests, that it is the most exposed and most threatened aspect of man's grandeur, the most prone to evil. Political "evil" is, in the literal sense, the madness of grandeur, that is to say the madness of what is great—Grandeur and culpability of power!

Henceforth, man cannot evade politics under penalty of evading his humanity. Throughout history, and by means of politics, man is faced with *his* grandeur and *his* culpability.

One could not infer a political "defeatism" on the basis of this lucidity. Such a reflection leads rather to a political *vigilance*. It is here that reflection, ending its long detour, comes back to actuality and moves from critique to praxis.

[3] THE PROBLEM OF POWER IN SOCIALIST REGIMES

IF OUR ANALYSIS of the paradox of power is correct, if the State is at once more rational and more passional than the individual, the great problem of democracy concerns the *control* of the State by the people. The problem of the control of the State, like that of its rationality, is equally irreducible to socio-economic history, as is its evilness irreducible to class contradictions. The problem of the control of the State consists in this: to devise institutional techniques especially designed to render possible the exercise of power and render its abuse impossible. The notion of "control" derives directly from the central paradox of man's political existence; it is the *practical* resolution of this paradox. To be sure, it is, of course, necessary that the State *be* but that it not be too much. It must direct, organize, and make decisions so that the political animal himself might be; but it must not lead to the tyrant.

Only a political philosophy which has perceived the specific nature of polity—the specific nature of its function and the specific nature of its evil—is in a position to pose correctly the problem of political control.

Thus the reduction of political alienation to economic alienation would seem to be the weak point in the political thought of Marxism. This reduction of political alienation has, in effect, led Marxism-Leninism to substitute another problem for the problem of State control, that of the *withering away* of the State. This substitution seems disastrous to me; it grounds the end of the iniquity of the State upon an indefinite future, whereas the true, practical political problem pertains to the limitation of this evil in the present. An eschatology of innocence takes the place of an ethic of limited violence. At one and the same time, the thesis of the withering away of the State, by promising too much for the future, equally tolerates too much in the present. The thesis of the future withering away of the State serves as a cloak and an alibi for the perpetuation of terrorism. By means of a sinister paradox, the thesis of the provisory character of the State turns into the best justification for the endless prolongation of the dictatorship of the proletariat and forms the essence of totalitarianism.

It is quite necessary to realize that the theory of the withering away of the State is a logical consequence of the reduction of political alienation to economic alienation. If the State is merely an organ of *repression,* which springs from class antagonisms and expresses the domination of one class, then the State will disappear along with all the aftereffects of the division of society into classes.

But the question is whether the end of the private appropriation of the means of production can bring about the end of *all* alienations. Perhaps appropriation itself is but one privileged form of the power of man over man; perhaps money itself is but one means of domination among others; perhaps the same spirit of domination is given expression in various forms: in economic exploitation, in bureaucratic tyranny, in intellectual dictatorship, and in clericalism.

Our concern here is not the hidden unity of all alienations. In any case, the reduction of the political form to the economic form is indirectly responsible for the myth of the withering away of the State.

It is true that Marx, Engels, and Lenin have attempted to elaborate this theory on the basis of experience. They interpreted the Paris Commune as the guarantee and the commencement of the experimental verification of the thesis of the withering away of the State; for them it demonstrated that the dictatorship of the proletariat may be something quite different than the mere transfer of the State's power into other hands, but indeed the overthrow of the State machine as the *"special force"* of repression. If the armed populace is substituted for the permanent army, if the police force is subject to dismissal at any moment, if bureaucracy is dismantled as an organized body and reduced to the lowest paid condition, then the general force of the majority of the people replaces the special force of repression found in the bourgeois State, and the beginning of the withering away of the State coincides with the dictatorship of the proletariat. As Lenin says, "it is impossible to pass from capitalism to socialism without a certain return to a primitive form of democracy." The withering away of the State is therefore contemporaneous to the dictatorship of the proletariat, in the measure that the latter is a truly popular revolution which smashes the repressive organs of the bourgeois State. Marx could even say: "The Commune was no longer a State in the literal sense of the word."

In the thought of Marx and Lenin, the thesis of the withering away of the State was therefore not a hypocritical thesis but a sincere one. To be sure, few men have demanded so little of the State as the great Marxists: "So long as the proletariat still has need of a State," reads the *letter to Bebel,* "it is not in order to secure freedom but to put down its adversaries; and the day when it becomes possible to speak of freedom, the State will cease to exist as such."

But if the withering away of the State is the critical test for the dictatorship of the proletariat, then the crucial question is posed: why has the withering away of the State not *in fact* coincided with the dictatorship of the proletariat? Why, in fact, has the socialist State reinforced the power of the State to the point of confirming the axiom which Marx believed to be applicable only to bourgeois revolutions: "All revolutions have only served to perfect this machine instead of smashing it." [11] The attempt to reply to this

11. Marx, *The Eighteenth Brumaire of Louis Bonaparte.*

question is at the same time to provide the missing link to the Khrushchev report, for it is to explain how the phenomenon of Stalin was possible in the midst of a socialist regime.

My working hypothesis, such as is suggested by the preceding reflection, is that Stalin was possible *because* there was no recognition of the permanence of the problematic of power in the transition from the old to the new society, because it was believed that the end of economic exploitation necessarily implied the end of political repression, because it was believed that the State is provisory, because one had substituted the problem of the withering away of the State for that of its control. In short, my working hypothesis is that the State cannot wither away and that, not being able to wither away, it must be controlled by a special institutional form of government.

Furthermore, it would seem that the socialist State, more than the bourgeois state, requires a vigilant, popular control precisely because its rationality is greater, because it enlarges its sphere of analyses and forecasts so as to encompass sectors of human existence which elsewhere and in former times were given over to chance and improvisation. The rationality of a socialist State, striving as it does to suppress class antagonisms and even aspiring to put an end to the division of society into classes, is certainly greater. But you see at once that its scope of power is also greater as well as the possibilities for tyranny.

It would seem that the task of a critique of socialist power should be to articulate lucidly and faithfully the new possibilities of political alienation, that is to say those which are opened up by the very battle against economic alienation as well as by the reinforcement of State power which this battle entails.

Here are some avenues of approach which might be pursued by an investigation of power in socialist regimes:

1. We should first have to determine in what measure "the administration of things" necessarily involves a "governing of persons" and in what measure the progress in the administration of things gives rise to an augmentation of political power of man over man.

For example: planning implies a choice of an economic character concerning the order of priority in the satisfaction of needs and the employment of means of production; but this choice is from the very outset *more* than a matter of economics. It is the function of a general politics, that is to say of a long-term project concerning the orientation of the human community engaged in the experience of planning. The proportion of the part reinvested and the part consumed, the proportion of cultural and material goods in the general equilibrium of the plan, spring from a "global strategic vision" in which economics is woven into politics. A plan is a technique serving a global project, a civilizing project animated by implicit values, in short, a project which in the last analysis pertains to man's very nature. Hence, insofar as it gives expression to *will* and power, polity is the soul of economics.

Thus the administration of things may not be substituted for the governing of persons, since the rational technique of ordering man's needs and activities on the macroscopic scale of the State cannot extricate itself from all ethico-cultural contexts. Consequently, in the last analysis, political power unites scales of value and technological possibilities, the latent aspirations of the human community, and the means unleashed by knowledge of economic laws. The connection between ethics and technics in the "task" of planning is the fundamental reason why the administration of things *implies* the governing of persons.

2. Next, we should have to determine how the reinforcement of State power, which is intimately linked to the expansion of the jurisdiction of the socialist State in comparison with the bourgeois State, fosters *abuses which are inherent to it in virtue of its nature as a socialist State.* This would constitute the elucidation of the idea mentioned earlier, that the most rational State possesses the most opportunities for being passional.

Engels pointed out in *Anti-Dühring* that the organization of production will remain authoritarian and repressive, even after the expropriation of expropriators, so long as there is a perpetuation of the old division of work and the other alienations which make working a burden and not a joy. When it is not spontaneous, the division of work still arises from constraint, and this constraint is precisely connected to the passage from hazard to rationality.

The temptation toward forced labor therefore becomes one of the major temptations of the socialist State. But it can easily be seen that the socialist State is the least protected against this temptation, since its method of global planning also endows it with the *economic* monopoly over psychological constraint (culture, the press, and propaganda are encompassed within the plan and are therefore *economically* determined by the State). Hence, the socialist State will have a whole arsenal of means at its disposal, including psychological means ranging from inducements and competition to deportation.

In addition to these opportunities for abuse provided by the organization of the means of production, there is the temptation to overcome irrational resistances by more expeditious means than those of education or discussion. In effect, the rational State encounters resistances of all kinds; some of these result from residual phenomena (described quite well by Chinese Marxists, in particular, and previously by Lenin in the *Infantile Disorder of Communism*). These resistances are typical of the peasantry and the lower middle class, demonstrating that the psychology of workers is not on the same plane as that of technocrats, but remains adapted to long standing situations. Thus we find resistances of a psychological character which do not spring from considerations of the general welfare of the people but from the habituation to outdated economic conditions. Yet all resistances are not subject to this explanation by backward mentalities. The socialist State has a more remote and more vast project than the individual whose interests are more immediate, limited to the horizon of his death or at the very most to that of his children. In the meantime, the State calculates by generations; since the State and the individual are not on the same wave length, the individual develops interests which are not naturally in accord with those of the State. We are familiar with at least two manifestations of this variance between the goal of the State and that of the individual: one concerns the division between investment and immediate consumption, the other the determination of standards and the rate of production. The micro-interests of individuals and the macro-decisions of power are in a state of constant tension, fostering a dialectic of individual demands and State constraint which is an occasion for abuse.

Thus we find tensions and contradictions which are not the remedies for the private appropriation of the means of production. Certain of these tensions and contradictions even derive from the new power of the State.

Lastly, the socialist State is more ideological than the "liberal" State. It may attribute to itself the ancient dreams of unifying the realm of truth within an orthodoxy encompassing all the manifestations of knowledge and all the expressions of the human word. Under the pretext of revolutionary discipline and technocratic efficacity, it can justify an entire militarization of minds; it can do it, that is to say, it has the temptation and the means to do so since it possesses the monopoly of provisions.

All of these reflections converge toward the same conclusion: if the socialist State does not abolish but rather revives the problematic of the State—if it serves to further its rationality while intensifying opportunities for perversion—the problem of the democratic *control* of the State is still more pressing in socialist regimes than in capitalistic regimes, and the myth of the *withering away* of the State stands in the way of a systematic treatment of this problem.

3. The third task of a critique of power in socialist regimes would then consist of coming back to the critique of the liberal state in light of this idea of democratic control. This would enable it to determine which institutional features of the liberal state were independent of the phenomenon of class domination and specifically adapted to the limitation of the abuse of power. No doubt this critique could not be carried out within the specifically critical phase of socialism; the liberal State had to appear almost inevitably as a hypocritical means of perpetuating economic exploitation. Yet today it is indispensable to discern between the instrument of class domination and democratic control in general, at least after the bitter experience of Stalinism. Perhaps it is the case that Marxism in itself embodies the ingredients for this revision when it propounds that a class in its ascending phase pursues a *universal* function. In giving expression to the problem of democratic controls, the "philosophers" of the eighteenth century devised the true *liberalism* which no doubt goes beyond the destiny of the bourgeoisie. It does not follow that just because the bourgeoisie had need of these controls in order to draw limits to monarchic and feudal power and to facilitate its own ascension, that these controls therefore exhaust their abiding significance within their provisory usage. In its profound intention, liberal politics comprised an element of universality, for it was adjusted to the *universal* problematic of the State, beyond the form of the bourgeois state. This explains how a return to liberal politics is possible within a socialist context.

I should like to cite a few examples of this *discernment* applied to the structures of the liberal State, examples of the division between the "universal" aspects and the "bourgeois" aspects of these structures. I shall present them in a problematic manner since we are practically at the end of a critique of socialist power of which the first postulates are scarcely certain:

a) Is not the independence of the "judge" the very first condition of permanent legal remedy against the abuse of power?

It seems to me that the judge is a personage who must be voluntarily placed, by the consent of all, on the fringes of the fundamental conflicts of society.

The independence of the judge, it will be objected, is an abstraction. Quite so. Society requires for its human respiration an "ideal" function, a deliberate, concerted abstraction in which it projects the ideal of legality that legitimates the reality of power. Without this projection, in which the State represents itself as legitimate, the individual is at the mercy of the State and power itself, without protection against its arbitrariness. It stands to reason that the proceedings of Moscow, of Budapest, of Prague, and elsewhere, were possible because the independence of the judge was not technically assured nor ideologically founded in a theory of the judge as a man above class, as an abstraction of human proportions, as the embodiment of law. Stalin was possible because there were always judges to judge in accordance with his decree.

b) The second condition of permanent legal remedy against the abuse of power is the citizen's free access to sources of information, knowledge, and science, independent of those of the State. As we have seen, the modern State determines the way of living since it orients economically all of man's choices by its macro-decisions, its global planning; but this power will become more and more indistinguishable from totalitarian power if the citizens are not able to *form, by themselves, an opinion* concerning the nature and the stakes involved in these macro-decisions.

More than any other, the socialist State requires the counterpart of *public opinion* in the strict sense of the word, that is to say, a public which has opinions and an opinion which is given public expression. It is quite plain what this involves: a press that belongs to its readers and not to the State, and a press whose freedom of information and of expression is constitutionally and economically guaranteed. Stalin was possible because no public opinion could launch a critique of him. But then again, the post-Stalin State alone has dared to utter that Stalin was evil, *not* the people.

The independent exercise of justice and the independent formation of opinion are the two lungs of a politically sound State. Without these, there is asphyxiation.

These two notions are so important that it was in virtue of them that the overthrow of Stalinism was accomplished; the notions of *justice* and *truth* gave birth to the revolt. This explains the role of intellectuals in the abortive revolution of Hungary and in the successful revolution of Poland. If intellectuals, writers, and artists played a decisive role in these events, it is because the stakes at issue were not economic and social, notwithstanding misery and low wages; the stakes were strictly political, or to be more precise, they were the new political "alienation" infecting socialist power. But the problem of political alienation, as we are well aware of since Plato's *Gorgias,* is the problem of untruth. We have also learned of this through the Marxist critique of the bourgeois State, situated, as it is, entirely upon the terrain of *untruth,* of being and appearance, of mystification, and of falsehood. It is just here that the intellectual as such becomes involved in politics. The intellectual is driven to the fore of a revolution, and not merely within its ranks, as soon as the incentive for this revolution is more political than economic, as soon as it touches upon the relation of power with truth and justice.

c) Next, it would seem to me that the democracy of work requires a certain dialectic between the State and labor councils. As we have seen, the long-term interests of the State, even apart from the consideration of money, do not immediately coincide with those of workers; this stands to reason in a socialist period, in the precise sense of the word, that is to say in a phase of inequality of wages, wherein professional specialization is in opposition to unskilled and skilled laborers, directors, and intellectuals; this also stands to reason in a period of rapid or even forced industrialization. Consequently, only a network of liasons between the State and associations representing the diverse interests of workers can consolidate the groping quests for a viable equilibrium, that is to say at once economically sound and humanly tolerable. The right to strike, in particular, would seem to be the sole recourse of workers against the State, *even against the State of workers.* The postulate of the immediate coincidence of the will of the socialist State with all interests of all workers seems to me to be a pernicious illusion and a dangerous alibi for the abuse of State power.

d) Lastly, the key problem is that of the control of the State by the people, by the democratically organized foundation. At this point, the reflections and experiences of the Yugoslavian and Polish communists ought to be consulted and analyzed very closely. The question is whether the pluralism of parties, the practice of "free elections," and the parliamentary form of government derive from this "universalism" of the liberal State, or whether they irremediably pertain to the bourgeois period of the liberal State. We must not have any preconceived ideas: neither for nor against; neither for Occidental custom, nor for radical criticism; we need not be in a hurry to answer. It is certain that planning techniques require that the socialist form of production not be given over to the hazard of popular vote; that it be irrevocable, as is the republican form of our government. The execution of the Plan calls for full powers, a government of long continuance, a long-term budget. Yet our parliamentary techniques, our manner of interchanging the majorities in power, would not appear very compatible with the modern rationality of the State. And yet, on the other hand, it is just as certain that *discussion* is a vital necessity for the State; through discussion it is given orientation and impetus; discussion curbs its tendency to abuse power. Democracy is discussion. Thus it is necessary that this discussion be *organized* in one way or another. Here we encounter the question concerning parties or the unique Party. What may argue in favor of the pluralism of parties is that this system has not only reflected tensions between social groups, determined by the division of society into classes, but it has also invested political discussion as such with organization, and it has therefore had a "universal" and not merely a "bourgeois" significance. An analysis of the notion of "party," on the sole basis of the socio-economic criterion, therefore seems to me dangerously inadequate and liable to encourage tyranny. This is why it is necessary to judge the theory of multiple parties and the theory of a single party not only from the standpoint of class dynamics, but equally from the viewpoint of the techniques of controlling the State. Only a critique of power in socialist regimes could further advance this question. Yet this critique has hardly been launched.

I do not know whether the term political "liberalism" can be saved from falling into disrepute. Perhaps its affinity with economic liberalism has compromised it once and for all, although of late, the label "liberal" tends to constitute a misdemeanor in the eyes of social fascists in Algeria and in Paris, and thus recovers its bygone freshness.

If the term could be saved, it would state rather well what ought to be said: that the central problem of politics is *freedom*: whether the State *founds* freedom by means of its rationality, or whether freedom *limits* the passions of power through its resistance.

Universal Civilization
and National Cultures

THE PROBLEM EVOKED HERE is equally pertinent to highly industrialized countries ruled by well-established governments, and to underdeveloped countries which have just attained their independence. The problem is this: mankind as a whole is on the brink of a single world civilization representing at once a gigantic progress for everyone and an overwhelming task of survival and adapting our cultural heritage to this new setting. To some extent, and in varying ways, everyone experiences the tension between the necessity for the free access to progress and, on the other hand, the exigency of safeguarding our heritage. Let it be said at the outset that my thought does not result from any contempt for universal modern civilization; there is a problem precisely because we are under the strain of two different necessities which are both pressing.

[1]

HOW CAN WE CHARACTERIZE this universal world civilization? Some have hastily characterized it as a technical civilization. Yet technics is not the decisive and fundamental factor; for the source of the spread of technics is the scientific spirit itself. Primarily, this is what unifies mankind at a very abstract and purely rational level, and which, on that basis, endows civilization with its universal character.

We have to keep in mind that if science is Greek in its origins

[271]

and European through Galileo, Descartes, Newton, etc., science does not foster this power of unifying mankind because it is Greek or European but because it is a human dimension. It manifests a sort of *de jure* unity which controls all the other features of civilization. When Pascal writes that "the whole of mankind may be looked upon as one single man who constantly learns and remembers," his statement simply means that every man, if confronted with a test of a geometrical or experimental character, is capable of arriving at the same conclusion providing he has had the required background. Hence, it is a purely abstract and rational unity of mankind which leads to all the other manifestations of modern civilization.

In second place we shall, of course, rank the development of technics. This development may be understood as a revival of traditional tools on the basis of the consequences and applications of this single science. These tools, which belong to the primitive cultural resources of mankind, have in themselves a very great inertia. Left to themselves they tend to coagulate in solid traditions. They are not transformed by something intrinsic to them, but by the repercussions of scientific knowledge; tools are revolutionized and become machines by means of thought. Here we encounter a second source of universality; mankind develops in nature like an artificial being, that is to say, like a being that creates all its relations with nature by means of tools which are constantly being revolutionized by scientific knowledge; man is a kind of universal contrivance. In this sense we can say that technics, considered as a revival of traditional tools in an applied science, has no fixed domain either. Even if it is possible to ascribe to such or such a country or culture the invention of writing, printing, the steam engine, etc., an invention rightfully belongs to mankind as a whole. Sooner or later it creates an irreversible situation for everyone; its spread may be delayed but not totally prevented. Thus we are confronted with a *de facto* universality of mankind: as soon as an invention appears in some part of the world we can be sure it will spread everywhere. Technical revolutions mount up and because they do, they escape cultural isolation. We can say that in spite of delays in certain parts of the world there is a single, world-wide technics. That is why national or nationalistic revolutions, in making a nation approach modernization, at the same time make it approach a certain cosmopolitanism. Even if—and we shall come back to this presently—the scope is national or nationalistic it is still a factor of communication to the extent that it is a factor of industrialization, for this makes it share in the universal technical civilization. It is thanks to this phenomenon of diffusion that we are able today to have a world-wide awareness and, so to speak, a lively sense of the earth's round-ness.

At the third stage of this universal civilization I would put what I call with caution, the existence of a rational politics. Naturally, I am not underrating the importance of political regimes, but one may say that amid the diversity of familiar political regimes there is the unfolding of a single experience of mankind and even a unique political technics. The modern State, *qua* State, has a recognizable universal structure. The first philosopher to have reflected on this form of universality is Hegel in the *Philosophy of Right*. Hegel is the first to have shown that one of the aspects of man's rationality and, at the same time, of his universality, is the growth of a State which institutes laws and develops the means for their enforcement in the form of an administration. Even if we should sharply criticize bureaucracy and technocracy, we only achieve the pathological form peculiar to the rational phenomenon which we are elucidating. Perhaps we must even go farther: not only is there the single political experience of mankind, but all regimes also have a certain path in common; as soon as certain levels of comfort, instruction, and culture are attained, we see them all inescapably evolve from a dictatorial form to a democratic form. We see them all in search of a balance between the necessity of concentrating power, or even of personalizing it, in order to make a decision possible, and on the other hand, the necessity of organizing discussion in order that the largest possible number of men can take part in this decision. But I want to come back to the concept of the rationalization of power represented by an adminis-tration, because it is a phenomenon seldom treated by political philosophy, even though it is a factor in the rationalization of history which could not be underestimated. It may be said that we are confronted with a State, a modern State, when we witness the power capable of effecting a public function, a body of civil servants who prepare decisions and enforce them without being themselves responsible for the political decision. This constitutes a rational aspect of politics which concerns absolutely all the nations of the world to the point that it constitutes one of the most decisive criteria of the accession of a State onto the world scene.

It may be dangerous to speak of the existence of a rational, universal economy as a fourth factor. Undoubtedly, it is necessary to speak of it with even more caution than of the previous phenom-enon, owing to the decisive importance of individual economic regimes as such. Nevertheless, a good deal takes place behind the scenes. Over and above the known massive oppositions, economic techniques of a truly universal character unfold. Calculations concerning contingencies, techniques of market-control, plans of forecasting and decisions, all of these have something in common despite the oppositions of capitalism and authoritarian socialism. We can speak of an economic science and an economic technics of international proportions; they are integrated in their different economic goals, but at the same time they create, whether we like it or not, converging phenomena whose effects seem to be inescapable. This convergence results from the fact that economics as well as politics is cultivated by the human sciences, which in their essence are supra-national, without a country. The original universality, with its scientific character, permeates all human technics with rationality.

Lastly, it can be said that throughout the world an equally universal way of living unfolds. This way of living is manifested by the unavoidable standardization of housing and clothing. These phenomena derive from the fact that ways of living are themselves rationalized by techniques which concern not only production but also transportation, human relationships, comfort, leisure, and news programming as well. Let us also mention the various techniques of elementary culture or, more exactly, the culture of consumption; there is a culture of consumption of world-wide dimensions, displaying a way of living which has a universal character.

[2]

Now what is the significance of this world civilization? Its significance is very ambiguous and it is this double meaning which creates the problem that we are treating here. On the one hand, it seems to constitute a real progress; still it is necessary for this term to be clearly defined. There is progress when two conditions are fulfilled: there is a phenomenon of accumulation and a phenomenon of improvement. The first is the easiest to distinguish, although its boundaries are unclear. I would readily say that there is progress wherever one can distinguish the phenomenon of the deposit of tools which we were just speaking about. But in that case, we have to take the expression "tools" in a very broad sense, covering both the properly technical realm of instruments and of machines. The whole network of organized mediations which are put into the service of science, politics, economics, and even of ways of living and means of leisure are dependent, in this sense, on the realm of tools.

The transformation of means into new means constitutes the phenomenon of accumulation, which is the reason why, moreover, there is human history. To be sure, there are many other reasons which account for human history; but the irreversible character of this history depends in large measure upon the fact that we work as fragments of tools; here nothing is lost and everything accumulates. This is the basic phenomenon, and it can be seen in fields which are on the surface quite removed from pure technics. Thus, unfortunate experiences and political failures constitute an experience which becomes, for the whole of mankind, something similar to a set of tools. It is possible that certain ways of careless planning, for example, those pertaining to rural populations, will spare other planners from making the same mistakes, at least if they follow the course of reason. Hence, there arises a phenomenon of rectification, an economy of means, which is one of the most striking aspects of progress.

But one could not attribute progress to any accumulation whatever. This development has to represent an improvement in various respects. Now it seems to me that this universalization is a good in itself. By itself, the awareness of a single humanity represents something positive; one might say that a sort of mutual recognition of men arises in the midst of all these phenomena. The multiplication of human relationships makes mankind a more and more compact network, more and more interdependent; and it makes all nations and all social groups a single humanity which develops its experience. It can even be said that the thought of nuclear destruction makes us a little more aware of the unity of mankind, since for the first time, we can feel ourselves totally threatened *en masse*.

On the other hand, universal civilization is a good because it represents the availability of elementary possessions to the masses of humanity. No kind of criticism of technics will be able to counterbalance the absolutely positive benefit of the freedom from want and of the massive access to comfort. Up to the present, mankind has lived, so to speak, by proxy, either through certain privileged civilizations or through some select groups. For the first time in two centuries in Europe, and since the second half of the twentieth century for the immense populations of Asia, Africa, and

South America, we can now detect the possibility of a massive access to at least a minimum degree of comfort.

Furthermore, this world civilization represents a good, owing to a sort of shift in the attitude of mankind taken as a whole with regard to its own history. Mankind as a whole has experienced its lot as a dreadful fate; this is probably still true for more than half of mankind. But the massive access of men to certain values of dignity and autonomy is an absolutely irreversible phenomenon, a good in itself. We are witnessing the advance onto the world scene of great human masses who were heretofore silent and downtrodden. It can be said that a growing number of men have the awareness of making their history, of making history; in this sense, one can say that these men are really joining the majority.

Lastly, I shall not scoff at what I earlier called the culture of consumption, from which we all benefit to some degree. It is certain that a growing number of men are today approaching that elementary level of culture of which the most noteworthy aspect is the fight against illiteracy and the development of means of consuming and a basic culture. Until these last few decades, only a small fraction of mankind knew how to read. Now, however, we may expect that in a few more decades, mankind will have surpassed the threshold of a first rudimentary culture by far, and this is unquestionably a good.

On the other hand, we have to admit that this same development presents a contrary character. The phenomenon of universalization, while being an advancement of mankind, at the same time constitutes a sort of subtle destruction, not only of traditional cultures, which might not be an irreparable wrong, but also of what I shall call for the time being the creative nucleus cf great civilizations and great cultures, that nucleus on the basis of which we interpret life, what I shall call in advance the ethical and mythical nucleus of mankind. The conflict springs up from there. We have the feeling that this single world civilization at the same time exerts a sort of attrition or wearing away at the expense of the cultural resources which have made the great civilizations of the past. This threat is expressed, among other disturbing effects, by the spreading before our eyes of a mediocre civilization which is the absurd counterpart of what I was just calling elementary culture. Everywhere throughout the world, one finds the same bad movie, the same slot machines, the same plastic or aluminum atrocities, the same twisting of language by propaganda, etc. It seems as if mankind, by approaching *en masse* a basic consumer culture, were also stopped *en masse* at a subcultural level. Thus we come to the crucial problem confronting nations just rising from underdevelopment. In order to get onto the road toward modernization, is it necessary to jettison the old cultural past which has been the *raison d'être* of a nation? The problem often comes up in the form of a dilemma or a vicious circle. The fight against colonial powers and the struggles for liberation were, to be sure, only carried through by laying claim to a separate personality; for these struggles were not only incited by economic exploitation but more fundamentally by the substitution of personality that the colonial era had given rise to. Hence, it was first necessary to unearth a country's profound personality and to replant it in its past in order to nurture national revendication. Whence the paradox: on the one hand, it has to root itself in the soil of its past, forge a national spirit, and unfurl this spiritual and cultural revendication before the colonialist's personality. But in order to take part in modern civilization, it is necessary at the same time to take part in scientific, technical, and political rationality, something which very often requires the pure and simple abandon of a whole cultural past. It is a fact: every culture cannot sustain and absorb the shock of modern civilization. There is the paradox: how to become modern and to return to sources; how to revive an old, dormant civilization and take part in universal civilization.

However, as I indicated at the outset, this same paradox is met by industrial nations who long ago worked out their political independence around long-standing political institutions. Indeed, meeting other traditional cultures is a serious test and, in a way, totally novel for European culture. The fact that universal civilization has for a long time originated from the European center has maintained the illusion that European culture was, in fact and by right, a universal culture. Its superiority over other civilizations seemed to provide the experimental verification of this postulate. Moreover, the encounter with other cultural traditions was itself the fruit of that advance and more generally the fruit of Occidental science itself. Did not Europe invent history, geography, ethnography, and sociology in their explicit scientific forms? But this encounter with other cultural traditions has been just as great a test for our culture and one from which we have not yet drawn all the consequences.

It is not easy to remain yourself and to practice tolerance toward other civilizations. However much we may be inclined toward foreign cultures—whether it is through a kind of scientific neutrality or through a curiosity and enthusiasm for the most remote civilizations, or whether it is caused by a nostalgia for the abolished past or even through a dream of innocence or youth—the discovery of the plurality of cultures is never a harmless experience. The disillusioning detachment with respect to our own past, or even self-criticism, both of which may nourish this exotic feeling, reveals rather well the kind of subtle danger which threatens us. When we discover that there are several cultures instead of just one and consequently at the time when we acknowledge the end of a sort of cultural monopoly, be it illusory or real, we are threatened with destruction by our own discovery. Suddenly it becomes possible that there are just *others*, that we ourselves are an "other" among others. All meaning and every goal having disappeared, it becomes possible to wander through civilizations as if through vestiges and ruins. The whole of mankind becomes a kind of imaginary museum: where shall we go this weekend—visit the Angkor ruins or take a stroll in the Tivoli of Copenhagen? We can very easily imagine a time close at hand when any fairly well-to-do person will be able to leave his country indefinitely in order to taste his own national death in an interminable, aimless voyage. At this extreme point, the triumph of the consumer culture, universally identical and wholly anonymous, would represent the lowest degree of creative culture. It would be skepticism on a world-wide scale, absolute nihilism in the triumph of comfort. We have to admit that this danger is at least equal and perhaps more likely than that of atomic destruction.

[3]

THIS CONTRASTING REFLECTION leads me to ask the following questions:
1. What constitutes the creative nucleus of a civilization?
2. Under what conditions may this creativity be pursued?
3. How is an encounter with different cultures possible?
The *first question* will give me the opportunity to analyze what I hurriedly called the ethico-mythical nucleus of a culture. It is not easy to grasp what is meant by the definition of culture as a complex of values or, if you prefer, of evaluations. We are too prone to look for the meaning of culture on an excessively rational or reflective level, for example, by starting with a written literature or an elaborated form of thought, as in the European tradition of philosophy. The values peculiar to a nation and which constitute

it as a nation must be looked for on a much lower level. When a philosopher works out an ethic, he gives himself to a work of a very reflective character; strictly speaking, he does not make up an ethic, but he mirrors the one which has a spontaneous existence in the people. Here, the values of which we are speaking reside in the concrete attitudes toward life, insofar as they form a system and are not radically called into question by influential and responsible people. Among the attitudes which interest us here, the most important are those concerning tradition, change, our behavior toward our fellow-citizens and foreigners, and more especially the use of available tools. Indeed, a set of tools, we said, is the sum total of all ways and means; consequently, we may immediately oppose it to value insofar as value represents the sum total of all goals. In fact, in the last analysis, these valorizing attitudes decide upon the meaning of the tools themselves. In *Tristes tropiques*, Lévi-Strauss analyzes the behavior of an ethnic group which, when suddenly confronted with a civilized set of tools, is incapable of assimilating it, not out of a lack of ability in the proper sense of the word, but rather because their fundamental conception of time, space, and interhuman relations does not allow them to give any kind of value to profit, comfort, or the capitalization of means. With all the strength of their fundamental preference, they hold out against the introduction of these means into their way of living. One may think that whole civilizations have thus sterilized technical inventions on the basis of a wholly static conception of time and history. Some time ago, Schuhl pointed out that Greek technics had been checked by the same conception of time which did not involve a positive evaluation of progress. The very abundance of slave-trading does not by itself constitute a purely technical explanation, because the brute fact of disposing of slaves must in addition be valorized in some way or another. If they did not bother to substitute machines for manpower, it is because the value had not been formulated: diminishing man's burden. That value did not belong to the group of preferences which made up Greek culture.

Thus, if a set of tools is put into use only by virtue of a process of valorization, then the question arises concerning where this deposit of values is to be found. I think we have to seek it out on several different levels. When I earlier spoke of a creative nucleus, it was with reference to this phenomenon, with reference to this multiplicity of successive layers which must be penetrated in order to reach the creative nucleus. At a quite superficial level, the values of a nation are expressed in its habitual customs and factual morality. But that is not the creative phenomenon; like primitive tools, customs represent a phenomenon of inertia; a nation maintains its initial impetus by means of its traditions. At a less superficial level, these values are manifested by means of traditional institutions, but these institutions are themselves only a reflection of the state of thought, will, and feeling of a human group at a certain point in history. The institutions are always abstract signs which need to be deciphered. It seems to me that if one wishes to attain the cultural nucleus, one has to cut through to that layer of images and symbols which make up the basic ideals of a nation. I use these concepts of image and symbol here in the psychoanalytic sense; indeed they are not discovered by immediate description; in this respect, the intuitions of sympathy and of the heart are misleading; what we need is an authentic deciphering, a methodical interpretation. All the phenomena directly accessible to immediate description are like symptoms or a dream to be analyzed. In the same way, we should have to be prepared to conduct our research up to the stable images and the permanent dreams which make up a nation's cultural resources and which feed its spontaneous judgments and its least elaborated reactions regarding experienced situations. Images and symbols constitute what might be called the awakened dream of a historical group. It is in this sense that I speak of the ethico-mythical nucleus which constitutes the cultural resources of a nation. One may, therefore, think that the riddle of human diversity lies in the structure of this subconscious or unconscious. The strange thing, in fact, is that there are many cultures and not a single humanity. The mere fact that there are different languages is already very disturbing and seems to indicate that as far back as history allows us to go, one finds historical shapes which are coherent and closed, constituted cultural wholes. Right from the start, so it seems, man is different from man; the shattered condition of languages is the most obvious sign of this primitive incohesion. This is the astonishing thing: humanity is not established in a single cultural style but has "congealed" in coherent, closed historical shapes: *the* cultures. The human condition is such that different contexts of civilization are possible. Yet this layer of images and symbols still does not make up the most radical phenomenon of creativity; it merely constitutes the outermost layer of it.

Unlike a set of tools which accumulates, sediments, and becomes deposited, a cultural tradition stays alive only if it constantly creates itself anew. Here we touch on the most unfathomable riddle in which one can merely recognize the style of temporality as is opposed to that of the deposit of tools. Here we have two ways for mankind to pass through time: civilization fosters a certain sense of time which is composed of accumulation and progress, whereas the way in which a nation develops its culture is based upon a law of fidelity and creation; a culture dies as soon as it is no longer renewed and recreated. One needs a writer, a thinker, a sage, or a religious man to rise up in order to start a culture anew and to chance it again with venture and total risk. Creativity eludes all definition, is not amenable to planning and the decisions of a party or State. The artist—to take him as one example of cultural creativity—gives expression to his nation only if he does not intend it and if no one orders him to do it. For if one could direct him to do it beforehand, that would mean that what he is going to produce has already been said in the language of everyday technical and political prose: his creation would be false. We can only know after the fact if the artist has really communicated with the stratum of fundamental images which have made the culture of his nation. Each time a new creation is born, we shall also know in what direction the culture of the artist's country is heading. As all great artistic creations always begin with some scandal, we can all the less forecast them: first of all, the false images which a nation or a regime form of themselves need to be shattered. The law of scandal answers the law of the "false consciousness." It is necessary to have scandals. A country will always tend to give itself a favorable image or a right-thinking image. The artist, contrary to the tendency to be a conformist in his own milieu, rejoins his people only when that crust of appearances is shattered; chances are that in his solitude, being in contention and misunderstood, he will bring about something which will be shocking and bewildering at first and which will be retained long after as the authentic expression of his people. Such is the tragic law of the creation of a culture, a law diametrically opposed to the steady accumulation of tools which make up the civilization.

Then the *second question* is raised: under what conditions can the cultural creativity of a nation continue?—a quite important question raised by the development of universal, scientific, technical, judicial, economic civilization. For if it is true that all traditional cultures undergo the pressure and erosive influence of this civilization, they all do not have the same capacity for resistance and above all the same capacity of absorption. It is to be feared that every culture is not compatible with the world civilization born of science and technics. It seems to me that we can distinguish certain conditions which are *sine qua non*. Only a culture capable of assimilating scientific rationality will be able to survive and revive; only a faith which calls upon the understanding of intelligence can "espouse" its time. I would even say that only a faith which integrates a desacralization of nature and brings the sacred back to man can take up the technical exploitation of nature. Likewise, only a faith which values time and change and puts man in the position of a master before the world, history, and his own life, seems fit to survive and endure. Otherwise, its fidelity to the past will be nothing more than a simple folkloric ornamentation. The problem is not simply to repeat the past, but rather to take root in it in order to ceaselessly invent.

There remains, then, the *third question:* how is the encounter with different cultures possible, that is to say an encounter which is not fatal for all? It would seem, in fact, that the result of the preceding reflections would be that cultures are incommunicable; and yet the strangeness of man to man is never total. Man is certainly a stranger to man, but always similiar. When we land in a totally foreign country, as I did a few years ago in China, we feel that in spite of the greatest change of elements we have never left mankind. But this feeling remains blind, one has to raise it to the rank of a wager and a voluntary affirmation of man's oneness. Such is the wager which Egyptologists formerly made when, in discovering incomprehensible markings, they postulated in principle that if these markings were made by man they could and should be *translated*. Certainly everything does not come out in a translation, but something always does. There is no reason or probability that a linguistic system is untranslatable. The belief that the translation is feasible up to a certain point is the affirmation that the foreigner is a man, the belief, in short, that communication is possible. What we have just said about language—signs—is also valid for values and the basic images and symbols which make up the cultural resources of a nation. Yes, I believe it is possible to understand those different from me by means of sympathy and imagination, just as I understand a character in a novel or at the theater or a real friend who is different from me. Moreover, I understand without repeating, portray without reliving, make myself different while remaining myself. To be a man is to be capable of this projection into another center of perspective.

Then the question of fidelity is raised: what happens to my values when I understand those of other nations? Understanding is a dangerous venture in which all cultural heritages risk being swallowed up in a vague syncretism. Nevertheless, it seems to me that we have given here the elements of a frail and provisional reply: only a living culture, at once faithful to its origins and ready for creativity on the levels of art, literature, philosophy and spirituality, is capable of sustaining the encounter of other cultures—not merely capable of sustaining but also of giving meaning to that encounter. When the meeting is a confrontation of creative impulses, then it is itself creative. I think that among all creations, there is a kind of harmony in the absence of all agreement. It is in this way that I understand Spinoza's excellent theorem: "the more we understand individual objects, the more we understand God." When one has penetrated to the depths of singularity, one feels that it is harmonious with every other in a way that cannot be put into words. I am convinced that a progressive Islamic or Hindu world in which old ways of thinking would inspire a new history, would have with our European culture and civilization that specific affinity that all creative men share. I think that skepticism ends here. For the European, in particular, the problem is not to share in a sort of vague belief which would be acceptable to everyone; his task is expressed by Heidegger: "We have to go back to our own origins," that is, we have to go back to our Greek, Hebrew, and Christian origins so as to be worthy participants in the great debate of cultures. In order to confront a self other than one's own self, one must first have a self.

Hence, nothing is further from the solution to our problem than some vague and inconsistent syncretism. At bottom, syncretisms are always residual phenomena; they do not involve anything creative; they are mere historical formations. Syncretisms must be opposed by communication, that is, a dramatic relation in which I affirm myself in my origins and give myself to another's imagination in accordance with his different civilization. Human truth lies only in this process in which civilizations confront each other more and more with what is most living and creative in them. Man's history will progressively become a vast explanation in which each civilization will work out its perception of the world by confronting all others. But this process has hardly begun. It is probably the great task of generations to come. No one can say what will become of our civilization when it has really met different civilizations by means other than the shock of conquest and domination. But we have to admit that this encounter has not yet taken place at the level of an authentic dialogue. That is why we are in a kind of lull or interregnum in which we can no longer practice the dogmatism of a single truth and in which we are not yet capable of conquering the skepticism into which we have stepped. We are in a tunnel, at the twilight of dogmatism and the dawn of real dialogues. Every philosophy of history is inside one of these cycles of civilizations. That is why we have not the where-withal to imagine the coexistence of these manifold styles; we do not possess a philosophy of history which is able to resolve the problems of coexistence. Thus if we do see the problem, we are not in a condition to anticipate the human totality, for this will be the fruit of the very history of the men who will take part in this formidable debate.

6 / The Power of Affirmation

True and False Anguish

PHILOSOPHICAL REFLECTION does not go astray when it concerns itself with poignant feelings. On the contrary, it is on solid ground as long as it directs the inquiry, interrogates the feeling, defines its implicit intention and, by means of this critical test, raises feeling to the status of truth.

Let us examine in common the anguish of our time. Our task would have no meaning if we should shrink back and collectively stir up panic among ourselves. We shall learn from anguish only if we try to understand it and if, by understanding it, we reestablish contact with the fount of truth and of life which nurtures our rejoinders to anguish. To experience in order to understand, to understand in order to go beyond—or, failing to go beyond, to confront—such would seem to be the maxim which ought to govern our meditation.

I shall first lay down as a very general definition, which will serve to limit the bounds of our investigation, that fear has a determined object or, in any case, one that is determinable, and that it anticipates a partial threat limited to a part of ourselves. Anguish, on the other hand, has an indetermined object and one which is all the more indeterminable as reflection attempts to coin its aim into fears with precise contours; but in return, this indetermined object of anguish signifies a threat for my totality over and above the division of my body into vulnerable parts, my psychism into discordant functions, my social personage into opposed roles, even over and above the scattering of my freedom into discontinuous acts. (We shall see that it is on such occasions that we seize ourselves as a totality suddenly summoned to unity by the threat.)

[287]

Thus, wherever fear becomes indeterminate, in respect to its object, and, on the other hand, moves toward myself so as to unfurl a total threat before me, at this point, fear turns into anguish.

In accordance with the rule laid down above, our task is to effect an actual recapturing of a feeling which is at once indetermined and massive. I propose to undertake an analysis into levels, that is to say to establish the various zones of menaces situated at levels which are progressively more profound. As anguish becomes more radical, reflection will also become more profound and will bring into view what I shall constantly be calling throughout the course of this meditation the "primary affirmation" [*l'affirmation originaire*], something which we shall also attempt to capture at its successive levels. This expression of M. Nabert, found in his *Eléments pour une Ethique,* seems quite fitting to designate the intense passion for existence which anguish puts into question and pursues from level to level in an uncertain battle. To meditate on anguish is, I believe, to use its hard schooling in order to explore and reachieve the primary affirmation, more primordial than all anguish which would lay claim to being original.

Still another word of introduction: we are invited to reflect upon *present-day anguish.* We have the duty to understand our time, if only to speak the language of its anxiety. Yet I do not think we should allow ourselves to be guided by the most emotional features of our epoch, but rather by the internal dynamism of the dialectic between anguish and what I shall call primary affirmation. By gradually advancing toward our time instead of immediately starting therefrom, perhaps we shall better be prepared to recognize it, that is, to situate its anguish and to assign to their rightful place emotions which are so much the more grievous as they are the less authentic. For it is quite possible that anguish is manifest in events of the moment only within a certain median zone of the levels of anguish, between two extremities of this scale of which one would be below the historical level—vital anguish—and the other above the historical level—metaphysical anguish. It is quite possible that our epoch, because it is very sensitized to a certain quality of anguish that we shall examine in this analysis, screens from itself other, more radical forms of anguish under an excessive and superficial pathos.

The foregoing explains why I have chosen a method which subordinates the meaning of current events to a reflection more detached from history; besides, we have become sensitized to anguish only through the work of thinkers and artists who most often were not in tune with the temper of their time, or, indeed, who were completely removed from their time: Aeschylus revived the terror of ancient myths when they were already disappearing from the collective consciousness of his time, when the city was attaching itself to gods less laden with enigma and anguish. Amos, Osee, and Isaiah, on the contrary, anticipated certain dreadful threats which they in turn foretold to their people. And Kierkegaard thundered out in the dead calm of Scandinavian bliss. Heidegger wrote *Sein und Zeit* without mention of the European crisis and within the framework of an ontology more allied to Parmenides than the contemporary public consciousness.

To the first maxim, experience in order to understand, understand in order to transcend, I therefore add the following: understand one's time, not by starting from it, but by gradually advancing toward modernity on the basis of a long tradition of anguish. These two maxims justify the reference of my title to truth: *True and False Anguish.*

At the lowest degree, at the vital level, anguish concerns life and death; or, to be more exact, it detects the proximity of death to life. This proximity is a relation that wavers between the exterior and the interior (we shall have to come back to this ambiguity of total threat which at one and the same time swoops down upon us and swells up as if from the very core of our being).

Death is an external threat in the sense that it is not necessarily implied by life; on the whole, life could be immortal. I learn of the necessity of my death empirically by witnessing the death of others, one after another. Thus every death, even the least expected, intervenes in life as a severance. My own death floats outside of me, I know not where, pointed against me by I know not what or whom.

And yet this very abstract knowledge—that all men die, *therefore* I, too—is such that anguish brings it closer to me to the point that my death appears to be fostered by my life, according to Rilke's extraordinary experience recorded in his *Notebooks.*

How can death, the intruder, appear inscribed within the depths of my being as my most ultimate possibility? It is, in part, the death of another which somehow transposes or shifts the threat from the outside to the inside. By means of the horror-stricken feeling which comes upon me from the silence of those who are absent and who will no longer respond, the death of another pierces me as an injury to our communal existence; death "touches" me; and in so far as I am also another for others, and ultimately for myself, I anticipate my future death as my eventual lack of response to all the words of all men. It is, therefore, by means of respect, which recognizes the irreplaceableness of loved ones, that I internalize anguish. When I feel myself involved within the compass of this mutual reverence, the anguish over my death acquires a sort of intensity that is more spiritual than biological and this is the truth of the emotion. Yet this is but one stage: there is no death of the other but for I who remain, and this survival of myself over my friend still screens the living part of myself from anguish.

But vital anguish already has an ally, namely, a certain vague experience of contingency that encircles the brute fact of existing and which I would connect, for my part, more to a meditation on birth than to a meditation on death. The fact of suffering already attests to me that I am divisible in space, an aggregate of parts, and soon to be dust. Growing older shows me that time is not merely the incessant creation of unforeseeable novelties, but rather that it distends and destroys. But above all, it is the necessity of being already born that reveals to me the non-necessity of being here; vertigo comes from the possibility there was of being different, of not having been at all. . . ; vertigo which is immediately obliterated by my unquestionable carnal presence, and yet vertigo that remains invincible before this presence: to come into the world is not an act which is the founder of myself by myself. I grant that this nothingness of contingency is not itself anguishing, because anguish is on the watch for eventualities and awaits the stroke of the future. But anguish, still external to death, pursues its approach toward my center of existence when it unites with this very inward experience of contingency; anguish receives from it the mark of inwardness while conferring upon it, that is to say upon contingency, the pathos which it lacks.

It remains that this anguish is unable to complete its approach toward me; in order for the possibility of dying to unite with the already acquired non-necessity of my birth, there must be an accident which actually makes me die, an accident that I cannot deduce from my contingency as such. Only my death will one day fulfill the contingency of my birth and will lay bare the nothingness of this non-necessity of having once been born. Thus, the anguish of death, the primal anguish that eats away at my being-in-the-world, is not completely immanent to my existence. Life has not yet been touched by it, and this allows me to joke about death with impunity: alcohol kills slowly, reads the poster; "we aren't in any hurry," replies the drunkard, whose grating humor, he thinks, embraces the wisdom of Epicurus: when death is here, you are no longer; when you are here, it hasn't yet arrived.

And yet this imperfect anguish—imperfect in the sense in which we speak of a perfect crime—is not vain: at its primal level, it calls forth a rejoiner in the form of this intense passion to exist whose degrees of depth are proportional to those of anguish. At this level, primary affirmation is revealed as will to live; it is embodied in will to live.

It is to be noted that the will to live is reflected and even given cohesion only under the threat of death, therefore in and through anguish. The expression "will to live" does not represent a simple or elementary "instinct." As a living being, I pursue goals which are disparate, heterogeneous, and, in the end, incoordinate: life, at least at the human stage, is a bundle of tendencies whose aims are neither clear nor concordant. Only in catastrophic situations, under the threat of the indetermined absolute—my death—does my life become determined as the totality of what is threatened. For the first time, I look upon myself as a threatened totality. The threat of death bestows upon life the greatest degree of simplicity of which it is capable.

But what is this "all" that anguish consolidates? Certainly it is here that reflection fulfills its true role: in the act of understanding, reflection goes beyond the initial situation. To understand this menaced whole is to evaluate it, to arm it with values. There is no will to live without a reason for living. We are well aware of this when we vainly attempt to restrain someone on the verge of committing suicide; in him, all incentive has been destroyed, and thus it is that discussion is useless. My life, my human life, as an incarnate affirmation, is what Bergson called the meaning of happiness and honor.

I therefore discover that my will to live evades anguish only when my reasons for living are placed above my life itself, when concrete values, which form the meaning of my happiness and my honor, transcend the very opposition between my life and my death. It stands to reason that this act of transcendence is achieved only within the comportment of sacrifice. Thus my life is at one and the same time threatened and transcended, threatened by death in the catastrophic situation, and transcended by its own reasons for living which have become reasons for dying. But in this matter, it is easier to speak than to live; reflection requires the aid of striking examples with which an epoch of extreme danger, such as ours, is surfeited.

Our dialectic resumes as soon as we attempt to probe the reasons for living contained in the will to live. Will the isolated consciousness find in itself the resources for the well-being and energy necessary to the maintainance of its equilibrium and its efficiency? It may prove helpful to pause momentarily at the purely psychological level to consider certain aspects of psychoanalysis. Yet I shall not delay here as long as would be required by the nature of this dialectic.

It must be said, at least in passing, that the narcissistic conscience is a source of anguish for itself. Psychoanalysis has taught us that fear of obscure forces, rejected by our social Superego, fosters neurotic tendencies latent in every psychism, even the most balanced. I am not a simple psychical energy, I bear division within me, and perhaps repression, aggression against myself. Plotinus did not realize just how right he was when he called the soul the One *and* the Many, in opposition to *Nous,* to intelligence, which is the One-Many. Thus, anguish springs from the very depths of my inner conflicts and from what might be called the *fragility* of the human psychism which redoubles the *contingency* of life. But the contingency of life was anguishing only through the mediation of death; the fragility of the psychism is a direct source of anguish, for what makes me afraid is an unknown and, as it were, buried visage of myself, the possibility of not recognizing myself, of being other, of being literally alienated.

I shall insist upon one point alone: upon the modern cast of this psychic anguish. Vital anguish merely varies in intensity from epoch to epoch, following the value given to individual life. But psychic anguish is more conspicuous throughout history by virtue of its very nature. It is indeed striking that it is within the most civilized societies, those best protected against danger and during peacetime, that this endogenous insecurity of the psychism makes its appearance, as if the most fragile of all psychisms were that of the civilized. In addition to the complexity of the psychism, I should like to invoke the role of what might be called the boredom of civilization. There has been no want of descriptions of this boredom that oozes out from societies most endowed with the products of civilization (I am thinking of E. Mounier's notions on Scandinavia, of Karl Stern's, in *The Pillar of Fire,* on the New World where the Jewish refugee from Germany disembarks, surprised to find, thousands of miles removed from the Nazi hell that he left, that here is a world more fragile psychically than the one that he left). Not only well-being, but also work, in its piecemeal form, diffuses boredom into industrial societies, as if a more acute psychic evil were taking the place of physical pain. I do not say that boredom is anguish, but it leads to anguish. By creating zones of freedom or at least areas of life organized apart from public order, from political and social security, the growth of civilization leaves man to himself, the prey of boredom; man who is less and less equipped to counter the dangers secreted by his psychism. To create leisure is very often to hand man over to the inanity of comfort, to a sort of civilized idleness, and, in the end, to his own vacuity, to his lack of purpose. The error of Narcissus is not far away.

These few notations—too short in my opinion—had but one goal: to show the insufficiency of an investigation of sanity and equilibrium based upon the mere concern for mental hygiene. A form of hygiene which fails to propose *tasks,* or a quest for equilibrium which does not impose *duties* is devoid of content. Man cannot avert the anguish of Narcissus if he does not associate himself to a work at once communal and personal, universal and subjective. The desertion of neurotics in time of war proves that the incipient pathology of every consciousness which isolates itself, fixes upon itself, entices itself, and evades itself, finds its recovery only in the consciousness of belonging to . . . , in loyalty to a "cause," in the words of Josiah Royce. Hegel gave the term "spirit" to this synthesis of the Universal and the singular, of the we and the I, of the in-itself of the human world and the for-itself of the consciousness which, according to Hegel, is at first unhappy consciousness.

We may call the new level of anguish which we have attained *historical,* for man appears herein as the protagonist—the craftsman and the sufferer—of the history of mankind on its collective level. It is by means of a veritable leap—which we can credit to Hegelianism and French sociologism—that we move from concerns over mental hygiene to the destiny of groups, nations, and classes.

Yet is this "true spirit," this "ethical substance"—to use Hegel's terminology—of great historical collectivities secure from anguish, from an anguish proportioned to this "spirit" (with which we are identifying our humanity)? Our epoch is uncommonly sensitized to a specific anguish which may well be called historical, as the level at which it is situated. But here it is important to remain faithful to our initial maxim: to advance toward present-day anguish rather than to start with it.

Let us make our approach toward anguish on the basis of the hope afforded to consciousness by Hegelian philosophy: no other philosophy has ever equalled its endeavor to integrate tragedy to logic; yet no other philosophy has ever rivalled its claim to surmount opposition by means of reconciliation, to transform all sterile negations into fruitful mediations. Thus Hegel thought he had formulated a more authentic idealism than that, for example, of Fichte. Every form of idealism promises the identity of thought and being. Yet not only did Hegel promise it, but he also thought he had actually constituted it, because the absolute knowledge in which there is the reconciliation of the in-itself and the for-itself, of being and subjectivity, is at the end of an itinerary wherein the throes of history are actually integrated. But in order for Hegel to have remained faithful to the promise of idealism, it was necessary for the spirit of his time itself to have been closer than another to absolute knowledge, for the spirit of his time to have offered, if not the actuality, at least a form, a sign, or, in short, the "phenomenon" of this spirit to which the throes of history raise the individual self. Recently, Jean Hyppolite quoted certain striking texts by Hegel on this alleged affinity between the spirit of his time and the dialectical synthesis of thought and being propounded by idealism.[1]

This hope afforded to us by Hegel has been belied by actual history. For us, his idealism and his absolute knowledge are just as much in the air as the idealism of Fichte was for him. We do not recognize in our awareness of the times, the form of the reconciliation of historical contradictions. The spirit of our time is not even the sign that the negative mediatizes an actual subsiding of the sundering of consciousness.

It would seem to me that present-day anguish may be discerned and understood in terms of the radical exigency formulated by idealism, notably that of Hegel: the hope is that our dreadful history is a ruse of reason heading toward higher syntheses. And here it is: anguish springs up at this precise point of our hope; a specific insecurity clings to history because we are not certain that it can bring about the coincidence of reason and existence, of logic and tragedy. A frightening possibility is discovered by anguish: what if *actual* history did not have meaning; what if Hegelian reconciliation were but a philosopher's contrivance? The nothingness with which the threat is announced is a nothingness of meaning, at the very level of "spirit," a nothingness of meaning at the core of this presumed meaning which was to give purpose and design to mental hygiene and to cure Narcissus.

I believe that by approaching the anguish of our time in this way, based upon the idealist exigency, we are better prepared to

<hr>

1. *Genèse et structure de la phénoménologie de l'esprit de Hegel* (Paris: Aubier, 1946), pp. 42–48.

distinguish the authentic from the unauthentic in contemporary anguish.

Contemporary pathos encompasses indiscriminately the best and the worst. A great deal of the anguish in face of history is but *La Petite Peur du XXe siècle.* I look upon E. Mounier's booklet, which bears this title, as one of the means best suited to reduce the emotional influence of the literature of castastrophe to its proper proportions. A certain confusion in face of machines, before the vast administrative techniques required by a politics of economic planning, of full employment, of socialized medicine and social security, is hardly more significant, no doubt, than the confusion of the adolescent cut adrift from the protective environment of the family and thrown into a larger and more rapid tempo of living. The dissolution of old customs, the toilsome assimilation of our own inventions, are perhaps but vicissitudes of adaptation which herald a new equilibrium between man and his environment. In any event, our very acquisition of industrial and administrative techniques is irreversible, and our duty is not to bemoan or to regret this, but rather to correct it and to compensate for it.[2]

But it is not enough to decry *La Petite Peur du XXe siècle;* it is necessary to assimilate and elucidate the authentic element of anguish that it conveys. Our generation is undoubtedly more sensitive than previous ones to a certain *ambiguity* of historical development. The truth of historical anguish is not decadence, but rather the ambivalence of human attainments, as if the ruse of history were to construct both positive *and* negative elements and in this way, cancel out our schemes of progress and decadence one by the other.

Hence, the very techniques that lighten man's burden also engender this obscure affliction of boredom in comfort and even in work, this boredom which, as we have seen, drives man to psychic anguish. But the ambiguity is especially anguishing at the strictly political level. A political consciousness has been evolving now for 150 years, the mainstay of which is the conviction that political authority is empowered to rectify freely and rationally the hazards of economic life, hazards which formerly were pompously called natural laws; empowered to eliminate the violence and injustice which preside over the distribution of wealth. But this political

---

2. In this respect, the studies on the psycho-sociology of work are a thousand times more useful than the literature of catastrophe for rectifying the evils of the division of piecemeal work. These studies are useful because from the outset they accept the value of the over-all orientation of human work and rectify it from within instead of criticizing it from without.

consciousness to which Asia is presently acceding, and to which Africa will accede tomorrow, is a sick consciousness from its very inception, generative of new violences. In this respect, the concentrationary regime is probably only the most glaring form of a totalitarian evil that is corrupting old forms of democracy such as new African nations and Soviet socialism. The ambiguity of the modern State is immense; our political consciousness is, so to speak, caught in a trap. Can the State be interventionist in social and economic affairs while still protecting the right of *habeas corpus*, freedom of thought, and the right to error won through bygone liberalism? Must we not say that political economics is more advanced than our reflection on polity as such, or our knowledge of its proper structure and the specific passions which cling to power? Thus it is that polity is the seat *par excellence* of the anguishing ambiguity of contemporary history, and those who dally over the malefaction of machines and technics lead us entirely astray; they lay blame upon things and instruments; they fail to perceive the specific evil of present-day history that assails the human operations constitutive of power and of State sovereignty.[3] Such is the anguish fostered by contemporary history through the instrumentality of our own political consciousness. We ourselves, as *homo politicus*, create the ambiguity of our own history. And thus our optimism on the level of technics, which was a sort of vital reflex, becomes, in the words of E. Mounier, a "tragic optimism." The scope of anguish has therefore expanded: in addition to the contingency of life and the fragility of the psychism, there is the ambiguity of history; in addition to the possibility of death and the possibility of alienation, there is the possibility of nonsense. This tertiary threat has repercussions in the secondary and primary threats: the peace and boredom of civilization cata-

3. It is quite obvious that the problem of atomic energy is a political and not a technical problem; the question is whether the great powers will continue to subject the production of atomic energy to secrecy and thereby to subjugate and reduce scientific research to their strategic designs, or whether they will be able to transfer in time this power to a world authority having a public and pacific character. Our fear on the threshold of the atomic age is not principally physical, nor even technical, but, in the last analysis, political. Behind the terror of the material destruction of the totality of mankind and all human attainments, even behind the vertigo engendered by the thought of the swelling of atomic energy, lurks the fear of the State power that possesses the secret, the will, and the power relative to this energy. Each man feels expropriated from a means of collective production by an authority which twists the meaning and usage of it and which seems to withhold the very secret of our death. The atomic threat has thus become the physical representation of the State, insofar as we no longer see in the State the delegation of our own political existence. The atomic threat is our political conscience, alienated into a hostile and murderous power.

lyzes psychic anguish; war and massive destruction endlessly breed the primary anguish of death. . . .

What is the power of reflection in face of this tertiary anguish? To separate the authentic from the unauthentic and to become aware of the ambiguity of current history, all of this is still to maintain the attitude of the disinterested and perhaps scoffing spectator who ponders the "way of the world." The ambiguity of history must turn away from this spectacle and become a modality of our will in the strictest sense of the word. I believe that it is here that we must seek out the truly therapeutic significance of French existentialism; it is by no means a prey to some penchant for the absurd, but is rather animated by a sort of courage before the uncertainty of the meaning of history. Only this historical courage is capable of coping with anguish by the act of incorporating this anguish within oneself and integrating it fully to freedom.

Hence, by raising the will to live to the level of the communal and social will, to the "spirit," in the Hegelian sense of the term, anguish transcended its first degrees. Likewise, by rejecting absolute knowledge and by assuming the hazards of an historical destiny, anguish may be conquered on its historical level. It falls to a philosophy of freedom to undertake this new step.

Should I be afraid of the "negative" of history—if I understand that I am the first "negative," if I resign myself to being the "negative" of the world, the negative of my own past, the negative of my own achievements, which, by dint of the force of custom, reinstates the in-itself within the core of myself? The theme of the *nothingness* of freedom, as we know, is the existentialist transposition of the Hegelian theme of the travail of the "negative"; but whereas for Hegel there was a movement from the unhappy self-consciousness to spirit as the synthesis of the universal and the singular, we here turn from a philosophy of history to a philosophy of freedom. At once we see that anguish is not transcended, the negative is not surmounted, but, in the words of this philosophy, it is "assumed," that is to say freedom is jointly anguish and upheaval, anguish over losing one's foothold, of being abandoned, without support or security, *and* the upsurge of projects, the openness of the future, and the making of history.

This is not the proper place to attempt to determine whether freedom is known in its true essence when its negativity is exalted; is freedom not a super-being rather than a lack of being? I shall pass over this discussion altogether. Let us merely ask whether the anguish inherent to choice is really the foundation of anguish and whether this anguish of the historical condition of all choice does not dissimulate a still more radical anguish. When I utter the glorious words: "to make, and in making, to make oneself" [*faire et en faisant se faire*], I am afraid of being incapable, of being prey to an inability, the victim of some evil influence, of an evil spell, of which I would be at once the author and the victim. Here reflection plunges into regions which events of the moment tend to mask; anguish springs from ancient myths, from Greek tragedy, and from the Hebraic Bible.[4]

This anguish, which we shall call the anguish of guilt, is not a form of fear provoked by a taboo, by a circumscribed prohibition. It becomes anguish precisely at the moment when I go beyond the strictly moral level of observance of commandments fixed by tradition; when I switch from the concern over moral rectitude to that of perfection and unlimited sanctity. Moral codes are transcended, but so too is the security of everyday duties and habitual obligations. I enter into this zone of absolute danger heralded by the tragic chorus and by the prophet of Israel:[5] I am a freedom in "odyssey," a "lost" freedom.

The problem of anguish, to be more precise, concerns only one of the two components of errant or lost freedom. The first looks to the past: I am "always already"—*immer schon*—a "fallen" freedom, as Heidegger expresses it in the novel pages devoted to the concept of *Verfallen* in *Sein und Zeit*. It is on the basis of the second feature, which looks toward the future, that guilt becomes anguishing: I who am always already bound, I create and recreate evil in the world by means of a free and yet unfree intention. It is this component that Kierkegaard elucidated in the celebrated *The Concept of Dread*. This dread or anguish over the imminence of guilt is not the consciousness of having sinned, which is moral sorrow and not anguish, but the consciousness of being able to sin. What is anguishing in guilt is the vertigo of seduction. In his *Études Kierkegaardiennes*, Jean Wahl clarified the nature of this anguish by Shelling's expression: "evil never is, but strives to be." This anguish therefore revolves, like all anguish, around the realm of the possible: but it is a possible that affects, in the second degree, the possibility that I am, as freedom. It is the imminent possibility of degrading myself as a possibility of being free. Herein

4. "Culpabilité tragique et culpabilité biblique," *Revue d'histoire et de philosophie religieuses* (1954).

5. Isaiah, exclaiming before the temple: "Woe unto me! I am lost, for my lips, and those of my countrymen, are defiled; and yet my eyes have looked upon the King, the Lord of hosts."—*Isaiah* vi:5.

we meet once again, although one degree higher, with the ambiguity of history. In point of fact, Kierkegaard saw in the anguish of guilt a mixture of attraction and repulsion, an antipathetic sympathy, he said, or a sympathetic antipathy. This ambiguity, transformed into ambivalence, is precisely that of vertigo, of seduction.

This anguish also uncovers nothingness—or a form of nothingness. But what is this nothingness? Here it is necessary, I believe, to dismember the all too enticing Hegelian negativity—"the jack-of-all-trades of Hegelian philosophy," in the words of Kierkegaard—and analyze it in accordance with the various divisions of anguish: the nothingness in question is neither death, nor madness, nor nonsense, nor even this active negation of being-there which constitutes freedom. It is rather the vanity of freedom itself, the nothingness of a bound freedom.

What is the power of reflection in face of this new anguish? Let us first lay down that this anguish does not fall outside of the scope of reflection. Kierkegaard's unique experience can be universalized and found in the most classic of philosophies. In the *Craytylus*, Plato called to mind those souls, tormented by vertigo, who invented by means of the language of motion the very illusion of motion. Further, in the *Phaedo*, Plato finds that the soul is "nailed" to the body only because it makes itself "its own prisoner." The primordial captivity of the soul is what makes a prison of desire: "And philosophy perceives that the most dreadful thing about this imprisonment is the fact that it is caused by the lusts of the flesh, so that the prisoner is perhaps the chief assistant in his own imprisonment." In Plotinus, we find extraordinary passages referring to the soul's fascination and its ensnarement; in turn, the soul appears hemmed in by absolute exteriority and inventive of this impulsion toward the exterior and toward the lower.

Thus, by universalizing the most singular experiences, reflection proceeds to this critique of authenticity which is ever preoccupying us; it calls upon the most diverse sciences to support this critique. I am thinking in particular of the idea of guilt presented by Dr. Hesnard in *L'Univers morbide de la faute*:[6] it is of the utmost importance that the experience of fault be thus purged by psychoanalysis; for real guilt emerges beyond the fear of self, of self-punishment, beyond the impulse to recede into neurosis; it springs up in this point of ourselves which Kant called *Willkür* and not *Freiheit*, within the heart of this subjective freedom defined by

6. Cf. "'Morale sans peché' ou peché sans moralisme," *Esprit* (September, 1954).

the birth of intentions, of "maxims" of the will, which today we would call the "project." The psychoanalytic critique of guilt, therefore, aids reflection in distinguishing a sane anguish from a merely neurotic anguish which would take us back to one of the already surpassed levels of the dialectic of anguish. The scientific critique of anguish should be supplemented by a strictly existential critique which would distinguish authentic anguish from this complacence in slavery which tradition has termed *baseness* and which Sartre analyzes in *Les Mouches* and elsewhere.

By means of this critique of authenticity, anguish approaches its truth; it is transformed into thought as much as possible. The model of such a reflection is found in Kant's essay on radical evil for which both Karl Barth and Karl Jaspers, oddly enough, have profound admiration. In this essay, Kant has, I believe, given expression to what Kierkegaard had lived and felt; Kant raises Kierkegaard's anguish to the status of conception and allows us to actually speak of the *Concept of Dread*.

For Kant, to reflect on radical evil is to reflect on a certain maxim of the free will which serves as a foundation for all the evil maxims in experience and in history. This foundation, this *Grund*, allows one to perceive the scattered forms of empirical evil (Kant even says that this *Grund* renders evil actions intelligible). But then this *Grund* is inscrutable (*unerforschbar*) as to its origin, for, he says, there is no comprehensible ground (*kein begreiflicher Grund*) from which evil could have arisen in the first place; it is anguish elevated to thought: a foundation of evil actions which is without foundation; a *Grund* which is *Abgrund*. And Kant himself compares this inscrutable foundation with the Biblical account of the Fall. In this respect, Kant anticipates Kierkegaard who later stressed the character of the actual occurrence of evil which commences and recommences; this character of the actual occurrence of fault therefore reveals its affinity with the mythical structure of the Fall recorded in the Bible as well as in Plato's writings.

But reflection—as we have already said in reference to the preceding degrees of anguish—does not limit itself to criticizing and to thinking anguish; Kant's essay is the model of a reflection which may well be termed recuperative. To reflect on the radical evil of freedom is to forge beyond successive intentions, beyond the discontinuous choices which time scatters in every which direction up to this totality of self; at the same time, I discover this origin of the action whence regeneration may surge forth. Thus anguish unbounds the self, deepens it to this root of acts which we have called primary affirmation [*l'affirmation originaire*].[7]

How is this possible? Kant demonstrated in his brilliant essay that it is the same free will, the same *Willkür*, that is both inclination toward evil—*Hang zum Bösen*—and destination for good—*Bestimmung zum Guten*. I am "inclined toward evil" and "destined to good"; *simul peccator et justus,* said Luther. I believe that this is the experience of repentence or, as Kant said, of regeneration; herein, anguish again acquires momentum. No doubt, the Kantian philosopher knows nothing of an assistance or grace which would be as a new creation and which the Christian calls "remission of sins"; but the reflective philosopher at least knows that the delicate point wherein the free bestowal upon us may connect with our freedom is the very one that anguish has laid bare.

In conclusion, I should like to replace this whole dialectic of anguish within the horizon of an ultimate anguish. Beyond the vital anguish of death, the psychic anguish of alienation, the historical anguish of nonsense, even beyond the strictly existential anguish of choice and guilt, there is the properly metaphysical anguish that is given expression mythically in the theme of the wrath of God: is it only by chance that God is not wicked? This alarming possibility is far from being beside the point: God's goodness is the last idea that is conquered, and perhaps only then in hope, as a last term, as the ἔσχατον [eschaton] of all tribulations. Too many "believers" are prone to take the idea of the benevolence of God for granted.

The crucial experience which introduces us to this anguish is, I believe, the experience of the *suffering just*. The Hebraic conscience reached this after the Exile; the Book of Job is the highest expression of it. Job represents the failure to explain suffering by punishment; here we are confronted, in effect, with innocence (innocence by hypothesis; Job is a dramatized hypothesis), the innocent one driven to desperation. The companions of Job, who are representative of an explanatory theodicy, try to make him confess that his misfortune is but an effect of his sin. Yet Job does not yield and his protestation exposes and intensifies the enigma of the misfortune which is out of proportion to his fault. The anguish of guilt is therefore not the last anguish: I had tried to assume evil, to regard myself as the one who establishes evil in the world, but

7. I should once again like to express my debt to M. Jean Nabert and his *Eléments pour une ethique* which starts out with a reflection on fault.

here is Job, righteous and yet suffering; here is evil which *happens* to man, the evil which is woe. And today, it is no doubt the sight of the afflicted infant that touches us the most; the infant epitomizes the whole destiny of man as *victim*, a destiny tangled up with that of *guilty* man, without the appearance of any correspondence or proportion between the woe and the fault. Is human existence in its natural state *The Plague?*

And suddenly this anguish, sweeping back from the summit of anguish toward its base, appears to recapitulate all the degrees of it. First, it seizes the anguish of guilt which it does not dislodge but which it retakes as from above: the φόβος [fear, terror] of Greek tragedy flows from this dreadful foreboding that man's guilt, his ὕβρις [violence], is at the same time the perfidy of a god who deliberately leads astray. Greek tragedy, at least that of Aeschylus, springs from the coalition of these two anguishes: the anguish of an evil foundation and the anguish of a guilty man.

Hebraic thought at first seems very far from this tragic conception. And yet the possibility of chaos, of original maleficence, resurges in many ways: the God of the Prophets reveals His absolute exigency in the thunder of destruction, in the fury of history; His holiness is a dreadful holiness. Jehovah is also the God who becomes indurate; and in the account of the Fall, the Serpent plays an enigmatic role which proves that man is not the absolute evildoer—he is never the evildoer but through seduction. Thus, outside of man there is a calling to fault which rises from his fragile affectivity and from the spectacle of chaos exhibited by creation; and if "Satan" precedes "Adam," how is "Satan" possible?

Step by step, the anguish of the evil foundation enlists the other anguishes: is not the nonsense of history the most stupendous display of chaos? The philosophers of history see in the "Negative" a mediation toward new syntheses; but they suppress all that is not recoverable in a vaster and higher signification; they say nothing of what has been of no use, of what is pure and simple loss by comparison to the rationality of history—the suffering of the innocent, of humble servants, the insignificance of lives without horizon and purpose. This "negative," which, it would seem, mediatizes nothing, is incorporated in the emotion of metaphysical anguish.

Lastly, the primary anguish of death is recaptured within the ultimate anguish. The very thought that man, who determines the meaning of things, who plans indefinite tasks, that this man *must* die is certainly the most flagrant sign of the apparent nonsense of the foundation. Thus, the *Apocalypse* speaks of death as the last enemy that will be conquered. Among all the forms of anguish there is, therefore, a sort of circularity or commutation which is such that the first anguish is also the last anguish.

How can reflection be recuperative reflection? Does it have the means to overcome the phantasm of the "evil God"? I shall not attempt to mask the leap that is represented in the access to the act of hope which alone would appear capable of affronting the last anguish. No apologetic, no explanatory theodicy can take the place of hope. In the end, Job is consoled not by an explanation but by meditation on his suffering which opens upon a sort of encounter of the living God.

Thus, reflection is not fulfilled in intuition; for even a conscience which would have integrally assumed its own sufferance and recognized therein the possible path of its own perfection, would have merely glimpsed that the wrath of God is the outward display of God's love. It would have merely glimpsed this, for the suffering of others would still remain the "mystery of iniquity." Only eschatological hope, not intuition, not knowledge, sees in the distance the end of the phantasm of the wrath of God.

But let us be mindful here that we cannot privilege this act and leave without misgivings as after the happy ending of a sad movie. The act of hope, to be sure, presages a good totality of being at the origin and at the end of the "breath of creation." But this foreboding is only the regulative idea of my metaphysical feeling; and it remains inextricably bound up with the anguish that forebodes a strictly senseless totality. That "it is good"—*wie auch es sei das Leben, es ist gut*—this I do not see: in the darkness, I hope it is. And then, do I have hope? Thus, although hope is the true contrary of anguish, I *hardly* differ from my friend who is in despair; I am riveted with silence, *like him*, before the mystery of iniquity. Nothing is closer to the anguish of nonsense than timid hope.

And yet this insignificant act works in silence and at one and the same time is hidden and reveals itself in its power to recapitulate all the degrees of primary affirmation. It is through this recapitulatory power that it comes to the level of reflection, as in a broken mirror; this is what secretly propels the resumption of momentum in the depths of the self lashed by the anguish of guilt; this is what regains possession of the tragic optimism before the ambiguity of history and what underlies psychic energy itself and the simple will to live of everyday, mortal existence.

Hope therefore enters into the scope of reflection, as reflection of reflection and through the regulative idea of the totality of the goodness of being. But unlike absolute knowledge, primary affirmation, secretly armed with hope, brings about no reassuring *Aufhebung;* it does not "surmount," but "affronts"; it does not "reconcile" but "consoles"; this is why anguish will accompany hope until the last day.

Negativity and Primary Affirmation

ONE SINGLE QUESTION dominates the whole of this meditation. It is difficult to formulate this question without some preliminary preparation; for not only the answer, but also the question itself will gradually become elaborated. It is easier to state what has given rise to the question: first, the desire for clarity amid my own reservations regarding philosophies which, since Hegel, have made negation the proper activity of reflection, or which indeed identify the human reality with negativity; secondly, the feeling that Hegel represents a break, a rupture with the sum total of previous philosophies, and that it is yet possible and necessary to reachieve a philosophy of the primacy of being and existing, a philosophy that gives serious consideration to this proliferation of philosophies of negation. Such is, in rough form, the subjective motivation of this study. But it is not yet a rigorously formulated question. Considered apart from the steps leading up to it, the question would be: does being have priority over the nothingness within the very core of man, that is, this being which manifests itself by a singular power of negation? Stated in these terms, the question destroys the stages of its own elaboration and therefore seems abstract. Yet as we shall see, it governs a whole philosophical style, a style of "yes" and not a style of "no," and perhaps even a style characterized by joy and not by anguish.[1]

Let us therefore put this last question aside and rather try to

1. In addition to this cardinal motive for interrogation on negation, there is the following one: is there not a negation, evil, whose foundation in affirmation cannot be understood? Is it not this negation which is infecting the whole of the philosophy of negation and which makes it appear primary? But this question must be held in abeyance so as to carry through with the one which is elaborated within these pages.

get a better grasp on what might constitute a gateway to the question. For we shall only recognize the question in the answer itself. Let us begin with reflection on the human reality. We shall try to transcend the act of reflecting, from the inside as it were, so as to retrieve the ontological conditions of reflection in the mode of nothingness and of being.

But what does it mean to start with reflection, with the act of reflection? It means precisely to start with the acts and operations in which we become *aware of our finitude by going beyond it.* Hence, it means to start with the connection between an *experience* of finitude and a *movement* which transgresses this finitude. This is where we shall find the principal and fundamental negation, the one which relates to the very constitution of reflection. The experience of finitude will be shown to be implied in an act of transcending which, in its turn, will show itself as denegation.

Once this negative moment is brought into view, the properly ontological question will be elaborated: does denegation attest to a Nothingness or a Being whose privileged mode of manifestation and attestation is negation?

[1] FINITUDE AND TRANSGRESSION

THUS, WE MUST NOW establish this initial proposition: that the specific experience of finitude at first presents itself as a correlative experience of limitation and of transgression of limitation.

This paradoxical structure of human existence must be described as it is and not broken in two; as if one could, in a first stage, work out a description of being-in-the-world (e.g. in perception or in affectivity) and then, in a second stage, initiate the transcendence of this being-in-the-world (e.g. through the word or the will). In one and the same movement, in one single flash, the act of existing becomes embodied and transcends its embodiment.

It is first of all within the strange and unusual relation that I have with my body and, by means of it, with the world, that I must seek out the nucleus of an experience of finitude. What are the features by which my relation to my body and, through it, to the world gives evidence of the finite? I think it is premature to answer that the function of the body's mediation is finite as such. Actually, what my body shows itself to be at first is an openness onto. . . . Far from being a closed shell, as Plato put it, or even less an Orphic Tomb, it is openness. And it is this in multiple ways: the openness of need by which I am wanting the world; the openness of suffering itself by which I find myself exposed to the outside, confronted by its threats, open like an unprotected flank; the openness of perception by which I receive the other; lacking, being vulnerable, receiving. Here already, then, are three irreducible ways of being open to the world. But this is not all: by means of expression, my body displays the inside upon the outside; as a sign for others, my body renders me decipherable and offered to the mutuality of consciousnesses. Lastly, my body offers to my will a set of powers, *savoir-faire*, expanded by the acquisition of habits, aroused and upset by emotion: now these powers make the world practicable for me and open me to the usability of the world by means of the grips which they give me upon the world.

Hence, what I first encounter is not finitude but openness. What are the features of this openness which qualify it as finite? Is it merely the dependence upon the world inscribed within openness? Is it the fact of wanting . . . , of experiencing . . . , of receiving . . . , of expressing . . . , of having ability? Kant seemed to tacitly admit this, for he called finite those beings who do not produce the reality of their thoughts but rather receive it, contrasting these beings to a being endowed with original intuition, in the sense of being creative, a being that would not have objects given to it but would create for itself what it sees (*Entstand* and not *Gegen-stand*). But can we really hold the world to be a *limit* of my existence? What is precisely bewildering in the mediating role of the body is that it opens me to the world; in other words, it is the organ of an intentional relation in which the world is not the boundary of my existence but its correlate.

It would seem, then, that it is necessary to look within openness itself for an additional feature which makes my body a finite openness. To remain within the image of openness, we must discern a principle of narrowness, a closing within the opening, so to speak, which is precisely finitude.

Among the five examples of openness which I have listed—wanting, experiencing, receiving, expressing, ability—the case of perception (receiving) is the most enlightening. We shall see how it may be generalized.

The special finitude of perception is linked to the notion of *point of view*. It is striking that this finitude is first noticed *on* the object itself; next, I turn back from the object toward myself as the finite center of perspective. Indeed, it is on the object that I perceive the perspectival character of perception; the object is perceived from a certain angle; every perspective is unilateral in the literal sense of the word. We can see how the unilateralness of the percept and its temporality are connected; it is because I always see the thing from one angle that I must deploy the flux of silhouettes in which the thing presents itself in succession from this angle, then from this other angle. Thus, the very inadequacy of perception as always being in process (and not its mere receptivity, taken as such) discloses the finitude of my point of view. By moving back from the percept to the perceiving—and, to be more precise, toward perceiving as embodied in organs—I form the idea of my perception as an act produced from somewhere; not that my body is one place among others; on the contrary, it is the "here" to which all places refer, the "here" for which all other places are "there." I always perceive "there" only from "here." This correlation between the "here" of perceiving and the unilateralness of a percept constitutes the specific finitude of receptivity. Hence, it is no longer merely the idea of creative intuition which serves as a counterpart to that of receptive intuition in the infinite-finite opposition; it is rather the idea of other points of view which are correlative or opposed to mine. Here it is the finite which limits the finite. We shall presently see precisely under what condition I can be opposed to another point of view.

How can I know my perspective as perspective in the very act of perceiving if I did not somehow escape it? It is this "somehow" which constitutes the essence of the whole question. We have suggested this in passing: to apprehend my point of view as finite is to situate it in relation to other possible perspectives which I anticipate, so to speak, emptily. I bring about this anticipation on the thing itself by disposing this side that I see in relation to those that I do not see but which I *know*. Thus I judge of the thing itself by transgressing the face of the thing into the thing itself. This transgression is the signifying intention, the meaning-giving act, the *Meinen*. By it I bring myself before a meaning which will never be perceived anywhere by anyone. If I now note that this intention, this *Meinen*, is the very possibility of *Saying*, then it would seem that I am not merely a passive onlooker but a being who intends and expresses. For when I speak, I speak of things in terms of their non-perceived sides and in their absence. Thus the finite perceptual intention, which gives me the fullness of the perceived at every moment, the present of the presence, is never alone and bare. In so far as this perceptual intention is saturated with presence, it is always enmeshed in a more-or-less complete relationship of fulfillment with regard to this other aim which penetrates it through and through, which literally passes right through it and to which the word is primordially linked. The mute look is caught up in discourse which articulates the meaning of it; and this ability to express meaning is a continual transcendence, at least in intention, of the perspectival aspect of the perceived here and now. This dialectic of signifying and perceiving, of saying and seeing, seems absolutely primal. And the project of a phenomenology of perception, in which the moment of saying is postponed and the reciprocity of saying and seeing destroyed, is, in the last analysis, a hopeless venture.

In other words, I am not wholly defined by my status of being-in-the-world: my insertion in the world is never so total that I lose the aloofness of signifying, of intending, the principle of expression. This aloofness is the very root of reflection on point of view as point of view; it is what allows me to convert my "here" from an absolute placement into any place whatever, relative to all the others, in a social and geometrical space in which there is no privileged emplacement. Henceforth I know that I am here; I am not merely the *Nullpunkt* but I also reflect on it: and I know at the same time that the presence of things is given to me from a point of view, because I intended the thing in its meaning, beyond all point of view.

Is it now possible to generalize this dialectic of finitude and transcendence? Yes, to the extent that one can find an equivalent for perspective in all the other aspects of bodily mediation: wanting, being threatened, expressing, being able. The specified and elective character of want is obvious. Yet I am equally characterized by a clearly defined complex of threats which delineate the contours of my fragility and make of my life an oriented fragility. Affectivity in its entirety tells me how I "find" myself in the world; this *Befindlichkeit* is at every moment the inverse opacity of this light which begins with the first clear perception, that is to say, what is offered and opened to me.

Thus the way one "feels" or "finding oneself in a certain mood" bestows upon the perspectival point of view a density which is the false profundity of existence, the body's dumb and inexpressible presence to itself. The "here" of my body, manifested by the opaque feeling, vibrates its presence. That "deep" sensibility shows that the body is more than the letting-in of the world, more than the letting-be of all things; the body is not pure mediation but also immediate for itself. The fact that the body cannot be pure mediation but is also immediate for itself constitutes its affective closing.

The same factor of closing is found in all the powers which

provide a foundation for the will's activities. Every power is a complex of potency and impotency; the habit, in fact, operates in accordance with this double line; it awakens aptitudes only by giving them form and fixing them. Ravaisson's excellent book on *Habitude* could certainly be used for our meditation on closure within openness. A power which has a form, such is the "I can." In this sense one may say that the "I can" is the practical perspective of the "I want."

Ultimately, all these notations on perspective, on the affective immediacy of the body to itself and on the contours of the "I can," could be summarized in character. A character is a finite figure or form; character is the finite openness of my existence, it is my existence as determined. But in order not to transform this character into a thing, it must not be separated from the idea of point of view or perspective. In the measure that perception is the light of affectivity, and of activity—hence of wanting, of being threatened, and of being able—it is the notion of perspective or point of view which best explains that of character, because this notion reminds us that finitude is not a spatial closure, not the contour of my body, nor even its structure, but rather a feature of its mediating function, a limit inherent to its openness, the original narrowness of its openness.

Now what was said earlier about "perspective" in the act of perceiving may be applied *mutatis mutandis* to all the manifestations of our finitude: I can only experience them in the movement which tends to "transcend" them. Can I experience some want, as a man and not merely as an animal, without beginning to evaluate it, that is, without approving or reproving it, and therefore without taking up a position with respect to it? Although I am immersed in suffering, I also judge and measure this suffering against a scale of values more precious than my body, values which will perhaps give me joy in the very depths of sorrow. Hence, through the experience of want and suffering, of desire and fear, we are led to look for the original transcendence of our finitude within the very act of volition. The act of taking a position, in order to evaluate, evinces affectivity in its entirety as a vital perspective, as a finite will to live. But I know this only in the will to signify and in the will to do.

Our analysis has thus reached a first level: the notion of limitation applied to human existence has a double significance. On the one hand, it designates my *limited being-there* as perspective; on the other hand, it designates my *limiting act* as an intention of signifying and willing. It is my act as limiting which reveals my being-there as limited, somewhat in the sense in which Kant maintained that it is not sensibility which limits reason, but reason which limits sensibility in its pretension to give phenomena the status of things-in-themselves.

[2] TRANSCENDENCE AS DENEGATION

HAVING COMPLETED this preliminary analysis, it is now possible to formulate the problem: what is the meaning of the mark of negativity which clings to the movement of the "transgression" of perspective by the signifying intention and, more generally, of the situation of finitude by human transcendence?

Let us go back to our reflective analysis of perspective. Perspective, we said, seemed to be involved within a contrasted experience of signifying and seeing; I *think* of the thing beyond this perspective which I *perceive* as a silhouette of the thing.

Where is the first negativity in this experience?—In the very act of transcending. I cannot *express* my transcendence over my perspective without expressing myself negatively: as transcendence, I am not what I am as point of view. In an abbreviated and paradoxical form: I am not what I am. But I reach this radical expression of my transcendence only by an indirect, reflective route: it is on the thing itself that I perceive the negative in which my transcendence consists, just as, earlier, it was on the thing itself that I understood the meaning of point of view, perspective, etc. Likewise, it is on the thing itself that its meaning is given as "*empty*" signification, as an empty intention, which is more-or-less "fulfilled" by the plenum of presence. The very first negation is therefore found in this void of signification, described by Husserl in the first of the *Logical Investigations:* I "mean" the thing in a way different than my perspective. It is to be noted that Husserl's great work does not begin with the presence of things but with the power of signifying them: the height of signification is therefore the one which cannot in principle be fulfilled, the absurd signification. I am a power of absurd significations. This single power attests that I do not exhaust myself in an intentionality of fulfilled presence, but that I am a twofold intentionality: on the one hand, an intentionality signifying emptily, an *élan* of signifying and a power of speaking in the absence of the this-here; on the other, a fulfilled intentionality, an openness to receiving and a power of seeing in the presence of the this-here. Fortunately, Husserl began his work not with a phenomenology of perception but with a phenomenology of signification whose horizon is the absurd signification without possible fulfillment.

But Husserl did not draw the consequences of his analysis for a philosophy of negation. These consequences come into view only when the first of the *Logical Investigations* is seen in light of the analyses which launch the *Phenomenology of Spirit*. The first negation which Hegel lists is the gap between certainty and truth. The "this is" remains the richest of certainties and the poorest of truths. In effect, as soon as I wish to *express* this plentitude of the totality offered to thought, this plentitude to which nothing can be added, it is first necessary that I cancel, in the universal, the *this* which pretended to express all this in a this; the truth of the thing is primarily the not-this, just as the universality of the concept I is the not-him. This analysis corresponds exactly with that of Husserl when he distinguishes the "meaning" of vision, the signification of presence. For it is from the phenomenological description of "meaning" that Hegel makes negation arise. Let us therefore say that meaning is non-vision; meaning is the non-point of view.

We may apply to the very act of signifying what we have just discovered on the thing itself. Let us therefore say, as previously, but with the awareness of having elaborated the sense of the formula: I am not, as transcendence, what I am as point of view.

What has just been said of the negation of point of view, inherent in my intention for truth, is even more applicable to the denegation of my will to live, which denegation belongs to the constitution of my will proper. If to take a position is to evaluate, to evaluate is to be able to refuse; it is to be able to resist and beat off my instantaneous impulsiveness, as well as my own habits which my duration secretes by a strange and deadly process of sedimentation. Refusal is thus the militant soul of the transcendence of the will. Volition is nolition.

It is not difficult to perceive the ramifications of this in the ethical realm: there is no will which does not reject, disapprove; reprobation and revolt are the first manifestations of ethics as protestation. Socrates' demon remained silent when he acquiesced; it only appeared in order to resist, to say no.

There is no volition without nolition: this also means that value expresses the absence of what is lacking to things when the will casts the shadow of its projects over these things. An analysis of value as a "negative" thus unexpectedly links up with what Kant wished to express when he interpreted practical reason as the limit of my faculty of desire. The analysis of value as a "negative," which the moderns undertake, paradoxically rejoins the analysis of the imperative, as a negative, which Kant had already elaborated. Its motive is the same: the negative sign is inherent to obligation (or defense) and to value (or lack) because of the transcendence of obligation over desire, of evaluation over will to live.

Lastly, it would be easy to show how this style of negativity, which characterizes all the aspects of my transcendence in relation to my finitude, also commands every possible analysis of my relation to another. It is not surprising: I transcend my point of view only by imagining this empty meaning of the signified thing, fulfilled by another presence, given to someone other than me. The sympathetic imagination of another perspective which limits mine belongs primordially to my transcendence. In effect, I can say, in the two senses, that I would not judge my perspective as a perspective if I did not imagine another perspective and that I would not imagine another perspective if I did not escape from mine and if I did not direct toward the thought-about and unseen object the empty intention of signifying it. It is this knowing of the other side which the perspective of another, imagined and non-perceived, fulfills in a different manner. Thus, my ability to transport myself imaginatively into another perspective and my ability to judge my perspective finite are one and the same power of transcendence; another limits me only in the measure that I actively establish his existence. I participate imaginatively in this limitation of myself; hereafter the apperception of another manifests my finitude as from the outside, transcended in another; but this is only one aspect—in the form of a sympathetic imagination turned toward another—of this power of transcendence correlative to my finitude. It is, therefore, not astonishing that the positing of another's existence involves the same mark of negativity as the movement of transcendence by which I transgress my perspective: another is the not-I *par excellence,* just as the universal is the not-this *par excellence.* These two negations are correlative and, you might say, co-original.

And, because they are co-original, they have the same extension: *all* the modes of transgression of my finitude and all the modes of negativity which accompany them have their double in a negative mark which equally affects the imagining of another. There is no volition without nolition, as we said earlier; and we recognize this "hollow" of the will, over and above my simple will to live, in the "lack" of value; but this "lack" of value, this denial of the fact inherent to the need to be, is distinctly correlative to the positing of another as denegation of all my transgressions. In terms similar to those of Kant: I escape perspective, both the perspectives of my looking and my desires, and I oppose other values to my ambition only through the imagination of the existence-value of another; it is the other's dignity that puts a limit to my pretension to use him merely as a means, as a commodity, or as a tool. The idea of humanity is thus the negative of my power of desiring insofar as it is the "supreme restrictive condition of all subjective ends." [2] We said that the will is not contained in the will to live, but rather that the will contains the will to live. This is possible through the mediation of another as a limit of my power of desiring: I limit myself by means of the recognition of the perspective and the value of another, and this limit belongs primordially to the power of denegation which raises my own transcendence over my own finitude.

Our reflection has led us to the point where the act of existing is perceived as a nihilating act. Up to this point, but no farther. What is in question is the right to hypostatize these nihilating acts into a nothingness which is, according to Sartre, the "ontological characteristic" of the human being, that is, this reality which evinces itself by means of questioning, of doubt, of absence, of anguish, of the petrifying retort to the petrifying gaze of another. I did not think it profitable to go over these celebrated analyses of the "negative." My preference was to start with a reflection on the perspective in perception and in the will. I believe I have thus established sufficient grounds for returning to the problem of the foundation of negation.

On the basis of the preceding analysis, I should like to outline a *reflection on reflection,* through which it would be possible to recapture, within the very core of denegation, the "primary affirmation," in the words of M. Nabert, *the primary affirmation* that is denoted by means of negations.

[3] Transcendence as Negation of Negation

IT WOULD SEEM that the first stage of this recuperative reflection consists in showing that denegation is not a simple negation but conceals by implication the negation of a negation. In other words, the first work of denegation is to expose the point of view itself as a first, prior negation. In retrospect, I discover that

2. Kant, *Foundations of the Metaphysics of Morals,* Section II.

what is primitively negative is not meaning in comparison with point of view, nor saying in comparison with seeing, nor the taking of an evaluating position in comparison with the will to live; it is rather the point of view, the perspective, the will to live. Descartes was correct when he said that the idea of the infinite was wholly positive and identical to being *plane et simpliciter*, and that the finite was at fault with respect to being. "And I should not imagine that I do not perceive the infinite by a true idea but only by the negation of the finite, just as I understand repose and darkness by the negation of movement and of light: for, on the contrary, I see that there is manifestly more reality in infinite substance than in finite substance, and therefore that in some way I have in me the notion of the infinite before that of the finite, the notion of God before that of myself." [3]

Total reflection, and in this sense, concrete reflection, encompasses not only the unquestionable certainty of the living present, but also the truth of this living present which is, again in the words of Descartes, "that I am something imperfect, incomplete, and dependent on another, which constantly aspires after something which is better and greater than myself." [4] Husserl says as much when he speaks of the inadequacy of perception, of the permanent possibility that one silhouette may cancel the preceding one and that thereby the world as meaning may be destroyed.

But then, what is the meaning of this negation anterior to the denegation of thinking and willing, this negation of finitude, if you will?

In saying that negation is of its essence adapted to finitude, and only as negation of negation to the transcendence of finitude by thought and by will, I do not mean that negation springs up entirely in living experience, in the experience of finitude. No doubt it goes farther back, back to the very sphere of objectivity; for negation is a word and it is necessary to constitute it in discourse itself.

But prior to the experience of finitude there is no radical negation, there is only the distinction between this and that, that is not yet negation but otherness: this is different from that. At least it must be granted that the negation of finitude presupposes the prior constitution of *negative language* at the level of distinction and difference. This constitution pertains to a formal ontology, that is to the categories of the "something in general." It would be vain to try to draw everything from the existential sphere, if the

3. Descartes, *Meditations*, III.
4. *Ibid.*

objective sphere were not already constituted. My thesis is therefore limited: before the denegation or negation of transcendence, there is a primal negation which is the negation of finitude; before this there is indeed a language of already constituted negation, but this language is that of otherness. Negation becomes an *experience of negation* only through the passage from the objective to the existential sphere, by means of the application of the "not," inherited from formal ontology, to the *experience of finitude*.

It will be sufficient, therefore, to recall how the language of negation is constituted in the operation of distinguishing. This operation is the first constitution of relation; but it is necessary to seek out the first expression of it, on the very level of perception, in the act of signifying interwoven with the perception of presences.

To be sure, there is no percept but where there is something distinct. Let us merely cite a few primitive modalities of the category of the distinct: the opposition in space between form and substance, qualitative contrasts (of sound, color, taste), appearance and disappearance. Let us note that we cannot express the distinct without recourse to negation: this is not that. It would be necessary to determine how this negation, which is constitutive of all order and which we have seen arise on a level with perception, becomes more involved as one rises from forms to things with their durable properties and their accidents, then to forces and their constant relations, to living beings as organized individuals, and to psychisms. In this way, we would witness the formation of a whole scale of the distinct, from distinct forms to distinct forces and distinct individuals. This investigation concerning successive levels of the negation constitutive of objectivity pertains to a logic of experience; but this does not interest us here. The birth of the negative in the distinct is sufficient for the continuation of this analysis.

This constituting function of negation must not, it seems, be inopportunely mixed up with the tragedy of anxiety, of death and battle: there is nothing tragic in this negation. At bottom, the passage from the first to the second part of the *Phenomenology of Spirit*, from consciousness to self-consciousness by means of the same negativity, is an illusion which is only maintained by a secularized theology wherein all negations flow from the very movement of the Absolute which limits itself and denies itself by determining itself so as to surmount its negation in the thought of its other. If we wish to protect ourselves from the pathos of negation, we must return to Plato and the thesis of the *Sophist* which reduces non-being to the other. Philosophical sobriety lies here, ebriety in the inverse reduction of otherness to negation.[5]

How, then, does negation come to the experience of finitude? If negation flows from otherness, from distinction, such as is implied by the constitution of the perceived thing, of living individuality, of the singular psyche, how does it steal into the heart of the experience of finitude to the point of becoming its privileged language and, to all appearances, its native land?

Why is want expressed negatively as an: "I don't have"? Why is the past, mediatized by regret, expressed in the "no longer," and the future, in tones of impatience, in a "not yet"? Why is death anticipated as the "nothingness" of my very existence? One can see how the "no longer" has been taken from the sphere of objective experience in which it designates the disappearing correlative to another appearing. But to speak of death requires the *mediation of an affect:* the let-down over something lost, the wound inflicted by the loss of an irreplaceable being. I direct this loss of another toward myself: I am in this anticipated future, the being who for another is lost. Thus from transpositions to transpositions, from the disappeared to the lost and from the lost to death, the "no longers" of things are shifted to the death of someone, and ultimately to my future death. Hence it must be granted that certain affects have an affinity for negation; that, for example, the burdening dread of death is found in the negative structure of discourse; this coalition is so adhesive that affects such as death dramatize all negations, as is so often seen in Hegel when he calls negation the death of determinations, and that in return, the tragedy of existence is recaptured in a dialectic of figures and forms, or even categories.

A rigid differentiation between the objective and the existential spheres renders this contamination void; at least it shows the inevitable genesis of it: the negation of finitude is born of the conjunction between a relation and an affect, that is between the category of the distinct, of the other, and certain affects by which finitude is suffered like a wound and no longer merely perceived as the limitation of point of view, or, to go back to an expression of the first part, as the closure inherent to our openness to the world.

We are thus brought back to those affects which we said had an affinity for negation: lack or need, regret, impatience, anguish. One cannot, it seems, go farther; it must be admitted, as a residue of our regressive analysis, that spoken negation, elaborated around

---

5. I have treated this problem of the priority of otherness over negation, after the fashion of Plato, or of negation over otherness, after the fashion of Hegel, in "Philosophie et ontologie," *Esprit* (August, 1955).

the idea of otherness, *exhibits* a negative in certain lived "moods." This negative, which lies deeper than all discourse, was called "sadness" by Spinoza. "By sadness," he says, "I mean a passion by which the soul passes to a lesser perfection." This *lessening of existence* affects the very effort through which the soul endeavors to persevere in its being and so may well be called a primitive affection.

Thus I come to form the idea of a default of subsistence, or contingency, which is the ontological characteristic of my existence as finite. It is an idea which I borrow from the sphere of things in which I distinguish the necessary from the non-necessary in the order of formulated determinations. I return to it and apply it to this obscure disturbance of my whole being, to this vague vertigo which flows from the joint meditation on birth and death, on need and oblivion, on growing old and the unconscious. I fail to be necessary, I could have not been, I can cease to be. I am the living non-necessity of existing.

It is therefore of this primal negation, which I now call contingency or insubsistence, that the act of transcendence is the second negation. Denegation is negation of negation. More exactly, the thought which aims at meaning beyond finite perspective, the taking up of a position which aims at validity beyond the point of view of the will itself, is, in comparison with the negation of finitude, in a specific relation which is stated rather well in an expression such as this: I think, I want, *in spite of* my finitude. *In spite of* . . . , such seems to me to be the most concrete relation between negation as transcendence and negation as finitude, between denegation and annihilation.

What have we gained from this analysis? This: the negativity which our reflection on meaning and point of view, on will and will to live, had brought to light is not an immediate negation, but rather a negation of negation. It is therefore *possible* to recognize therein an affirmation which is retrieved by resisting resistance, as Bergson would say.

[4] DENEGATION AND AFFIRMATION

IT IS NOW the task of our reflective analysis to show that the soul of refusal, of recrimination, of contestation, and, lastly, of interrogation and doubt, is fundamentally affirmation; to show that denegation is never but the reverse of a more primordial affirmation, only half an act.

To say that human transcendence is rightly negation is to be authorized to pass from nihilation to nothingness. It is this passage which must be brought into question. Now the whole of Sartre's philosophy rests on the right to call "nothingness" what our previous analyses only allowed us to name "nihilating acts." [6]

Sartre starts with this remark, directed against Hegel, that being and nothingness are not logically contemporary and that there is no passage from one to the other; being does not pass to nothingness nor nothingness to being. Being is being and negation will never bite into it, since it must be denied in order to think nonbeing. The whole and full positivity of being is therefore unbreakable. It remains, then, if one wishes to account for "the origin of negation," that nothingness "lies coiled in the very core of being, like a worm." [7] In other words, it is necessary that nothingness be "given in some way, given at the core of being." [8] If, in fact, being excludes nothingness and is even established without relation to it, it is necessary that there be a being whose property is to "nihilate nothingness, to support it in its being, to sustain it perpetually with its very existence, a being through which nothingness comes to things." Parodying and twisting a well-known expression of Heidegger, Sartre calls it: "a being such that in its being, it is question of the nothingness of its being." [9]

Let us be clear about what Sartre expects from his analysis: not merely a series of nihilating acts which, he admits, would in turn require a foundation in being, but "an ontological characteristic of being required." [10] In short, a *nothingness* and not merely a *nihilating act*. The question is right here: do the numerous nihilating acts which Sartre describes with an extraordinary virtuosity—from interrogation, doubt, absence, and anguish to the petrifying retort to another's petrifying gaze—postulate such a nothingness of being as an ontological characteristic?

Sartre believes that this nothingness, the source of nihilating acts, is found in freedom: "Descartes, following the stoics, gives the name 'freedom' to this possibility for the human reality to secrete a nothingness which isolates it." [11]

To what is Sartre alluding here? To the connection which Descartes himself established between doubt and freedom. It is true that Sartre neglects to note that for Descartes himself, the

6. Cf. J.-P. Sartre, *L'Être et le néant* (Paris, 1948).
7. *Ibid.*, p. 57.
8. *Ibid.*, p. 58.
9. *Ibid.*, p. 59.
10. *Ibid.*
11. *Ibid.*, p. 61.

freedom to which doubt leads is only the "lowest degree of freedom," which he calls the freedom of indifference. However that may be, in this freedom of doubt, Sartre finds traces of the Stoic ἐποχή—the "suspension" of judgment which delivers the soul of the sage from his passions—and of the sign of the Husserlian epoché by which the thinking I withdraws itself from the natural and the factual. This gesture of disconnecting, of uprooting, of disentangling, this "nihilating withdrawal," is found by Sartre in every authentically human act; he returns to his past analyses of the imagination which nihilates the whole of the real for the benefit of absence and the unreal; he reinterprets time and finds, between the past and the present, this cleavage which is not an obstacle but actually nothing; this nothing is precisely my freedom. He means that nothing in my past compels me nor justifies me: "Freedom is the human being putting his past out of play by secreting his own nothingness." [12]

Having centered all nihilating acts on nothingness as freedom, he thus sees in anguish the consciousness of being the nothingness of one's own past as freedom: "Anguish is precisely the consciousness of being one's own future in the mode of not-being." [13] We may note the example of the gambler who swore never to gamble again and who, right before the gaming table, realized the emptiness of such a past and surpassed decision; for nothing prevents him from gambling, and this is his freedom; it is this nothing which anguishes him. Thus, within the consciousness of nothingness as freedom, there is a recovery of the anguish which Kierkegaard linked to fault and which Heidegger discovered in his search for being as being.

Lastly, the concept of nothingness clarifies the famous thesis of the priority of essence over existence. If my essence is what I "am been [est été] [14]—according to an expressive barbarism which renders Hegel's expression: *Wesen ist, was gewesen ist*—then the nothing which separates freedom from the past, from everything acquired, is also the nothing which puts existence beyond all essence: "essence is all that human reality apprehends in itself as having been" and anguish is an "apprehension of self in so far as it exists as a perpetual mode of wrenching away from what is." [15]

Let us not oppose speculative objections to Sartre but, if possible, propose a better description. Later, we may have to come

---

12. *Ibid.*, p. 66.
13. *Ibid.*, p. 69.
14. Literally "is been" or "is-was." Cf. *L'Être et le néant*, pp. 71–72—Trans.
15. *Ibid.*, pp. 72–73.

back to the question concerning the presuppositions which inter-
fere with his description and prevent it from giving its true
meaning.

The question I raise is this: is the origin of refusal the refusal
itself? Can a negation begin of itself? I shall bring the description
to bear upon two points: on the relation of decision to its motives
which are, so to speak, behind the decision, and secondly on the
project in front of the decision.

Let us reflect on the *"nothing"* which points up the
insufficiency of every motive to bind me, that is to release me of all
responsibility, providing me with an excuse, an alibi. This "nothing" has always been known: the classicists introduced it into the
very definition of motives when they said they inclined *without
necessitating*. What does this mean? In no wise, it seems to me,
that decision "is wrenched away" during the course of motivation;
nowhere do I encounter an act which breaks with the totality of the
incitements and solicitations of consciousness. I break with the
power of solicitation of one group of motives only because I fall in
with other motives. The relation of decision to motives is not a
relation of rupture but one of support; it breaks here only because
it takes support there; to decide is always to decide because
of. . . . The idea of *refusal* is therefore not the key to this "nothing" which causes the insufficiency of motives. What is it then? This
nothing appears only if I project my motives on the background of
things and interpret them in a language of things, that is in terms
of physical causality. Hence I say: a motive is not a cause. But in
that case, nothingness is not, in my act, between motive and
decision, but in my reflection between cause and motive. There is a
huge difference between motivation and causality; yet decision
does not escape psychological motivation. Thus, when I insist on
the negative aspect of freedom, I simply mean that self-
determination is a determination by motives and *not* by causes.
This is the gist of the "inclining without necessitating." Negation is
only in the definition, not in the act.

It may be objected that authentic decisions do not support
themselves upon . . . , that they are, on the contrary, the upsurge of an act, an innovation which "nihilates" the past such as it
is given. One may then attempt to make subversive decisions,
insurrectional decisions, if you will, model decisions, canonical
decisions. Let us grant this and ask under what conditions we can
nihilate our past as given.

Let us take the most extreme case, that of a conversion which
in the eyes of my friends would assume the form of a *repudiation*

of all that I had until then affirmed and believed. Under what conditions can my negations, which I oppose to my former convictions and to the set of reasons which supported them, be viewed as a denial, as an act of reversing my judgment, but not as an act of repudiating myself? If in my opinion I have not repudiated myself, this is because my decision is not the universal nihilation of my past. However radical a conversion can be imagined to be, it nihilates a dead past only to discover and stir up behind it a living past which the "crisis" has liberated. The conversion effects a change of appearance in my past, making of the form the substance, of the substance the form. Thus I repudiate a past of myself only because I assume another past. This very word "assume" is not foreign to the existentialist vocabulary; it marks the return in force of affirmation into a philosophy of negation. By means of this assumption, I carry myself on amid the most radical "crises" of existence. A conversion is not a consciousness of severance; rather, I am aware of liberating in myself what remained inhibited, refused, impeded. I have only repudiated shackles, denied negations. Hence, by means of negations, and in a way that is more profound than all my refusals, I believe that by converting myself I have constituted a better continuation of myself, a more fully affirmative continuation.

What we have just said of denegation in relation to the past causes us to turn toward the future and to consider decision as project. It is from here that the primacy of negation in freedom seems to draw all its strength. For what is a project? Is it not an event which is *lacking* to things? As a being of projects, am I not he who, according to Sartre's percussive image, brings about a sort of decompression in the plenitude of things? Is not value this lack, this hole, which I hollow out before me and which I fill by acts, in the sense that one fulfills a wish, completes a program, or fulfills a promise?

Let us grant that the project has this negative sense, that value is what is lacking to given facts. All this is quite true and the Sartrian analysis does not call for a refutation, but rather a sort of critical renewal which justifies it while transcending it.

I believe it is possible to show that in every contestation of the real, which is the way in which a value surges forth into the world, an affirmation of being is included. This can be shown by an analysis of the valorizing attitudes, such as indignation, protestation, recrimination, and revolt which, on the surface, are the most "nihilating."

What is it to rebel? No doubt it is to say *no:* no, I shall no longer tolerate this, I shall not endure such and such any more. But the slave who rebels against the master not only repudiates the master, but he also affirms that he is right; as Camus so rightly expressed it, without perceiving all the metaphysical implications of it: "In every act of rebellion, man experiences not only a feeling of revulsion at the infringement of his rights, but also a complete and spontaneous adhesion to a certain part of himself." And he adds: "Not every value leads to rebellion, but every rebellion tacitly invokes a value." Adhesion, invocation—words which are supremely positive. Shall we say that the object of adhesion is precisely what does not exist, since that part of himself which the slave raises before the master has no place in this world? This part has no place in the realm of the factual, in being-there, but the adhesion which foments rebellion is the testimonial of an "I am" beyond factual being, an "I am" which is strictly equal to an "I have worth." Adhesion goes straight to the existence-value, to dignity, which is not mere absence from the world but the very tension of being. The wish that "another might be" is merely abridged in the expression "that is to be done." Thus, the "to be done" of value and the "that he be" of the other's existence are strictly reciprocal.

From this standpoint, it would seem that we can no longer hold value for a mere lack, if it is the active positing of the existence of another as correlative of mine. Through value, I surpass myself into another. I accept his existence so that I, too might exist, that I might exist not only as a will to live, but also as an existence-value. Let us not say therefore that value is lack, but that scandalous situations lack value, fall short of value. It is a question of things which have no value and not of values which fail to exist.

This discussion has not been in vain: if existentialism privileges the moment of refusal, of wrenching away from the factual, of disentanglement, this is because the moment of the *nihilation of the factual* is always obscured by a will guilty of the *annihilation of another*. But philosophical reflection is purifying in this: that it discerns the nucleus of affirmation shrouded in anger, the generosity concealed in the implicit will of murder. On the other hand, the moment of the *existence-value of another,* which is the soul of respect, is always clouded by a mystifying tendency to hide this affirmation under the cloak of solemn abstractions: justice, liberty, etc. But the positing of existence by existence, of the existence of the other as a condition of my full and complete existence, does not condemn me to a philosophy of essences, but rather orients me toward a philosophy of the act of existing. The illusion of existentialism is twofold: it confuses denegation with the passions which inclose it within the negative; it believes that the only alternative to freedom-nothingness is being petrified into essence.

At this stage of our recuperative reflection, in the very bosom of nihilating reflection, let us pause to get our bearings. We said at the outset: the power of the denegation of consciousness is a second degree negation; it is a negation of negation; the nothingness of finitude being the first degree negation. The *possibility* of finding an affirmation within denegation was thus opened up by this analysis. Then we said: *in fact* one can always find an affirmation implicit to the most virulent negations of consciousness: break with the past, entrance into the future by rebellion. Is it necessary to go farther? Can one show the *necessary* subordination of negation to affirmation? In other words, does affirmation have value as foundation?

[5] "Primary" Affirmation

Hence, it is the *originary* character of affirmation that is at stake. It would seem that if we reach an impasse here, it is because we have at the outset a very narrow and crude idea of being, reduced to the status of the *thing,* the brute fact—or of *essence,* itself grossly identified with some immutable paradigm without relations, like Platonic Ideas interpreted by the "Friends of the Form" who were combated by Plato in the *Sophist.* This point is quite clear in Sartre: his notion of being-in-itself, which serves as a foil to his notion of nothingness, is too flimsy and already reified. From this standpoint, the nothingness which the human reality is in itself is not the nothingness of the whole of being, but of the reification which invades my body, my past, and this promotes a sort of compression, of sedimentation, of relapse into the slumber of the mineral. If Sartre has thus been able to contrive a sort of hypostasis of the nihilating act into an actual nothingness, this is because he has previously confined being to the factual, to the mundane outside of me and in me. Consequently, what he has demonstrated is that in order to be free, one must be constituted as no-thing; but nothing is not not-being. In my opinion, this is the crucial point of his philosophy. His philosophy of nothingness is the consequence of an inadequate philosophy of being. In particular, his whole theory of value is encumbered with this flimsy conception of being. If being is the brute fact, then the value which aerifies, so to speak, the factual, which introduces a *need-to-be* into being, can only be lacuna and lack. All possibility of grounding nihilating acts in a higher affirmation is ruled out under penalty of falling back into the initial ensnarement. Being can no longer be a refuge, it is a trap; snare, but not *élan* and foundation. Value derives its being from its exigency and not its exigency from its being; and so it only remains to rely on the nothingness of freedom to make value exist as value, "by the sole fact of recognizing it as such." [16] "As the being by whom values exist, I am unjustifiable" and my freedom is anguished at being "the foundation of values while itself without foundation." [17]

Hence, is it not necessary to proceed in the inverse direction? Instead of prematurely sealing off our idea of being, of closing it up within the notion of the in-itself wholly constructed upon the model of the thing, let us rather ask what being ought to be in order for it to be the soul of denegation, of doubt and rebellion, of interrogation and contestation.

The benefit of a meditation on negation is not to lead us to a philosophy of nothingness, but rather to carry our idea of being beyond a phenomenology of the thing or a metaphysics of essence up to this act of existing of which it may be equally said that it is without essence or that all its essence is to exist. But is this affirmation a *necessary* one?

Philosophy was born with the pre-Socratics in the great discovery that "*to think*" is to think being, and that to think *being* is to think ἀρχή [18] in the double sense of the beginning and the foundation of all that we can establish and disestablish, believe and put into doubt. If we are to believe the doxographers, Anaximander was the first to see this. Aristotle, who seems at this point to have a collection of pre-Socratic texts before him, says: "Everything is either a source or derived from a source. But there cannot be a source of the infinite, for that would be a limit of it." And again: "It has no source, but it is this which is held to be the principle of other things and to encompass and govern all." [19] The idea of something which is the source of other things without itself having a beginning puts a stop to this endless regression in the generations of the gods of mythology. At the same time, one can find in this philosophical archaism two features which are decisive for our meditation. First, the conviction that this ἀρχή, this "principle," is χοσμός and δική, "order" and "justice." In effect, this principle is the common source of the intelligibility of physics, ethics, and politics.

16. *Ibid.*, p. 76.
17. *Ibid.*
18. The Greek can mean beginning, origin, first cause, principle—Trans.
19. *Physics*, III, 203b; cf. Diels, *Vorsokratiker*, A 9 and A 15.

What we take for a confusion between the real and the ideal, between fact and value, is the conviction that ontology, under penalty of breaking in two, is the common root of being in the sense of the factual, and of being in the sense of value. The second feature which matters to us here is that the same meditation on ἀρχή founds negation on the ground of affirmation. The First, says Anaximander, does not comprise the determinations of what comes after the First; it is not-this, not-that, precisely because it is, purely and simply. Thus the ἀρχή of the pre-Socratics is ἄπειρον, unlimited, undetermined, *inessential;* the movement from negation is secretly animated by the avowal of ἀρχή. Xenophanes was the first to formulate the critique of anthropomorphism in the representation of the divine; for us, God may no longer be represented in animal or human forms; He is rather essence or value; the critique is the same.

The *cantus firmus* of being and the thought of being presses on, from the Greeks up to our time, in a way that is more fundamental than the differences between schools of philosophy. It matters little that Parmenides held the "(it) is"—which the goddess reveals to him at the end of his voyage beyond the gates of Night and Day—for a physical sphere; it matters little that Plato called the Good that which leads to the known Ideas of being and existence; and that Aristotle called it "being as being." All defined man by this act which they called νοεῖν or φρονεῖν—thinking or meditating. For them, the affirmation of being founds man's existence and puts an end to what Parmenides called "wandering," that is to say beyond error, the condition of wandering.

But, it will be objected, can I not interrogate over and over again and raise the question of the origin of origin? Does not this possibility alone testify that man is this endless interrogation, capable of calling into question and of nihilating the very possibility of a principle of being? Plotinus was familiar with this kind of vertigo and established the false prestige of it: are we asking what is the principle of the principle? This question is not without answer, it is not a question at all. The notion of the First is the very extinction of the question of the origin of the First. In the eighth Tractate of the Sixth *Ennead,* entitled "The Freedom of the One," Plotinus says, as did Anaximander eight centuries before him: "To ask after its cause is to seek another principle for it; but the principle of all has no principle"; then, in attempting to get at the motive behind the question, he finds it in a spatializing illusion which would make being arise as within an anterior void which it would close up; it is this arrival of a stranger, suddenly haunting its prior absence, which gives rise to the vain question of its origin (*Enneads*, VI, 8, 11). Philosophy thus proclaims itself as the thought which suppresses the motive of the aporia of being.

It was to be the inestimable glory of Kant to confirm that thought is thought of the Unconditioned, for it is the limit—*Grenze*—of all thought by the object, of all phenomenal thought, animated by the pretension of sensibility. Thereby Kant came back to Anaximander's intuition—being is primordially dialectical: determining and undetermined. It is through this dialectical structure that he puts an end to interrogation concerning its origin and founds the possibility of interrogating upon all else.

If such is the case, we may consider our whole itinerary on the basis of its terminal and founding act. It seems to me that a philosophy of being which is not swallowed up in a metaphysics of essence, and still less in a phenomenology of the thing, is alone capable of both *justifying* and *limiting* the pact of human reality with negativity.

On the one hand, primary affirmation must be recuperated by negativity, for my incarnation on the whole plays the role of an obturator; it is the temptation of dissimulating the foundation; only the temptation—not fault. The meaning of incarnation remains ambiguous: on the one hand, my body opens me to the world, to reality in its entirety; but, at the same time, it prompts me to define myself by my being-there, by my being-in-the-world. The very thing that opens me to the factual also dissimulates from me the thought of origin. This is what Kant called the "pretension" (*Anmassung*) of sensibility. Thus primary affirmation is, through my own fault, primordially lost. This is a point that Heidegger strongly emphasized: the dissimulation of non-truth is part of the essence of truth. Hence, negativity is the privileged road of the climb back to foundation; and this explains the necessity of this complex train of thought: to discover human transcendence in the transgression of point of view, and negativity in transcendence; then to discover in this negation a double negation, the second negation of point of view as primary negation; and then to discover primary affirmation within this negation of negation.

But the same recuperative reflection which justifies a philosophy of negativity also shows its limit: the dissimulated and lost character of the question of being is such that I not only *must* wrench myself away from things by nihilation, but also that I *can* apprehend this negativity of man without foundation in being. A mutilated philosophy remains possible. This mutilated philosophy is the philosophy of Nothingness. But this is only the philosophy of the transition from things to being. All the Sartrian expressions—wrenching away, detachment, disentanglement, nihilating retreat—testify with genius to this philosophy of transition; nihilation represents the obscure side of a total act whose illuminated side has not been disclosed. Thus, an expression such as "to be one's own nothingness" is ultimately devoid of meaning. On the surface, it would seem that Plotinus uses the same terminology in describing the soul captivated by fascination for its body and when he sums up the approach toward the One in the heroic precept: τὰ ἄλλα πάντα ἄφες—"suppress everything else" (*Enneads*, VI, 8, 21). But the same words convey another meaning, since they are caught up in the movement of affirmation.

No doubt, the virtue of the philosophies of negativity since Hegel is to have put us back on the road toward a philosophy of being which cuts away from the thing and essence. All classic philosophies are, in varying degrees, philosophies of the form, whether the form be interpreted as Idea or as Substance and quiddity. The function of negation is to render the philosophy of being difficult, as Plato was the first to have recognized in the *Sophist*: "being and non-being embarrass us equally." Under the pressure of the negative, of negative experiences, we must re-achieve a notion of being which is *act* rather than *form*, living affirmation, the power of existing and of making exist.

Let us call upon Plato one last time, through the personage of the Stranger in the *Sophist*: "But tell me, in heaven's name! Are we to be so easily convinced that change, life, soul, and mind actually have no place within the core of universal being, that it has neither life nor thought, but stands immutable in solemn aloofness, devoid of intelligence?—That, sir, would be an appalling doctrine to accept." [20]

20. *Sophist*, 248 E.

Bibliographic Note

IN THEIR ORIGINAL FORM, the essays that constitute this volume appeared in the following publications:

"Objectivity and Subjectivity in History" (Objectivité et subjectivité en histoire) is the text of an address before *Journées pédagogiques de coordination entre l'enseignement de la philosophie et celui de l'histoire* (Sèvres: Centre International d'Études Pédagogiques, December, 1952).

"The History of Philosophy and the Unity of Truth" (L'Histoire de la philosophie et l'unité du vrai), first published in German in *Offener Horizont, Mélanges en l'honneur de Karl Jaspers* (Münich: Piper, February, 1953), later appeared in the *Revue internationale de philosophie*, no. 29 (1954).

"Note on the History of Philosophy and the Sociology of Knowledge" (Note sur l'historie de la philosophie et la sociologie de la connaissance) appeared in *L'Homme et l'histoire*, Actes du VIᵉ Congrès des Sociétés de philosophie de langue française (Strasbourg: September, 1952).

"The History of Philosophy and Historicity" (Histoire de la philosophie et historicité *) appeared in *L'Historie et ses interprétations*, conversations with Toynbee (Paris–La Haye: Mouton, 1961).

"Christianity and the Meaning of History" (Le Christianisme et le sens de l'histoire) appeared in the review *Christianisme social* (April, 1951).

"The *Socius* and the Neighbor" (Le Socius et le prochain) is taken from *Amour du prochain*, a special edition of *La vie spirituelle* (1954).

* Added to the French second edition of 1964.

[329]

"The Image of God and the Epic of Man" (L'Image de Dieu et l'épopée humaine *) appeared in *Christianisme social,* (1960), pp. 493–514.

"Emmanuel Mounier: A Personalist Philosopher" (Emmanuel Mounier: Une philosophie personnaliste) appeared in *Esprit* (December, 1950).

"Truth and Falsehood" (Verité et mensonge) appeared in *Esprit* (December, 1951).

"Note on the Wish and Endeavor for Unity" (Note sur le voeu et la tâche de l'unité) is taken from an article entitled "The Scientific Man and the Man of Faith" published in *Le Semeur* (November, 1952) and the cahiers of the C.I.C.

"Work and the Word" (Travail et parole) appeared in *Esprit* (January, 1953).

"Non-violent Man and His Presence to History" (L'Homme non violent et sa présence à l'histoire) appeared in *Esprit* (February, 1949).

"State and Violence" (État et violence *) appeared in *Les conférences annuelles du foyer John Knox* (Geneva, 1957).

"The Political Paradox" (Le Paradoxe politique *) appeared in *Esprit* (May, 1957).

"Universal Civilization and National Cultures" (Civilisation universelle et cultures nationales *) appeared in *Esprit* (October, 1961).

"True and False Anguish" (Vraie et fausse angoisse) is taken from *L'Angoisse du temps présent et les devoirs de l'esprit* (Rencontres Internationales de Genève, Éditions de la Baconnière (September, 1953).

"Negativity and Primary Affirmation" (Négativité et affirmation originaire *) appeared in *Aspects de la dialectique,* Recherches de philosophie, II (Desclée de Brouwer, 1956, pp. 101–24).

Index